RETHINKING MARKETING

THE ENTREPRENEURIAL IMPERATIVE

Minet Schindehutte, Ph.D.

Associate Professor of Entrepreneurship
Whitman School of Management
Syracuse University

Michael H. Morris, Ph.D.

Professor and Chris J. Witting Chairholder in Entrepreneurship
Whitman School of Management
Syracuse University

Leyland F. Pitt, Ph.D.

Professor of Marketing and Academic Chair of the EMBA Program
Segal Graduate School of Business
Simon Fraser University

PEARSON

Prentice
Hall

UPPER SADDLE RIVER, NEW JERSEY 07458

Library of Congress Cataloging-in-Publication Data

Schindehutte, Minet.
  Rethinking marketing : the entrepreneurial imperative / Minet Schindehutte,
Michael H. Morris, Leyland F. Pitt.
    p. cm.
  ISBN-13: 978-0-13-239389-8 (pbk.)
  ISBN-10: 0-13-239389-1 (pbk.)
  1. Marketing.   2. Marketing—Management.   I. Morris, Michael H.   II. Pitt,
Leyland F.   III. Title.
  HF5415.S326 2009
  658.8—dc22   2007047241

Editor-in-Chief: *David Parker*
Acquisitions Editor: *Jennifer M. Collins*
Product Development Manager: *Ashley Santora*
Editorial Assistant: *Elizabeth Davis*
Marketing Assistant: *Ian Gold*
Associate Managing Editor: *Suzanne Grappi*
Permissions Project Manager: *Charles Morris*
Senior Operations Supervisor: *Arnold Vila*
Operations Specialist: *Carol O'Rourke*
Senior Art Director: *Janet Slowik*
Cover Design: *Karen Quigley*
Cover Photo: *Angelo Cavalli/Digital Vision/Getty Images*
Composition: *ICC Macmillan Inc.*
Full-Service Project Management: *Winifred Sanchez/ICC Macmillan Inc.*
Printer/Binder: *STP/RR Donnelley/Harrisonburg*
Typeface: *10/12 Times Ten Roman*

Credits and acknowledgments borrowed from other sources and reproduced, with
permission, in this textbook appear on appropriate page within text.

Pearson Education Ltd., London
Pearson Education Singapore, Pte. Ltd.
Pearson Education, Canada, Ltd.
Pearson Education–Japan

Pearson Education Australia PTY, Limited
Pearson Education North Asia Ltd.
Pearson Educación de Mexico, S.A. de C.V.
Pearson Education Malaysia, Pte. Ltd.

10 9 8 7 6 5 4 3 2 1
ISBN-13: 978-0-13-239389-8
ISBN-10:   0-13-239389-1

Dedication

To the ones who see things differently.
(Minet Schindehutte)

For Nola, a truly entrepreneurial marketer and so much more.
(Michael Morris)

For Lise, Linda, and Christine.
(Leyland F. Pitt)

BRIEF CONTENTS

PART I   **THE NEW MARKETING SPACE   1**

Chapter 1   Picture the Future: *The Janus-Face of Trends*   1
Chapter 2   The Rules Have Changed: *The Emergence of Entrepreneurial Marketing*   21

PART II   **INNOVATE OR DIE: CREATING MARKETS AND LEADING CUSTOMERS   43**

Chapter 3   The Customer of the Future   43
Chapter 4   Do the Dogs Like the Dog Food? Entrepreneurial Market Research   63
Chapter 5   Creating Markets . . . and the People Creating Them   85
Chapter 6   Strategic Innovation and the Marketer: *Or, Why the Marketing Concept Is Misconceptualized*   109
Chapter 7   Running a Different Race: *From Innovative Products to Revolutionary Business Models*   129

PART III   **THE ESSENCE: THINK, FEEL, AND DO MARKETING   145**

Chapter 8   Trends in Customer Communication Practices   145
Chapter 9   The Magic of Marketing Juju   169
Chapter 10   Lessons from the Red Queen   197

PART IV   **PLAYING AT THE EDGE: THE DESIGN OF MARKETING PROGRAMS   219**

Chapter 11   Pricing Secrets of Market Shapers   219
Chapter 12   Changing Channels: *Redefining Distribution Strategy*   235
Chapter 13   Real Gold Goes to the Bold: *The Entrepreneurial Sales Force*   251
Chapter 14   Marketing Strategy in the Digital Age: *The Internet Changes Everything*   271
Chapter 15   Customer Capital: *When the Relationship Comes First*   289

PART V   **HAVING AN IMPACT: THE NEW METRICS   309**

Chapter 16   The Acid Test   309
Name Index   337
Subject Index   341

CONTENTS

Preface   xvii

About the Authors   xxxi

PART I   THE NEW MARKETING SPACE   1

CHAPTER 1   Picture the Future: *The Janus-Face of Trends*   1

Beginnings and Ends   1

Trend 1: Growth and Prosperity versus Poverty and Despair   2
More Wealth . . .   2
Poverty and Despair?   2

Trend 2: Free Markets versus Growing Protectionism   3
Free Markets . . .   3
Growing Protectionism   3

Trend 3: Population Growth versus Population Shortages   4
Population Growth   4
Population Shortages   5

Trend 4: Global Bliss versus Global Gloom   6
Global Bliss   6
Global Gloom   8

Trend 5: Power of Multinational Corporations versus Fragility of
Multinational Corporations   9
The Power of Multinational Corporations   9
Fragility of Multinational Corporations   10

Trend 6: Worldwide Media Reach versus Fragmentation of Media
and Audiences   10
Worldwide Media Reach   10
Fragmentation of Media and Audiences   11

Trend 7: Enhanced Service versus Diminished Service   12
Enhanced Service   12
Diminished Service   12

Trend 8: Brands versus Anti-Brands   14
The Age of Brands   14
The Era of the Anti-Brand   15

So What's a Marketer to Do? Managing in an Era of Janus Trends   16

Key Terms   18

Questions   18

Resources and References   18

CHAPTER 2   The Rules Have Changed: *The Emergence of Entrepreneurial Marketing*   **21**

The Shift: From Monolinear Information to Polyrhythmic Interactions   21

Developments in Marketing Thought and Practice   22
Developing Cracks in Marketing's Façade   23
Marketing Theory Tries to Keep Pace   23

The Four P's Are Dead: Long Live the New Four C's   24

The Nature of, and Need for, Entrepreneurship   27

The Entrepreneurial Marketing Construct   28

Underlying Dimensions of Entrepreneurial Marketing   31
Proactiveness   31
Obsession with Opportunity   32
Customer Intimacy   32
Innovativeness   33
Calculated Risk-Taking   33
Resource Leveraging   34
Exceptional Value Creation   34

Interactions among Components and Ongoing Dynamics   34

Market-Driven or Market-Driving: A Strategic Choice or Part of the DNA?   37

Summary and Conclusions   38

Key Terms   40

Questions   40

Resources and References   41

PART II   INNOVATE OR DIE: CREATING MARKETS AND LEADING CUSTOMERS   43

CHAPTER 3   The Customer of the Future   43

As Smart as Marketers Know They Are   43

The Paths That Products Take: What Products Do to Customers   44
Offerings as Means Extension   47
Offerings as Emergence: Intentional Subversion   48
Diversion   48

Offerings as Emergence: Unintentional Emersion 49
Aspersion 49
The Interrelationships of Processes 50
Marketing and Technology 50

When Customers Get Clever—What's a Manager to Do? 50
Clever Customers Aren't Lead Users 52
Consumer Creativity Does Not Equal Creative Consumers 55
Firms' Stances toward Creative Consumers 56

Capturing and Creating Value from Creative Consumers 59

Summary and Conclusions 60

Key Terms 60

Questions 60

Resources and References 61

**CHAPTER 4 Do the Dogs Like the Dog Food? Entrepreneurial Market
Research 63**

What You Don't Know Can Hurt You 63

Start by Thinking Logically 64
The Set Up 64
The Measurement 67
The Management Decision 68

Now Try a Backward Approach 68

The Entrepreneurial Researcher 70

Some Principles to Guide the Entrepreneurial
Research Process 72
Think Like a Guerrilla 72
Make Use of Your Surroundings 72
Find Insights in the Ordinary 72
Explore the Unconscious 73
Build Research into Daily Operations 74
Use Technology Creatively 74
Create and Mine Databases 75

Less Costly but Effective Measurement Approaches 76
Observe Customers in Action 76
Create Web-Based Surveys 77
Use Focus Groups 78
Form Consumer Panels 78
Talk to Lead Users 78
Build Snowballs 79
Check the Garbage 79
Sift the Archives 80
Monitor Weblogs 80
Conduct Simple Experiments 81
Explore Other Ethnographic Approaches 81

Summary and Conclusions   81

Key Terms   82

Questions   82

Resources and References   83

CHAPTER 5   Creating Markets ... and the People Creating Them   85

Change: The Genesis of Opportunities   85

Creative Destruction: The Kissing Cousin of Opportunity   88

Frequently Asked Questions about Opportunity   90
  Question #1: What Is an Opportunity?   90
  *Question #2: When Is It an Entrepreneurial Opportunity and Not Just an
    Opportunity?   90*
  Question #3: Where Do Opportunities Come From?   91
  *Question #4: What Is the Difference between an Idea and
    an Opportunity?   91*
  Question #5: When Is an Idea Also an Opportunity?   91
  Question #6: What Is the "Window of Opportunity"?   92
  Question #7: Who Finds or How Does One Find Opportunities?   93
  *Question #8: What Is the Difference between an Opportunity and a
    Business Concept?   93*
  *Question #9: How Does One Get Better at Identifying Attractive
    Opportunities for New Ventures?   94*
  Question #10: How Do I Know It Is a "Good" Opportunity?   95

Capitalizing on Change by Recognizing, Discovering, and Creating
Opportunities   96
  Opportunity Creation (in the Land of Possibilities)   97
  Opportunity Discovery (in the Hot Spots)   97
  Opportunity Recognition (in the Cool Places)   98

Value Creation: That's What It's All About   98

Breaking Rules and the People Who Break Them   102

Summary and Conclusions   104

Key Terms   105

Questions   105

Resources and References   106

**CHAPTER 6   Strategic Innovation and the Marketer: *Or, Why the
            Marketing Concept Is Misconceptualized*   109**

Is Customer Orientation All That Matters?   109

The Customer-Product Debate   110

To Serve or Create? A Reexamination of Customer
Orientation   110

Beyond Customer Orientation: The Return to
Innovation   112

Marketing and Innovation   113

Competitive Advantage   114

Changing Needs and Environments   115
  Isolate   116
  Follow   116
  Shape   117
  Interact   118

Choosing a Mode of Focus   119
  Environmental Factors   120
  Economic Power of Existing Customers   120
  Competitive Factors   120
  Political Factors   120

Understanding Strategic Dynamics   121

Understanding the Implications of Changes of Mode   123

Summary and Conclusions   124

Key Terms   125

Questions   125

Resources and References   126

**CHAPTER 7   Running a Different Race: *From Innovative Products to
Revolutionary Business Models*   129**

Cool Businesses Are Built on Unique Models   129

Products, Concepts, and Models   130
  The Product or Service   130
  The Business Concept   133
  The Business Model   133

Breaking It Down: Elements That Define a Business Model   134

Beyond the Basics: Making Decisions at Three Levels   137
  Exploring the Proprietary Level: Creating Unique Combinations   138
  Understanding the Rules Level: Establishing Guiding Principles   138
  Applying the Framework in a Mainstream Industry   139

The Importance of Internal and External Fit   141

How Business Models Emerge   142

Summary and Conclusions   143

Key Terms   144

Questions   144

Resources and References   144

PART III THE ESSENCE: THINK, FEEL, AND DO MARKETING 145

CHAPTER 8 Trends in Customer Communication Practices 145

Lessons from the Marketplace 145

Effects of These Changes—New Developments in Marketing Practice 147

1. Bootstrap/Grassroots Methods 150

2. Conversation-Starter Methods 151

3. Technology-Facilitated Methods 152

4. Visionary Methods 153

Evolution of the Internet: From Information to Interaction 153

1. From Advertisement to In-game Advertising 154

2. Emergence of New Media 156

3. Consumer-Generated Media: Complement, Substitute, or Threat? 156

4. The Mobile Marketing Ecosystem 159

Summary and Conclusions 162

Key Terms 164

Questions 164

Resources and References 165

CHAPTER 9 The Magic of Marketing Juju 169

The Changing Role of Brands 169

The Brand in the Eyes of Its Creator 171

1. The Brand as a Product/Company Identity 172

2. Increasing Brand Relevance: From Product Identity to Trustmark 173

3. The Brand as a Relationship Builder 174

4. Improved Customer Interactions: From Identity to Experience 174

5. Loyalty beyond Reason: From Trustmark to Lovemark 175

6. The Brand as a Character in a Story 176

Evolution of Brands and Branding: The Story of Procter & Gamble 177

From Brand as Source of Value to Value Co-creation and Value Exchange 179

The Company and Its Network as Co-creator of Value 180

The Customer as Co-creators of Value 181

The Customer Community as Co-creator of Value 181

The Brand in the Eyes of Its Beholder 183

Representational Space (symbolic domain) 186

Ideological Space (cognitive domain) 186

Transformational Space (experiential domain) 188

Reciprocal Space (affective domain) 188

The Magic of Marketing Juju   189

Summary and Conclusions   192

Key Terms   193

Questions   193

Resources and References   194

CHAPTER 10   Lessons from the Red Queen   197

The Red Queen Effect   197

Crafting a Strategy Is an Exercise in Entrepreneurship   198

Escaping the Red Queen Effect: Five Lessons   202
  Lesson #1: Every Battle Is Won before It Is Ever Fought   203
  Lesson #2: Step Backward to Go Forward   205
  Lesson #3: Ready! Fire! Aim!   206
  Lesson #4: It Takes Two to Pass One   209
  Lesson #5: Don't Play Hardball — Throw a Curveball   210

Summary and Conclusions   212

Key Terms   214

Questions   214

Resources and References   215

**PART IV   PLAYING AT THE EDGE: THE DESIGN OF
MARKETING PROGRAMS   219**

CHAPTER 11   Pricing Secrets of Market Shapers   219

The Magic of Pricing   219

What Is a Price?   220

A Strategic Perspective on Pricing   221

The Underlying Pricing Orientation of a Company:
Toward Entrepreneurial Pricing   222

The New Pricing: Examples of Emerging Practices   224

Why Entrepreneurial Pricing Has Come of Age   225

Applying an Entrepreneurial Orientation to the Firm's Pricing
Program   228

Summary and Conclusions   230

Key Terms   232

Questions   232

Resources and References   233

CHAPTER 12   **Changing Channels:** *Redefining Distribution Strategy*   **235**

In Times of Change . . . Nothing Changes   235

Searching for a Way Out—and Being Creative   236

The Massive Challenge of Channel Inertia   237

Are Channels of Distribution What the Textbooks Say?   237

So . . . Is Anything Happening?   238

Back to Basics: What Is the Purpose of a Distribution Strategy?   238

What Does Technology Do to Distribution?   240
   The Death of Distance   *240*
   The Homogenization of Time   *240*
   The Irrelevance of Location   *241*

Filling in the Blocks: The Effects of Technological Changes on the Function of Distribution Channels   242
   The Death of Distance and Reassortment/Sorting   *243*
   The Death of Distance and Routinization   *243*
   The Death of Distance and Searching   *243*
   The Homogenization of Time and Reassortment/Sorting   *244*
   The Homogenization of Time and Routinization   *244*
   The Homogenization of Time and Searching   *245*
   The Irrelevance of Location and Reassortment/Sorting   *246*
   The Irrelevance of Location and Routinization   *246*
   The Irrelevance of Location and Searching   *247*

Long-Term Effects of the Impact of Technology on Distribution Channels   247

Key Terms   249

Questions   250

Resources and References   250

CHAPTER 13   **Real Gold Goes to the Bold:** *The Entrepreneurial Sales Force*   **251**

The Need for a New Mindset   251

Dominant Forces of Change   252

A New Concept of the Sales Force   255
   The Creative Sales Force   *256*
   The Expeditionary (or Innovating) Sales Force   *257*
   The Empowered Sales Force   *258*
   The Strategic Sales Force   *260*
   The Technological Sales Force   *261*
   The Collaborative Sales Force   *262*

Putting It All Together: Sales as the Home for Entrepreneurship   263

How Much Entrepreneurship Is Enough?   265

Examples of Entrepreneurship in Sales   267

Summary and Conclusions   268

Key Terms   270

Questions   270

Resources and References   270

CHAPTER 14   Marketing Strategy in the Digital Age: *The Internet Changes Everything*   271

Introduction—Traditional Strategy and Killer Applications   271

The Five New Forces   272
Moore's Law   273
Metcalfe's Law   275
Coasian Economics   276
The Flock-of-Birds Phenomenon   278
The Fish Tank Phenomenon   278

How the New Five Forces Work in Industries and Markets   279
How Moore's Law Affects Music and Gambling   280
Metcalfe's Law–Networks in Music and Wagering   281
Coasian Economics: Transaction Costs in Online Music and Wagering   282
The Flock-of-Birds Phenomenon: Lawlessness in Music and Gambling   282
The Fish Tank Phenomenon: The Power of Creative Individuals in Music and Wagering   284

Summary and Conclusions   286

Key Terms   287

Questions   288

Resources and References   288

CHAPTER 15   Customer Capital: *When the Relationship Comes First*   289

Beyond Making a Sale   289

Making Sense of the Ways Firms Interact with Customers   290

Building a Foundation: Customer Loyalty   292

From Loyalty to Relationships   294

Myths and Realities of Relationship Marketing   296

Relationships Lead to Changes in Goals: The Lifetime Value Concept   297

Types and Degrees of Relationships   299

Underlying Characteristics of Relationships   302

Creating a Relationship Management Program   303

The Need for Imagination in Managing Relationships   306

Summary and Conclusions   307

Key Terms   308

Questions   308

PART V   HAVING AN IMPACT: THE NEW METRICS   309

CHAPTER 16   The Acid Test   309

Introduction: Dilemmas Facing the Corporation   309

A Transformation: From Efficiency and Effectiveness to Sustainability   311

The New Calculus: People, Planet, and Profits   313

People: Mirror, Mirror, on the Wall, Who Is the Greatest Spin-Master of All?   315

Pillar #1: Honesty   316
Pillar #2: Responsibility   317
Pillar #3: Caring   318
Pillar #4: Respect   318
Pillar #5: Fairness   319
Pillar #6: Citizenship   319

Planet: It Might be a Blue Ocean, but the Future Is G-R-E-E-N   320

Profit: Retooling the Marketing Dashboard   324

Rethinking the Profit Maxim: The Entrepreneurial Imperative   330

Summary and Conclusions   333

Key Terms   334

Resources and References   335

Name Index   337

Subject Index   341

PREFACE

WHY THIS BOOK?

Marketing thinking and practice are in a state of change, redirection, and refocus. Conventional marketing approaches have been turned on their heads by a variety of new techniques, methods, and theories.[1] Likewise, rapid changes in people's needs and behaviors, new technologies, mass availability of information, radical and discontinuous innovations, virtualization of products and services, complex supply chains with multiple channels, increased uncertainty, and a plethora of brands and competitors have resulted in a growing gap between marketing practice and relevant frameworks in marketing textbooks. Today, "built to last" is nothing more than a mirage — "built to change tomorrow" is closer to reality. This situation has affected the discipline, educators, students, and practitioners in fascinating ways.

On one side of the spectrum, the discipline's search for relevance and applicability has drawn new insights from academic researchers and leading practitioners around such fundamental questions as "What is marketing and what should its role be in the firm?" Such questioning led to a new official definition from the American Marketing Association (AMA) in 2004. On the other side of the spectrum, practitioners have tried to stay abreast of popular new trends proposed by so-called gurus on best-seller lists (e.g., guerrilla marketing, buzz marketing). But relying on simple success recipes represents a trap. The marketer can find that he or she is on a runaway train, attempting what thousands of others are learning to do as well — and thus no better off than before. Educators and students who seek to understand changes in marketing practices and new ways of marketing thinking have found themselves caught in the middle between those who challenge the basic precepts of marketing and those who push the latest fads — an unenviable position. Trying to play catch-up on both sides requires sifting through piles of information in journals, the popular press, and online sources such as marketing blogs and consultant websites, only to discover that the new ideas become outdated in a few short months.

Entrepreneurial upstarts like Google and entrepreneurial veterans like Apple have shown that staying ahead means embracing their entrepreneurial DNA while thinking and doing differently, not by embarking on a relentless pursuit of the new "new thing." In these changing times, marketers do not need more tools to add to an abundance of theories, principles, and 2×2 matrices. If anything, there is already an oversupply of knowledge related to marketing. However, paradigm-shifting thinking that results in entrepreneurial opportunities is in short supply. In developing this book, the authors sought to discover under-lying patterns by exploring marketing from a variety of perspectives. This process revealed uncommon marketing wisdom along a number of themes, and these have been organized into the chapters of the book. Each theme brings a distinc-tive perspective to thinking about the evolving practice of marketing and about the potential—the imperative—of entrepreneurial thinking and acting in the marketing approaches of pioneers and thought leaders.

This book provides a thread that can be woven through the voices of the mar-keting gurus with their top-selling books and the best of academic research in marketing, strategy, and entrepreneurship so that these are no longer separate islands in the sea of marketing. In an age characterized by many divergent paths, we seek to offer clear signposts for your journey into the new world of marketing. This book provides a framework for making sense of the many new contributions that have redefined marketing—and that framework is entrepreneurship. It is not a book of new "tricks" or buzzwords. Instead, it provides a snapshot of an ap-proach to marketing that is an antidote to traditional marketing practices and thinking. It does not attempt to offer a simple formula to ensure future market success. It is a book about marketers who have blazed a new path, and, as such, it invites you to be a part of the next paradigm shift in marketing. We argue that un-questioning obedience to rules and conventional wisdom is synonymous with fear of failure—and, ironically, is likely to result in failure. The incessant pace of mod-ern change highlights the need to avoid conformance to existing patterns of think-ing. Moreover, the realities of the marketplace of today and tomorrow require marketers who are capable of entertaining, and creating, multiple interpretations of reality for a variety of stakeholders. It has therefore become critically important for marketers to broaden their repertoire of response by *rethinking* marketing.

The remainder of this introduction explains the book's starting points with rethinking as the centerpiece. First, we look back in time to lay the foundation and overall structure on which the new perspectives are built. After a brief look into the crystal ball to consider implications of lessons from the past for marketing in the future, a new worldview is proposed in an effort to repattern marketing. Summary overviews of each chapter suggest ways to rethink the basic building blocks of marketing such as the marketing mix, the role of brands and branding, customer relationships, and so forth.

REFLECTING ON THE PAST: THE SEVEN DEADLY SINS OF CONVENTIONAL MARKETING

The fact of the matter is that marketing must admit to itself that all the rule sets—the entire collection of values that determine how marketing activity unfolds—are completely out of sync with reality and logic.

—JOHN SINGER

In 1990, Regis McKenna proclaimed enthusiastically that "marketing is every-thing."[2] Since the start of the new millennium, several others have made equally convincing claims that marketing has in fact become irrelevant.[3] The list of titles of marketing-related publications paints a grim picture: "The End of Marketing"; "Marketing—In Chaos or Transition?"; "How Market Research Discourages Major Innovations"; "Do Marketing Educators Have a Future?"; "Marketing's Limited Role in New Product Development"; "Marketing at the Crossroads"; "Marketing—A Mid-Life Crisis"; "Rethinking Marketing, Our Disciplines, Our Practice, Our Methods"; "We Don't Do Marketing Here Anymore"; and "The Decline and Fall of Market Research in Corporate America" (among others).

The list is endless—although the titles keep changing, the main conclusions remain unchanged. Traditional methods employed in marketing practice today fall short of expectations—leading to a long list of criticisms[4] that are well-captured in the following "seven deadly sins":

1. Overreliance on established rules of thumb and formula-based thinking.
2. Marketing research that involves meaningless averages that distort reality as marketers try to give customers what they want.
3. Lack of accountability for marketing expenditures.
4. An overemphasis on the promotion element of the marketing mix without adequate responsibility for performance.
5. A focus on superficial and transitory whims of customers.
6. Marketing as a functional silo with static and reactive approaches that result in tendencies to imitate instead of innovate and to serve existing markets instead of creating new ones.
7. A concentration on short-term, low-risk payoffs or on winning marketing accolades rather than making sustainable sales happen.

Some of these criticisms are not new; marketers have been criticized for not being sufficiently innovative and entrepreneurial in their thinking and decision making for several decades. Yet, the volume has been turned up on these and other criticisms, as firms find the competitive landscape to be in a permanent state of flux, while also discovering that they face opportunities that never existed before. Stated differently, even if Regis McKenna is right and "marketing is everything," everything that has been marketing is no longer relevant in today's environment. And in the final analysis, it is people who will change how marketing is done—how they think and behave both as consumers of products and as creators of products.

IMAGINING THE FUTURE: A NEW WAY OF THINKING AND A NEW WORLDVIEW

The marketing imagination is the starting point of success in marketing. It is distinguished from other forms of imagination by the unique insights it brings to understanding customers.
—THEODORE LEVITT

The Internet has essentially changed our relationship with time and space.[5] In the ongoing rhetoric of "new," each type of "new economy" requires the marketer to cultivate a new set of skills to cope effectively in a "world of re-everything."[6]

Changes in people's behavior and shifts in marketing thinking are surface indicators of some larger cultural undercurrent; this deeper movement constitutes a paradigm shift—a shift in the whole set of interlinked cultural values, beliefs, and attitudes. With each paradigm shift, the difference between success and failure often depends on marketers' ability to question the dominant logic within the company and/or within the industry—to rethink their business models and redesign their marketing practices. Competitive survival and sustainability depend on the ability to continuously redefine and adapt goals, purposes, and "ways of doing things." Quite often this means finding a way to balance old-world thinking based on predetermined and predefined recipes of success side-by-side with the new world of re-everything.

Philip Kotler views marketing as "a societal process by which individuals and groups obtain what they need and want through creating, offering, and freely exchanging products and services of value with others."[7] The doomsayers argue that media moguls control news coverage, which in turn creates a vision for society. The pessimists assert that the market is politics, the office is society, and the brand has become a symbol of personal identity. According to this view, mass media (and, by inference, marketing) have a dual role—they reflect, as well as shape, societal values, thus affirming C. Wright Mills's classic definition of a mass society: ever fewer voices talking to an ever larger and an ever more passive audience.[8]

This book shares the perspective that marketing is a societal process. However, it diverges from the view that marketers reflect and shape society as so many would have us believe. That was the old model. Rather, society interacts with, and shapes, marketing—marketing is "a societal force belonging primarily to society and not simply the economy."[9] This is the brave new world facing the marketer today. The consumer is no longer a faceless, mindless, and powerless pawn who can be manipulated by marketers. She or he is demanding a voice and is not waiting for permission to speak. The rise of social networking is evidence of the consumer reasserting herself or himself, insisting on being heard and reclaiming her or his rights as the decision maker of what, where, when, how, why, and who should be part of the conversation as well as what she or he needs from a product or service. The consumer is taking a stand against exploitation, untruthfulness and manipulation—holding companies to a higher standard than companies held themselves in the past. While some might argue this is a counterintuitive position, we believe that social media radically decentralize culture—ending the nightmare of the mass society for good.

With hindsight, the notion of marketing and entrepreneurship as societal forces seems rather obvious, and we wonder why it has taken companies so long to realize this. However, marketing is largely still approached as if it were an organizational function. Many marketers have not yet accepted the need for reform or the need to rethink their basic purpose—not creating demand and fighting off competitors to increase profits, but fulfilling important needs. Innovation results from a new way of thinking and a new way of doing things. Marketing has to transcend the limitations of a linear process of cause and effect with the brand at the center of strategy making. Instead, it is time to adopt an aggregated view of strategic action at the systems level.

When viewed holistically, marketing is an art, a science, a philosophy, and politics—it is cross-disciplinary and it is part of culture. The cultural paradigm at any one time is a consequence of the interaction of dynamic social forces: economic, technological, political, social, demographic—all combining together to influence and, in some ways, reshape the *zeitgeist* (the spirit of the age) and its expression through that society's own particular forms of "popular culture." And so this book attempts to make sense of the paradigm movements, to capture the emerging culture of marketing—a culture of interconnectedness driven by radical innovation and entrepreneurship on all fronts.

THE ENTREPRENEURIAL IMPERATIVE— CHALLENGING ORTHODOXY AND REMAPPING REALITY

Entrepreneurship is fundamentally *a process of genesis:* it creates order, change, activity, novelty, and structure.[10] Thus, entrepreneurship is first and foremost about creation and becoming—it involves the creation of new markets, new value, new goods (products, services, or processes), new wealth, and so forth. Essentially, entrepreneurship is an act of world creation:[11] it creates new worlds by reconstituting meaning from a systems perspective. It is the energy (emotion) that starts and sustains the motion (change). The entrepreneur is an active initiator who thinks *in action.* Thus, entrepreneurship is something people *do*—it emphasizes an approach that puts action (creation) first, not thinking (creativity).[12] An entrepreneurial approach calls for improvisation, playful experimentation, and practice instead of striving to reach a utopia (something that doesn't exist) such as sustainable competitive advantage.

In this book, we explore marketing from an entrepreneurial perspective using a "what-if" compass in which the emphasis is on *asking the right questions,* rather than *finding the right answers.* The "what-if" question demands a fundamental rethinking of the "entire constellation of beliefs, values, techniques, and so on shared by the members of a given [scientific] community"[13]—in this case, marketing. We look at marketing practices through new lenses that are based on conceptual systems and social practices learned in the field, rather than from theoretical principles or marketing genius as precursors for success.

The entrepreneurial imperative for marketing suggests a new way of thinking and acting—it is a paradigm change that helps the marketer cross the great divide between binary opposites: marketer versus customer; competitor versus collaborator; supply versus demand; thinking versus doing. Instead of opposite poles in an "either-or" perspective, an entrepreneurial approach leads to "both-and" perspectives. In a world filled with entrepreneurial practice and experimentation, marketers explore new ideas by doing them first and formulating theories later. An entrepreneurial approach is generative, not inductive or deductive. Asking

"What if we try doing this instead?" generates numerous possibilities that go beyond mere "thought experiments." This deeper movement creates the pathway for marketing as a complementary (not dominant) social force that interacts, intersects, and interconnects with society—and in turn is shaped by society.

This entrepreneurial approach to marketing is as much an attitude and a philosophy as it is a set of tools and techniques. In the "world of re-everything" success and failure depend on a willingness to question everything incessantly— (re)pattern programmed logic through (re)assessment of customers and competitors, (re)conceptualization of the marketer and brands' role, (re)definition of organizational goals, and (re)purposing of products and service.[14] Goals become hypotheses, organizational memory the enemy, and experience a theory that requires ongoing reappraisal. Instead of the traditional information-processing paradigm with its focus on rational, analytical thinking, the marketer adopts the sense-making paradigm of knowledge management with a synergistic view of rational, experiential, and affective aspects of human cognition. This enables the marketer to go beyond knowledge discovery to create the new knowledge that is necessary for a radical redefinition of the game and the rules governing it.

OVERVIEW OF THE CHAPTERS AHEAD

Each chapter highlights new perspectives, paradigms, challenges, and directions taken by entrepreneurial thinkers as they developed revolutionary marketing practices to meet the needs of future customers. As such, each provides an assessment of what has changed in terms of traditional marketing practices and suggests entrepreneurial alternatives that might resolve particular challenges related to a specific marketing activity. Further support for these alternatives is provided through brief examples of marketing trendsetters, which are supplemented by suggestions for additional sources of information.

It is our belief that the practice of "doing" marketing that can eclipse old-school marketing thinking is seriously overdue for a new breed of marketers. Although examples are useful illustrations for learning from others' successes and failures, the underlying premise in this book is that each reader will develop his or her own unique point of view with which to think about marketing. This is not a book of theories and principles, facts and figures, rules of thumb or recipes for success. It is not another how-to book, either. Rather, it is an important book of *why*. To facilitate this understanding, the specific rethinking tool that is embedded in the contents of each chapter follows a summary overview of that chapter. Persistent use of these rethinking tools will enhance the quality and quantity of novel solutions to most problems in marketing practice, as well as everyday situations in which entrepreneurial alternatives are called for.

In Chapter 1, "Picture the Future," the focus is on a revolutionary approach to marketing strategy. In times of conventional marketing, trends were linear and only seemed to go in one direction at a time. Those who rethink marketing discover that in the 21st century, trends are paradoxical. Trends have mirror images that also seem to contradict them: growing populations in some countries, serious declines in populations in others; rapid growth in wealth among the rich, and a countervailing increase in dire poverty among those already poor; growing global bliss counteracted by rising universal gloom. Marketers who rethink marketing realize that they have to achieve a strategic balance. They recognize that when facing revolutionary change, orthodox marketing approaches might not present optimal solutions.

(Re)think tool #1: *Think at the crossroads of disciplines to discover breakthrough ideas where different worlds collide.*

Any conversation about "entrepreneurial marketing" is generally riddled with confusion because invariably people refer to one of four different things when they use this term: marketing for startups, high-tech marketing, marketing for small businesses, or marketing efforts that have entrepreneurial characteristics. Chapter 2, "The Rules Have Changed," clarifies the misconceptions around the term *entrepreneurial marketing.* Seven components associated with entrepreneurial marketing are used to analyze the marketing practices at Harley-Davidson, a champion of the unconventional. Entrepreneurial marketers such as Virgin defy conventional wisdom and disrupt the status quo to become market drivers—they are no longer driven by the market. Over time, they are not only market leaders but are also viewed as market owners.

(Re)think tool #2: *Think differently about thinking differently—experiment!*

In very oversimplified terms, customers are probably not as clever as economists tell us they are, nor as dumb as psychologists imply they are. In all likelihood, they are as smart as marketers know they are. Rather than examine customer behavior from the perspectives of economic rational choice models, or the behavioral and information processing perspectives of consumer psychology, Chapter 3, "The Customer of the Future," considers customer behavior from the perspectives of what products and services (offerings) do to customers and what customers do to the offerings of marketers. Rather than seeing customers as mere passive recipients of the offerings of marketers, those who rethink marketing recognize that offerings can be an active force on the behavior of customers. They also acknowledge that customers are increasingly fooling with their offerings in amusing, creative, and sometimes dangerous ways, and that it is better to have policies and practices in place to deal with this reality than to suffer the consequences later.

(Re)think tool #3: *Use intuition, imagination, inspiration, and ideation to think the unthinkable.*

Chapter 4, "Do the Dogs Like the Dog Food?" defines marketing research as a tool for reducing the uncertainty that surrounds the pursuit of novel, innovative actions. It is argued that research is more likely to produce useful, actionable results when it is performed backward, and when it relies on entrepreneurial research techniques . These techniques are distinguished from the ways that companies have historically satisfied their research needs. With an entrepreneurial approach, the firm is encouraged to conduct research in ways that are less complex and costly, and yet more creative and more richly connected to customers and the marketplace. Guerrilla skills are applied within the research context, as the marketer is encouraged to make optimal use of his or her surroundings, find insights in the ordinary, and build research into the everyday operations of the enterprise. A number of creative ways to gain insights about markets and customers without spending large amounts of money are introduced.

> **(Re)think tool #4:** *Create new alternatives and perspectives by thinking sideways using the six thinking hats for lateral thinking.*

Chapter 5, "Creating Markets. . . . and the People Creating Them," looks at the role of opportunities in driving and creating change. Entrepreneurial thinkers create, discover, or identify new opportunities that are associated with new markets. Yet, the real nature of opportunity is not well understood by many in marketing. When new markets offer customers quantum leap increases in value, companies are able to break free from constraints imposed by industry "rules" to create a new playing field.

> **(Re)think tool #5:** *Use forward-looking thinking to define and communicate a compelling vision as part of entrepreneurial leadership.*

In Chapter 6, "Strategic Innovation and the Marketer," the focus shifts to innovation as a source of value creation. Conventional marketing's perspective is that firms succeed by finding out what customers want and giving it to them. Supposedly this is following a corporate philosophy loosely known as the *marketing concept.* Those who rethink marketing, however, realize that this ignores Drucker's view that the purpose of a firm is not only to serve customers, but also to create them. Products and services create customers as much as they are created for them. This view permits the construction of a matrix of strategic archetypes that allows managers to identify their organization's mode of focus. Of course, those who really rethink marketing then ask whether this mode of focus is appropriate to the business environment in which the firm finds itself and whether it will permit the organization to innovate in the most effective manner.

> **(Re)think tool #6:** *Develop a balance between science and art, logic and imagination, using "whole-brain thinking" like Leonardo da Vinci.*

Chapter 7, "Running a Different Race," examines the role of business models in creating a sustainable competitive advantage. The business model has emerged as one of the most important strategic concepts in 21st century organizations. Marketing decisions play a key role in defining business models that allow firms to disrupt the status quo. Yet, virtually all marketing textbooks ignore the concept of a business model. Further, there are disparate views regarding the nature of a business model. In this chapter, an integrated method for building a business model for a new venture is introduced. It is argued that business models consist of six key decision areas and that these must be well coordinated and internally consistent. Further, decisions are made at the foundation and proprietary levels.

This approach enables the business model to serve as a major platform for innovation. The chapter emphasizes the idea that firms must innovate not just in the products and services they sell, or with their internal processes, but in the fundamental ways in which they design the business itself.

> **(Re)think tool #7:** *Think holistically by approaching marketing as a system with various ecosystems.*

The list of adjectives used in combination with the word *marketing* continues to increase (listed here in alphabetical order): brand-in-the-hand, buzz, expeditionary, experiential, guerrilla, mobile, neuro-, online, permission, radical, roachbait, street, subversive, viral, under-the-radar, and so forth. No doubt this trend will continue. More recently, consumer-generated marketing and mobile marketing have taken center stage, and major marketers are trying to figure out how to work around, work with, or counteract this powerful new force. Chapter 8, "Trends in Customer Communication Practices," creates some order in this constantly evolving hodgepodge of new marketing practices.

> **(Re)think tool #8:** *Think in 4D—beyond the limitations of the three dimensions inside and outside the box.*

Differentiation and positioning are two topics associated with every type of marketing. Being different and setting your brand apart are important. No doubt. However, some companies seem to have the Midas touch when it comes to "different" so much so that people become voluntary evangelists for a brand that resonates with their lifestyle or philosophy on life. Chapter 9 explores "The Magic of Marketing Juju" of brands that capture people's imagination—brands that create meaning and inspire action. In contrast to traditional perspectives on the brand from the company's perspective, this chapter examines how people have "hijacked" the brand, where the customer, not the company, endows it with meaning based on his or her respective worldview. Marketers are encouraged to find the edge—the charisma or energy associated with the brand, "that extra something" that inspires and captivates.

> **(Re)think tool #9:** *Solve problems in novel ways using pictures as part of kaleidoscopic thinking.*

Chapter 10, "Lessons from the Red Queen," draws on Lewis Carroll's inspirational lessons in his book *Through the Looking Glass* to get a fresh perspective on what it takes to win in the contemporary marketing space. How does a radical marketer think about strategy? Radical marketers are architects of transformation—they employ strategies that go beyond the military lexicon of being on the offensive or defensive and beyond standard categories as market leader or fast follower. They know that if there was a formula for success, others could follow, and it would lose its effectiveness. Consequently, they typically do the opposite of what everyone else in the industry is doing. Their strategies are imaginative, counterintuitive, original, and unique—marked by a considerable departure from the usual or traditional, far beyond the norm, uncompromising, revolutionary. These marketers create, shape, and accelerate markets by rethinking customer expectations, value propositions, and business processes. Rather than trying to avoid or do away with the escalating Red Queen race, this chapter focuses on how to craft strategies that put the company not simply ahead of the race, but enable it to play an entirely different game.

(Re)think tool #10: *Use the mind's eye, myths, memories, mystery, and magic to think metaphorically.*

Price represents one of the most underutilized elements in the marketer's toolkit. Yet, it is an area that easily lends itself to significant creativity and imagination. Chapter 11, "Pricing Secrets of Market Shapers," encourages the marketer to move away from traditional cost-based approaches to the setting of prices and adopt what we call value-based pricing. The value-based approach centers on pricing to capture a customer's perceived value in a product or service, which is a moving target. A logical framework is provided for building pricing programs that capture customer value. The framework includes price objectives, price strategy, price structure, price levels, and price promotions. Using this framework, we demonstrate how a firm can move toward entrepreneurial pricing, defined as an approach that is market based, proactive, risk assumptive, and flexible. Numerous examples of entrepreneurial pricing are provided. Attention is also devoted to exploring ways in which the Internet is revolutionizing how pricing should be approached.

(Re)think tool #11: *Think in reverse by reversing assumptions about cause and effect to remove obstacles.*

The ways in which distribution has been redefined again and again are examined in Chapter 12, "Changing Channels." Conventional marketers are often frustrated by the enormous inertia of a firm's chosen channels of distribution. Once established, it takes a brave, and sometimes foolhardy, marketer to change an existing channel. Marketers who rethink distribution, however, realize that changing channels is often the only way to survive. To help marketers rethink channel changing, this chapter introduces the Internet distribution matrix, a 3×3 tool that considers the three basic functions of distribution channels (reassortment, routinization, and searching), and what information technology does to them (kills distance, homogenizes time, and makes location irrelevant). Those who rethink distribution channels can use the approach to identify competitive threats, as well as to discover the new opportunities needed to overcome the burden of inertia.

(Re)think tool #12: *Think "leapfrog" to develop creative leverage that overcomes inertia.*

Entrepreneurial selling is the focus of Chapter 13, "Real Gold Goes to the Bold." The sales force in contemporary organizations is at risk of becoming obsolete. Fundamental changes in the competitive environment have made it increasingly attractive to use technology to replace salespeople and to outsource key aspects of a firm's selling and customer support operations. Yet, if approached properly, the sales force has never been more important. The key to avoiding obsolescence is to adopt an entirely new concept of the sales force—one where sales is the home of the entrepreneurial process in organizations. We argue for a sales force that is creative, empowered, expeditionary, technologically savvy, strategic, and collaborative. We examine how entrepreneurial thinking can be applied both to sales management and to the activities of individual salespeople. Further, we encourage that sales territories be viewed as entrepreneurial ventures. The concept of entrepreneurial intensity is applied to describe different types of sales forces. Examples of innovations when managing sales are explored.

> **(Re)think tool #13:** *Use unconventional wisdom to develop a whole new mindset that channels thinking and action.*

Most marketers have used Porter's well-known five forces model to better understand the competitive environment in which they operate. The approach offers a robust means of understanding the nature of rivalry, as well as possible ways of competing in markets where change has been relatively slow. The emergence of so-called killer apps (disruptive technologies that don't just offer a new offering but change whole markets and industries) has made the five forces approach a little more difficult to use. Chapter 14, "Marketing Strategy in the Digital Age," offers a "new five forces" approach to those who want to rethink marketing, particularly in terms of how disruptive technologies will influence their organizations and offerings.

> **(Re)think tool #14:** *Be a revolutionary for the sake of marketing—embrace ambiguity, paradox, and uncertainty to learn adaptively by thinking with tenacity.*

Perhaps the most fundamental change in modern marketing is a move from viewing the customer as an object to be caught to approaching the customer as an extension of the firm. In this vein, the transaction has been replaced by the relationship as a key goal of marketers. In Chapter 15, "Customer Capital," we argue that relationships represent one of the most misunderstood and misapplied concepts in marketing. A relationship with a customer is not a one-way street—it involves two-way interaction, with mutual investments. Further, relationships are dynamic, evolving over time to new and different forms. Having true relationships with customers is a strategic decision that requires a basic change in the mindset of managers. Based on an understanding of the fundamental nature of relationships, we argue that different types of relationships are possible and that firms should not strive to have the same type of relationship with all of its customers. The determination of the type of relationship to have, and how much to invest in the relationship, is tied to the concept of customer lifetime value. We review a simple method for calculating the value of a customer. Following this, a logical process for building relationships is presented. Using this process, we demonstrate the critical role of creativity and innovation in managing relationships.

Think Different

Here's to the crazy ones.

The misfits.
The rebels.
The troublemakers.
The round pegs in the square holes.
The ones who see things differently.

They're not fond of rules.
And they have no respect for the status quo.

You can praise them, disagree with them, quote them, disbelieve them,
glorify or vilify them.
About the only thing you can't do is ignore them.
Because they change things.

They invent. They imagine. They heal.

They explore. They create. They inspire.
They push the human race forward.

Maybe they have to be crazy.

How else can you stare at an empty canvas and see a work of art?
Or sit in silence and hear a song that's never been written?
Or gaze at a red planet and see a laboratory on wheels?

We make tools for these kinds of people.

While some see them as the crazy ones, we see genius.

Because the people who are crazy enough to think they can change the world . . .
are the ones who do.

Source: Apple Computer's original "Think Different" campaign.

(Re)think tool #15: *Develop empathy—think with the heart!*

Putting people before profits and considering the ecological footprint of the company as part of a triple bottom line require marketers to rethink their products, customers, and the role played by the company in society. The three elements contributing to the triple bottom line as part of a marketing dashboard move to the center of attention in Chapter 16, "The Acid Test." At the end of the day, it is about people and ethics, planet and sustainability, profits and metrics.

(Re)think tool #16: *Think about the new 3 P's—people, planet, and profits— to assess all angles and cultivate an appreciation of the interconnectedness of things.*

Welcome to the new path. We hope it is an exciting and enriching journey.

References and Suggestions for Additional Information

1. Day, G. S., & Montgomery, D. B. (1999). Charting new directions for marketing. *Journal of Marketing* 63: 3–13.
2. McKenna, R. (1991). Marketing is everything. *Harvard Business Review* 69(1): 65–79.
3. Singer, J. (2006). Framing brand management for marketing ecosystems. *Journal of Business Strategy* 27(5): 50–57.
4. Hill, S., & Rifkin, G. (1999). *Radical marketing: From Harvard to Harley. Lessons from ten that broke the rules and made it big.* New York: Harper.
5. Virilio, P. (1994). *The vision machine.* Bloomington, IN: Indiana University Press.
6. Malhotra, Y. (1998). Knowledge management, knowledge organizations & knowledge workers: A view from the front lines. Accessed November 14, 2007, http://www.brint.com/ interview/maeil.htm.
7. Kotler, P. (2000). *Marketing management.* Englewood Cliffs, NJ: Prentice Hall.
8. Mills, C. W. (1956). People, power, politics. New York: Oxford University Press.
9. Ireland, R. D., Hitt, M. A., & Sirmon, D. G. (2003). A model of strategic entrepreneurship: The construct and its dimensions. *Journal of Management* 29(6): 963–989.
10. Schindehutte, M., & Morris, M. H. (2007, June). Strategic entrepreneurship: Conceptualization as a multi-dimensional opportunity space. Paper presented at the Max Planck Institute of Economics Annual Schloß Ringberg Conference on Strategic Entrepreneurship.
11. Steyaert, C. (2000). *Creating Worlds: Political Agendas of Entrepreneurship.* Paper presented at the 11th Nordic Conference on Small Business Research, Aarhus, Denmark.
12. Mintzberg, H., & Westley, F. (2001). Decision making: It's not what you think. *Sloan Management Review* 42(3): 89–94.
13. Kuhn, T. S. (1970). *The structure of scientific revolutions,* 2nd ed. Chicago: Chicago University Press.
14. Arthur, W. B. (1996). Increasing returns and the new world of business. *Harvard Business Review* 74(4): 100–109.

ABOUT THE AUTHORS

Minet Schindehutte is Associate Professor of Entrepreneurship in the Department of Entrepreneurship and Emerging Enterprises at the Whitman School of Management, Syracuse University. She received her Ph.D. in Chemistry at the University of Pretoria. A South African national, she has worked both in academia and in the private sector, and her professional background includes technical marketing, brand management, and entrepreneurship-related activities. Dr. Schindehutte has received recognition for her innovative teaching and pedagogical advances. She is co-director of the annual Experiential Classroom for Entrepreneurship Educators. She has also served as a Vice President of the United States Association for Small Business and Entrepreneurship. Her current research interests include the interface between entrepreneurship, innovation, and strategy; entrepreneurship under conditions of adversity; and factors affecting performance in entrepreneurial companies. Dr. Schindehutte has numerous refereed publications, research monographs, and book chapters, and her articles have appeared in such journals as the *Journal of Marketing Theory and Practice*, *Small Business Economics*, *Journal of Small Business Management*, *Business Horizons*, and the *Journal of Business Research*, among others.

Michael Morris is Professor and Chris J. Witting Chairholder in Entrepreneurship at Syracuse University. He previously held endowed chairs at the University of Hawaii and Miami University. He is a former Fulbright Scholar, and spent two years as Gordon Professor of Entrepreneurship at the University of Cape Town (South Africa), where he created the Supporting Emerging Enterprises Program. In addition, he has been a principal in three entrepreneurial startups. Professor Morris has published six books and numerous academic articles in such publications as the *Journal of Management*, *Journal of Business Venturing*, *Entrepreneurship Theory and Practice*, *Journal of Small Business Management*, *Small Business Economics*, *Journal of Business Research*, *Long Range Planning*, *Journal of Business Ethics*, *Journal of the Academy of Marketing Science*, *Journal of International Business Studies*, *European Journal of Marketing*, and *Industrial Marketing Management*. He created and annually organizes the Experiential Classroom, a faculty clinic on best practices in entrepreneurship education. He is the President-elect of the United States Association for Small Business and Entrepreneurship. He also serves as co-Series Editor for a fifteen-book entrepreneurship series with Prentice-Hall. He has chaired the American Marketing Association's Task Force on the Marketing and Entrepreneurship Interface, and was editor of the *Journal of Developmental Entrepreneurship* for five years. Dr. Morris has received recognition for his teaching and research, including receiving the Oberwager Prize for impacting students beyond the classroom, and has been honored by Pi Sigma Epsilon as national Faculty Advisor of the Year. He has been inducted as a "21st Century Entrepreneurship Research Fellow," and received the Edwin and Gloria Appel Prize for contributions to the field of entrepreneurship.

Leyland Pitt is Professor of Marketing and Academic Chair of the EMBA Program, Segal Graduate School of Business, Simon Fraser University, Vancouver, Canada, and is a Senior Research Fellow of the Leeds University Business School in the United Kingdom. He has also taught on executive and MBA programs at major international business schools such as the Graham School of Continuing Studies at the University of Chicago, the Graduate School of Business of Columbia University, and London Business School. His work has been accepted for publication by such journals as *The Journal of Advertising Research, The Journal of Advertising, Information Systems Research, Journal of the Academy of Marketing Science, Sloan Management Review, Business Horizons, California Management Review, Communications of the ACM,* and *MIS Quarterly* (of which he also served as Associate Editor), and in 2000 he was the recipient of the Tamer Cavusgil Award of the American Marketing Association for the best article in the *Journal of International Marketing.* Professor Pitt has won many awards for teaching excellence, including Best Lecturer on the MBA Program, Henley Management College, UK; the Dean's Teaching Honor Roll, Faculty of Business Administration, Simon Fraser University, Canada; best professor and MBA Teacher of the year, Copenhagen Business School, Denmark; and Best Professor of Program, Joint Executive MBA, University of Vienna, Austria, and Carlson School of Management, University of Minnesota, USA. In 2002, Leyland Pitt was awarded the Outstanding Marketing Teacher of the Academy of Marketing Science. In 2006, he was awarded the TD Canada Trust award for outstanding teachers. He was listed as one of Canada's top MBA professors in the magazine *Canadian Business* in 2005. Leyland Pitt has also presented in-house management development programs in major organizations worldwide, including British Airways, Unilever, Hong Kong Shanghai Bank, Lloyds TSB, Dixons, Volkswagen, SABMiller, Armstrong World Industries, Kone, Siemens, and the Royal Metropolitan Police.

CHAPTER

PICTURE THE FUTURE
THE JANUS-FACE OF TRENDS*

BEGINNINGS AND ENDS

Throughout the 1980s and 1990s, trend spotters like John Naisbitt[1] and Faith Popcorn[2] established major reputations and amassed significant fortunes by identifying and foretelling trends that would change lives, change business, and change the world. With the 20-20 vision that hindsight provides, we can now look back and say that generally they did a fair job. Many of their predictions proved to be correct as their envisaged developments materialized. Firms that followed these predictions prospered as they either capitalized on the opportunities that one or more of the trends foretold, or acted to ensure that the risks that the trends presaged were eliminated or negated. It is tempting to look and hope for a new Naisbitt or an up-to-the-minute Popcorn for the 21st century. The problem is that trends aren't what they used to be.

The trends of the modern age were linear—more, or less, of something that was either good for most actors or bad for everyone. A social trend in our concern for health was good for almost everyone, including firms and consumers. The trend to urbanization meant larger cities, pollution, social problems, and massive changes in lifestyle. Like most post-modern phenomena, however, the trends of the post-modern 21st century are paradoxical. They are neither universally positive nor negative, nor are they bad for everyone or good for everyone. They are a lot like Janus.

Janus is the Roman god of gates and doors (*ianua*), beginnings and endings. He is always represented with a double-faced head, with each face looking in

---

*Leyland Pitt is indebted to Dr. Bodo Schegelmilch, dean of the Wirtschaftsuniversität Wien Executive Academy and chair of International Marketing & Management at the Wirtschaftsuniversität Wien (Vienna University of Economics and Business Administration) for co-authoring this chapter.

opposite directions. He was worshipped at the beginning of the harvest time, planting, marriage, birth, and other types of beginnings—especially the beginnings of important events in a person's life. Janus also represents the transition between primitive life and civilization, countryside and city, peace and war, and the growing-up of young people. Janus was frequently used to symbolize change and transitions such as the progression of past to future, of one condition to another, of one vision to another, of one universe to another. As former vice president Dan Quayle is once alleged to have said, "I believe we are on an irreversible trend toward more freedom and democracy—but that could change."

Marketers and entrepreneurs of the 21st century need to understand trends to capitalize on the opportunities they provide and to minimize the threats they represent. However, they must also recognize that, like Janus, the trends are paradoxical and seldom function solely in one direction or the other. In this chapter, we identify and describe eight Janus trends for the early 21st century:

1. Growth and prosperity versus poverty and despair
2. Free markets versus growing protectionism
3. Population growth versus population shortages
4. Global bliss versus global gloom
5. Power of multinational corporations versus fragility of multinational corporations
6. Worldwide media reach versus fragmentation of media and audiences
7. Enhanced service versus diminished service
8. Brands versus anti-brands

TREND 1: GROWTH AND PROSPERITY VERSUS POVERTY AND DESPAIR

MORE WEALTH...

The world is wealthier now than it has been at any previous time in history. Growth and prosperity abound, and there are now more than 7.7 million people globally who hold more than US$1 million in financial assets. Merrill Lynch's World Wealth Report 2004 (see **www.ml.com**) expects that the average growth rate of high net worth individuals (HNWIs) will be 7% per annum until 2008. The firm also reports that there are 236,000 millionaires in China and 61,000 in India. In China, the real gross domestic product (GDP) has grown by around 10.7% per annum (p.a.) during the past 10 years, and in very recent years India's growth rate has either equaled or exceeded this.

POVERTY AND DESPAIR?

Despite this, the gap between the rich and the poor has never been larger, and it is widening at an alarming rate. In 2001, some 2.7 billion people in the world survived on less than $2 daily, and the media report regularly on the huge numbers of children who starve each day, or eke out meager livings by foraging in the garbage dumps of large cities. In 1960, the average income of the wealthiest 20% of the world's population was 30 times higher than that of the poorest 20%. By 2001, the average income of the wealthiest 20% of the world population was 82 times higher!

The effects of these disparities are observable in a range of key areas. There has been a huge rise in elective cosmetic surgery, as being able to change the physical nature of one's body becomes not only possible but very affordable to affluent people. Facelifts, breast enhancements, and liposuction are passé, and regular botox treatments (at many hundreds of dollars each time) are a part of many wealthy individuals' health and beauty routines. On the other hand, in various parts of the world, measles, malaria, and diarrhea are three of the biggest killers of children—yet all are preventable or treatable. More than 30 million children in the world are not immunized against treatable or preventable diseases, and 6 million children under the age of 5 die every year as a result of hunger.

Education is one of the most rapidly growing sectors of developed work economies, and the returns on investment in good education have never been greater. For every year of education, wages increase by a worldwide average of 10%. Yet 134 million children in the world between the ages of 7 and 18 have never been to school. Girls are more likely to go without schooling than boys—in the Middle East and North Africa, girls are three times more likely than boys to be denied education.[3]

TREND 2: FREE MARKETS VERSUS GROWING PROTECTIONISM

FREE MARKETS...

Worldwide there has been a trend toward the freeing up of markets. This has been observable on a national scale, where many countries have privatized and liberalized industries and services providers ranging from airlines to power utilities, and banking to telecommunications. It has also been a prominent global trend, as nations seek to free up their trading with each other by working to remove a host of barriers. The World Trade Organization (WTO) now has 147 members representing more than 90% of the world's trade. Since 1950, the average tariffs for manufactured goods fell from 40% to below 4%. Over the past decades, freight and communication costs declined rapidly, as can be seen from Figure 1-1.

GROWING PROTECTIONISM

Paradoxically, nations have become much more protectionist in many ways. European Union tariffs for agricultural products remain at the 20% level, which hampers the developing world severely, considering that some 70% of the exports

FIGURE 1-1 How Transport and Communication Costs Have Declined

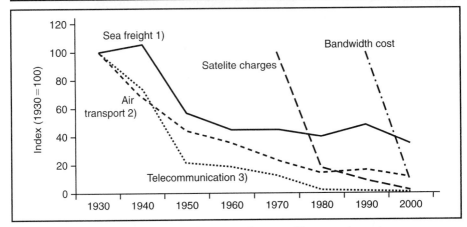

Note: 1) Average ocean freight and port charges per short ton of import and export cargo. 2) Average air transport per passenger mile. Cost for 1920 not available. 3) Cost of a 3 minute telephone call New York to London. Cost for 1920 not available.

Source: Georg Hufbauer: World Economic Integration. The Long View, In Economic Insights, Vol. 30 (1991), pp. 26–27, Globalisation and the Competitiveness of Regional Blocs, Bernhard Fisher, Intereconomics 1998/04, and Tariffs, Transport Costs and the WTO Doha Round: The Case of Developing Countries, Mattlas Busse, In Journal of International Law and Trade Policy, Vol. 4 (2003), No. 1, pp. 15–31.

from the poorest countries are agricultural products and textiles. The U.S. government enacts "safeguard quotas" against Chinese textile imports, and the early years of this millennium witnessed an ongoing row regarding Boeing and Airbus subsidies between Europe and the United States. The effect of protectionism by developed world countries on the economic progress of poorer countries is considerable, and is almost inevitably to the detriment of the less fortunate nation. What gives even greater cause for concern is the considerable degree of "lip-service" paid to trade liberalization by wealthy nations. Developing nations expressed their outrage in 2001 by saying that they remained "deeply disappointed and concerned. . . . Seven years from the Uruguay Round on Textiles and Clothing, few quota restrictions have been phased out."[4]

TREND 3: POPULATION GROWTH VERSUS POPULATION SHORTAGES

POPULATION GROWTH

During the past 40 years, the world's population has doubled from 3 billion to 6 billion, and it is expected to reach 9 billion by the year 2050, as shown in Figure 1-2. The world's 50 poorest countries will triple in population size by 2050. Five countries alone accounted for around half of the world's total inhabitants (see Figure 1-3a),

FIGURE 1-2 The World's Population

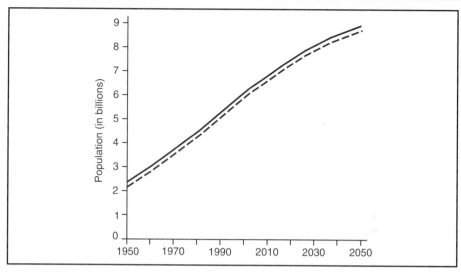

Source: UN Population Division

and the populations of the world's five largest cities exceeded or almost matched those of the majority of the world's nations (including geographically large nations such as Australia and Canada; see Figure 1-3b).

POPULATION SHORTAGES

While the world's population continues to grow, this growth is not uniformly distributed across countries, and indeed, many nations are suffering and will continues to suffer from population declines and population shortages. The population of the 27 countries that should be members of the EU by 2007 will decrease by

FIGURE 1-3 Population Figures

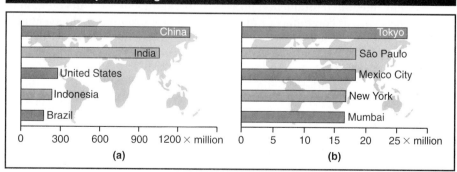

(a) Most populated countries **(b)** Most populated cities

Source: http://www.geohive.com/

6% until 2050. If those trends hold (and there is no reason to believe they won't), then simple arithmetic allows us to predict that Italy's total population will decline by 12.5 million, and Spain's by 3 million. Immigration doesn't always solve the problem: even assuming (no doubt unrealistically high) annual immigration of 250,000, Germany's population could still decline to 50 million by 2100. The effects of population shortages are already being felt in many parts of the world. For example, the energy boom in Canada's Alberta province has meant that despite major economic growth, firms such as McDonald's have actually had to close branches because they are unable to find workers, despite offering far better pay than branches in other parts of the world.

TREND 4: GLOBAL BLISS VERSUS GLOBAL GLOOM

GLOBAL BLISS

There is good reason for a general state of bliss in today's world. In many ways, the cultures and countries of the globe are realizing that the similarities between them are greater than the differences, and that they all have more to gain from cooperation than conflict. Whereas a traveler in the 1950s would have been bewildered by the visual impact of visiting another country, where few signs and logos were recognizable, today's tourists are familiar with their surroundings even when visiting a new foreign city for the first time. Global brands abound— Coca-Cola, Sony, and Mercedes Benz are everywhere. The television set in the hotel room broadcasts the same CNN and BBC World as the television set back home. Not only do the McDonald's burger and Starbucks coffee taste the same as those at home, but the stores and personnel look the same as those back home, and the tourist can "speak" McDonald's or Starbucks despite not being able to converse in the local language. Visa and MasterCard are accepted just about everywhere, so the traveler of today doesn't have to struggle nearly as much with currency conversions or the charges attached to cashing a traveler's check (which are hardly used any more in any case).

Globally integrated production processes abound, and it is not uncommon to find products such as computers or digital cameras, for example, that have multiple sources of origin. The box was assembled in China, the monitor was produced in Japan, the mouse and keyboard came from Malaysia, and the instruction booklet was printed in Ireland.

In lots of ways, traditional boundaries have become meaningless. Geographic boundaries have disappeared in many parts of the world; for example, travelers in the so-called Schengen zone in Europe no longer need to proceed through border formalities when moving from one country to another. Spectacular advances in logistics have led to a dramatic lowering of transportation costs. Container shipping produced a massive decrease in port handling costs, contributing significantly to lower freight charges and, in turn, boosting trade flows. Almost every manufactured product humans consume spends some time in a container (see Table 1-1).

TABLE 1-1 **Biggest Container Companies**			
Top 10 container shipping companies in order of TEU* capacity, 1st January 2006			
Company	*TEU Capacity*	*Market Share (%)*	*Number of Ships*
A.P. Moller-Maersk Group	1,665,272	18.2	549
Mediterranean Shipping Company S.A.	865,890	8.6	299
CMA CGM	507,954	5.6	256
Evergreen Marine Corporation	477,911	5.2	153
Hapag-Lloyd	412,344	4.5	140
China Shipping Container Lines	346,493	3.8	111
American President Lines	331,437	3.6	99
Hanjin-Senator	328,794	3.6	145
COSCO	322,326	3.5	118
NYK Line	302,213	3.3	105

* "Twenty Foot Equivalent Unit"

Source: http://en.wikipedia.org/wiki/Containerization

As a result of containerization, shipping costs today represent only a very small proportion of the final price consumers pay for imported products.

Not only have distance boundaries been reduced substantially, but to all intents and purposes time boundaries have been all but eliminated. This has been referred to as the "homogenization of time," which essentially means that time is the same for everyone, regardless of where they are in the world[5] (this is discussed in more detail in Chapter 12). This has been facilitated by a plethora of advances in communication technologies, including the Internet and cell phones, which permit anyone to communicate at low or zero cost with anyone else, anywhere in the world. In the pre-Internet world, a firm in the United States wishing to order products from a firm in Australia would have to wait until the firm opened, or there was someone to take the call, or rely on regular mail. Using a website, the customer firm can glean information, place or change orders, and track the progress of the order—all while the company on the side of the world is physically closed and its personnel fast asleep.

Regulatory boundaries between countries have also fallen, as nations seek ways of enhancing trade and the frictionless movement of goods between them. Examples abound: the North American Free Trade Agreement (NAFTA), the European Union (EU), the Association of Southeast Asian Nations (ASEAN), and the Southern African Development and Economic Community (SADEC). Not only is there a freer movement of goods, there is also a striving to unbind the interchange of monetary and intellectual capital across borders. In the European Union, for example, professions and qualifications are now recognized across borders. German industrial technology (IT) firms recognize that their survival depends on the skills of programmers in and from India, as the pool of local talent depletes due to low population growth.

GLOBAL GLOOM

Despite the bliss occasioned by the world becoming a smaller place, there is also a pervasive sense of global gloom or pessimism. Many people feel that globalization is a bad thing, and that the majority of the world's population is worse, not better, off as a result. These days, anti-globalization protesters attend almost every major meeting of political and business leaders in the world, united in their opposition to the political power of large corporations, as exercised in trade agreements and elsewhere. They allege that globalization undermines the environment, labor rights, national sovereignty, and the great majority of people in the developing world.

Some critics have argued that globalization undermines local cultures,[6] not only as local diets are replaced by global fast-food brands, but as pervasive global technologies dilute languages, interests, arts, and beliefs. There is also a strong argument that globalization promotes unsustainable consumption, and contributes to unhealthy dietary patterns and unsafe food technologies. Consumption in the world's richest countries can take a great but often hidden toll on distant peoples and places. Today's global economy has a tendency to insulate consumers from the various negative impacts of their purchases by stretching the distance between different phases of a product's lifecycle—from raw material extraction to processing, use, and finally disposal. As Benjamin Barber[7] puts it, in what he refers to as "McWorld" (see Exhibit 1-1), ". . . onrushing economic, technological, and ecological forces . . . demand integration and uniformity, mesmerize peoples everywhere with fast music, fast computers, and fast food . . . , one McWorld tied together by communications, information, entertainment, and commerce." At the heart of all these allegations lies the assertion that globalization places profits ahead of human rights.

EXHIBIT 1-1   McWorld

The Spread of "McWorld"

- McDonald's operates 30,000 restaurants in 119 countries and serves 46 million customers each day. Its total revenue was $15.4 billion in 2002. On opening day in Kuwait City, the line for the McDonald's drive-through was more than 10 km long.

- Siemens, the German manufacturer of mobile phones, computers, medical supplies, lighting, and transportation systems, employs 426,000 people and is represented in 190 countries. In 2002, Siemens' net sales amounted to $96.4 billion, of which 79% were international.

- Levi Strauss sells clothing in more than 100 countries, and its trademark is registered in 160 countries. It employs 12,400 people worldwide. It reported total sales of $4.1 billion in 2002 and a net income of $151 million in 2001.

- Coca-Cola sells more than 300 drink brands in more than 200 countries. More than 70% of the corporation's income originates outside of the United States, and its net revenues reached $19.6 billion in 2002. Coca-Cola employs 60,000 people in Africa alone.

Source: http://www.worldwatch.org/node/814

TREND 5: POWER OF MULTINATIONAL CORPORATIONS VERSUS FRAGILITY OF MULTINATIONAL CORPORATIONS

THE POWER OF MULTINATIONAL CORPORATIONS

Multinational corporations (MNCs), or firms whose reach extends across the nations of the world to the extent that it is sometimes difficult to pinpoint their original nationality, have considerable power and influence. While some would argue against a simple comparison of the GDP of a country with the revenues of a firm, when this is done, "of the 100 largest economies, 51 are corporations and 49 are nation states," according to economist Noreena Hertz.[8] She goes on to point out that the sales of General Motors and Ford exceed the GDP of the entire sub-Saharan Africa region, and that Wal-Mart has higher revenues than most of the economies of Eastern Europe.

As can be seen from Figure 1-4, the power of MNCs increases further as they merge with and acquire firms across the world; the graph simply shows that the number of cross-border mergers and acquisitions (M&As) continues to grow rapidly. This leads to significant concentration of power within industries, as a small number of firms dominate world markets within these industries. For example, the combined markets share of the 10 largest companies in the automobile industry is 80%; in pharmaceuticals, it is 50%; in computers, 70%; in telecommunications, 86%; and in pesticides, 85%. MNCs fortify their competitive positions through a strong emphasis on research and development (R&D), as well as aggressive intellectual property protection.

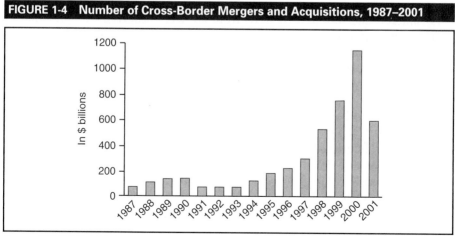

FIGURE 1-4   Number of Cross-Border Mergers and Acquisitions, 1987–2001

Source: UNCTAD 2002: 337

FRAGILITY OF MULTINATIONAL CORPORATIONS

While the power and dominance of MNCs in so many fields is without question, they are simultaneously fragile and vulnerable to a host of threats. The modularization of value chain activities has meant that smaller players can now compete — either by providing the specialist activities in a value chain that are attractive to many customers or by accessing these in a way previously available only to major firms. MNCs are now also vulnerable to "brand companies" — firms that outsource every activity (especially manufacturing) except the management of the brand itself. Brand companies are especially flexible in that they don't have to bear the burden of overhead cost and investment in major infrastructure.

MNCs are also susceptible to the activities of so-called hidden champions — small- to medium-sized firms with strong global orientation. Hidden champions (a term that entered European business lingo after the publication in 1996 of a book with that title by Bonn consultant Hermann Simon[9]) can be found all over Europe, North America, and parts of Asia. These firms tend to pursue a clearer strategy, manage their finances more professionally, provide superior customer service, and invest more in R&D than many poorer-performing MNCs.

Another problem faced increasingly by MNCs is that of intellectual property protection. In many countries, legal systems don't afford MNCs adequate patent and copyright protection, and their significant investments in intellectual resources are at risk. Simultaneously, while attempting to protect these assets, MNCs risk looking like bullies in their pursuit of legal recourse.

TREND 6: WORLDWIDE MEDIA REACH VERSUS FRAGMENTATION OF MEDIA AND AUDIENCES

WORLDWIDE MEDIA REACH

Throughout much of the 20th century, mass media such as television and newspapers gathered and reported on news from all over the world by stationing reporters in all its far-flung corners. The news people received really did depend on the newspaper they read or the television channel they watched. From the 1980s on, however, media began to concentrate significantly as smaller newspapers and television stations realized the significant savings to be gained from "buying" news. Without actually having a journalistic presence in Beijing or Bahrain, a television station could still report on events in those places by purchasing footage from CNN, Sky, or the BBC. Likewise, the news people read in a newspaper, at least on international or national events, is far more likely to come from a supplier such as Reuters, or be syndicated from the *Financial Times, Time,* or *The Economist.*

In the domain of newspapers and magazines, publications such as the *Financial Times, The Economist,* and *Time* are now published simultaneously throughout the world's countries. There is provision for local advertising, which means that an edition of *Time* published in Australia will have some different ads (and some catering to local taste) than an edition of *Time* published in Canada, but essentially the content and approach will be identical. Television channels such as CNN and MTV broadcast news and music, respectively, to the world. CNN is to be found on just about every hotel television set in the world, if there are hotels and television is broadcast. The *Financial Times* (originally a British newspaper) now has a far larger distribution throughout the world than it does in the United Kingdom, and it is standard reading fare in the business class sections of most of the world's airlines. It is now possible to reach huge portions of the world's population by using only a select few media.

FRAGMENTATION OF MEDIA AND AUDIENCES

While it can be argued that the world's media have become concentrated, standardized, and homogenized, simultaneously, and paradoxically, media and the audiences that consume them have been fragmented and personalized on an unprecedented level. An array of media and communication reach the "audience of one." Video games enable each player to be exposed to different messages from different sponsors, depending on how they play the game and the stage they are at in a game at any particular time. Advertisers pay large sums for product placement in games so that players will be exposed to realistic billboards for brands such as Sony, Shell, and Motorola as they round a bend or pass a grandstand in a car racing game. The characters in a soccer game not only look like David Beckham or Ronaldinho, they also sport the same brands as the real players on their "sponsored" jerseys.

E-mail marketing permits highly personalized messages to be targeted at individuals. These are not awful, pervasive, "spam"; they are usually messages sent because the recipient previously indicated that he or she wished to receive details on new books published by favorite authors, updates on the latest software, or details of the newest online games. These types of strategies, falling under the umbrella of "permission marketing,"[10] have also migrated into what has been termed M(or mobile)-media, where personalized messages are posted to cell phones and other portable devices. Some observers have termed this "U-commerce,"[11] or commerce that is ubiquitous, universal, unique, and in unison with the individual's circumstances.

The Internet has further fragmented media and its impact in the development of technologies such as "podcasting," which allows everyone to be a broadcaster and to permit the downloading of content (audio or video) onto PCs and playback devices such as iPods. Similarly, video streaming services such as YouTube and MySpace permit anyone to upload video content onto web servers, and this can in turn be downloaded by others. While these services began their lives as platforms for people to share home movies, they are now seen as very viable media by advertisers and viral marketers who wish to generate "buzz" about their offerings and brands.

TREND 7: ENHANCED SERVICE VERSUS DIMINISHED SERVICE

ENHANCED SERVICE

Since the publication of *In Search of Excellence* by Peters and Waterman[12] in the 1980s, in which being "close to the customer" was identified as a driving force in corporate success, many firms have been obsessed with delivering great service and delighting customers. The 1980s and 1990s saw a fixation on service quality, as firms measured what customers perceived their service to be, and then subtracted that from what they really expected. This gap served as an accurate and usually telling indication of how far firms were from meeting their customers' desires. No longer is it merely enough to satisfy customers: they have to be delighted and surprised. No longer is it sufficient to deliver service: firms are admonished to "stage" customer "experiences.[13]

Stories are told of the great service deliverers: Nordstrom, with its legendary returns policy and dedicated personal shoppers; Singapore Airlines, whose elegant "Singapore girls" pamper business class passengers as they sip the finest wines and eat gourmet meals in the lap of luxury at 35,000 feet; Four Seasons Hotels, where staff are trained to recall the names of returning guests and to remember their personal preferences; and Federal Express, which guarantees package delivery and compensates for lateness. Many organizations attempt to motivate employees to deliver great service using campaigns such as the one illustrated in Exhibit 1-2.

DIMINISHED SERVICE

Simultaneously, there is a push for diminished service wherever we look. This is not simply because firms don't care about service (at least most of them do), or in a simple desire to cut costs, but because in many arenas, there is a realization that customers don't want more service, they want less. Some years ago, Ted Levitt,[14] in a prescient article, "The Industrialization of Service," argued that firms would not be more successful if they provided more service, but if they provided less of it. They should, he suggested, industrialize themselves and become more similar to mass producers of goods than be benevolent panderers to the whims of individuals. Rather than try to solve the problems that arise in service firms, they should try to eliminate them; not fix the system, but change it. Putting "more people" into a service setting doesn't solve problems, it creates them. When firms do this, they will be giving the customer what they really want: not more service, but less service! To many marketers in general and service providers in particular, this might sound like heresy. Some simple examples enable us to illustrate Levitt's points vividly, however:

• Just 30 years ago, telephoning London from New York would have required calling an operator and waiting to be connected, which could take a long time if there weren't enough operators on shift. Today, we dial directly, effortlessly.

EXHIBIT 1-2   Delivering Great Customer Service

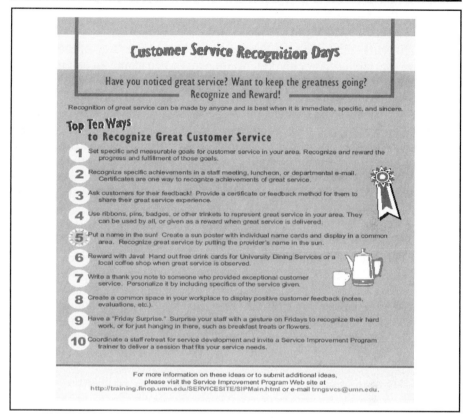

Source: University of Minnesota

• Just 30 years ago, a customer wishing to withdraw cash from a bank account would have had to wait until the bank opened and then stand in line to be served by a bank teller. And there never seemed to be enough tellers on duty. Today, we use an automated teller machine, wherever there is one, at any time of the day or night.

• Just 10 years ago, a frequent flyer wishing to obtain his or her latest air miles balance would have had to wait for a statement to be mailed. When the statement did arrive, it didn't record the last few flights, and thus was immediately out of date. Today, the same individual can log on the airline's website and get his or her latest balance with ease.

It is clear from these examples (and countless more like them) that customers don't always want warm, delightful service; they often simply want solutions to their problems. They don't always want more people to help them; they are very often prepared to help themselves. They want the speed, efficiency, and, most importantly, control that helping themselves provides.

TREND 8: BRANDS VERSUS ANTI-BRANDS

THE AGE OF BRANDS

The past 10 years could quite easily be characterized as the "Age of the Brand." Brands are everything. Savvy marketers argue that when all the great innovations have been imitated, and the services offered by firms not only look the same but are all of equally high quality, it is the strongest brands that will win.

Firms have focused on brand equity—the value of their brand, and the meanings it occupies in the mind of the market. The management consulting firm Interbrand (**www.interbrand.com**) has built its worldwide business (and also its own brand) by using a simple formula to calculate brand equity, or the monetary value, of all of the world's largest brands. Disregarding the fact that the firm's methodology has been criticized as being overly simplistic, if not just flawed, marketers, managers, the media, and the public at large are fascinated by reports that "brand X is worth Y million dollars, and that brand Z has lost a lot of value over the past year." An example of the type of research Interbrand conducts is to be seen in Figure 1-5, in which it can be seen that the brand equity, or brand value, of brands such as Coca-Cola and Microsoft is larger than the GDPs of many nation-states.

It is not just the brands of for-profit firms that have attracted attention; it has been argued that brands such as the Red Cross, Amnesty International, and Greenpeace possess more equity than many *Fortune* 500 firms. One study cites

FIGURE 1-5 Brand Values of the World's 10 Most Valuable Brands

Brand	2006 brand value ($ millions)
Marlboro	21,795
McDonald's	27,501
Disney	27,848
Toyota	27,941
Nokia	30,131
Intel	32,319
GE	48,907
IBM	56,201
Microsoft	56,926
Coca-Cola	67,000

Source: Interbrand, 2006.

the charity Habitat for Humanity as having the same brand value as Starbucks.[15] Certainly, they are more recognizable to the world's citizens than a great many of the brands of for-profit firms. The potential to extend these brands to goods and services that can be sold, either to gather funds or to make profits, is considerable.

THE ERA OF THE ANTI-BRAND

While brands may be "everything," what they stand for and represent is not appreciated by everyone. There has been an active anti-branding movement throughout the world directed at the better-known brands that has accused them of a multitude of sins, ranging from anti-competitive stances to outright bullying. In many countries, there are consumer groups that resent the dilution that they perceive global brands exert on their cultures. There has been considerable effort targeted at major brands:

• The longest civil or criminal action in British legal history was triggered when McDonald's sued former gardener Helen Steel, 39, and former postman David Morris, 50. The pair had been handing out leaflets containing numerous allegations about the corporation's policies and practices. Neither Ms. Steel nor Mr. Morris wrote the leaflets, but they became embroiled in the libel action launched in 1990 and ending only in 1997—with 314 days spent in court. At the end of the case, the British High Court ruled McDonald's had been libeled and awarded the company £60,000 in damages, later reduced to £40,000 on appeal. McDonald's came out looking like a bully for its efforts.

• Massachusetts Institute of Technology student Jonah Peretti tried to order a customized pair of Nike shoes off the firm's special customization website, NikeID. The special slogan he chose to have embossed on his shoes was "Sweatshop." Nike declined to take his order; they termed his chosen watchword "inappropriate slang." His subsequent e-mail dealings with the firm found their way to the Internet, where anti-globalization and anti-brand cognoscenti had a field day making fun of the firm. The e-mail exchanges were forwarded to thousands of inboxes all over the world (see the story at **http://www.shey.net/niked.html**).

• Despite the fact that Starbucks has been shown in many ways to be more "diverse" than the participants in the anti-brand and anti-globalization movements, the firm has been the focus of much protest. Although Starbucks has actively pursued a number of socially responsible operating policies such as the purchase of Fair-Trade coffee, the subsidization of health care facilities in Central America, and the introduction of a number of socially responsible coffee products in its stores, it continues to be the target of anti-globalization activities.

• Naomi Klein's[16] successful anti-branding book, *No Logo,* argues that "free speech is meaningless if the commercial cacophony has risen to the point where no one can hear you." Far from delivering on the choice promised by the information age, she contends that the brands marketed by large MNCs limit, rather than extend, the options open to the world's consumers. The Vancouver, Canada-based anti-advertising action group Adbusters publishes a magazine and a website that parody the advertising of many of the world's best-known brands. Adbusters targets Nike especially, and now markets its own brand of casual footwear, called Blackspot Unswooshers, as an alternative to Nike's Swoosh products. Of course, cynics might argue that both Klein and the Adbusters group are really doing what commercial brand builders have always done—creating brands for themselves.

SO WHAT'S A MARKETER TO DO? MANAGING IN AN ERA OF JANUS TRENDS

Given the uncertainty that paradoxical trends like those considered earlier create, marketers might be forgiven for contending that it is impossible to plan and that the only thing certain about the future is uncertainty. Some pessimists might even paraphrase Arthur Clarke's observation that "this is the first age that's paid much attention to the future, which is a little ironic since we may not have one." We prefer Theodor Seuss Geisel's (better known as Dr. Seuss) little rhyme, "Today was good. Today was fun. Tomorrow is another one." Never before has the time for an aggressive market entry strategy been so good. Yet never before has the value of incumbency within a market or an industry been so low.

Diverging global trends and the accelerated rate of change result in dramatically raised uncertainty. At an elementary level, managers routinely need to monitor changes in the global business environment and to explore new paradigms for organizational success. Similarly, global marketing managers need to balance the tensions between global-scale efficiency and multinational flexibility. There is also a need to continually explore innovations and leverage knowledge on a worldwide basis.

At a more complex level, and as illustrated in Figure 1-6, marketers have to achieve a strategic balance. Ideally, firms need to evolve, making relatively slow changes to what they do and how they do it, so that they don't rush and don't end up simply fixing what isn't broken. We might term this approach "strategic evolution by creeps." On the other hand, because business life is seldom ideal, firms must acknowledge the need for, and indeed attempt "evolution by jerks,"[17] or more radically, revolution. In the language of evolutionary biology, this would be

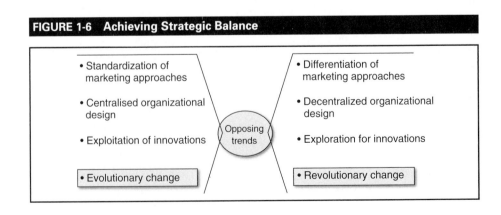

FIGURE 1-6   Achieving Strategic Balance

- Standardization of marketing approaches
- Centralised organizational design
- Exploitation of innovations
- Evolutionary change

Opposing trends

- Differentiation of marketing approaches
- Decentralized organizational design
- Exploration for innovations
- Revolutionary change

known as "punctuated equilibrium,"[18] a theory which states that most reproducing species will show little to no evolutionary change throughout their history. When evolution does occur, it happens sporadically, and it occurs relatively quickly compared with the species' full duration on earth.

Figure 1-6 shows that there is a paradoxical tension to maintain evolutionary change on the one hand and to achieve a process of revolutionary change on the other. Under the evolutionary change scenario, the firm manages a slow and determined process of exploiting innovations. The pace of innovation is relatively slow, and each viable advance is milked for all it's worth. Many of these types of innovations are customer led: marketing research reveals customer desires and preferences, and the firm innovates to satisfy these. When the focus is on revolutionary change, the firm explores for innovations much as gold miners of old staked as many claims as they could and panned for all they were worth. While much of what is found will simply be dirt and dust, every now and then an innovation will be unearthed like a large nugget. The firm places many bets, knowing that while many of them will lose, the gains made on the winners will more than compensate for the exploration losses. These types of innovation are seldom customer driven; they usually result from a "build it and they will come" philosophy that has faith in the power of great innovations to woo and seduce customers.

Under the evolutionary change scenario, firms tend to be hierarchical and somewhat static in structure. Roles are assigned, tasks are performed, and individuals in the firm know where they fit and how things are held together. Often, the firm is organized along the lines of functional silos, with departments such as human resources (HR), operations, finance, and marketing all having assigned tasks and purposes. Firms in a revolutionary mode are structurally fluid, with roles frequently changing and often unassigned. Functions such as HR and marketing are frequently undetectable in an organization chart (if there is one) and are usually seen as general management functions and part of everyone's job.

Marketing, under an evolutionary scenario in a firm, will follow a standardized approach. Marketing scholars and practitioners would recognize this as familiar, orthodox, "textbook" marketing. The firm positions itself in a familiar market within a well-defined industry. It carefully segments this market by means of common market segmentation techniques to identify homogenous groups of customers that it can best serve given its limited resources. To better serve these customers, the firm conducts marketing research and identifies the articulated needs and wants of these customers. Then it constructs a marketing mix, the familiar "4 P's" of marketing: the right *product,* at the right *price,* available at the right *place* (distribution), with the best *promotion* strategy (advertising, personal selling, publicity, sales promotion) to build its ongoing relationships with this market.

When firms face revolutionary change, orthodox marketing approaches might not present optimal solutions. In this book, the focus is on a revolutionary approach to marketing strategy. The firm might not be in a familiar market, nor might it be in a well-defined industry—indeed, the market might not yet exist, and the industry might still be experiencing the pangs of an uncertain birth. There might not be a well-defined target market; moreover, conventional marketing research might even reveal that customers don't want the offering! And yet, when the innovation is released it might have the power of being able to create customers. Pricing strategies might have to be entrepreneurial rather than conventional, and distribution might be through channels that need to be invented and created. Standard mass media advertising and conventional selling techniques will give way to edgy communication strategies such as guerilla marketing, ambush marketing, and viral marketing, and will use media that never existed 10 years ago.

Key Terms

- trends
- future
- paradox
- strategic balance

Questions

1. What is meant by the observation that trends are "paradoxical"?
2. Choose any one of the trends identified, and analyze how the trend will affect an industry, market, or firm of your choice. Will it be good or bad for that industry, firm, or market?
3. List and describe other trends that you can currently identify. Are they paradoxical? Why, and how?
4. How would you determine whether an organization had achieved "strategic balance"? Can you think of any steps you would go through or processes that you would use?
5. The chapter talks about the need for achieving strategic balance. Take any three of the paradoxical trends discussed, and map how a firm of your choice can still manage to achieve strategic balance with regard to those trends.

Resources and References

RESOURCE

Interbrand. (2006). *Best global brands 2006: A ranking by value.* Report accessed April 30, 2007, www.interbrand.com.

REFERENCES

1. Naisbitt, J. (1988). *Megatrends: Ten new directions transforming our lives.* New York: Warner Books.
2. Popcorn, F. (1992). *The Popcorn report: Faith Popcorn on the future of your company, your world, your life.* New York: HarperCollins Publishers.
3. http://www.care.org/campaigns/childrenpoverty/facts.asp.
4. "Stitched up: How rich country protectionism in textiles and clothing prevents poverty alleviation." Oxfam Briefing Paper, April 2004.
5. Pitt, L. F., Berthon, P. R., & Berthon, J. P. (1999, March–April). Changing channels: The impact of the Internet on distribution strategy. *Business Horizons* 42(2): 19–28.

6. Cowen, T. (2002). *Creative destruction: How globalization is changing the world's culture*. Princeton, NJ: Princeton University Press.
7. Barber, B. (1995). *Jihad vs. McWorld: How globalism and tribalism are reshaping the world*. New York: Random House.
8. Hertz, N. (2003). *The silent takeover: Global capitalism and the death of democracy*. New York: HarperCollins Publishers.
9. Simon, H. (1996). *Hidden champions: Lessons from 500 of the world's best unknown companies*. Boston: Harvard Business School Press.
10. Godin, S. (1999). *Permission marketing: Turning strangers into friends, and friends into customers*. New York: Simon & Schuster.
11. Watson, R. T., Pitt, L. F., Berthon, P. R., & Zinkhan, G. M. (2002, Fall). U-commerce: Extending the universe of marketing. *Journal of the Academy of Marketing Science:* 329–343.
12. Peters, T. J., & Waterman, R. H. Jr. (1982). *In search of excellence: Lessons from America's best run companies*. New York: HarperCollins Publishers.
13. Pine, B. J., & Gilmore, J. H. (1999). *The experience economy: Work is theatre & every business a stage*. Boston: Harvard Business School Press.
14. Levitt, T. (1976). The industrialization of service. *Harvard Business Review* 54(5): 63–74.
15. Quelch, J. A., & Laidler-Kylander, N. (2006). *The new global brands: Managing non-governmental organizations in the 21st century*. New York: Thomson South-Western.
16. Klein, N. (1999). *No logo*. New York, NY: Picador.
17. Ghiselin, M. T. (1986, December 14). We are all contraptions. *New York Times*.
18. Eldredge, N., & Gould, S. J. (1972). Punctuated equilibria: An alternative to phyletic gradualism. In T. J. M. Schopf, ed., *Models in paleobiology* (pp. 82–115). San Francisco: Freeman Cooper. Reprinted in N. Eldredge. (1985). *Time frames*. Princeton, NJ: Princeton University Press.

CHAPTER 2

THE RULES HAVE CHANGED
The Emergence of Entrepreneurial Marketing

Armed with concepts like segmentation, the value chain, competitor benchmarking, strategic groups, and mobility barriers, many managers have become better and better at drawing industry maps. But while they have been busy mapmaking, their competitors have been moving entire continents. The strategist's goal is not to find a niche within the existing industry space but to create new space that is uniquely suited to the company's own strengths—space that is off the map.

— Gary Hamel and C. K. Prahalad

THE SHIFT: FROM MONOLINEAR INFORMATION TO POLYRHYTHMIC INTERACTIONS

Companies today must operate in an environment consisting of increased risk, decreased ability to forecast, fluid firm and industry boundaries, a managerial mindset that must unlearn traditional management principles, and new business structures that not only allow for change, but also help create it. It is a competitive landscape that has been characterized by four overriding forces: change, complexity, chaos, and contradiction. Chapter 1 introduced a number of paradoxical forces that affect markets on a global scale. These forces are also having an important effect on marketing. Markets are shifting, overlapping, fragmenting, and becoming frictionless; distribution channels are being reshaped, reconfigured, and bypassed; firms interact as competitors, customers, and collaborators in a global, knowledge economy; and customers are becoming more demanding than ever. Marketing is context dependent, but the context is continually changing. Time, location, market, or competition-centric law-like generalizations and rules-of-thumb no longer apply. A proliferation of communication vehicles seems to be making marketing more costly, less effective, more complex, and increasingly more difficult to measure. In the midst of these challenges, marketing thought and practice have been criticized as focusing on mundane issues, defining problems narrowly, and emphasizing tactical responses to strategic challenges.[1]

Some have argued that the fundamental precepts of marketing are not the problem, but that more attention must be given to two specific areas:

1. Customization, one-to-one approaches, and personal relationships in a more personalized approach.
2. Networking, strategic alliances, integration, and technology in an increasingly global effort.

Others claim that marketing itself should be reconceptualized, arguing that simply extending existing theoretical frameworks is no longer sufficient to reflect marketplace shifts or to guide marketing practice in the fundamentally new competitive context and conditions of the 21st century.[2] In the meantime, power has shifted away from the marketer toward the market as a result of changes in consumer behavior, technological advances, and unabated evolution of the Internet, resulting in time-shifting and asynchronous communications. Some companies have realized the urgency to restructure their marketing efforts significantly. But how? In this chapter, we consider how the current forces and trends predicted for the future are affecting the way in which companies and customers are thinking about marketing in an effort to make sense of what marketers can do amidst the cacophony in the market space.

DEVELOPMENTS IN MARKETING THOUGHT AND PRACTICE

Historically, the American Marketing Association (AMA) defined marketing as "the process of planning and executing the conception, pricing, promotion, and distribution of ideas, goods, and services to create exchanges that satisfy individual and organizational goals."[3] This definition has formed the foundation for much of conventional marketing practice. Typically, marketers attempt to blend product, price, promotion, and distribution decisions into an integrated mix that meets the needs of target customers better than competitive offerings. In this environment, salespeople and customer service representatives interface with customers, while the marketing department operates in isolation—far removed from the sales department—using mass media (e.g., TV, radio, or print advertising) to move potential target customers through the buying process. At best, the marketer *might* interact with customers in focus groups or product testing—if these activities are not performed by a third party (e.g., a marketing research firm).

DEVELOPING CRACKS IN MARKETING'S FAÇADE

In an attempt to break through the clutter and achieve more impact, while also responding to customers' retaliation against marketing communications (e.g., using devices such as TiVo) and harnessing the power of the Internet, a number of alternative marketing approaches have appeared in recent years. Examples include expeditionary marketing, guerrilla marketing, radical marketing, convergence marketing, buzz marketing, and viral marketing (see Chapter 8). These alternative approaches have captured the attention of marketers looking for new ways to market effectively in a difficult environment. They vary in terms of tactical versus strategic considerations, the emphasis on promotion versus the entire marketing mix, and the extent to which they focus on smaller ventures versus established firms. Yet, there are several commonalities among these approaches that represent enduring characteristics of successful marketing efforts in the new age: efficiency in marketing expenditures by leveraging resources, creative and alternative approaches to managing marketing variables, ongoing product and process innovation, customer intensity, and an emphasis on changing the rules of the competitive game. However, none of these new marketing approaches, by themselves, represents a framework comprehensive enough to guide marketing practice in the future.

MARKETING THEORY TRIES TO KEEP PACE

In the closing years of the 20th century, experts were beginning to recognize the need for marketing thought to move in new directions.[4] There was increasing evidence marketing should embrace a more cross-functional, cross-border, and cross-disciplinary orientation and focus on networks of strategic alliances and relationships.[5] Further, the relationship paradigm suggested marketing must replace a focus on short-term exchange with an emphasis on acquiring and retaining customers[6] and building customer equity in the long run.[7] It was also being argued that marketing must play an important role at the organizational level in product development, supply chain management, and customer relationship management, as well as at the functional level with processes that link a firm to its customers such as customer-product, customer-service, and customer-financial.[8] These developments in marketing thought emphasized the importance of intra- and interorganizational partnerships to acquire and retain desired customers as part of a market orientation.[9] Moreover, marketing efforts had to be more closely linked with financial considerations, with marketing playing a leading role both at the overall business level and as a functional area.

After much debate and disagreement, the AMA in 2004 acknowledged some of these fundamental changes by redefining marketing as "an organizational function and a set of processes for creating, communicating, and delivering value to customers and for managing customer relationships in ways that benefit the organization and its stakeholders."[10] This new definition reflects a shift in emphasis from process, planning, and transactions to the creation and communication of value in search of long-lasting customer relationships. Marketing's role is to make people aware of the brand and to generate and grow demand. Yet, as we will discuss later, those in the marketing profession are struggling to keep abreast of customers. Customers are constantly redefining the marketer's role in their lives: they are no longer passive recipients, but active co-creators. This shift from an enterprise value chain (at the company level) to a personal value chain (at the customer level) makes it imperative for marketers to rethink everything they do. It also means that marketing matters more than ever before.

THE FOUR P's ARE DEAD: LONG LIVE THE NEW FOUR C's

The time has come to slay the sacred cows of conventional marketing. As the Cluetrain Manifesto[11] notes, it is "the end of business as usual." The formulaic, predictable world of the marketing mix (better known as the 4 P's), with its unidirectional, horizontal communication mechanisms, is blocking potential. For too long marketers accepted the unquestioned rules prescribed by marketing textbooks; dogmatic systems seemed off-limits to change. The dominant paradigm or way of thinking in marketing acknowledges the importance of getting and keeping the customer. It assumes the marketer accomplishes this after segmenting the market, positioning the product relative to its competitors, and targeting potential customers using the 4 P's (product, price, place, and promotion). Traditional marketing logic was simple: the marketer acts as agent of the company by managing the 4 P's as variables with which to attract customers and build loyalties—the customer is viewed as a fish to be caught, a pawn in the ongoing struggle between competing firms in search of superior profits for their stakeholders. This is inherently a linear, supply-based view.

But this marketing logic is broken. Some skeptics even refer to the 4 P's as *prescriptive, polemical, permanent, and problematical*—generally ill-equipped to deal with the challenges facing marketers today in which *paradox, profusion, plurivalence, and poligny* prevail. Consider this: Information is available instantaneously, either structured or unstructured (via Google, Yahoo!, MSN, CNN, or thousands of other sources); every person (customer or not) can be heard and his/her online voice has the power to tell the world about a given company. This means the marketer no longer controls brand communications; changes in products or prices are immediate and available in real time to customers and competitors alike. Products and services look more and more alike, with the only noticeable difference often being the price. Everyone is connected—conversations online are accompanied with offline exchanges through multiple media, compounding the complexity of a marketing world that revolves around a static and fixed marketing mix in which the only creative variable is promotion through full-color brochures, expensive media campaigns, or clever websites.

The old marketing logic cannot be fixed; all the reactionary band-aid remedies have proven to be ineffective. The new marketing logic requires a fundamental *rethinking* of the old rules that applied in a world of stability and hierarchical control. Marketing velocity (the speed of transactions) is higher: it is dynamic and happening in real time. In a polyrhythmic, demand-based view, customers insist that marketers act as an agent with their best interest at heart; then, and only then, will the customer cooperate (by opening purse strings, and heart strings in some instances). This requires the marketer to accept that the customer is in control, and therefore drives decisions, not the product and definitely not the marketer. It also requires reconceptualization of the marketing mix from the perspective of the customer: beyond customer-centric to customer-made. The customer is no longer the object of a sale, or the subject of a loyalty scheme. To capture what is important to the customer, we must shift from the 4 P's to the 4 C's:

- From *product* to *co-created* solutions/experiences (don't presume you can understand me — don't try to capture me; captivate and engage me!).
- From *promotion* to communication within *communities* (I want interconnected interactions with like-minded others, not information).
- From *price* to *customizable* personal value (I am not a cost-to-serve or one of many).
- From *place* to *choice* and convenience (I am here; why are you not?).

In short, marketers must act as servers of customers rather than suppliers of products. In this blurring of roles between customer and company in which the customer's view of value trumps the marketer's perception of brand or customer value, marketing's sole purpose becomes one of value creation for the customer — no other stakeholders come first. How can this be achieved? By engaging the customer, by creating meaning, by making the seemingly impossible possible. Jones Soda is such a marketer (see Exhibit 2-1). This company has the new 4 C's as its foundation; it exemplifies a new marketing logic that challenges old assumptions and conventional wisdom.

This is the era of Generation C, [12] where *C* stands for *content*. This generation is *connected, creative, collaborative,* and *contextual.* It's no wonder the shift is away from the tangible hardware of the traditional 4 P's toward the new 4 C's, which are abstract and conceptual: the watchwords have changed to *co-creation, community, customization,* and *choice* in which the *customer* is at the *center* of marketing activity, not the brand or the marketer. Note that the word *consumer* is not in this list: people are taking charge, becoming content creators, reviewers, producers, champions, inventors, designers, and critics.

"Customer-made" is becoming as ubiquitous as "Made in China." Outsourcing is being replaced by crowd-sourcing, the act of taking a job traditionally performed by a designated agent (usually an employee) and outsourcing it to an undefined, often large group of people in the form of an open call.[13] This means that to create content, solve problems, even do corporate R&D, a massive collaboration of professionals, amateurs, volunteers, and tinkerers in an online community can use their spare time to solve problems better, and at a lower cost, regardless of where they are located. Moreover, these open systems can produce

EXHIBIT 2-1 Jones Soda—The Story of a Sacred Cow Slayer

Jones Soda Co. (founded in 1987 as Urban Juice and Soda Company Ltd) started as a distributor of other companies' beverage lines such as Arizona Iced Tea and Thomas Kemper sodas. Utilizing experience and knowledge gained in distribution, Jones Soda Co. started launching its own brands in 1995 when it entered the emerging new-age beverage industry. Shortly thereafter, the company launched several noncarbonated soft drinks with unusual colors and added a distinct fashion component to the drink, which created a new category (all natural soda) in the new-age or alternative beverage market. Since 2001, Jones Soda Co. has focused on product line extensions (new flavors like Fufu Berry, Blue Bubblegum, WhoopAss, and special holiday drinks like Brussels Sprout with Prosciutto, etc.) and the addition of new product lines (e.g., energy drinks, diet sodas, carbonated soft drinks, organic tea line) to maintain the vitality of the product range. In 2004, the company entered the mainstream carbonated soft-drink industry in which Pepsi and Coca-Cola dominate and extended the brand into nonalternative beverage products and nonbeverage products (e.g., lip balms).

However, founder Peter van Stolk thinks very differently about the company, its products, and its customers. Instead of creating another soda company, Jones has used its soda as a platform for social interaction. To cement this connection, Jones launched a website called Jones Independent Music, where bands post songs, images, bios, and contact information. A virtual community of fans gathers at the company's website to create new products, chat, blog, enter contests, share movie reviews, and download freebies. In 2002, Jones Soda Co. was issued a patent for its myjones.com business operation.

Talk about a new marketing logic!

Why would a soda company offer a music service? To answer this question, it is important to understand Jones' philosophy—it has never been about selling soda. Everything the company does demonstrates its commitment to a shared ownership of the brand with the customer that goes beyond merely listening to the customer. Instead of extolling the virtues of its brand, Jones unleashes the energy and creativity of its customers to give the brand its virtues. As a result Jones Soda has created a cult following—soda drinkers, employees, directors, and shareholders alike share this passion for music. Its radical approaches to brand management have redefined the market space and changed consumers' perceptions through brand ownership and several rule-breaking behaviors.

Talk about customer-made!

At Jones Soda the customer creates the product—the flavors as well as the unique packaging that features constantly changing labels. Customers are encouraged to submit photos for consideration to the company's website and then vote to determine the most popular photos for the labels. Jones has received more than 4 million photos from customers. Customers also e-mail favorite sayings, aphorisms, and messages, which are then used as under-the-cap fortunes. Customers are active participants in a customer community, which creates a lasting emotional bond with customers. Participation among customers themselves shape Jones's personality and products, giving them an even greater stake in what the company does.

Talk about being different!

Distribution of Jones Soda is *the* alternative—the firm sells its products where Pepsi and Coca-Cola do not. Moreover, Jones Soda Co. places it own coolers, bearing signature flames, in unique venues such as skate-, surf- and snowboarding shops, tattoo and piercing parlors, individual fashion stores, and national retail clothing and music stores.

Talk about being unique!

Jones Soda incorporated unique marketing initiatives in its strategy through the Jones Team Riders: extreme athletes BMXer Matt Hoffman, surfboarder Kahea Hart, and skateboarder Willy Santos. These champions promote the brand by sporting the Jones logo at extreme sporting events across the country. The firm also uses various street marketing tactics to connect with its customers.

Source: Jones Soda Company, accessed October 22, 2006, http://www.secinfo.com/dRqWm.3vf8.htm; http://en.wikipedia.org/wiki/Jones_Soda; and http://www.jonessoda.com/.

faster and more powerful results than the traditional closed proprietary systems, because "billions of connected individuals can now actively participate in innovation, wealth creation, and social development in ways we once only dreamed of. And when these masses of people collaborate they effectively can advance the arts, culture, science, education, government, and the economy in surprising but ultimately profitable ways."[14]

Who is crowd-sourcing? Just about every industry has discovered ways to harness the creativity of distributed labor available from everyday people. John Fluevog Shoes (**www.fluevog.com**) produces chunky, funky shoes from designs submitted by Fluevog fanatics—the start of Open Source Footwear. The Japanese specialty furniture retailer Muji (**www.muji.net**) asks the member base on its community site of approximately 500,000 people to submit radical new product ideas and then pre-evaluate these designs before passing the highest-ranked ideas on to professional designers for further development. Zazzle (**www.zazzle.com**) allows you to create calendars, mugs, shirts, and posters based on your own designs— and if other Zazzlers like your work enough to order products with your design, you get a cut. The Beastie Boys' most recent concert movie was filmed by 50 fans wielding Hi-8 cameras. Other examples include Peugeot (solicited car designs and built a prototype of the winners) and IKEA (developed 14 new products from 5,000 design ideas for storing home media) and even the Human Genome Project.

THE NATURE OF, AND NEED FOR, ENTREPRENEURSHIP

Ultimately, all of this is about entrepreneurship. *Entrepreneurship* has been defined as "the process of creating value by bringing together a unique package of resources to exploit an opportunity."[15] It results not only in the creation of new, growth-oriented ventures, but also in the strategic renewal of existing firms. The process includes the set of activities necessary to identify an opportunity, define a business concept, assess and acquire the necessary resources, and then manage and harvest the venture. But entrepreneurship is not limited to someone who starts or owns a business. An entrepreneur uncovers new approaches and better ways to get things done. At its core, entrepreneurship is

> a subversive activity. It upsets the status quo, disrupts accepted ways of doing things and alters traditional patterns of behavior. It is at heart a change process that undermines current market conditions by introducing something new or different in response to perceived needs. It is sometimes chaotic, often unpredictable. Because of the dynamic nature of entrepreneurship and because of the entrepreneur's ability to initiate change and create value . . . the concept of "creative destruction" is an apt description of the process. . . . The entrepreneur thus disrupts the economic status quo, and as a result creates new market opportunities.[16]

Various observers have suggested that entrepreneurship is the principal agent of change operating from within any economic system. Such change comes in the form of new combinations of resources, or innovations, which eventually displace existing products and processes through "creative destruction"[17] — the continual disruption of economic equilibrium brought on by entrepreneurial activity. An entrepreneurial perspective is reflected in Sony founder Akio Morito's conclusion that "the nature of business is to make your own product obsolete."

Entrepreneurship has also been viewed as an organizational orientation exhibiting three underlying dimensions: innovativeness, calculated risk-taking, and proactiveness.[18] *Innovativeness* refers to the seeking of creative, unusual, or novel solutions to problems and needs. *Calculated risk-taking* involves the willingness to commit significant resources to opportunities that have a reasonable chance of costly failure, but it also includes creative attempts to mitigate, leverage, or share the various risks. *Proactiveness* is making things happen through whatever means are necessary. The more innovative, risk-taking, and proactive the activities of the firm, the more entrepreneurial it is. Thus, entrepreneurship is not an either-or determination, but a question of degree. A growing body of evidence suggests the more successful firms over time are the ones that engage in higher levels of entrepreneurial activity. The need for entrepreneurship is greatest when firms face diminishing opportunity streams, as well as rapid changes in technology, consumer needs, social values, and political roles. The same is true when firms are confronted with short decision windows, unpredictable resource needs, lack of long-term control over the environment, increased resource specialization, and employee demands for independence.

THE ENTREPRENEURIAL MARKETING CONSTRUCT[19]

The term *entrepreneurial marketing* has been most frequently associated with marketing activities in firms that are small and resource constrained and therefore must rely on creative and often unsophisticated marketing tactics that make heavy use of personal networks. Alternatively, the term has been employed to describe the unplanned, nonlinear, visionary marketing actions of the entrepreneur. Leading universities, including Stanford and Harvard, have built entrepreneurial marketing courses around the act of market creation by high-growth, high-technology firms. Yet another perspective distinguishes marketing at different stages of a firm's development, referring to "entrepreneurial marketing" or guerrilla, grassroots approaches in the early stages of company development, and "intrapreneurial marketing" or creative, nonformulaic marketing in the later stages. In spite of these various uses of the term, a consistent definition has not been promulgated, nor have the underlying components of the concept been specified.

For our purposes, *entrepreneurial marketing (EM)* is proposed as an integrative construct for conceptualizing marketing in an era of change, complexity, chaos, contradiction, and diminishing resources, and one that will manifest itself differently as companies age and grow. It fuses key aspects of recent developments in marketing thought and practice with those in the entrepreneurship area into one comprehensive construct. As such, it provides an umbrella term for capturing many of the new forms of marketing discussed earlier.

> Entrepreneurial marketing (EM) is defined as the proactive identification, evaluation, and exploitation of opportunities for acquiring and retaining profitable customers through innovative approaches to risk management, resource leveraging, and value creation.

EM represents an opportunistic perspective wherein the marketer proactively seeks novel ways to create value for desired customers and build customer equity. The marketer is not constrained by resources currently controlled, and product/market innovation represents the core marketing responsibility and the key means to sustainable competitive advantage. A comparison of specific aspects of conventional and entrepreneurial marketing approaches is presented in Table 2-1.

While the juxtaposition in Table 2-1 serves to distinguish EM, in reality a continuum exists from a more responsive, risk-avoidant, control-oriented approach to one that is highly entrepreneurial. Hence, rather than a simple dichotomy, a spectrum of marketing approaches exists. The differences lie in concepts of "frequency" (or the number of entrepreneurial actions pursued by the marketer) and "degree" (or the extent to which these activities are more innovative, risky, and proactive). Thus, EM implies innovation or leveraging efforts that are more frequent and that represent greater departures from current norms or standards. A company's position on this spectrum is context specific, reflecting the firm's particular circumstances and environment. EM is most needed when facing contexts that are more fragmented, dynamic, or hostile, as well as in emerging markets, where the marketer must act as innovator and change agent. Alternatively, the context for conventional marketing is more stable for established markets where the marketer is principally concerned with the efficiency and effectiveness of the marketing mix.

TABLE 2-1 Contrasting Conventional and Entrepreneurial Marketing

	Conventional Marketing	*Entrepreneurial Marketing*
Basic premise	Facilitation of transactions and market control	Sustainable competitive advantage through value-creating innovation
Orientation	Marketing as objective, dispassionate science	Central role of passion, zeal, persistence, and creativity in marketing
Context	Established, relatively stable markets	Envisioned, emerging, and fragmented markets with high levels of turbulence
Marketer's role	Coordinator of marketing mix; builder of the brand	Internal and external change agent; creator of the category
Market approach	Reactive and adaptive approach to current market situation with incremental innovation	Proactive approach, leading the customer with dynamic innovation
Customer needs	Articulated, assumed, expressed by customers through survey research	Unarticulated, discovered, identified through lead users
Risk perspective	Risk minimization in marketing actions	Marketing as vehicle for calculated risk-taking; emphasis on finding ways to mitigate, stage, or share risks
Resource management	Efficient use of existing resources, scarcity mentality	Leveraging, creative use of the resources of others; doing more with less; actions are not constrained by resources currently controlled
New product/ service development	Marketing supports new product/service development activities of R&D and other technical departments	Marketing is the home of innovation; customer is co-active producer
Customer's role	External source of intelligence and feedback	Active participant in firm's marketing decision process, defining product, price, distribution, and communications approaches

The differences highlighted in Table 2-1 also suggest that an EM approach requires changes not only in behavior but also in the underlying mindset and attitudes held by those responsible for marketing activities. Engaging in actions that are innovative, entail risks, or are more proactive implies that managers understand and have positive attitudes toward these kinds of behaviors and that they develop skill sets to support these activities. Thus, EM is more than simply an examination of the role of marketing in entrepreneurship or the role of entrepreneurship in marketing. It entails a shift from the use of the word *entrepreneurial* as the marketing efforts of an entrepreneurial company[20] (e.g., a high-tech, start-up, or small firm) to EM as a central concept that integrates the two disciplines of marketing and entrepreneurship. It represents an alternative approach to marketing under certain conditions.

EM lies at the interface between a market orientation and an entrepreneurial orientation. It consists of "matching up the products of human imagination (as embedded in products, firms, and other potential means of supply) with human aspirations (i.e., latent demand that derives from unmet market needs or problems that are poorly satisfied) to create markets for goods and services that did not exist before the entrepreneurial act."[21] Thus, integrating a customer focus throughout the firm and continuous innovation and leading rather than following are interdependent elements that must work hand in hand. The correlation between the two orientations suggests they may jointly contribute to a single, overriding organizational philosophy.[22]

UNDERLYING DIMENSIONS OF ENTREPRENEURIAL MARKETING

Entrepreneurial marketing has seven underlying dimensions. Three of these dimensions—proactiveness, calculated risk-taking, and innovativeness—were mentioned earlier in our discussion of the entrepreneurial orientation of the firm. The fourth dimension concerns the entrepreneur as a change agent who is opportunity-obsessed. A fifth dimension—resource leveraging—is also a common theme within the entrepreneurship literature. The final two dimensions—customer intimacy and value creation—are consistent with the market orientation of the firm. Moreover, as conceptualized, customer intensity has a visceral and emotional component, as reflected in many of the emerging perspectives, most notably customer-centric, radical and expeditionary marketing. Further, value creation is a core element of commonly accepted definitions of entrepreneurship because innovative efforts that do not convey market value lack commercial potential. Let us examine each of these dimensions in further detail.

Proactiveness

Marketing's conventional role is to assess existing or anticipated environmental conditions and then make recommendations for changes to the marketing mix that will enable the firm to best capitalize on those conditions. Entrepreneurial marketing does not consider the external environment as a given or as a set of circumstances to which the firm can only react or adjust. Proactive behavior concerns differences among people based on the extent to which they take action to influence their environments, and it can be thought of as "purposeful enactment."[23] The environment is viewed as an opportunity horizon where the marketer attempts to redefine external conditions in ways that reduce uncertainty and lessen the firm's dependency and vulnerability. Marketing variables are used as a means of both creating change and adapting to change.

OBSESSION WITH OPPORTUNITY

A continuum exists of managerial approaches to marketing, ranging from an emphasis on pursuing opportunity regardless of resources currently controlled (i.e., behavior that is more entrepreneurial) to a focus on the efficient utilization of existing resources (i.e., behavior that is more administrative).[24] The recognition and pursuit of opportunity is fundamental to entrepreneurship and is a core dimension of EM. Opportunities represent unnoticed market openings that are sources of sustainable profit potential. They derive from market imperfections, where knowledge about these imperfections and how to exploit them distinguish the entrepreneurial marketer. The availability of opportunities tends to correlate with rates of environmental change, indicating a need for marketers to engage in heightened levels of both active search and discovery. Further, exploitation of opportunity entails learning and ongoing adaptation by marketers before, during, and after the actual implementation of an innovative concept. Marketing scholars principally focused on environmental scanning activity have devoted relatively little attention to issues surrounding the identification and pursuit of opportunity. With EM, the need for an external focus and environmental scanning are viewed as critical, but the identification of opportunity is actually approached as a special case of the creative process. Scanning activities can help identify trends and developments, but the ability to recognize underlying patterns that represent unnoticed market positions or market imperfections requires creative insight. Further, the marketer strives to expand the opportunity horizon beyond that dictated by current customers/products. Stated differently, they strive to "escape the tyranny of the served market."[25]

CUSTOMER INTIMACY

Beyond conventional perspectives on the need to be customer oriented, entrepreneurial marketing emphasizes customer equity, visceral relationships, and an emotional dimension to the firm's marketing efforts. EM incorporates creative approaches to customer acquisition, retention, and relationship development. Evolving estimates of lifetime value and customer equity guide decisions regarding customer investment and customization levels. A philosophy of customer intimacy produces a dynamic knowledge base of changing customer circumstances and requirements. Relationship marketing focuses predominantly on managing existing relationships, while EM focuses on innovative approaches to creating new relationships or using existing relationships to create new markets.

A second aspect of the customer intensity dimension is the goal of establishing visceral relationships with the firm's customer base. The relationship is dyadic, where the firm identifies with the customer at a fundamental level and the customer similarly identifies with the firm. Examples include the symbiotic relationships between customers and such companies as Harley Davidson and Apple Computer.

Largely ignored in marketing theory and empirical research is an emotional aspect to successful market actions. Southwest Airlines represents a case in point. The company uses the concept of "spirituality" to capture profound convictions regarding the role of the employee, the nature of the customer experience, and how the two are interrelated. EM reflects a deeply felt sense of purpose and conviction, resulting in a different marketing consciousness. Marketing efforts incorporate a sense of conviction, passion, zeal, and belief in where the marketing effort is attempting to take the firm. As such, it often involves serendipity, intuition, flair, and insight instead of the rational decision making that underlies mainstream marketing theory.

INNOVATIVENESS

Relentless and sustained innovation involves the ability, at an organizational level, to maintain a flow of internally and externally motivated new ideas that are translatable into new products, services, processes, technology applications, and/or markets. With EM, the marketing function plays an integral part in sustainable innovation. By providing leadership in managing an innovation portfolio, a marketer's roles range from opportunity identification and concept generation to technical support and creative augmentation of the firm's resource base to support innovation. Further, EM seeks discontinuous and dynamically continuous initiatives that lead the customer, as well as the more conventional marketing emphasis on incremental improvements and line extensions that follow customers. Within marketing operations, process innovation is ongoing. Managers continually champion new approaches to segmentation, pricing, brand management, packaging, customer communication and relationship management, credit, logistics, and service levels, among other operational activities.

CALCULATED RISK-TAKING

Company operations can be characterized in terms of a risk profile. Risks are reflected in the various resource allocation decisions made by an organization, as well as in the choice of products, services, and markets to be emphasized. Entrepreneurship is associated with calculated risk-taking, which implies overt efforts to identify risk factors and then mitigate or share these risks. Toward this end, the marketer attempts to redefine elements of the external environment in ways that reduce environmental uncertainty, lessen the firm's dependency and vulnerability, and/or modify the task environment in which the firm operates. Further, resources are managed in ways such that they can be quickly committed to or withdrawn from new projects, thereby enhancing the firm's flexibility. Examples of efforts that can achieve one or more of these outcomes include collaborative marketing programs with other firms, joint development projects, creative test market experiments, staged product roll-outs, working with lead customers, strategic alliances, outsourcing of key marketing activities, and resource expenditures that are tied to performance. As a risk manager, the marketer is enhancing the firm's level of control over its destiny. Such a role for marketing can be contrasted with the more conventional orientation of trying to minimize risk through a focus on increasing sales of existing products within existing markets, with priority given to aggressive advertising and promotional tactics.

RESOURCE LEVERAGING

At its most basic level, leveraging refers to doing more with less. Entrepreneurial marketers are not constrained by the resources they currently have at their disposal. They are able to leverage resources in a number of different ways, including stretching resources much farther than others have done in the past, getting uses out of resources that others are unable to realize, using other people's (or firms') resources to accomplish their own purpose, complementing one resource with another to create higher combined value, and using certain resources to obtain other resources. Entrepreneurial marketers develop a creative capacity for resource leveraging. The ability to recognize a resource not being used optimally, see how the resource could be used in a nonconventional way, and convince those that control the resource to let the marketer use it involves insight, experience, and skill. Perhaps the most critical form of leveraging involves the ability to use other people's resources to accomplish the marketer's purpose. Examples of leveraging include bartering, borrowing, renting, leasing, sharing, recycling, contracting, and outsourcing.

EXCEPTIONAL VALUE CREATION

The focal point of marketing has historically been the transaction and, more recently, the relationship. The focal point of EM is innovative value creation, based on the assumption that value creation is a prerequisite for transactions and relationships. The task of the marketer is to discover untapped sources of customer value and to create unique combinations of resources to produce value. In dynamic markets, the value equation is continually redefined. Moreover, the amount of new value being created is the benchmark for judging marketing initiatives. The ongoing responsibility of the marketer is to explore each marketing mix element in a search for new sources of customer value. This requires the marketer to see the customer differently than others do but, more importantly, to see the product differently than others do.

INTERACTIONS AMONG COMPONENTS AND ONGOING DYNAMICS

It is important to note that the seven components that comprise entrepreneurial marketing are not independent. For instance, there is evidence that increased innovation, with numerous market incursions that involve exploring multiple market niches, actually reduces a firm's risk profile. Similarly, risk and innovation interact with the opportunity-driven dimension. This can be seen in the distinction between "sinking-the-boat risk," or the risk of pursuing an opportunity and failing, and "missing-the-boat risk," or the risk of loss from not pursuing an opportunity until too late.[26] In periods of rapid environmental change, missing-the-boat risks increase, which suggests a need for more opportunism. Another example of interactions includes the possibility that risks are mitigated through resource leveraging in the form of outsourcing; innovation may be facilitated through resource leveraging in the form of a strategic partnership, but this might increase the firm's dependency on an outside party. In addition, not all of the dimensions need to be operating at once for entrepreneurial marketing to occur. The marketer could engage in significant innovation that redefines environmental conditions, is highly customer-centric, and includes numerous risks (some of which the marketer can mitigate), but resources are not being leveraged, and the required approach involves a heavy, fixed commitment. EM is a matter of degree, and various combinations of the underlying dimensions will result in marketing that is more, or less, entrepreneurial. Finally, entrepreneurial marketing manifests itself in different ways as organizations evolve through stages of development, including stages of marketing development. That is, marketing efforts within firms tend to develop over time, moving through stages as they become more formalized, strategic, sophisticated, and integrated.[27] It is likely that the different underlying components of entrepreneurial marketing (i.e., resource leveraging versus risk-taking) will receive more emphasis either in degree or amount and will take different forms depending on the stage of organizational development.

A good example of the various interactions and evolution of marketing within a firm is Harley-Davidson. A detailed analysis of this "poster child" of EM is provided in Exhibit 2-2. Harley-Davidson illustrates how a truly entrepreneurial marketer manages to create a sustainable competitive advantage through its marketing practices. After being on the brink of bankruptcy in the 1980s, Harley Davidson[28] reconceptualized every aspect of its marketing activities to emerge as a "tattoo brand" (one of a kind) that transcends socioeconomic, gender, generational, cultural, and a host of other traditional divides. It is important to note that it isn't a matter of demonstrating one or more of the seven components of EM: if all seven components are not present to some degree, then a firm's marketing practices are not entrepreneurial. Harley-Davidson exhibits all components of EM in its marketing strategy—positioning the company for success.

A perusal of the Harley-Davidson company website **www.harley-davidson .com** demonstrates how the motorcycle business has expanded entrepreneurially to include retail merchandise, biker education, and financing advice. Instead of focusing simply on managing the product, price, place, and promotion to influence customers through advertising, Harley-Davidson takes the more unconventional approach of redefining the industry by setting its own standards, regardless of actions taken by competitors. As a result, the brand appeals to a diverse group of individuals: men and women, young and old, wealthy and poor. Its approach to marketing activities demonstrates how an organizational philosophy that fuses an entrepreneurial orientation with that of a marketing orientation leads to extraordinary outcomes.

EXHIBIT 2-2 Harley-Davidson – An Entrepreneurial Marketer Par Excellence

Harley-Davidson (H-D) has created a unique experience associated with owning a bike, in addition to the motorcycle experience of riding a Harley. Instead of focusing simply on managing the product, price, place, and promotion to influence customers through advertising, Harley-Davidson takes the more unconventional approach of redefining the industry by setting its own standards, regardless of actions taken by competitors.

Proactive Orientation

With a philosophy of being the alternative, H-D created radical change in the biker industry. Owning a Harley-Davidson is a dream way of life—changing perceptions of the motorcycles to become a lifestyle, a piece of Americana. The brand symbolizes freedom, rugged individualism, excitement, and bad boy rebellion. H-D turns negatives into positives by changing the negative connotations of noisy Hogs into adorable piggy banks to encourage Harley owners' kids to save.

Sustained Innovation

New models are introduced at regular intervals; Harley owners are co-creators of products through customization and personalization of their own motorcycles. H-D offers tips on maintenance and service through the wrenching department online and developed an online wish list for those still waiting for bikes—raising customer expectations as well as gathering ideas about unsatisfied or new needs.

Risk Management

Analogous to the Dell model and a just-in-time policy, H-D makes fewer fixed commitments and uses others' resources. For instance, the company builds motorcycles only from advance orders, not based on projected demand. The customer's down payment is used to purchase materials or to finance other buyers' loans.

Resource Leveraging

H-D uses nontraditional policies to keep quality high and costs low. One approach to resource leveraging includes using customers and employees to do marketing, thereby keeping the marketing department small. The brand name associated with Harley-Davidson is leveraged to reach and expand into new markets.

Customer Intimacy

H-D has strong emotional ties with its customers as seen by the Harley Ownership Group (HOG) and Rider's Edge programs, which have created a growing community of customers. The CEO and top managers ride their bikes to the various events across the country as part of a policy that states, "You have to ride to decide." This increases face-to-face contact and enables decision makers to conduct continuous marketing research.

Exploitation of Opportunities

H-D has made itself the centerpiece of a lifestyle. The Harley-Davidson company has expanded its product range to include related offerings such as retail merchandise, biker education, and financing advice. Merchandise includes men's, women's, and children's clothing and accessories; home collectibles; and toys and games.

Value Creation

H-D created long-lasting customer relationships as a result of a mutual understanding between the company and its customers. The brand is sustained through a consistent design and a recognizable identity loved by generations. As a result, the brand appeals to a diverse group of individuals: men and women, young and old, wealthy and poor.

Source: Hill, S., & Rifkin, G. (1999). *Radical marketing: From Harvard to Harley. Lessons from ten that broke the rules and made it big.* New York: Harper Collins.

MARKET-DRIVEN OR MARKET-DRIVING: A STRATEGIC CHOICE OR PART OF THE DNA?

At the nexus of the interface between entrepreneurship and marketing is value creation and value appropriation within the market. It is the market that provides signals both to the entrepreneur and marketer regarding what value is needed, when it is needed, and how it should be delivered. The market represents a control system that determines the success or failure of entrepreneurs and marketers. Yet, the fundamental nature of the market poses a vexing challenge. There may be a tendency to think of markets as a given. Thus, it might be assumed that an amorphous market exists (e.g., the market for farm products or televisions) and that this market reacts to the efforts of entrepreneurs and marketers. These types of existing markets tend to evolve and can be quite dynamic at times, therefore requiring firms to be efficient and develop their adaptive capabilities. In this scenario, the needs in question tend to be fairly observable or articulated, and success is associated with superior abilities to attract, serve, and retain customers. This is referred to as "market-driven behavior."[29] Numerous companies exhibit market-driven behavior, including IBM, Canon, and Xerox. The market-driven approach (which can be responsive or proactive) involves learning, understanding, and responding to stakeholder perceptions and behaviors within a given market structure. The firm develops skills at market sensing and adapting internal capabilities to meet customer demands.

The challenge comes into play when the market does not yet exist or is being radically redefined. While market-driven behavior centers on following customers and keeping abreast of competitors, it isn't very entrepreneurial. Moreover, there are instances in which markets are fundamentally redefined and the competitive rules are changed. What has been labeled "market-driving behavior" refers to firms that shape the structure, preferences, and behaviors of all market stakeholders.[30] Some examples of market drivers include the following: instead of traditional marketing research, The Body Shop was guided by the vision of its founder, Anita Roddick, to redefine customer needs; Southwest Airlines created new price points that compared flying with the cost of traveling by car or bus; IKEA introduced innovative product concepts and a unique delivery system; and FedEx completely reconfigured channels. The market-driving firm creates entirely new markets, produces discontinuous leaps in customer value, designs unique business systems, raises service to unprecedented levels, and fundamentally changes the rules of the competitive game. Market-driving behavior is predicated on dynamics requiring superior integration of multiple factors that are ultimately forged by a manager's market sensing, visioning, and entrepreneurial capabilities. All market-driving companies started small, but their market-driving potential was inscribed in their DNA. While market-driven companies are excellent in generating incremental innovation, market-drivers produce radical innovations in products, business models, or value creation networks. Key differences between market-driven and market-driving companies are summarized in Table 2-2.[31]

TABLE 2-2 A Summary of Differences between a Market-Driven and a Market-Driving Approach

Characteristics Associated with Market-Driven	Characteristics Associated with Market-Driving
1. Respond to market demand	1. Create market and new standards
2. Incremental innovation	2. Breakthrough, revolutionary innovation
3. Reinforce brand loyalty; increase market share	3. Redefine customer needs
4. Brand = Identifier (name, logo, slogan and awareness)	4. Brand = Experience provider (engagement of customer − events not products)
5. Functional features and benefits of product/service	5. Affective, cognitive, and sensory aspects of experience; lifestyle
6. Transaction and relationships; full channel cooperation	6. Holistic and community; embedded network of customers and collaborator relationships
7. Leverage existing resources	7. Expand alliances
8. Market leadership	8. Market ownership
9. Customer is external source of intelligence and feedback	9. Customer is co-active partner in marketing decision process
10. Methods are analytical and quantitative	10. Research methods are eclectic

Firms attempt to achieve a sustainable advantage by responding to the market, fundamentally modifying the market, or attempting to create a new market. The latter two options may result in market-driving behavior. Market-driving behavior requires special skills, capabilities, and resources of the firm. Additionally, the ability to drive markets can be hindered or facilitated by the firm's culture and a host of internal work environment variables. These factors can constrain a firm's ability to become market-driving when it starts out as market-driven, with corresponding implications for performance and sustainable competitive advantage.

Summary and Conclusions

In the 21st century, high-performing firms need both a market orientation and an entrepreneurial orientation. Building on the distinctions made between market-driven versus market-driving behavior, it is important to also consider two other concepts: market leadership and market ownership. IBM is an example of a market-driver that fell from grace and has not been able to regain market-driver status. Market-driven companies fight for market leadership and alternate between leader and fast follower (e.g., Procter & Gamble and Kimberley-Clark with disposable diapers) or may eventually decide to exit the market. Alternatively, a market orientation can cause the leader(s) to be so focused on the served market that it loses sight of emerging markets that seem unattractive at first (e.g., Xerox and Kodak both relinquishing the market for smaller copiers to Canon, or Sears misinterpreting the threat of Wal-Mart). A company with a technology orientation (e.g., a biotech start-up) could be neither market-driven nor market-driving. Similarly, many firms are only market-driven at a given point in time (e.g., Target, Nordstrom) or market-driving for a period of time (e.g., Wal-Mart). Hence, at one time early in their respective histories, Sears, McDonald's and Xerox were arguably market-driving, and all three became market-driven.

Market leaders emphasize responsiveness to the needs of channel members and existing customers. The primary objectives of a market-driven company are to gain full channel-member support of a product launch and to leverage existing customers in adopting an incremental innovation, often through the use of product/service migration strategies. The result of a successful market-driven strategy is expanded market share or share of wallet/budget, reinforced brand loyalty, and enhanced customer satisfaction. While firms can maintain competitive advantage by being market-driven in existing markets, they become vulnerable to firms pursuing a market-driving strategy.

Market-driving companies are usually new entrants to the industry, although there are exceptions. The history of innovation is a pattern in which bursts of breakthrough innovation that reshape an industry are interspersed by flows of less dramatic incremental improvements. Once the radical innovation phase is over, improvements to the existing offering and business system become the primary, immediate challenge. Furthermore, other firms ultimately emerge with competitive, or even superior, value propositions and business systems modeled after the new market leader. It is at this stage that market-driving firms must search for their next market-driving innovation or lose their competitive advantage to a new incumbent. Yet, certain market-driving companies continue to be market-driving for an extended period of time—they might engage in market-driven behavior in the short term as an underlying strategy, but the overall result is that they are market-driving. Companies such as IKEA, Southwest Airlines, and Starbucks literally "own the market,"[32] achieving long-run equilibrium with supra-normal profits and hence a sustained competitive advantage. They started as small, insignificant companies with revolutionary ideas (not products) and poor financial performance. Once they recognized sources of sustainable advantage, they became market-drivers and never looked back.

Market-owners are opportunistic and collaborative. They are generally new entrants that revolutionize an industry by delivering a substantial leap in customer value through a breakthrough technology or through a marketing system made possible by a unique business process. Firms that launch radical product and process innovations create, shape, and accelerate markets for these radical innovations and redefine customer expectations, value propositions, and business processes. Successful market-drivers develop, grow, and strategically leverage networks of alliances and key customers. The most successful radical innovations produce a "lock-out," where a technology or technology-based business process becomes an industry standard that is extremely difficult to dislodge (e.g., Apple, eBay, Dell, Starbucks).

The challenge with a market-driven orientation lies in understanding how it can be achieved and sustained through better generation, dissemination, and response to market intelligence throughout the organization. By contrast, the challenge with market-driving lies in ensuring that others cannot achieve or sustain it by constantly leading the market and exploring the "white space"—by creating the new maps mentioned in the quotation at the beginning of this chapter.[33] One such example is Apple—iMac, iPod, iTunes, iPhone, iWhat'sNext?— always market-driving regardless of industry, competitor, customer, size, or time. Market-driving is not a benchmarking activity. Nor is it something other organizations can learn. The market-driver innovates at a faster rate with higher frequency and greater disruptive force, thereby ensuring an enduring sustainable competitive advantage. Some of the strategies through which this is achieved are covered in Chapter 10.

Key Terms

- new marketing logic
- entrepreneurial marketing
- market-driven
- market-driving
- market ownership

Questions

1. It has been argued that contemporary marketing practices are no longer adequate. What is the principal reason for this? Are there circumstances where contemporary practices make sense?
2. Answer the six universal questions about the change in rules as they affect marketing: Why? When? What? Who? Where? How?
3. It is clear that the conventional static approaches to marketing in a dynamic world are outdated. Do you see solutions for marketing practice that have not been offered in this chapter?
4. Analyze a relatively young, growing company such as Jones Soda or Cirque du Soleil using the seven components described in this chapter. Determine whether the company is an entrepreneurial marketer or not.
5. Based on the distinctions between market-driven and market-driving companies, which of the following companies should be considered as market-drivers: Amazon, Swatch, General Electric, Enterprise Rent-a-Car, Virgin, Disney, Toyota, Sony? In each instance, consider what does (or does not) make the firm a market-driver.
6. Is an entrepreneurial marketer by definition also a market-driver? Why or why not? Having determined whether Jones Soda and Cirque du Soleil are entrepreneurial marketers, evaluate them as potential candidates that qualify as market-drivers.
7. Do you believe market drivers have enduring competitive advantages, or can you foresee a situation in which a market-driver loses its footing? Take Starbucks, for example, Can you imagine a future in which Starbucks no longer enjoys the prominence it has at the moment? Why or why not?

Resources and References

1. Deshpande, R. (1999). Foreseeing marketing. *Journal of Marketing* 63: 164–167.
2. Srivastava, R. K., Shervani, T. A., & Fahey, L. (1998, January). Market-based assets and shareholder value: A framework for analysis. *Journal of Marketing* 62(1): 2–18, 168.
3. Bennet, P. D., ed. (1988). *Dictionary of marketing terms.* Chicago: American Marketing Association.
4. Day, G. S., & Montgomery, D. B. (1999). Charting new directions for marketing. *Journal of Marketing* 63: 3–13.
5. Achrol, R. S., & Kotler, P. (1999). Marketing in the network economy. *Journal of Marketing* 63(Special Issue): 146–163.
6. Grönroos, C. (1999). Relationship marketing: Challenges for the organization. *Journal of Business Research* 46: 327–335.
7. Blattberg, R. C., Getz, G., & Thomas, J. S. (2001, October). Managing customer acquisition. *Direct Marketing* 64(6): 41–54.
8. Moorman, C., & Rust, R. T. (1999). The role of marketing. *Journal of Marketing* 63 (Special Issue): 180–197.
9. Narver, J. C., & Slater, S. F. (1990, October). The effect of a market orientation on business profitability. *Journal of Marketing*: 20–35.
10. *AMA Adopts New Definition of Marketing.* http://www.marketingpower.com/content21257.php, Accessed on October 30, 2007.
11. Locke, C., Levine, R., Searls, D., & Weinberger, D. (2001). *The Cluetrain Manifesto: The end of business as usual.* New York: Perseus Books Group.
12. Springwise. (2006). Generation C. Accessed April 12, 2007, http://www.trendwatching.com/trends/GENERATION_C.htm.
13. Howe, J. (2006). The rise of crowdsourcing. *Wired* Blog Network. Accessed March 3, 2007, http://www.wired.com/wired/archive/14.06/crowds_pr.html.
14. Tapscott, D. (2006). *Wikinomics: How mass collaboration changes everything.* New York: Portfolio.
15. Stevenson, H. H., Roberts, M. J., & Grousbeck, H. I. (1989). *Business ventures and the entrepreneur.* Homewood, IL: Irwin.
16. Smilor, R. W. (1997). Entrepreneurship: Reflections on a subversive activity. *Journal of Business Venturing* 12(5): 341–346.
17. Schumpeter, J. (1950). *Capitalism, socialism, and democracy.* New York.: Harper and Row.
18. Miller, D., & Friesen, P. H. (1983). Innovation in conservative and entrepreneurial firms: Two models of strategic momentum. *Strategic Management Journal* 3: 1–25.
19. Morris, M. H., Schindehutte, M., & LaForge, R. W. (2002). Entrepreneurial marketing: A framework for integrating emerging perspectives on the nature and role of marketing. *Journal of Marketing Theory and Practice* 10(4): 1–22.
20. Lodish, L., Morgan, H. L., & Kallianpur, A. (2001). *Entrepreneurial marketing: Lessons from Wharton's pioneering MBA course,* New York: John Wiley and Sons.
21. Venkataraman, S., & Sarasvathy, S. D. (2001). Strategy and entrepreneurship: Outlines of an untold story. In M. Hitt, E. Freeman, & J. Harrison, eds., *Handbook of Strategic Management* (pp. 650–668). Malden, MA: Blackwell.
22. Deshpande, R., Farley, J. U., & Webster, F. E. Jr. (1993, January). Corporate culture, customer orientation, and innovativeness in Japanese firms: A quadrad analysis. *Journal of Marketing* 57: 23–27.
23. Van de Ven, A. H., & Poole, M. S. (1995). Explaining development and change in organizations. *Academy of Management Review* 20(3): 510–529.

24. Stevenson, H. H., Roberts, M. J., & Grousbeck, H. I. (1989). *Business ventures and the entrepreneur*. Homewood, IL: Irwin.
25. Hamel, G., & Prahalad, C. K. (1994). *Competing for the future*. Boston: HBS Press.
26. Dickson, P., & Giglierano, J. J. (1986). Missing the boat and sinking the boat: A conceptual model of entrepreneurial risk. *Journal of Marketing* 50(3): 43–51.
27. Tyebjee, T. T., Bruno A. V., & McIntyre S. (1983). Growing ventures can anticipate marketing stages. *Harvard Business Review* 61(1): 62–64.
28. Hill, S., & Rifkin, G. (1999). *Radical marketing: From Harvard to Harley. Lessons from ten that broke the rules and made it big*. New York: Harper Collins.
29. Jaworski, B., Kohli, A. K., & Sahay, A. (2000). Market-driven versus driving markets. *Academy of Marketing Science* 28(1): 45–54.
30. Kumar, N., Scheer, L., & Kotler, P. (2000). From market driven to market driving. *European Management Journal* 18(2): 129–142.
31. Schindehutte, M., Morris, M. H., & Kocak, M. (forthcoming). Understanding market-driving behavior: The role of entrepreneurship. Special Issue. *Journal of Small Business Management*.
32. McKenna, R. (1991). Marketing is everything. *Harvard Business Review* 69(1): 65–79.
33. Hamel, G., & Prahalad, C. K. (1994). *Competing for the future*. Boston: HBS Press.

CHAPTER

THE CUSTOMER
OF THE FUTURE

AS SMART AS MARKETERS KNOW THEY ARE

Economists of the classical and neoclassical schools have, since the 18th century, used the model of *homo economicus*, or "economic man," to explain human behavior and, by definition, the behavior of customers and consumers. The conjecture is that people act in their own self-interest, and pursue their own well-being in a rational way. At its most extreme, the rational choice theory employed by many economists assumes that an individual has precise information about exactly what will occur under any choice made. Furthermore, it assumes that individuals have the cognitive ability to weigh every choice against every other choice, and also that individuals are aware of all possible choices. These assumptions work well in mathematical models, but our everyday observation of what happens in the real world leads us to suspect that people are not as smart as economists would have us believe they are.

Consumer psychologists have spent many years studying customer purchasing behavior. Much of this research has been grounded in behavioral, stimulus-response models and views the consumer as a more or less passive recipient of, and responder to, marketing stimuli. Because it is so difficult to study customers in their natural surroundings, researchers conduct experiments in contrived settings, so much of what we think we know about consumer behavior is actually what we know about the behavior of undergraduate university students in controlled environments. From the 1970s onward, information processing approaches to the study of consumer behavior became prominent, and the customer began to be viewed as a problem solver. Faced with a dilemma that could be solved by consumption, customers engaged in phases of problem definition, a search for information, information processing, decision making, action, and then a feedback loop whereby they learned from experience before embarking on the next cycle. Thus, customers are, in all likelihood, not as simple as psychologists seem to tell us they are.

Consumers and customers are certainly as smart as marketers suggest. Sure, they do lots of seemingly dumb things—they are emotional rather than rational in many cases, and they buy products no one ever thought they would, and don't buy some of the best offerings ever invented. They use products in ingenious way—ways that the producers of these products had never intended. They pay prices no one ever expected them to for offerings that don't seem to be worth the money, but don't want to snap up bargains when these are thrust in their faces. They patronize outlets that no self-respecting customer should support, but are also intensely loyal to stores that have been there forever. Supposedly they hate advertising, yet spend hours watching it, posting it on sites like YouTube, and sending it to their friends online. They are frustrating, but endlessly fascinating, and honest marketers admit that they never fully understand them but that they will die trying.

In this chapter we will take an unconventional look at customer behavior from two perspectives. First, we will revisit the standpoint that products and services are offerings designed and conceptualized in response to customer needs. We will contemplate whether, in fact, offerings have the potential to "create" or "consume" customers, bearing in mind that when they are released into marketplaces they often assume very different flight paths from those intended by marketers. Like most exciting phenomena in dynamic marketplaces, this occurrence has the potential to either destroy whole firms or create spectacular business opportunities. Second, we will explore the fact that many customers interact with a firm's products to an extent that they change them, alter them, and modify them in undreamed-of ways that can be of great benefit, merely playful, or downright dangerous. This behavior can hold enormous potential for firms that are alert to it, but it can also represent a considerable hazard, which means that firms should have a view and policy in this regard.

THE PATHS THAT PRODUCTS TAKE: WHAT PRODUCTS DO TO CUSTOMERS*

Marketing has emphasized technology as a means (to meeting customer needs and wants) and has consequently focused on the traditional role of consumers "consuming" and users "using" offerings.** Indeed, modern marketing has excelled at developing techniques for eliciting consumers' needs and wants. Asking, listening, observing, and interacting with customers provide invaluable insights

---

*This section of the chapter is based largely on Berthon, P. R., Hulbert J. M., & Pitt, L. F. (2005, Fall). Consuming technology: Why marketers sometimes get it wrong. *California Management Review* 88(1): 110–128.
**We use the term *offering* to refer broadly to what firms bring to market – products, services, ideas, and concepts.

EXHIBIT 3-1   How Offerings Create Customers

Cup Holder

The humble and ubiquitous car cup holder is a simple device that has changed the consumption patterns and lifestyles of an entire nation. Initially a nonessential accessory, it is now an indispensable part of a passenger vehicle and a deciding factor in automobile purchase. Now an estimated one out of every five meals in the United States is consumed in the automobile, and the drive-in revenues of restaurants have soared. Indeed, the car cup holder is a facilitating factor in America's dependence on fast food; the enabling of an auto-centric, sedentary lifestyle; and the concomitant rise in obesity and the explosion of related health care costs.

SMS

Short message system, or text messaging, was introduced in 1995 as a way to let cellular network operators communicate important service messages to their subscribers. The intention was not to have customers using the technology to communicate with each other, but that is what happened. It involves sending a text message (typically not exceeding 150 characters) from a computer or cell phone to another cell phone. It sounds simple — and it is. It is also instantaneous, cheap, discrete, and fun — most people are surprised at what can be communicated in 150 characters. The discrete nature of text messaging makes it a popular way to flirt and socialize. In December 2001, well over 1 billion messages were sent in England as the traditional Christmas card was dumped in favor of seasonal text messages. This simple technology has had subtle yet profound effects on consumers and society. Consider these examples (in chronological order):

- In January 2001, Joseph Estrada was forced to resign as president of the Philippines. The popular campaign against him was widely reported to have been coordinated with SMS chain letters.

- In July 2001, Malaysia's government decreed that an Islamic divorce (which consists of saying "I divorce you" three times in succession) was not valid if sent by SMS.

- In June 2004, a British punk rock fan was questioned by police, who had intercepted a text message containing lyrics from "Tommy Gun" by The Clash — confirming that text messages are being monitored for terrorist activity.

Source: Berthon, P. R., Hulbert, J. M., & Pitt, L. F. (2005, Fall). Consuming technology: Why marketers sometimes get it wrong. *California Management Review* 88(1): 110–128; Petroski, H. (2004, March 15). Drink me: How Americans came to have cup holders in their cars, *Slate.com.*

into the design and development of offerings to meet these needs. The role that offerings play in the revealing, eliciting, and creating of new realities has received far less attention. Yet the offerings that firms bring to market are not passive "substances" but active "forces" — they both "consume" and "create" consumers; they are created and create. The two simple yet profound examples in Exhibit 3-1 illustrate our points: the humble car cup holder and the more exotic, but no less ubiquitous, mobile phone text messaging system or short message system (SMS).

In similar manner, we might contemplate the influence of the "pill," the PC, and the automobile itself. It can be said that society is as technology does, meaning society tends to become what technology dictates. In other words, technology results in capabilities and creates intentions, and new capabilities also create unintentions. Yet marketing has underplayed the morphing power of offerings, simply sticking to its normative guns that offerings should serve the customer and that by asking the customers what they want, the best offerings to serve them can be conceptualized.

Most product or service offerings are typically created from an instrumental perspective—that is, they are created as "means to ends," the means of fulfilling some need. However, once "released" into society, the offering can be subject to a number of forces or processes that change its path in new and surprising directions. Thus, over time the offering and the society evolve in an emergent series of exchanges, and the number of possible paths it takes expands.

The processes or mechanisms by which an offering evolves consist of two categories: intentional and unintentional. Intentional processes are where people change the offering; unintentional processes are where the offering changes people. This schema is shown in Figure 3-1.

Intentional processes can be further broken down into three main groups: further extension by the initial creator of the offering, subversion by the consumer, and diversion by some third party. Further extension is a path with which most marketers would be familiar—typically it is the "new and improved" approach to product development, and it enhances an existing design or concept by making it better. For example, automobile manufacturers followed producers such as Alfa Romeo in installing five-speed manual gearboxes to boost acceleration, increase top speed, and cut fuel consumption. Now many manufacturers are following Formula 1 racing car design by producing models with electronic "paddle shift" manual gearboxes, which offer six or seven gears and shift many times faster than conventional manual boxes. Subversion occurs when a consumer or third party changes or adapts the offering so as to use it in a manner quite at odds

FIGURE 3-1 The Paths That Offerings Can Take

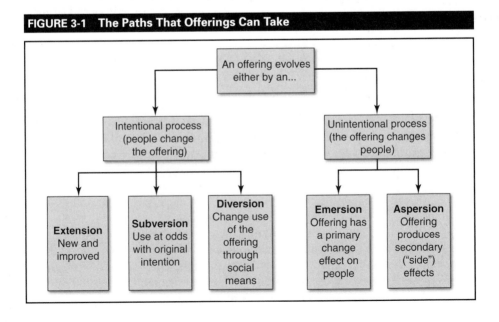

with that for which it was originally intended; that is, the original use is subverted. In South Africa, for example, the rampant theft of copper wire—which was previously used in telecommunications systems—presented a huge problem.[1] Service providers thought they had solved the problem when they began to use optical fiber cable—which after all, should have no scrap value (it's just raw glass in a plastic sheath). The thieves have remained undaunted, and steal optical fiber as enthusiastically as they stole its copper predecessor. The protective glass fiber sheathing of the optical strands is shredded and woven into waistcoats that are, supposedly, bulletproof. In addition, the glass strands in the optical cable itself are melted and twisted into very attractive ornaments for resale. Diversion occurs when a consumer, group, or some other third party (firm, government regulatory agent) seeks to effect changes in the offering and/or restrictions in the use of the offering through social, legal, or political means. The original use of technology is delimited or diverted. Many schools and health clubs have banned mobile phones equipped with cameras as these can be used to photograph unsuspecting fellow students or club members in various stages of undress and then to broadcast the images to the world. Companies, too, are following suit as they recognize the threat posed by the synthesis of photographic and instant communications technologies.[2]

Unintentional processes can be broken down into two main groups: emersion and aspersion. Emersion is where the offering has a primary change effect on people, such that there is a positive feedback loop between society and the offering and where the offering and society then assume a very different path. The interaction of product or service offering and society proceed in an unforeseen, creative, and emergent manner. For example, SMS is predicted to become the major truancy control mechanism in Australia, where schools will simply text-message parents to inform them of and/or confirm a child's absence from school. In British Columbia, Canada, a new SMS service is being tested that will send a text message to a motorist reporting where the cheapest fuel is to be had within a particular radius of the motorist's location. The system uses the cell phone's geographic position to send the appropriate message. Aspersion, in contrast, is where the offering produces secondary effects ("side effects" to the main effect) on people and society, which are typically managed in a negative feedback loop so as to be balanced or minimized. Enthusiasm for outdoor adventure in 4 × 4 vehicles has affected wilderness areas and beaches in many parts of the world to the extent that governments, local communities, and 4 × 4 enthusiasts alike have agreed either to impose bans on their use or to establish severe restrictions. We employ the term *aspersion,* as it stems from the Latin *aspergere,* meaning to spread or scatter, typically in a negative sense.

OFFERINGS AS MEANS EXTENSION

This is the traditional domain of marketing and offerings. A company's offerings have the effect intended by marketers and are used by consumers in ways consistent with marketers' intentions. For example, consumers use digital satellite radio technology as envisaged and intended by marketers.

OFFERINGS AS EMERGENCE: INTENTIONAL SUBVERSION

Subversion—the process of intentional change of offerings by social actors—can range from incremental translation to radical transformation. Consider the case of Nike. The company's objective was to produce shoes for professional and amateur sports people. However, consumers soon adopted the shoes not as sports items, but as fashion accessories. The initial intention of the offering was subverted by consumers. Indeed, as late as the 1990s, the CEO of Nike went on record to say that Nike was not in the business of making fashion items and that Nike would continue its sole focus on sports technology for the athlete. Yet come the millennium, Nike had capitulated to the market and increasingly differentiated its shoe line into real sports and overt fashion items. Indeed, it now differentiates its shoes by outlet, with some shoes being available only through certain stores. For example the recent Landreth running shoe is available only through selected sports stores catering to the serious runner.

What is important to observe in these cases is the fact that consumers did not change the physical artifact itself, but rather the use and meaning of the item. Thus, while no dramatic change was wrought in the offering (the physical shoes remained the same), there was dramatic change in what the shoe meant and symbolized to the individual consumer and to society.

DIVERSION

In diversion, a third party (e.g., an individual, a pressure group, a competitor, or a government) changes the intended use of an offering through political, social, or legal intervention. This can range from the modifying or delimiting of an offering to its outright ban. The Internet company Third Voice, one of the most newsworthy sites on the Internet at the turn of the century, provides a recent example of diversion. Third Voice allowed consumers to post comments on the websites of companies providing products and services, without the owner of the website being able to do anything about this. These comments could be positive, negative, or simply informative. However, in 2002, due to huge pressure (in the form of legal suits) from firms that received negative Third Voice postings, the service was morphed into an also-ran shopping service; and by late 2004, the website was inactive. The music file-sharing provider Napster was forced to suspend its services by the music industry and the judiciary, outraged by the fact that Napster permitted almost unlimited copying and sharing of free music content. The brand has been revived as just one more online paid music download service. As the website now says, "Napster is the legal, safe, and easy way to discover and share the most music" (**www.napster.com**). This is small consolation to the almost 25 million users who previously formed the original Napster network (who really could discover and share music easily, if not safely and legally). Similarly, in Formula 1 motor racing, competing teams often seek to block, through appealing to the sport's regulatory body, technological innovations that give an innovating team a decisive advantage. Such was the case when Brabham introduced fan-assisted ground-effect to enable faster cornering in the 1980s.

OFFERINGS AS EMERGENCE: UNINTENTIONAL EMERSION

This category describes the emersion (or revealing) of phenomena. Here offerings change the way in which consumers and society behave in often radical and profound ways. They create new "ways of being" for consumers. The automobile, the Internet, and the mobile phone all provide classic examples of technological emersion, where the offerings have deep, unforeseen effects on consumers and society. E-mail has dramatically changed the ways in which our business and private lives are conducted and the ways in which we communicate with each other. Similarly, the mobile phone has significantly changed the way we do business (allowing multitasking), the way we find mates (text messaging is becoming a primary initiator of romantic contact in countries such as Norway), and the way we manage social situations (talking on the phone in public makes statements as to our social status and our availability for, and the likely mode of, subsequent interaction with others).

Toothing describes an activity where strangers on trains and buses and at bars and concerts hook up for clandestine romantic interactions by text messaging each other with their cell phones or personal digital assistants (PDAs). Toothing takes advantage of the capabilities of Bluetooth, a wireless technology that allows two devices to communicate with each other over short distances. Many mobile phones and PDAs now have built-in Bluetooth functionality that allows users to automatically locate other such devices in their vicinity. Having discovered another device, the expression "toothing?" is normally sent as an initial greeting. This was certainly not the intention of the Bluetooth company when originally conceptualizing its offering, nor that of mobile phone and PDA manufacturers such as Nokia or Palm.

ASPERSION

Aspersion involves the myriad unintended consequences of offerings on consumers, society, and the environment. These consequences are the unanticipated side effects of the interaction of the offering and society. Examples range from cases of repetitive stress injury from long-term use of computer keyboards; through the use of mobile phones in cars having deleterious effects on drivers' concentration; to environmental health hazards created by leaded paints, asbestos, or diesel engine particulate emissions. Furthermore, the development of antibiotics has created drug-resistant "super-bacteria," the use of DDT has produced strains of pesticide-resistant mosquitoes, and the anti-depression drug Prozac is suspected of inducing suicidal behavior in certain people. Amongst the young, television and video games are often charged with contributing to attention deficit disorder (ADD) and a plethora of related problems, such as truancy and violence.

There is an epidemic of obesity in many affluent countries today, linked to the pervasiveness of convenient fast foods. Humans crave fats and sugars because, in prehistoric times, these ensured survival by providing warmth and energy. Pleistocene man hunted fat in the form of wild animals (who weren't as fat as today's purpose-bred cattle and poultry) and fueled himself by the fruit sugars obtained from wild berries he foraged for en route (not the refined sugars found in candy bars, soft drinks, and ice creams). When consumers of today have ready and easy access to saturated fats and endless quantities of cultivated and modified sugar—and don't exert any physical energy in going to hunt for it—then corpulence is an all-too-obvious consequence.[3]

THE INTERRELATIONSHIPS OF PROCESSES

Finally, these processes of emergence, subversion, diversion, emersion, and aspersion are reciprocally interlinked such that they feed back into each other over time, thus sustaining a social-technological evolution. Consider the production and consumption of music. Once upon a time, a few companies, based on their control of the physical distribution of music, dominated the entire industry—from artist to consumer. With the advent of the Internet, consumers subverted open-source file compression technology and peer-to-peer networks to electronically share songs. The major record companies are responding to this threat by trying to divert the use of the technology, through legal suits, while at the same time trying to extend the very same technologies to solve the problem of file copying and maintain their revenue streams.

MARKETING AND TECHNOLOGY

Unfortunately, marketers have tended to view offerings primarily as a means, not as a mode of revelation or a process of emergence. Seeing offerings as a means has the following implications:

- The customer is seen as the passive "consumer" of offerings.
- The firm is seen as the "active" force, the producer of the offerings.
- The offerings are seen as an instrumental means, as passive objects, owned and controlled by the firm.

The paradigm is thus predicated on these assumptions: firms produce offerings, which customers consume. However, this is a partial truth and has blinded marketing to a deeper understanding of how offerings and markets interact, which we will explore further in Chapter 6.

WHEN CUSTOMERS GET CLEVER—WHAT'S A MANAGER TO DO?*

Once we understand that customers are not merely passive recipients of offerings, and that they don't always use them in the ways marketers intend, we can ask an intriguing question: What happens when customers get clever? As an

---

*Based on Berthon, P. R., Pitt, L. F., McCarthy, I., & Kates, S. M. (2007, January/February). When customers get clever: Managerial approaches to dealing with creative consumers, *Business Horizons* 50(1): 39–47.

example, what should a firm do when creative consumers start to modify products, hack code, and adjust services to suit themselves? The examples below illustrate the dilemmas managers face and the very different strategies firms employ in dealing with the phenomenon.

• Jim Hill was barred from the Magic Kingdom—an incident that for him was hardly an enchanted one. A devoted fan, he writes a blog on Disney, and for the past few years, he has offered guided but unauthorized tours of Disneyland, charging $25 per person. In March 2005, he had a rather different captivating experience when park security at Disneyland in Anaheim, California, informed him that he was being barred from the park and all other Disney venues. "In the 25 years that I have been writing and telling stories about the Walt Disney Co., this is the first time ever that Mickey has made an effort to gag me. And—to be honest—it wasn't a very pleasant experience," Hill wrote in his blog (**www.jimhillmedia.com**).

• A pink-haired computer developer in Tempe, Arizona, named Jose Avila made furniture for his apartment exclusively from Federal Express boxes. However, when he displayed pictures of the furniture on his website (**www.fedexfurniture .com**), the firm promptly overnighted a cease and desist letter to him, demanding that he take down the website.[4] While the website has indeed been removed, consumer comments on weblogs persist: "This really brightened my day! The letters are classic lawyer exchange. My husband and I laughed and laughed. Lawyers jousting at windmills . . .", and, "FedEx needs to lighten up. Jose is a bright and innovative young man, and instead of making his life miserable, they should give him a great job. With his kind of thinking, he can only improve the company . . . the first thing he should do is fire the lawyers" (see **http://www .bookofjoe.com/2005/ 08/fedexfurniturec.html**).

• Ron Gremban's car looks like a typical Toyota Prius hybrid, but in its trunk an additional stack of 18 brick-sized batteries boosts the car's already high mileage with an extra electrical charge so it can burn even less fuel. An electrical engineer and committed environmentalist, he spent several months and $3,000 tinkering with his car. The extra batteries let him store extra power by plugging the car into a wall outlet at his home, all for about 25 cents. Toyota Motor Corporation initially frowned on people altering its cars, but now says it may be able to learn from them. "They're like the hot rodders of yesterday who did everything to soup up their cars. It was all about horsepower and bling-bling, lots of chrome and accessories," said Cindy Knight, a Toyota spokeswoman.[5]

• The BBC is giving web developers and designers outside of the organization access to its content so that they can "create cool new things." Called **backstage .bbc.co.uk**, website gives people who create computer programs, applications, or graphics the chance to put their stamp on BBC digital content. While the beta-stage project is only informal at the moment, it aims to drum up interest and proposals for prototypes. Launched in the summer of 2005, there has been significant interest already (see **http://news.bbc.co.uk/2/hi/technology/4538111.stm**).

Four different kinds of customer initiatives in four very different industries, and four very different corporate responses to customer inventiveness. The organizations' reactions range from a simple quashing, to threat of legal actions, to a begrudging condescension, to an active embracing of customer creativity. So what is a firm to do?

Creative consumers—customers who adapt, modify, or transform a proprietary offering—represent an intriguing paradox for business. They can be a black hole for future revenue. Breach of copyright is rife, and the notion of intellectual property is often treated with cavalier disregard. There is also the distinct possibility that customers who meddle with proprietary products can produce something truly dangerous! On the other hand, they can be a gold mine of ideas and business prospects, as customers identify opportunities and implementations that become sources of revenue, apart from being significant improvements.

The modern business environment provides unprecedented occasions for customers to get clever. The Internet permits the rapid dissemination and communication of customer innovations. Hobby programmers delight in improvising and improving carefully written code. Modular products that embody high levels of reconfigurability plus inexpensive hardware, particularly in the form of computer chips and storage media, enable enthusiasts to tinker with technologies. The problem is central to business—because a business needs to both *create* and *capture* value. By capture, we mean they must be able to extract some returns from the marketplace for the value they create. The dilemma is that creative consumers demand a shift in the managerial mindsets and business models of how firms create and capture value. We provide a framework for thinking about the phenomenon, which also enables managers to identify their own corporate stance toward customer creativity and develop strategies for dealing with it.

CLEVER CUSTOMERS AREN'T LEAD USERS

The creative consumer *is an individual, or group, who adapts, modifies, or transforms a proprietary offering (such as a product or service).* As a phenomenon, the creative consumer has a long and illustrious history; indeed it is as old as products and services themselves. The automobile serves as an excellent example of a product that, since its inception, has lived in a generally symbiotic relationship with creative consumers. The early Model T Ford was regularly adapted by farmers as a power source for driving generators, mills, and lathes. In the 1960s, the motor racing team BRM modified a jet engine to power a successful Le Mans race car; today, thousands of "petrol heads" reprogram the engine management chips on their turbo cars to extract (sometimes fatal) amounts of extra horsepower! Yet while the phenomenon is old, it has received somewhat limited inspection by researchers and business leaders. Only recently has it begun to get attention in the serious management literature—for example, Mollick[6] refers to creative consumers as "underground innovators."

The related concept of "lead user" has been the primary focus of management and researcher attention. The notion of a lead user was coined by von Hippel[7] around 20 years ago, when he defined it as a user whose current strong needs will become widespread in a marketplace only months or years in the future. Because lead users experience a need that they often try to fulfill by using or adapting novel products in unusual ways, they can be a source of new product concepts and design data as well. The lead user is (1) a user of a novel or enhanced product who (2) faces needs that will be general in a marketplace—but faces them months or years before the bulk of that marketplace encounters them—and (3) is positioned to benefit significantly from obtaining a solution.[8] It is important to note, however, that the terms *creative consumer* and *lead user* are far from synonymous. If we compare and contrast the concepts of creative consumer and lead user, the following four observations can be made:

1. Creative consumers *work with all types of offerings*—not just novel or enhanced products that are the focus of the lead user. Creative consumers sometimes work with old, and even the simplest, de-featured products. For example, while Apple ceased production of its unsuccessful Newton PDA in the mid-1990s, there is still today an active community surrounding the product that continues to find ways to change the product's functionality, write software for it, and share their observations and experiences with others.[9]

2. Creative consumers *don't necessarily face needs that will become general;* they often work on personal interests that can remain personal or expand in use to a subset of users. Consumers who use their car alternators to generate electricity for their homes are likely to remain a minority subset! Indeed, the notion of "will become general" is potentially a major problem for managers working with lead users; managers have to identify those users they think will encounter "needs that will become general." Second, they need to monitor and act on the exploits and advice of these users, while noting that lead users can all too often mislead—a point well articulated in the work of Christensen and his colleagues.[10] Moreover, creative consumers often innovate from a love of experimentation and creativity and not to solve some specific need. In other words, while the innovation can be seen as fulfilling some instrumental need, it (the innovation) was not necessarily driven by a need.

3. Creative consumers *need not benefit directly from their innovations,* although they may obviously benefit indirectly through thanks, peer recognition, and so forth. This is often referred to as "symbolic capital."[11] Conversely to economic capital, the more one "gives away," the more symbolic capital one accumulates in the form of prestige, status, and reputation. BMW now gathers the ideas of its customers and invites the most inspired among them to meet with its engineers in Munich on a regular basis. Joerg Reimann, the firm's head of marketing innovation management, is quoted as saying, "They were so happy to be invited by us, and that our technical experts were interested in their ideas. They didn't want any money."[12] Others may be the primary beneficiaries; this process can be both

conscious (a consumer adapts or modifies a product for the benefit of another consumer or group) or serendipitous (a consumer, while "playing around" with a product, produces a modification that is adopted by other consumers; see point 2). The open-source software community is replete with examples.[13] Volunteers have created a very viable alternative to Microsoft Windows in the operating system Linux, with no personal reward other than the kudos of friends and users—and, of course, the challenge of solving a problem.

4. Firms tend to use a formal and disciplined process to find, screen, and select lead users. For example, 3M involved many medical specialists from differing professional environments in a strict four-stage process to develop a new disposable surgical draping product.[14] In contrast creative consumers *rarely ask permission to experiment with a firm's offering,* and critically it is they who select the product, the firm, and the innovation. They certainly don't observe a formal process. Whereas the firm remains in control with lead users, the situation is reversed with creative consumers; this lack of control over the creative consumer can represent major challenges to some firms.

Lead users garnered managerial attention in the 1970s and 1980s because they were seen as a viable means of reducing the risks and costs involved in new-product development. The creative consumer phenomenon has been given attention more recently only because a confluence of factors has pushed it to the fore. These include the advent of the Internet, which allows connections between creative consumers and dissemination of their ideas; the programmability and malleability of software and components, which have evolved in the last two decades; and an overall cultural shift toward customization and individualization.

Creative consumers and lead users are two distinct groups of customers, but there is potential for an overlap between them, especially when management incorporates and adapts their ideas into offerings. Moreover, creative consumers tend to be more difficult to manage, because their innovations tend to be more idiosyncratic and stochastic than lead user efforts, which are more focused and controlled by the firm. Creative consumers are usually independent of the organization. Lead users, on the other hand, are contacted by and communicated to, and the process of their interaction with the firm is controlled by the organization. In short, creative consumers represent an important and overlooked group. The reasons for treating them strategically include the following:

1. They exist and are here to stay; as the technology in products becomes more and more digitized, atomized, and interconnected, the potential for consumers to reprogram, adapt, modify, and transform offerings also becomes greater. In simple terms, this phenomenon is growing and will continue to grow.

2. Creative consumers are a rich source of innovation. Indeed, they are a hothouse of imaginative ideas that a firm might not have the resources or the time to cultivate by itself. They offer an alternative to formal product development programs, which survey consumer needs and preferences and then design and manufacture corresponding product offerings. Creative consumers will simply

innovate for firms—but are unlikely to tell them about it. Thus, the challenge for firms involves recognizing that creative consumers exist, identifying their actions, and understanding how to capture and create value from them. Ignoring or mismanaging creative consumers can lead to failure. At the very least, it may give customers the impression that what they say and do doesn't matter to the firm. At a more serious level, the firm may lose out on innovative ideas and the revenues that these may represent. At worst, firms could find that competitors do identify and exploit the innovations that customers develop on the firm's offerings.

3. Recognizing and utilizing creative consumers is a form of outsourcing, whereby the process of new-product development is informally contracted out to the market. In a self-governing manner, this extended enterprise is able to lengthen the life cycles of existing products by overcoming the boundary between design production and design consumption. The cost benefits are potentially much better than those of "in-house" innovation, but a significant risk is that the R&D is done in public. Therefore, without appropriate processes for capturing value from creative consumers, there is no guarantee that the firm that originally developed the product will be the one that can successfully appropriate the value created by the creative consumer. There is a very real risk that competitors might be able to capitalize on the opportunities identified by creative consumers. That alone might be a good reason for the firm not to ignore the phenomenon.

Consumer Creativity Does Not Equal Creative Consumers

Consumer researchers have certainly not ignored customer creativity. They have defined it and identified its traits, its antecedents, and its consequences. The problem is that almost all of the research has been done at a conceptual level. While this is laudable from a scholarly perspective, it tells managers little about how customers mess with their products and what happens as a result. It also gives them very little advice about what they should do. "Consumer creativity" (the study of consumer problem solving and creativity traits) and "creative consumers" (the reality of how consumers adapt, modify, or transform proprietary offerings) are related but still very different phenomena.

In summary, the important notion of lead users has received considerable research attention and application in practice. However, while lead users and creative consumers have some things in common, they are not synonymous. Studying lead users alone does not provide all the answers to a firm wishing to become aware of consumer creativity, to develop a stance toward it, and to be able to formulate and implement action plans regarding it. Similarly, the study of consumer creativity by marketing psychologists, mostly in laboratory settings using student samples, yields many important insights into what motivates consumer creativity and the environmental conditions that enhance it. However, the work is not very helpful to practicing managers. It certainly doesn't tell them what to do about creative consumers.

Having defined and established the importance of the creative consumer, we now go on to explore the stances that firms adopt toward this important group; stances that, as we will see, range from nonmanagement through to mismanagement and proactive management.

FIRMS' STANCES TOWARD CREATIVE CONSUMERS

As outlined in the introduction to this chapter, firms adopt a range of stances toward creative consumers. Some see them as threatening and try to prevent them from being innovative with their products; others see them as an opportunity and actively facilitate consumers' creativity. In thinking about firms' reactions to this phenomenon, it is useful to differentiate using two axes: a firm's *attitude* toward, and its *action* on, consumer innovation. Attitude to consumer innovation is a firm's *espoused* policy or philosophy toward the phenomenon in principle; it can range from positive to negative. The espoused philosophy typically reflects the mental mindset of top management, but it can also range from a subtle form of politicking to poor organizational communication. Action on consumer innovation comprises what a firm does once the phenomenon has actually been detected. This can range from *active* to *passive*.

These two axes delineate a fourfold typology of firm postures to consumer innovation, comprising the stances of discourage, resist, encourage, and enable. The four stances are illustrated with examples in Figure 3-2 and discussed in turn in the following sections.

DISCOURAGE

In barring Jim Hill from its parks, Disney's espoused policy was very evidently one that didn't welcome independent customer involvement in its offering. On the other hand, the firm did not choose to prosecute or to resort to legal means in its efforts to thwart Hill's association—it simply instituted an internal measure to stem much of his creativity. We refer to this first stance as *discourage*. Here a firm's attitude toward consumer innovation is negative, but the firm's actions are *de facto* passive. Firms verbally berate consumer innovation, but take no overt action. Instead, their approach can range from ignorance to reluctant tolerance to an unreceptive internal reaction. This is perhaps the default or initial stance for many firms. Examples are legion. After Sony released the PSP (Portable PlayStation) game player, consumers soon began hacking the proprietary operating system so that they could surf the web, check e-mails, and run retro and other nonproprietary games on the device. Sony's reaction was swift condemnation, but other than making its attitude to the innovation crystal clear, they took no further action. Apple's espoused attitude to podcasting (using its iPod devices to broadcast Internet radio stations) represents a further example. Initially, Apple, perhaps fearful of the legal repercussions over copyright, sought to distance itself from early podcasting. Subsequently, this position has evolved into a more proactive stance with iPod players being shipped with legally approved podcasting subscriptions and downloads as part of the iTunes package.

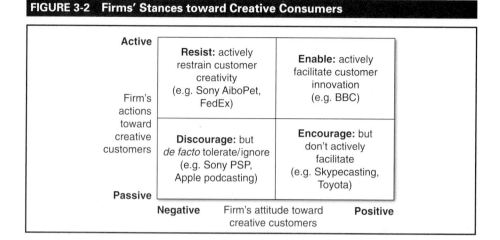

FIGURE 3-2   Firms' Stances toward Creative Consumers

RESIST

FedEx not only disapproved of Jose Avila's furniture construction methods and materials, it acted directly by serving him with legal instructions to desist and take down his website. This is an example of what we term the *resist* stance. What distinguishes this stance from the discourage posture is that while the firm's attitude toward consumer innovation is still negative, the firm's responses are active. Thus, firms verbally berate consumer innovation and also follow up their espoused position with punitive action. The firm actively seeks to minimize or eliminate consumer innovations. A long-established embodiment of resistance is invalidation of warranty. In the past the Ford Motor Company refused to honor warranties on vehicles that they suspected had been adapted for alternative farming applications. Many Model T owners were farmers, who used the power of the car, transferred through the rear axle, to drive small milling and threshing machines and other agricultural equipment. Currently, as will be seen in a later example, Ford is more open to customer creativity. From warranty invalidation, firms then move on to taking proactive legal steps against innovating consumers. AiboPet is a rather expensive (around $2,000) robot dog, marketed by Sony, that can perform a number of pre-programmed tricks such as following its owner around and responding to voice commands. Sony initially sued consumers who had hacked the AiboPet operating system to make their cyberpet dance, jive, and perform a wide host of "unauthorized" actions![15]

ENCOURAGE

While Toyota was favorably disposed toward the experimentation of Ron Gremban on his new Prius, the firm did nothing to actively assist him either financially or materially. It was content to sit on the sidelines and observe. This third stance is the *encourage* position. The firm's attitude toward consumer innovation is primarily positive, but the firm's actions are again *de facto* passive.

In this instance firms verbally laud and applaud consumer innovation but take no overt action to facilitate it; this stance is a positive but "hands-off" approach to the phenomenon. Examples of this are becoming increasingly common. Skype, the voice over Internet protocol (VOIP) pioneer, recently made it known that it was delighted with the innovation of Skypecasting—a synchronized combination of podcasting and live VOIP broadcast. While Skype applauded this clever use of its service, the company has made no modifications to the software to facilitate and further encourage the phenomenon.[16]

ENABLE

When the BBC became aware that users were appropriating and using its content, the organization followed the mantra of "If you can't beat them, join them." Not only did the BBC demonstrate its positive attitude by making content freely available, it also actively facilitated the use of this content through the provision of software and other tools. This fourth stance is the *enable* position. Here a firm's attitude toward consumer innovation is positive, but in contrast to the previous encourage stance, the firm's posture is overtly active. In this instance, firms verbally laud and applaud consumer innovation and back words with deeds to actively help consumers innovate with their products. This is very much a "hands-on," positive approach to the phenomenon. This stance can perhaps most clearly be seen among leaders in the gaming industry. For example, Valve Software, producers of the popular game Half-Life, faced with consumers hacking into the encrypted software, took the overt, positive action of releasing the code to the community. The result was the creation of Counter-Strike, the most played online game in Internet history.[17] The Ford Motor Company also seems to have changed its stance since the days of the Model T and is working with individuals such as Chip Foose, who has been so successful at modifying Ford Mustangs that he went on to start his own business, Foose Design. His modified cars not only have the support of Ford, they are displayed at motor shows by Ford and sold through select Ford dealers.[18]

It would be ideal if there was "one correct" stance (see the matrix in Figure 3-2) that would be simple to follow and easy to implement. Like most important and complex issues in management, however, there is no simple and easy solution. Rather than provide straightforward answers, the matrix, instead, should prompt a series of questions that will require a firm to evaluate whether it has the appropriate stance for the set of environmental circumstances under which it operates. Legal, branding, and strategic considerations will be paramount, as well as a consideration of the resources available. There may be good reasons to follow a discourage stance. For example, where a firm is not positive toward a particular form of consumer creativity (and perhaps for good reason), but wishes to avoid the bad publicity that acting like a bully might cause, it can adopt a discourage posture. Where the consequences of the consumer creativity can be more severe, however, the firm might actively resist. It is not clear why FedEx has resisted Jose Avila, and the publicity surrounding the example has indeed made the firm appear to be a tyrant. However, it could be that the firm wishes to avoid the possible litigation that might result from injuries caused by furniture that was not intended to be . . . furniture. There are also cases when brand protection is paramount. In the case of Mattel Inc. versus Susanne Pitt,* the makers of the Barbie doll sued a woman who had transformed a child's toy into an adult parody—"Dominatrix Barbie." Firms that follow the encourage stance might do so because, while they support the consumers' creativity efforts, they don't wish to spoil its spontaneity by getting too involved. They would rather observe passively—and cheer—from the sidelines. Finally, in the case of firms adopting an enable stance, the intention is obviously to engage and promote creative consumers as much as possible, and to benefit as far as possible from the innovations that flow from this.

CAPTURING AND CREATING VALUE FROM CREATIVE CONSUMERS

Creative consumers comprise a more general category of offering innovators than lead users. When creative consumers innovate, they either benefit from their innovation in terms of new functionality and new applications, or they simply enjoy the thrill and challenge of experimenting with and altering a firm's offerings. They do not merely buy and obediently use products or watch other consumers struggle with product inadequacies. They have a curiosity that drives them to become participants in the evolution and destiny of the offering. Predicting and identifying creative consumer activity may be difficult, but a typology based on possible firm stances and actions toward customer innovation can help in the diagnosis and formulation of strategy. We have also outlined the difficulty of predicting and identifying creative consumer activity and proffer a typology of possible firm stances based on their attitude and action toward consumer innovation. So once more: What's a firm to do? Three things: be aware, analyze, and respond.

Ironically, many firms are blissfully unaware that consumers are modifying their products. Although, with the advent of the Internet, this ignorance is becoming less common, it is still widespread. Once managers are aware that consumers are adapting offerings, the next phase is to analyze the phenomenon. This is where the matrix outlined in Figure 3-2 is essential. What are the implications for the firm? Should our attitude be positive or negative? Should we pursue a hands-off approach or actively engage with the phenomenon?

Finally, as soon as management is aware of the phenomenon and has analyzed it extensively, a response is required. The response should be unambiguous and send appropriate messages to all stakeholders. Employees and shareholders will want to know that while their intellectual capital and other assets are being protected, they also won't run the risk that the firm will make a public relations

---

*No relation to the third author!

fool of itself by antagonizing the media and appearing to be an unfeeling bully. The public at large is entitled to having its concerns for safety considered by responsible management, when technology tinkerers threaten to get out of hand. Creative customers might want to know when their genuine efforts are rightfully applauded and appreciated. When indeed their inventiveness is regarded as harmful and threatening, they also need to be informed in no uncertain terms of the consequences of their behavior.

Summary and Conclusions

Customers are probably not as clever as economists think they are, but also not as dumb as psychologists suggest. They are about as smart as marketers know they are. They may do some seemingly irrational things, but they will always be a source of surprise. It is only naïve marketers who believe that the road to business success is paved with a simple understanding of what customers want. Bringing offerings to market that merely respond to articulated customer needs will succeed only some of the time, and probably not enough of the time. Astute marketers recognize that there is a far more complex interplay between offerings and customers: offerings can shape and change customers, and customers will shape and change offerings in ways that marketers never intended. Products and services, once launched, will frequently take paths into marketplaces that their marketers never intended them to take.

Customers will also change the proprietary offerings of firms in often destructive, frequently creative ways. This will happen whether marketers want it to or not, so it is best that firms at least understand their current stance toward customer creativity if they are to plan for, and live with, this dynamic future.

Key Terms

- customers
- consumers
- behavior
- understanding

- clever customers
- extension
- subversion
- diversion

- aspersion
- emersion

Questions

1. Consider the diagram in Figure 3-1. Now identify your own examples of each of the different paths that an offering can take, and describe them briefly. Consider whether this has presented an opportunity or a threat to the firm concerned, what the firm has done about it, and whether this has worked or not.
2. Identify three examples of where firms have done extensive market research before launching a new product or service to determine whether it would be acceptable or not, and where the market has "misled" the firm. In other words, despite the marketing research, the new offering has not been successful.

Also identify as many examples as you can of a firm doing marketing research to establish the potential of a new offering, and *launching* the new offering *despite* the market indicating that it would not be successful. Is there anything the firm could have done differently in these cases?

3. Collect and describe examples of your own of the four stances toward customer creativity according to the matrix in Figure 3-2.

4. Identify three examples of where customers have modified the offerings of firms with dangerous or unfortunate results. Describe these and what the firms did about this in each case. Were the actions taken by the firm acceptable in your opinion?

5. As an entrepreneur, how would you stay abreast of what creative customers were doing with your product? How would you formalize a process for dealing with this on an ongoing basis?

Resources and References

1. Hudson, E. E. (2002, January–March). Solving the connectivity problem. *TechKnowLogia:* 13–15.

2. "ASK ANNIE—Can my employer really ban camera phones?" *Fortune,* July 26, 2004, p. 14.

3. Winston, R. (2002). *Human instinct.* London: Bantam Books.

4. Morrissey, B. (2005). Crowd control: Handing creative to the masses. *Adweek* 46(7): 10.

5. Molloy, T. (2005, August 11). Engineers modify hybrid cars to get up to 250 mpg, Associated Press, p. 1.

6. Mollick, E. (2005). Tapping into the underground. *Sloan Management Review* 46(4): 21–24.

7. von Hippel, E. (1986). Lead users: A source of novel product concepts. *Management Science* 32(7): 791–805.

8. von Hippel, E. (2005). *Democratizing innovation.* Cambridge, MA: MIT Press.

9. Muniz, A. M. Jr., & Schau, H. J. (2005). Religiosity in the abandoned Apple Newton brand community. *Journal of Consumer Research* 31(4): 737–747.

10. Christensen, C. (1997). *The innovator's dilemma.* Boston, MA: Harvard Business School Press; Christensen, C., & Bower, J. (1996). Customer power, strategic investment, and the failure of leading firms. *Strategic Management Journal* 17(3): 197–218.

11. Bourdieu, P. (1977). *Outline of a theory of practice.* Cambridge, UK: Cambridge University Press.

12. "The future of innovation: The rise of the creative consumer." *The Economist,* March 12, 2005, p. 75.

13. Pitt, L. F., Watson, R. T., Berthon, P. R., Wynne, D., & Zinkhan, G. (2006). The penguin's window: Corporate brands from an OS perspective, *Journal of the Academy of Marketing Science* 34: 115–127.

14. von Hippel, E., Thomke, S., & Sonnack, M. (1999). Creating breakthroughs at 3M. *Harvard Business Review* 43(4): 47–55.

15. "PSP hackers go retro." *Wired,* June 7, 2005.

16. Biever, C. (2005, April 16). Software killed the radio star. *New Scientist:* 26.

17. "Will Sony crack down on PSP hacks?" *Technology Review,* April 8, 2005.

18. Sawyer, C. A. (2005). Chip Foose: Humble genius. *Automotive Design & Production* 117(4): 38–41.

CHAPTER 4

DO THE DOGS LIKE THE DOG FOOD? ENTREPRENEURIAL MARKET RESEARCH

WHAT YOU DON'T KNOW CAN HURT YOU

Entrepreneurs and managers make lots of marketing decisions. When creating something new or different, decisions have to be made about product features, target audiences, prices, communication methods, distribution approaches, and much more. Every one of these decisions has certain basic characteristics: a choice must be made between two or more options (often many more), and it is not clear which is the "right" choice. Typically, there is no one right answer, but there are a number of wrong ones. These wrong choices have severe costs and can often lead to failure.

Imagine being in the middle of trying to start a venture or attempting to develop a new product or service. Think about the day-to-day experience. Keep in mind that customers are complicated and have needs that continually change. Further, markets are complex, competitors are unpredictable, economic conditions fluctuate, and new (often disruptive) technologies keep emerging. Yet, decisions have to be made. They must be made under conditions of uncertainty, ambiguity, lack of control, and stress—and usually fairly quickly. Most critically, there is almost never enough information to conclusively determine which choices are superior.

It is these uncertain conditions that define the role of marketing research. The best means for reducing uncertainty is to develop better information. It has been said that "any reliable information that improves marketing decisions can be considered marketing research."[1] Without quality information, the marketing decision process becomes little more than guesswork. Whether one is surveying customers, studying competitors, examining sales data, reviewing government statistics on various industries, or interviewing technical experts, the goal is to develop insights that improve the ability to make a decision. The greater the uncertainty, the more critical becomes the research.

Of course, we can never remove all of the uncertainty surrounding a given decision. Further, managers face time and cost constraints. Marketing decisions usually cannot be delayed long enough to conduct an exhaustive search for information. Even if they could, the costs of performing the research and generating useful information can rapidly become prohibitive. This brings us to a fundamental truism: *marketing research is about trade-offs*. Trade-offs must be made between how much information is collected, from which sources, collected in what manner, at what cost, and completed by what date.

Entrepreneurs especially face significant time and money constraints. As a result, they make far too many decisions without proper research—meaning they make their best guess. Unfortunately, the simple laws of probability apply, and many of these decisions turn out to be wrong. Prices are set too high, the wrong customer is targeted, or a lot of money is wasted on advertisements in the wrong medium. Sometimes, the entrepreneur can react quickly, learn from incorrect decisions, and make appropriate adjustments. Just as often, though, the entrepreneur has little room for error, and finds him- or herself out of time, out of money, and out of business.

It is our contention that there is a better way. Between the need to spend large amounts of money on expensive, time-consuming research projects and the tendency to make decisions based on intuition or best guesses lies a more entrepreneurial solution. It combines a disciplined search for critical information with an innovative, clever mindset. We call this approach *entrepreneurial research*. To appreciate this approach, we begin with the basic logic of any research project.

START BY THINKING LOGICALLY

The best research projects, no matter how simple, are approached as a logical process. Figure 4-1 presents a picture of the interdependent steps in the process. This systematic approach provides a platform for ensuring the research is valid and reliable. Using this platform, the marketer can then apply innovation and creativity to perform research that reflects time and budget constraints.

THE SET UP

The beginning point should be a managerial decision that has to be made. Research is not done because it might produce some interesting insights; it is done because it will enhance the ability to make a decision. So we begin by

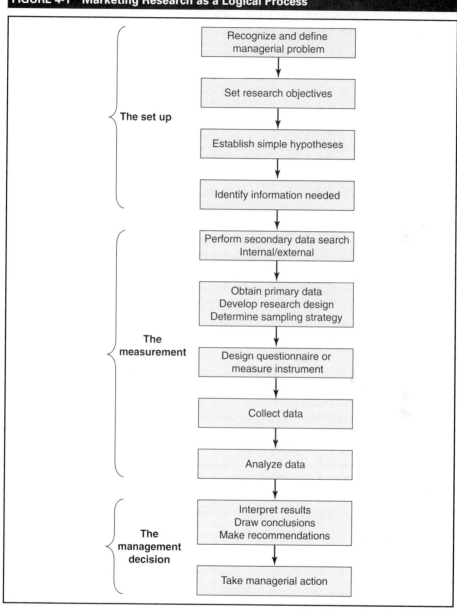

FIGURE 4-1   Marketing Research as a Logical Process

The set up
- Recognize and define managerial problem
- Set research objectives
- Establish simple hypotheses
- Identify information needed

The measurement
- Perform secondary data search Internal/external
- Obtain primary data Develop research design Determine sampling strategy
- Design questionnaire or measure instrument
- Collect data
- Analyze data

The management decision
- Interpret results Draw conclusions Make recommendations
- Take managerial action

determining "What is the decision we are facing?" Consider some examples of such decisions:

- Should I pursue this opportunity? How big is the dollar potential?
- What's the best way to position my company in the marketplace?

- Does it make sense to advertise in the same media used by competitors?
- Who are the likely early adopters I should target with my initial marketing efforts?
- How much should I charge, and should my prices be different depending on the target audience?
- Should I create a sales force or sell through distributors?

Each of these is a common decision confronting entrepreneurs and companies in general. With each, there is no place to simply look up the answer and no fixed formula for how to perform the kind of research that will shed light on the question. In fact, when one is creating new products and new markets, the research approach has to be more imaginative.

Let's use as an example the pricing question from the preceding list. Assume that an entrepreneur perceives an opportunity based on the growing trend for parents to home-school their children. She has created a venture that offers web-based testing services tied to particular courses, subjects, and grade levels. The tests are taken online and can be downloaded, with a score immediately reported to the user. Assume that she is uncertain whether to sell this service on a subscription basis, where the parent/student subscribes for a semester or year and gets unlimited access, or to charge based on each test taken. So the managerial decision concerns which of two pricing systems to adopt. Of course, there are other options available as well. We should note that the managerial question sometimes has clearly identifiable decision alternatives (e.g., Should I enter this market?), while in other instances the research itself must produce the decision alternatives (e.g., How should I position my product?).

Once the specific decision driving the research is determined, research objectives should be established. Here, the question is simply "What do we want to measure?" Research is ultimately a measurement process. Whether attempting to understand market size, customer perceptions, buyer behaviors, or anything else in marketing, the end result of research is a qualitative or quantitative measurement. Clearly defining what needs to be measured helps ensure that research quality is not undermined by including information on all kinds of things unrelated to the real question. In the case of the home-schooling venture, our measurement needs might involve seven key areas:

1. The types of courses a parent is currently teaching.
2. Materials used to support these courses.
3. Awareness of Internet-based materials.
4. Customer perceptions of pricing options when buying such services.
5. Payment preferences.
6. Likely usage behavior.
7. The financial implications of using one pricing option over the other.

After this, the manager formulates simple hypotheses to guide the research. A hypothesis is a statement of what a study is expected to reveal. With the home-schooling example, the key hypotheses might be that the two pricing approaches will differ

- in terms of whether they are perceived to be fair, easy to understand, or expensive.

- in how much they are preferred by likely users of the web-based testing service.

- with regard to the number of users each would attract, and the amount of revenue each would generate.

Other, more specific, hypotheses might be developed regarding differences among various market segments when it comes to the preference for a given approach. These initial steps enable the researcher to clarify exactly what information is needed to address the research problem. If, based on the hypotheses, the manager seeks to understand differences between key segments of potential users with regard to the desirability of these two pricing approaches, then the information needs may include certain demographic variables, together with different measures of desirability and behavioral intention. It is important that the information sought constitutes a clearly delineated set.

THE MEASUREMENT

Oftentimes, data may already exist that provide enough insight for making the managerial decision. This is called secondary data. It is information that has previously been collected, such as that found in government reports, trade association studies, past marketing research studies, or internal company data files. Creativity and tenacity in seeking out secondary information sources can save the firm a lot of money. With the home-schooling software, there may be information in Internet trade magazines regarding usage pattern trends for websites that are subscription-based versus usage-based.

Even where it exists, however, the secondary data can be too old, unreliable, aggregated, or in the wrong units of analysis. In these instances, it becomes necessary to pursue primary research. Primary data refer to new information generated by the researcher to address a particular problem. Use of such primary data requires the researcher to come up with a research design. This is where trade-offs in the research process become most evident. Can we use a simple focus group, or is it necessary to perform a national survey? Might some type of simple experiment be possible, or is there a way to actually observe the behavior we are interested in? The research design will also include decisions about where to take a sample from, how sample members are selected, and how large the sample should be—each of which creates additional trade-offs. A questionnaire or measurement instrument is designed, and a method for collecting data is determined, again requiring trade-off decisions.

Returning to our pricing dilemma, the marketer might construct a list of parents who home-school their children based on public records, membership lists from organizations that these parents tend to join, or subscriptions lists to publications that serve home-schooled children. The next step is to contact parents by e-mail after randomly selecting every other name on the constructed list; those who participate might be promised an incentive for completing a survey on home-schooling preferences, such as a free booklet on testing methods. A simple Internet-based questionnaire might be set up that includes questions on each of the seven key measurement areas identified earlier. Tabulation of the data involves transforming the raw responses into computer input. Analysis of the data is then guided by the research hypotheses and begins with the calculations of means and percentages for the responses. Further analyses might then be run to examine relationships between the variables being measured. This analysis can be performed quickly and efficiently, and at a minimum cost, using a personal computer and an inexpensive statistical software package.

THE MANAGEMENT DECISION

Let's assume the results of the survey indicate that approximately 50% of the respondents actually use Internet-based materials to support their home-schooling efforts, with 20% indicating they would likely use them in the future. Of the current users, two-thirds express a clear preference for subscription-based services with unlimited use, where one can subscribe for 3 months or less at a time. Pricing based on the number of tests is perceived by a majority to be both expensive and unfair, as it appears they are unsure how many tests they'll need or which are the right tests. However, a clear difference is identified between parents who currently use online materials and those who do not, with the nonusers clearly favoring pricing per test taken. Female respondents, which the secondary research indicated are more likely to make decisions about home-schooling materials, had a stronger tendency than males to favor subscription-based services. No other differences in perceptions or preferences could be found between survey respondents representing different demographic categories. Based on these and other findings from the survey, the marketer decides to offer subscription-based pricing on a monthly basis, with a lower monthly rate for those who will subscribe for 6 or 12 months at a time. A special incentive is offered where the first five tests across all courses are free.

NOW TRY A BACKWARD APPROACH

One of the primary reasons entrepreneurs and managers avoid marketing research concerns their skepticism that the findings will be *actionable*. When all is said and done and the research is complete, they know a managerial decision still must be made. They do not believe doing the research will significantly improve their ability to take the right course of action. And they have a point. The reality is that far too many research projects produce results that, while interesting, shed little light on the correct course of action a company should take. One approach to improving the chances that research will be actionable is called "backward marketing research."[2] This approach can be especially powerful when taking bold actions, such as the creation of entrepreneurial ventures.

As the name implies, the process we just introduced is done backward before it is done forward. Figure 4-2 provides an illustration. The manager starts again

FIGURE 4-2   Backward Marketing Research

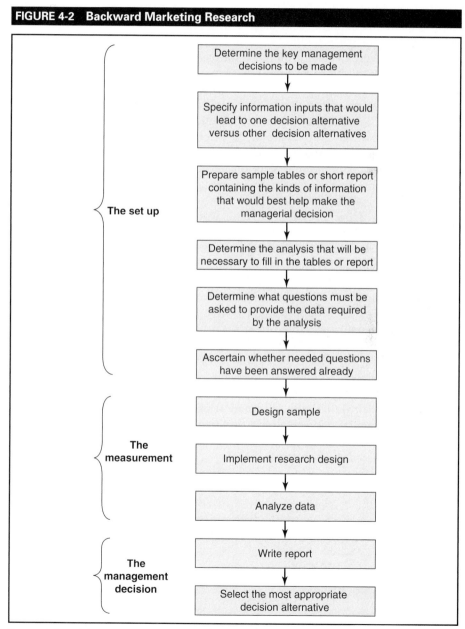

Source: Adapted from A. R. Andreasen. (1988), *Cheap but good marketing research.* Homewood, IL. Dow-Jones Irwin.

with the managerial decision to be made, such as the pricing methods question we discussed earlier. However, he or she then asks a vital question: "What would the data need to look like for me to make this decision?" This means envisioning specific numbers that would lead to the selection of one decision alternative over another, and the form those numbers would take. Thus, a certain percentage of people responding to four specific questions in a particular way might be sufficient to make the manager comfortable with one of the decision alternatives. It may be that he or she is looking for a certain percentage of each of five market segments to indicate a clear preference for one of the alternatives. Continuing to work backward, the manager next envisions the final report from the research project. Such reports typically have summary tables that capture key findings and relationships. For one clear choice to emerge, it is necessary to think about how these tables must look, including the hypothetical (at least at this point) data that would be in the tables. In the case of the pricing method problem, the manager might be looking for a table that summarizes average responses across a representative sample of home-schoolers on questions concerning preferences and behavioral intentions regarding a given pricing option. The manager might also be looking for a statistically significant difference between particular groups of people in terms of their preferences. Again working backward, the manager must then think about the kinds of statistical analysis that would produce these kinds of findings and relationships. Then the manager specifies what sort of data would be needed to conduct this analysis. This then leads to a determination of the kinds of questions that would have to be asked to produce this kind of data. The manager then attempts to find whether answers to these questions already exist and, if not, what would be an appropriate sample from which to obtain answers. In terms of the originally presented research process, we are now back on track in terms of coming up with and implementing a research design.

Approaching the research process backward, and then forward, greatly increases the likelihood that the manager is not left with a research report packed with interesting numbers and analyses, but is no better off in terms of making some critical marketing decision. It can also help ensure the research is not done in ways far more complicated than necessary. Finally, the backward approach can save a lot of time and effort. There is a tendency for research projects, once initiated, to become fishing expeditions. All kinds of variables and questions are thrown into the research design because they are intriguing, not because they have anything to do with the managerial question on the table. Unfortunately, these irrelevant questions frequently serve to muddy the water, potentially influencing how respondents answer other questions, and detracting from the reliability and validity of the research.

THE ENTREPRENEURIAL RESEARCHER

The forward and backward approaches provide a platform for conducting research. With this platform in hand, the manager still must come up with a research design that is appropriate for the problem being addressed. He or she must pick from among the myriad ways available for performing the research. Here, we distinguish traditional market research methods from entrepreneurial research.

Traditional research methods are heavily reliant on surveys. They employ large samples, often implemented by a professional research firm or the marketing research department within a company. They primarily involve direct questioning of subjects, with a focus on the conscious mind of these subjects. Customers are assumed to be rational decision makers. The research is fairly "arms length" or impersonal. Very often, the researcher has a product or service in mind when conducting the research, and this product or service drives the design of the research. A series of questions are asked regarding attributes, features, functions, and benefits. Methods are analytical and quantitative, with decisions typically determined by the rules of statistical math.

Research does not have to be this way. An alternative approach is what we might call "entrepreneurial marketing research." Here, the research is done in ways that often provide richer insights, but at lower cost and usually with less complexity. There is no single model employed here because each research question requires a new innovative design. Unlike traditional research, the entrepreneurial approach recognizes that customers are emotional, not just rational, and their feelings and instincts influence their behavior. A real challenge is to creatively tap into the unconscious mind of buyers, developing insights based on how customers formulate their thoughts and preferences. The reality is that there are unconscious dynamics to how customers think. As such, it is important to start with the customer and explore his or her problems, needs, wants, desires, and wishes. Further, the manager must think beyond surveys, where they ask respondents to project what they might do or recall what they might have done. When possible, direct observation of behavior is desirable, and the research is performed in real contexts—such as happens when a person is buying or consuming an item. Whenever possible, the research is personal; it is conducted face to face, with no intermediaries, and a visceral connection is sought. There is a recognition that emotional responses matter as much or more than rational processing. Customers are emotional animals, with perhaps only 20% of their actions explainable by careful rational analysis.

The research methods themselves are eclectic. They may rely on indirect techniques, such as the zoo that determined its target audience by monitoring automobile license plates over 2 months. They then tracked the plate numbers to specific geographic locales. Or, the method may be direct and immediate, such as the approach pursued by Leslie Blodgett of Bare Escentuals, who uses QVC television to market cosmetics and to reach out to customers who tell her what sells and what does not.[3] Some 3 million women tune into her program on QVC every other month and purchase up to $1 million worth of eyeliner, blush, and lipstick while watching—nearly a quarter of her annual sales. But these viewers, at the same time, provide immediate feedback, telling tell her what is wrong with new products and actually saving her from launching a perfume they dislike.

SOME PRINCIPLES TO GUIDE THE ENTREPRENEURIAL RESEARCH PROCESS

How do we become more entrepreneurial when conducting research? There is no formula for doing so. However, by adopting some basic principles, the likelihood of producing entrepreneurial solutions can be greatly enhanced. Let's consider seven of these principles.

THINK LIKE A GUERRILLA

Guerrilla warfare is a term used to describe the fighting of battles through the use of nonconventional tactics and unorthodox practices. When applied to marketing research, the researcher tries to think and act as a guerrilla warrior would. He or she realizes that there are an unlimited number of ways in which to collect information regarding a given managerial question. The guerrilla thrives on doing more with less, tapping into unutilized sources of information, and collecting information in very creative ways. An example of guerrilla thinking can be seen in the car rental company that picks up its customers and brings them to the rental agency, but the driver doing the pickup has been trained in interviewing techniques. Assuming the average commute time from pickup back to the agency is 15 minutes, the driver is given five probing questions regarding customer problems and needs that he or she is to weave into the conversation during the trip.

MAKE USE OF YOUR SURROUNDINGS

The term *guerrilla warfare* is also used to describe situations in which combatants make clever use of their surroundings. To illustrate this principle, consider the soldiers who hide inside carved-out tree trunks and then surprise the enemy, the army that moves all of its supplies through hidden underground tunnels, or the general who disguises large boxes to look like military tanks so that the other side miscalculates what they are up against. This kind of thinking can be extremely valuable when doing market research. Take the example of the auto repair shop that wanted to determine where to advertise. The shop first assessed secondary data regarding attributes of different media, including costs, audience reach, audience demographics, and usage patterns. Having determined radio would be the best way to reach the intended target audience at an acceptable cost, the shop owner then needed to determine on which stations to advertise. To do so, he generated primary data by simply turning on the radios of the cars brought into the repair shop and recording the stations customers had preset on their radio buttons. After doing this for 30 days, he was able to clearly identify the top three stations.

FIND INSIGHTS IN THE ORDINARY

Patterns are all around us, but we fail to recognize and learn from most of them. In business, the main reason patterns are missed is that managers are not looking for them. Rather, they take situations as they come. The entrepreneurial marketer understands that patterns emerge over time and becomes adept at identifying and tracking the variables that form patterns. Consider just a few of the identifiable trends the alert marketer might attempt to capture:

- Patterns in what customers are buying at certain times of the month or year.
- Patterns in the questions that customers ask employees.
- Patterns in the information sources customers rely on for different types of purchases.
- Patterns in complaints from customers, or in the types of customers who more frequently return items they have purchased.
- Patterns in the characteristics of repeat users.
- Patterns in the methods customers rely on to reduce risk when they are purchasing certain product categories.

In each of these cases, when noticeable commonalities emerge over time, there is a clear marketing message. Not only can the recognition of these patterns lead the marketer to make corrections to current marketing programs, but opportunities for value creation can be uncovered.

EXPLORE THE UNCONSCIOUS

Most marketing research efforts implicitly assume that buyers make careful rational choices—that their buying decisions are the result of logical cognitive processes. Based on this assumption, the researcher asks current or potential customers a series of questions regarding why they act they way they do; how they make decisions; and their preferences, perceptions, and intentions. In effect, these questions emphasize the rational left brain, while largely ignoring the emotional, feeling right brain. One of the leading thinkers in this area, Gerald Zaltman, explains that it is much easier to record, process, and analyze what consumers say directly about their needs and motivations than to probe into the deeper, shadowy emotions of the buyer.[4] He cites evidence that emotional arousal is critical for there to be sustained interest in anything, including product choices and brands. This means the researcher must be more adept at behavioral science and how the mind works than at statistical analysis.

Yet, emotional and intuitive aspects of buyers are not easy to decipher. As a beginning point, Zaltman argues against the traditional method of direct questioning.[5] Instead, he encourages researchers to develop research questions that speak to the unconscious brain and that address the factors that stir customer emotions. For instance, it may be possible to evoke valuable meaning by observing the metaphors used by customers because these metaphors give rise to images that can be used in marketing efforts. Similarly, underlying emotions and motives might be uncovered by asking customers to respond to visual stimuli, such as photographs, to determine the associations they make with particular products. Zaltman also recommends finding ways to measure consumer reactions to various marketing stimuli at the time these stimuli are processed. Given that the majority of human communication is nonverbal, valuable insights may come from finding ways to monitor the nonverbal cues provided by customers when they are in buying situations.

BUILD RESEARCH INTO DAILY OPERATIONS

In highly innovative companies, research should be a 24/7 activity. The firm should always be gathering information; learning; and obtaining a richer, more visceral understanding of users and their needs. In some of the more proactive companies, the goal is to know customers better than they know themselves, at least in terms of their problems and preferences. The quest to know more about markets and customers pervades all facets of the organization. In a sense, every employee is viewed as a market researcher. That is, beyond those responsible for customer service or marketing research, any employee who interfaces with or observes current or potential customers is challenged to be attentive to customer nuances, ask about their areas of dissatisfaction, and recognize potential areas for value creation. The key to these efforts is to create systems for recording and tracking insights as they are uncovered by employees.

As a case in point, consider the firm that receives numerous phone calls from customers requesting information or ordering products. Every time the company receives a call from a customer about anything, a point is made to learn some-thing new from that customer—and to record those data. A question is asked that goes to some aspect of their unmet needs, the broader challenges they face, and their future wishes. The point of these efforts is not to intrude or violate the customer's privacy. Rather, it is to better anticipate ways to delight customers, enhance their value proposition, and get to where customers want to go before they get there.

USE TECHNOLOGY CREATIVELY

Managers who embrace technology are able to be much more entrepreneurial in their research efforts. Many of the available technological tools are relatively simple to grasp and apply, while others are much more complex. Some may not actually be intended as marketing research tools but can be creatively adapted for this purpose. On the simpler side, consider the use of tracking software to see exactly how a visitor to the firm's website behaves, what features he or she examines, and how long he or she is on the site. Another relatively simple use of technology might find the marketer offering customers some kind of attrac-tive incentive if they will wear a GPS tracking device when they enter a mall. Such research might explain how the way people shop in a given retail store is influenced by their shopping patterns prior to entering the store. Other tech-nology is available to facilitate simple online surveys, such Survey Monkey, or to conduct simple experiments with subjects sitting at different computer stations, where certain stimuli are varied at only some of the stations. The emergence of cell phones that allow customers to take pictures of things that interest them or that they do not like represents yet another research tool with rich potential. New tools are also on the market to track response rates to advertisements or promotions placed in certain media, especially the Internet.

Somewhat more sophisticated is the use of emerging observational methodologies in marketing research. New technologies make possible direct, in-depth observation of behavior as well as internal processes that result in behavior. For instance, eye-tracking methodologies are available for understanding visual attention and internal responses to various aspects of a stimulus. Researchers are using neuroscience tools (such as the electroencephalogram and mapping and functional magnetic-resonance imaging) to develop richer insights into the mental processing of consumers. Virtual reality presentation techniques are also being used to create more realistic and engaging research contexts when assessing how consumers behave.

CREATE AND MINE DATABASES

An important application of technology for research purposes involves the creation and mining of databases. The ability to capture, categorize, sort, update, and analyze data on literally anything has never been so great—or so relatively easy. Entrepreneurial marketers understand the need to build databases on prospects, customers, product contribution margins, promotional efforts, sales force performance, price changes and their impacts, and more. While most of these can be built from scratch, there are also numerous off-the-shelf software packages available. For instance, packages available for managing customers and prospects can serve as important sources of marketing research inputs, such as in identifying the characteristics of customers who buy, buy more, and do not buy at all. When combined with company financial data, such databases can assist in calculating the costs of acquiring and retaining a customer, as well as getting a customer back once he or she has left. More companies are focusing on using such data to estimate the lifetime value of customers from different market segments. Such data are then used to determine how much to invest in a given segment.

A major vehicle for producing valuable databases is the point-of-sale system that connects a firm's cash register to inventory systems, financial statements, financial institutions, and suppliers. These systems are also sources of inputs into product and customer databases, helping to identify who is buying what, when, and in response to what incentives. Another tool is the retail store discount card. By using this card as much more than a way to provide standard discounts to repeat customers, entrepreneur Gary Hawkins has linked the card in his grocery store to customer databases that allow him to segment his customer base into four categories based on their projected lifetime value. He then uses these data to determine unique pricing and promotional strategies for customers in each of the four segments and has the ability to do so at the level of the individual customer.

For some firms, creative use of databases has become a major source of competitive advantage. Amazon.com is a case in point, with its ability to assess patterns in what people buy, for whom, and when, and then to implement proactive communications that make tailored suggestions to customers tied to particular buying situations. Netflix built an aggressive-growth movie rental firm around a similar capability.

An important dimension of database management is the creation of a regular stream of managerial reports. By regularly generating reports from the data that summarize activity and performance of products, customer segments, territories, middlemen, and other units of analysis, the manager is in a much stronger position to identify the patterns and trends that lead to opportunity recognition, as we discussed earlier.

LESS COSTLY BUT EFFECTIVE MEASUREMENT APPROACHES

Certainly, the research process we have outlined *can* lead to large survey projects with random samples, complex approaches to the development of items on a questionnaire, and very involved methodologies for data analysis. But the entrepreneurial researcher understands that there is no law requiring research to have big budgets and take long periods of time to complete in order to be effective. For example, showing alternative versions of a print advertisement to relatively small groups of customers can quickly determine which is best, while generating some fresh ideas for consideration. Or, unique customer insights can be obtained by performing simple content analyses on e-mails sent to the firm. Approaches such as these can be highly effective, but only if approached using a logical, systematic process such as the one we discussed earlier in the chapter. Let's consider some other cheap, but effective, ways to reduce uncertainty around marketing decisions (see also Table 4-1).

OBSERVE CUSTOMERS IN ACTION

Sometime the best insights come from simply observing real-world situations as they occur. Observational approaches can take many creative forms. They can be obtrusive, where the subject is aware that he or she is being observed, or unobtrusive, where he or she is not aware. An example of the former might find a retailer giving customers small handheld tape recorders as they come in, asking them to record their thoughts, questions, and observations as they walk through the store. In terms of the latter, a sales rep might take an assistant along on sales calls, and the assistant makes notes regarding the kinds of questions or objections raised by the prospective customer, or the way in which the person responded to different statements or pitches. Or, the researcher might simply count cars or people that pass a given location at certain times of the day. The key to these methods is to systematically organize the procedures and means of capturing the information.

TABLE 4-1 Organizing Ways to Conduct Low-Cost but Effective Research	
Techniques That Tend to Be More Qualitative	*Techniques That Tend to Be More Quantitative*
Natural Observation • Real-time observation 　• Unobtrusive 　• Obtrusive • Protocols • Trace studies • Garbology	**Survey Research** • Mail • Telephone • Face-to-face (e.g., mall intercepts) • Internet surveys • Consumer panels
In-depth Interviews • Individual • Focus groups	**Experimentation** • Laboratory experiments • Field experiments • Quasi-experiments
Projective Techniques • Collage • Picture completion • Metaphors and analogies • Psycho drawing • Personalization	**Archival Studies (secondary data)** • Internal archives (company records) • External archives

Sources: Adapted from Otlacan, O. (2005). Qualitative data collection techniques in international marketing research, http://EzineArticles.com/?expert=Otilia_Otlacan; and Andreasen. A. (1988). *Cheap but good marketing research.* Homewood, IL: Dow Jones-Irwin.

CREATE WEB-BASED SURVEYS

Earlier, we mentioned Survey Monkey, which is just one of a growing number of easy-to-use tools for creating online surveys. Most likely, they will become the dominant form of data collection for marketers in the coming years. These services allow literally anyone to design a survey, drop it into an established online questionnaire format, and post it on a secure website. Those individuals having web access and whom the researcher has made aware of the survey (and the URL address where the survey can be found) can then log on and complete the questionnaire. Usually some sort of deadline is established for completing the survey. These types of services will format the data into a spreadsheet format, which can then be analyzed using any basic statistical package. Some of them provide the statistical analysis as well, with the researcher simply indicating the analysis they require. Web-based surveys are extremely inexpensive and can reach very large numbers of people in a short period of time. They are also quite flexible, allowing for interaction with respondents as they complete a survey. They also permit the presentation of images (rather than just words) in a survey, which tends to produce much higher response rates. An example might be presenting different advertising images, or direct-mail pieces, to determine which ones customers find most interesting. Such studies can also help identify different clusters of customers based on common responses.

USE FOCUS GROUPS

Focus groups are an especially flexible way to get richer insights from customers than is possible from traditional surveys. They involve bringing together a small group of subjects (usually 6 to 10) for 90 minutes or so for an in-depth discussion of issues that the researcher cares about. While they may frame their answers to reflect the group nature of the conversation, participants are able to elaborate on their underlying feelings, beliefs, perceptions, and experiences. The sessions are typically tape recorded and sometimes filmed so that the researcher can go back and identify patterns and insights that help address the managerial decision that underlies the research. Because they are small and less representative of entire market segments, focus groups are valuable ways for getting preliminary insights, determining relevant issues that surround a particular managerial decision, and exploring reasons that underlie why people think or act in particular ways.

FORM CONSUMER PANELS

A consumer panel usually consists of a large number of buyers of a particular product category who have agreed to participate in a research project, often on an ongoing basis. For instance, a sample of 1,000 beer consumers might be asked to participate in a panel, where they will be interviewed by telephone twice per year over the next 3 years. It is a methodology that allows researchers to work with consumers who are giving more thought to the product category because of their ongoing involvement. The researcher is able to track changes in perceptions and opinions over time and identify underlying patterns in consumer input that emerge with subsequent iterations of the panel interviews.

The panel methodology lends itself to experimentation, especially where technologies are employed that empower the researcher. With the Internet, firms are finding it is possible to create sizable panels quickly and easily and to ensure that key segments are not left out. Another benefit finds the input from the panel immediately available to the manager facing some significant marketing decision. Or, consider the major market research firm in Chicago that has created mobile-phone-based panels that use short message service text messages.[6] In effect, panel members can participate from anywhere at any time, and the insights from the panel are produced in real time.

TALK TO LEAD USERS

An interesting methodology for discovering opportunities for radical innovations is called *lead user research*. In essence, the researcher attempts to find lead users in the marketplace or in particular industries—people who have needs for which no solution exists and who often have ideas for effective products that have not yet been developed. They sometimes are experimenting with prototype solutions, frequently products or services on the market that were developed for some other application but that, with modification, have the potential for addressing the lead user's needs. While these hybrid experiments are promising, they are not producing satisfactory solutions. This creates the opportunity for innovation.

Eric von Hippel, the pioneer in lead user research, notes that many new products originate not in innovative companies but in the minds and workplaces of everyday people.[7] These everyday people are ahead of market developments and trends. They are often experienced in a particular field of endeavor and have an intense need for a solution to a problem they face in their work. The lead user approach finds the researcher taking bits and pieces of information from experts about the future and combining them in novel ways. In essence, the researcher finds an important trend, identifies a number of lead users, interviews them regarding their needs and the solutions they are experimenting with, and then creates solutions that address their needs. It is an approach that has been adopted by 3M, a company with a strong track record of producing breakthrough innovation. As good as they have become at innovating, they have found that bringing lead users into the process, and learning from them, opens new opportunity windows that they otherwise would have missed.

BUILD SNOWBALLS

While sampling can be a very complex and time-consuming process, one highly effective way for identifying individuals who have the relevant experience or insights needed to make a marketing decision is called *snowball sampling.* Its use can be seen by considering a common problem faced by marketers who sell to organizations rather than to households. These business-to-business marketers struggle to determine the identities of the relevant role-players in major purchase decisions. This is especially challenging for new-to-the-market products or services. With snowball sampling, the researcher might identify one or more contacts inside the buying organization (say, a large regional hospital). The initial contact is telephoned and asked to identify four people inside the organization who would probably be meaningfully involved in a buying decision for the type of product in question. Then, these four people are contacted and asked to identify four key role-players. Then these 16 people are contacted and again asked the same thing. The size of the group of identified people is, in effect, snowballing or rapidly growing. The researcher then makes a tally of the two or three names that were mentioned the most times, and these people then become the focus of marketing efforts. The same method could be used to build the sample for our earlier research problem involving different pricing methods for a testing service sold to parents of home-schooled children. By contacting the parents of one home-schooled child and asking them to identify five other home-schooling parents who struggle with testing challenges, and then contacting these parents and again asking for five names, the researcher is able to create a highly qualified sample from the ground up.

CHECK THE GARBAGE

While it has other connotations, *garbology* can be thought of as the study of a market by examining what it discards. Once disposed of, garbage is in the public domain. While going through it sounds like a nasty business, there are ways to develop insights quickly without the process becoming too onerous. For instance, a company that wants to assess market shares of different soft-drink beverages in a local area might go to public parks and take a count of the littered bottles and cans for the purposes of identifying market leaders. Garbage studies can reveal the proportion of customers who actually open a direct-mail piece, read certain magazines, or fail to recycle certain products.

SIFT THE ARCHIVES

An archive is a collection of records that has been created or accumulated over time. Most archives, but not all, include information designated for long-term preservation. Records can be from virtually any medium, including written documents, magazines, videos, computer files, online databases, patent records, and more. While some involve a fee, access to most archives is free, and the information is objective. They are a type of secondary information that can reveal important insights to the creative researcher. A perusal of newspapers over a 3-year period might enable the researcher to estimate how much a competitor is spending on advertising, the positioning and differentiation strategy of the competitor, and assumptions that the competitor makes about the market. Use of a government archive, such as the historical records of *Country Business Patterns* from the Bureau of the Census, can reveal growth patterns for certain industries in different regions of the country. Within a company's own archives, an examination of 5 years of sales invoices can enable the researcher to clarify sales patterns across seasons and within a given month, while also providing a perspective on which types of customers tend to purchase certain products or at certain times.

MONITOR WEBLOGS

The huge popularity of weblogs, or "blogs," in recent years has produced a new source of research insights. A blog is a website that includes user-generated content, typically on some focused topic. Virtually anyone can post opinions or information to a blog, and discussions can be interactive. Further, text, pictures, videos, audio inputs, and links to other websites can sometimes be posted, depending on the nature of the blog. The millions of weblogs now in existence address virtually every sphere of life, from political discourse and video gaming discussions to scientific debates and insights on cooking and gardening. The text of a blog can be a valuable source of intelligence about customer perceptions, needs, and behaviors. Simple content analysis can be applied to identify prominent terms and themes that appear in blog discussions. New technologies allow for the structural or linguistic analysis of these texts. Linguistic observation and social network analysis have emerged as useful methodologies as well. With the latter, it is possible to observe who communicates with whom about what. Such insights can be helpful in designing viral marketing campaigns, a topic we discuss in later chapters. An example of a more sophisticated methodology involved researchers monitoring ongoing dialogues between customers and web-based virtual advisers (i.e., Kelley Blue Book's *Auto Choice Advisor*). In a major published study, Urban and

Hauser were able to identify major opportunities in the truck market based on new combinations of customer needs that emerged from these online discussions.[8]

CONDUCT SIMPLE EXPERIMENTS

Experimentation is a useful tool when the researcher has some ability to exert control over variables of interest. The conduct of experiments is usually associated with laboratories and rigorously managed conditions. However, marketers sometimes find themselves in "living laboratories," and simple technologies can enable the researcher to monitor the effects of changes in certain variables (e.g., promotional messages) on other variables (e.g., sales). Earlier we mentioned point-of-sale systems as a source of useful databases. Such systems can create a living laboratory for conducting experiments. With all products and prices entered into the system, the marketer can run advertisements or promotions for certain products and immediately track the impact. The same advertising message can be placed in different media, and again the results can be immediately tracked. Similarly, the impact of in-store promotions can be monitored by the hour. Many other scenarios exist that lend themselves to experimentation. When doing direct-mail campaigns, the themes can be varied for different geographic regions or target audiences and the differential impact can easily be evaluated. Where the marketer has multiple stores or outlets, it becomes possible to employ certain pricing or promotional tactics in one set of locations while not using them in other locations, again generating quick information on what works and does not work.

EXPLORE OTHER ETHNOGRAPHIC APPROACHES

A number of the methods we have described fall under the general rubric of *ethnography,* which is the use of field work to capture behavior and human reactions in natural settings, or as they occur. These settings allow the research to be holistic, allowing for an entire range of factors that come into play in real-world situations. Having researchers fly on airplanes acting as passengers to get a sense of other passengers' behaviors and perspectives would be an example. "Mystery shoppers," used in retail environments to observe customer service practices in action or to capture behaviors of other customers while shopping, would be a related form of this approach. Another ethnographic method is called the "disposable camera technique." Here, cameras are distributed to research staff or research participants, and they are asked to record snapshots of their social peers using or interacting with particular products or services. The goal is to capture others behaving naturally. These photographs can be useful both in product design and in designing advertisements.

Summary and Conclusions

The entrepreneurial marketer has two overarching responsibilities: continually recognizing emerging opportunities and effectively capitalizing on the most promising opportunities. Marketing research should play an instrumental role in both of these responsibility areas. New opportunities emerge from unexpected places, and spotting them requires that firms be proactive in gathering and interpreting inputs from the external environment. Further, in pursing a given opportunity, new "opportunity doors" open up. Research helps define and then screen these opportunities. Marketers must also be creative in the ways they exploit those opportunities, which again suggests a need for ongoing intelligence on customers, markets, distributors, and competitors. New marketing initiatives almost always involve considerable adaptation. Innovation starts with a bold new vision, but then requires numerous adjustments and refinements as things evolve. Changes must be made in how the market is defined, who is being targeted, the products or services being sold, the prices being charged, the selling and advertising approaches, and more. Market research provides the insights that lead to the smart adaptation decisions.

In the final analysis, marketing research serves to reduce the uncertainty surrounding managerial decisions. We have argued that this uncertainty can best be reduced when research is approached as a logical process and also that it can be helpful to implement the process using a backward methodology. Using this process as a platform, this chapter has argued that research itself can be an entrepreneurial pursuit. The entrepreneurial perspective on research emphasizes lower cost and greater ingenuity. New innovative research designs are explored through a process of trial and error. These designs are invented by the researcher, reflecting a guerrilla mindset and the leveraging of limited resources. We have reviewed a number of principles to guide this type of guerrilla thinking when it comes to research. In addition, the chapter has summarized 11 ways in which cheap but effective research can be conducted.

When approached in this manner, research facilitates action. It bridges the gap between companies suffering from the so-called paralysis of analysis and companies who simply believe that you should go with your gut. The first type of company uses the need for more research, often complex and expensive research, as an excuse for not acting. The second type blindly moves forward with little guidance regarding where and where not to go. By embracing the entrepreneurial research perspective, the manager is using research to continually ask questions, seek opportunities, experiment in the marketplace, learn from customers and competitors, and discover new ways to create value. In the final analysis, research makes possible the *calculated* part of calculated risk-taking.

Key Terms

- backward research process
- entrepreneurial research
- experimentation
- ethnography
- guerrilla thinking
- lead users
- observational techniques

Questions

1. When faced with an opportunity or critical marketing decision, how does the marketer determine whether it is worth performing market research?

2. In what sense is marketing research nothing but a series of trade-off decisions? What does this say about achieving accurate insights regarding a given research question?
3. Why is it helpful to approach the marketing research process from a "backward" approach? How can this backward approach lead to more useful research findings?
4. What does it mean to "think like a guerrilla," "make use of your surroundings," and "find insights in the ordinary" when conducing market research? Provide examples of each, assuming you were conducting research on whether people would feel comfortable visiting a doctor over a computer rather than in person.
5. Think about the less costly but effective research methods discussed in this chapter. One of them was simple experiments. We normally think of experimentation as a complex research methodology requiring a laboratory and highly controlled circumstances, with control groups and multiple treatments. Assume you were trying to discover how customers respond to the layout of your company's website. Can you think of a way to conduct experiments that are simple, low cost, but insightful?

Resources and References

1. Andreasen, A. (1988). *Cheap but good marketing research.* Homewood, IL: Dow Jones-Irwin.
2. Ibid.
3. Haire, T. (2005), Building a bare empire. Response. Accessed April 1, 2007, from www.responsemagazine.com/responsemag/article/articleDetail.jsp?id=154874&pageID=1.
4. Zaltman, G. (2003). *How customers think: Essential insights into the mind of the markets.* Boston: Harvard Business School Press.
5. Ibid.
6. Fielding, M. (2007, February 1). The consumer panel reinvented. *Marketing News.*
7. von Hippel, E. (2005). *Democratizing innovation.* Cambridge, MA: MIT Press.
8. Urban, G.L., & Hauser, J. R. (2004). Listening in to find and explore new combinations of customer needs. *Journal of Marketing* 68(2): 72–87.

CHAPTER 5

CREATING MARKETS... AND THE PEOPLE CREATING THEM

CHANGE: THE GENESIS OF OPPORTUNITIES

Change is constant. Proliferation of choice, rapid imitation of products, and shortened life cycles cause complex and fast-changing markets that are more connected than ever. Technology is a key driver of change—it facilitates interactivity and virtual networks, compresses time and distance, blurs industry boundaries through convergence, and increases the speed of change. Globalization highlights the irrelevance of geography, borders, and hierarchies. Traditional markets disappear overnight, leaving leading players blindsided by entrepreneurial startups that create new markets, new value propositions, and new products, services or processes—driving change and growth in a completely new direction. The music industry is in disarray and faces stiff competition from a "computer company" (Apple), while an "online book company" (Amazon.com) challenges Wal-Mart. Competitor today, collaborator tomorrow; among the *Inc.* 500 companies today, top of the *Fortune* 500 list tomorrow; profitable today, unprofitable tomorrow; major player today, gone tomorrow. These are the lessons Kodak had to learn the hard way when it missed the sign of the times and fell prey to nimble, new competitors who were hungry for digital change (see Exhibit 5-1).

Meanwhile the market is not merely responding to change, it is stimulating change as well. People are viewing technology as a menace as well as a blessing—it intrudes into private lives, yet enhances individuals' power in a battle of the people versus advertisers in an age of consumer distrust and retaliation. The extent to which marketers have had to relinquish control of marketing due to increased in consumer power is covered in more detail in Chapters 2 and 8. The

EXHIBIT 5-1   A Black Hole Filled with Old Markets That Die: Kodak

Founded in 1881, Kodak became synonymous with photographic film by making photography cheaper, better, and available to everyone—allowing people to take, print, and share their pictures. Markets, competitors, customers, and products were known or predictable. Although camera film came in different formats and sizes, Kodak film was considered the brand leader and by all accounts was better than its competitors, Fujifilm or Agfa.

But then two things happened that disrupted industry dynamics: First, in the 1970s, the photographic film market matured amidst slower growth and lower innovation rates. Second, new digital technology started to displace traditional film, causing convergence of hardware devices, software and processing, and imaging and printing—all of which were previously separate markets.

Suddenly Kodak did not know what market it was in, who the competitors were, what customers wanted, or which products to focus on. Digital cameras now come from Sony or Dell, and images are stored on the hard drive of a PC (not photographic film) and shared by e-mail (not physical copies), are processed by Snapfish or Jessops (not Kodak labs), printed from HP or Epson devices, and shared in digital photo albums with easy duplication (not costly copies by Kodak).

Kodak tried to respond on all fronts: Kodak cameras, Kodak online wallets, Kodak printers, Kodak print kiosks. It tried to transform itself into an imaging company, but neither its focus nor its future is clear. The company waited too long to enter the emerging digital market, causing it to miss the digital photography wave, despite being a pioneer in digital photography with more than 1,000 patents.

By the time Kodak was ready to respond to market challenges, the film market was already past its peak—a big black hole that had already sucked a former competitor, Polaroid, into its swirling void. The gap between Kodak's existing business (film) and the new market opportunity (digital) was too treacherous to traverse with ease. Additionally, when Kodak finally introduced a digital camera line in 2001, the digital market was filled with well-entrenched competitors in the digital space.

Kodak's turnaround plan with which to enter digital imaging included acquisitions that raised costs more than margins. The impact was disastrous. It's share price dropped from a peak of $95/share in the late 1990s to $25/share in 2004 when it was kicked off the Dow Jones Industrial Average. The prognosis for its survival is still uncertain.

Source: www.kodak.com

popularity of Facebook is but one example (see Exhibit 5-2) of the prominent new and evolving trend of social networking. Globalization is homogenizing cultures, resulting in cultural sameness and classlessness. Excessive choice breeds a bigger craving for even more choice, resulting in increasingly rapid changes in people's preferences and behavior.

While these changes are clearly threatening, they are also an endless source of new opportunities. This is the key to understanding marketing in the 21st century. Victory goes to those who see the opportunities and capitalize on them by innovating. The continuous interaction of new technological capabilities and new market knowledge amid dramatic alterations to the competitive landscape makes entrepreneurship not an option, but an imperative. Structural and behavioral changes fundamentally reshape markets—blending, converging, hybridizing,

---

EXHIBIT 5-2 The People Have the Power: Facebook

Founded in February 2004 by Mark Zuckerberg, Facebook (a social utility) is free to anyone with an e-mail account. This popular online social network expanded its reach from an initial 800 colleges and universities in the United States to more than 10 million members primarily in the 17–25 age group worldwide. People use Facebook to keep up with friends; learn more about the people they meet; and share photos, blogs, links, and videos from anywhere on the web—all within a network through which individuals have control over how and with whom they share information. Users can also speak out on personal and life topics through user-generated video that will be featured in a TV series, *Facebook Diaries*, through Comcast's partner, Ziddio. Facebook generates revenues in excess of $1.5 million per week from advertisers.

Source: www.facebook.com/

evolving—demanding a fresh approach from incumbents as new market spaces open up with new challenges. Realizing long ago that if they didn't make their own products obsolete, their competitors would, Sony's Akio Morita asserted, "We don't serve markets. We make markets." This quest required the company to identify market discontinuities that would enable it to create new markets and transform the industry. Any company faces three challenges simultaneously:

1. It must anticipate and respond to change.
2. It must leverage core competencies to exploit new market realities.
3. It must learn faster and innovate better to explore new territory.

Creativity is a basic survival tool, for it enables the successful innovations that help firms cope with change.[1] In the words of John Sculley, former chief executive officer of Pepsi and Apple Computer, "The future belongs to those who see possibilities before they become obvious." The future remains forever unforeseeable, unpredictable, and unknowable. But that does not mean the future is unimaginable. Companies must participate in shaping the future while actively preparing for the uncertain future.

Innovation requires a fresh way of looking at things, an understanding of people, and an entrepreneurial willingness to take risks and to work hard. An idea doesn't become an innovation until it is widely adopted and incorporated into people's daily lives. Most people resist change, so a key part of innovating is convincing other people that your idea is a good one— by enlisting their help, and, in doing so, by helping them see the usefulness of the idea.

—ART FRY, CORPORATE SCIENTIST, 3M,
AND INVENTOR OF POST-IT NOTES

This chapter examines opportunities that arise as a result of change—change is both the starting point and a fundamental part of opportunity. The spotlight is first on the nexus between change and opportunity—how opportunities come about and the role played by entrepreneurship. This is followed by answers to 10 questions that are frequently asked about opportunities, and an examination of three different processes whereby new opportunities come about. The attention then shifts to the people involved in opportunities—marketers, inventors, customers, and others—everyone with an entrepreneurial mindset who creates change that leads to new sources of value. This type of change requires rule-breaking behavior that underpins change. The entrepreneur breaks rules underlying people's perception (a paradigm shift), breaks rules related to industry boundaries, and breaks rules of what is possible and what is not.

CREATIVE DESTRUCTION: THE KISSING COUSIN OF OPPORTUNITY

The entrepreneur is the innovator who "shocks" and disturbs the economic equilibrium—both exploiting and creating uncertainty. Entrepreneurial activity is associated with "creative destruction"[2] in which the new replaces the old: the entrepreneur creates change by breaking free from existing competitive dynamics to carve out a competitive advantage in a new marketspace. For the purpose of this discussion of opportunity, *entrepreneurship* is defined as follows: *"entrepreneurship seeks to understand how opportunities to bring into existence future goods and services are discovered, created, and exploited, by whom and with what consequences."*[3] This definition stresses the important role played by *creativity* (how opportunities are discovered, created, and exploited) and focuses on the *social consequences* of this *action* (by whom and with what consequences) that involves innovation, growth, and unique value-creation methods.

The opportunity emerges from the process of creative destruction and continually evolves as new insights recast it in a new, more densely textured form. Thus, the opportunity is always under construction, and it is entrepreneurial action that makes it so—entrepreneurship is the transformation mechanism. As illustrated in Figure 5-1, entrepreneurial action includes the following: introduction of new operating processes and methods of production, new goods or services, or new qualities of existing goods and services; the opening up of new markets; utilization of new sources of supply of raw materials or intermediate goods; and the crafting of new organizational forms in the industry.[4] Without entrepreneurial action nothing happens; *the opportunity must be shaped by taking action.*

Entrepreneurship is *not* limited to creating and managing businesses. That is a common, but limiting, perception of the innate ability of every individual to think and act entrepreneurially. Similar to creativity, entrepreneurship is an everyday activity. It might be helpful to draw an analogy between entrepreneurship and sports to explain this point. Most people have an innate ability to run the 100-meter sprint, but not all are Olympic athletes. Similarly, most people have a natural ability to think and act in an entrepreneurial manner without becoming Richard Branson (Virgin) or emulating Michael Dell (Dell Incorporated), both of whom appear to be larger than life. It is a matter of exercising your entrepreneurial muscle: the more you practice, the better you will be prepared for the time when you participate in the entrepreneurship race. Moreover, entrepreneurship is

FIGURE 5-1   Seven Different Outcomes of Entrepreneurial Creativity

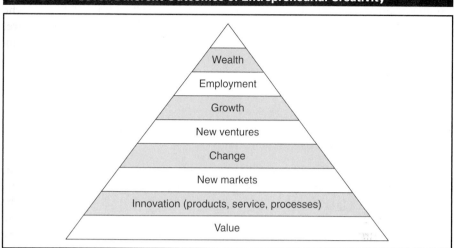

not restricted to an elite group of people with superhero abilities related to risk-taking, innovativeness, and proactiveness.

Entrepreneurial behavior begins with opportunity. Opportunity recognition (i.e. discovery, identification, and creation) is associated with creativity and imagination. However, entrepreneurship is not about creative-thinking tools and techniques related to general problem solving. There are many creativity techniques that can be used during idea-generation sessions, but ideas are always the starting point. There are three types of (entrepreneurial) creativity[5]:

1. Origination, or the act of pure invention.
2. Synthesis, or the creative act of joining together two previously unrelated things.
3. Modification, which occurs when a thing or process is improved or gains a new application.

However, as seen in Figure 5-1, the outcome of entrepreneurial action is not ideas (thinking) but change (action), new value creation, innovation, and so forth. This distinction makes it clear that the entrepreneur is not necessarily concerned with breaking new ground. Opportunity can also be found in a new mix of old ideas or in the creative application of traditional approaches.

The most important point to remember is that entrepreneurship is a multidimensional form of everyday world-making, not merely an economic activity. Entrepreneurship is not the exclusive purview of company founders who are celebrated for their heroic journeys. Consider the following insight:

> [T]he way the world is made—seen on a scale of everyday living—is an effect of entrepreneurial activity. The mobile home cars required new concepts of "what is a house" and "what is a car for." Indeed, I go as far

as to say that in this example, changing our ways of traveling and making love, are entrepreneurially effected. If I open a bottle, the bottle-opener is a cultural practice that has come to exist at a certain time, and so it is for the bottle itself, because I should resist my being used to bottles. All my habits have once been invented and cannot be taken for granted, as one studies entrepreneurship. Making products and services are always ways of world-making.[6]

In short, entrepreneurial activity produces social change—it is the "creative stream and energy of a society."[7] The remainder of this chapter examines how entrepreneurial actors create new worlds.

FREQUENTLY ASKED QUESTIONS ABOUT OPPORTUNITY

Many new ventures fail because they were started with an idea for a product or service for which no real profit-making opportunity existed. The entrepreneurial process starts with the identification of an opportunity, *not* a product or service as the basis for a new venture. For this reason it is important to make a clear distinction between what an opportunity is and how this differs from an idea, as well as from a concept for a new business venture. There are 10 basic questions the marketer needs to be able to answer about opportunities, each of which is addressed here.

QUESTION #1: WHAT IS AN OPPORTUNITY?

Answer: Opportunities are those situations in which goods, services, raw materials, markets, and organizing methods can be introduced and sold through the formation of new means, ends, or means-ends relationships.[8] It typically implies a favorable set of circumstances in the environment that create a need or opening for an innovative business concept.

QUESTION #2: WHEN IS IT AN ENTREPRENEURIAL OPPORTUNITY AND NOT JUST AN OPPORTUNITY?

Answer: What differentiates *entrepreneurial opportunities* from other opportunities is that to exploit entrepreneurial opportunities one must discover a new means to an end, with unknown outcomes and resources not yet under the control of the entrepreneur.[9] Entrepreneurial opportunities are therefore opportunities to *act* in the *creation of value*. They consist of a set of (1) ideas, (2) beliefs, and (3) actions that enable the creation of value.[10] New ideas may or may not actually lead to value creation (in terms of positive economic value), but actions should aspire (underpinned by beliefs) to achieve this end (the outcomes mentioned in Figure 5-1). Whether the opportunity will lead to the intended outcomes can be known only in retrospect—failure may be due to poor exploitation or due to the lack of a real opportunity.[11]

QUESTION #3: WHERE DO OPPORTUNITIES COME FROM?

Answer: The market, or more broadly the environment, is the source of opportunities in the form of gaps that exist as a consequence of change.[12] The potential sources of opportunity include the following:

1. Unexpected changes such as 9/11 creating a gap for new products and services.
2. A change necessitated by an incongruency or inconsistency in expectations.
3. Industry changes that result in supply shortages in raw materials or changes in industry market structures such as deregulation/regulation (e.g., rule changes in the airline industry and telecommunications).
4. Market change due to changing demographics such as smaller families, people staying single longer, or older people traveling more and living longer.
5. Changes in perception, mood, or meaning. For instance, people's need to have healthier eating habits made the Atkins diet hugely popular and changed menu options at restaurants.
6. Changes in knowledge due to scientific or technological advances such as the laser that can be used for eye surgery and fat and hair removal, as well as for precision diamond cutting.
7. Changes in process needs such as the need for an electronic switchboard to replace the huge number of manual operators when call volumes on the telephone skyrocketed.

QUESTION #4: WHAT IS THE DIFFERENCE BETWEEN AN IDEA AND AN OPPORTUNITY?

Answer: Misconceptions about the differences among an idea, an entrepreneurial opportunity, and a business concept can be fatal. First, ideas are like dreams— they last forever, they are free, everybody has them, and they don't need customers to survive. Opportunities, on the other hand, are perishable, they require effort (they must be identified, evaluated, and exploited), only some people are interested in pursuing them, and they are directed at creating markets and products/services for customers. If you were to ask people about a particular problem they wish they could solve, you would get a lot of ideas. Some examples of what they might say include the following: my car uses too much gas; I wish I could lose weight faster; my shoes never seem to fit properly; I dislike people letting their dogs run free in my neighborhood. Each of these ideas relates to a need they have or a problem in search of a solution, but not all of them are entrepreneurial opportunities. This brings us to the next question.

QUESTION #5: WHEN IS AN IDEA ALSO AN OPPORTUNITY?

Answer: Unfortunately, many ideas for new ventures are unrelated to a real entrepreneurial opportunity. They turn out to be based on wishful thinking or dreams instead of profitable commercial activity. To be considered as a possible opportunity, the idea must be timely (as determined by the window of opportunity), attractive (with profit-making potential), durable (sustainable over a period of time), and anchored in an offering (product, service, or process) that creates or increases value for its buyer and/or user. Something might be a good idea, but an unattractive opportunity, if it has any of the following characteristics:

1. There is no market need (i.e., it is a better mousetrap).
2. Customers are generally satisfied with their current option(s).
3. Customer loyalty to existing options is very strong.
4. Customer switching costs are high.
5. Customers are hard to reach.
6. There is intense competition.
7. It is easy to enter the industry (often the case with service businesses).
8. Customers are too demanding for what they are willing to pay.

QUESTION #6: WHAT IS THE "WINDOW OF OPPORTUNITY"?

Answer: As seen in question #5, a particular version of an opportunity has a life. That is, it only lasts so long before it ceases to be attractive. The term *window of opportunity* is used to capture this life, as windows open and they close. For as long as the window is open (time-sensitive), profits can be extracted from the opportunity (i.e., durable). Thus, the window of opportunity is the optimal time period during which to pursue an opportunity with a given business concept. For example, in Figure 5-2, there are two curves, A and B. In curve A, the optimal time period to enter a new opportunity is during the shaded area (i.e., between time period *t(a)1* and time period *t(a)2*). The same applies to the shaded area for

FIGURE 5-2   The Window of Opportunity—Timing, Duration, and Erosion

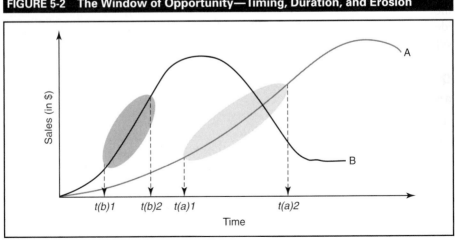

curve B. However, the window of opportunity is open for longer in curve A than it is in curve B, while the sales revenue potential for both curve A and curve B is similar. (A question for you: Which of the two situations, curve A or curve B, is the more attractive opportunity of the two?)

Let us consider another scenario, which is most noticeable in curve B. Getting in too early (i.e., before $t(b)1$ on curve B) will result in poor sales revenues, which might cause the company to abandon the opportunity prematurely. The original maker of automated teller machines (ATMs) was in the market before both banks and bank customers were ready to move to transactions not involving humans. Getting in too late (i.e., after $t(b)2$ on curve B) will result in heavy price-based competition that quickly levels off as the opportunity fades away over time. Video games are a case in point. An opportunity is uncovered for a new type of game, and following the pioneering firm, a slew of imitators enters with slight variations on the new concept. They all make money. However, the window closes rapidly in this type of market, and introducing a very creative new product to exploit the same opportunity might fail, because it entered the market a few months too late.

QUESTION #7: WHO FINDS OR HOW DOES ONE FIND OPPORTUNITIES?

Answer: This question relates to two different issues. First, when and how do opportunities for the creation of new value come into existence? Opportunities exist out there, independently of particular actors, but not as complete, identifiable, or separate entities. Instead, opportunities exist as potentiality in the form of technological possibilities and unfilled human needs. Second, why do some people but not others discover and exploit these opportunities? Seeing the potentiality embedded in an opportunity and recognizing ideas for new worlds based on the opportunity are the creations of actors who interact with each other, technologies, and their environments. Differences in knowledge, skills, attitudes, motivation, and other dispositions of individuals and/or firms result in different ideas for new ventures that match these personal characteristics, as well as perceptions of external conditions.

QUESTION #8: WHAT IS THE DIFFERENCE BETWEEN AN OPPORTUNITY AND A BUSINESS CONCEPT?

Answer: An opportunity is a favorable set of circumstances in the external environment creating a need or opening for a new business concept (venture idea). The business concept is a unique combination that is a specific, value-creating method for capitalizing on the opportunity. Note here that the combination must be unique and offer a new value proposition—this does not imply that it must be an invention or a radical innovation. A business concept can relate to modifications to an existing business, licensing, a franchise, an innovation (new product, service, or process), an existing product that is altered to fit the needs of a particular market segment (or niche), a new packaging solution, a new distribution approach, and so forth. Most successful new business concepts (1) solve a *problem*, (2) fill an important *need* in an unserved or underserved market, or (3) take advantage of an environmental *trend* that creates the opportunity for a new business idea. Not surprisingly, then, marketers with a problem-solving bias are likely to produce many new innovations.

QUESTION #9: HOW DOES ONE GET BETTER AT IDENTIFYING ATTRACTIVE OPPORTUNITIES FOR NEW VENTURES?

Answer: Opportunity identification demands knowledge, preferably first-hand knowledge, of the market: who buys; why they buy; and when, how, and where they buy. Current or potential customer needs and buying behavior are paramount; only when this information is in hand can the product or service with which to create value better than competitive offerings be considered. The marketer's personal experience and a deep understanding of important trends and forecasts based on market research form a powerful combination that facilitates the process of opportunity identification. An appreciation for existing and emerging technologies, and their potential applications, is also valuable. Beyond knowledge, a number of situational factors come into play, such as "being in the right place at the right time" to access information from one's own personal network, as was the case with Microsoft at startup.

One of the most intriguing aspects of opportunity recognition is captured in the notion of a "corridor principle."[13] In essence, the act of recognizing and pursuing an opportunity tends to make a person more opportunity aware. All of us are surrounded by opportunities in our daily lives—but we miss most of these opportunities. We are preoccupied with deadlines, immediate crises, and day-to-day responsibilities. But the person who takes the plunge and acts on a given opportunity starts to see the world differently. He or she recognize opportunities in places he or she never would have noticed before. It is like walking down a corridor that you are familiar with, but this time you notice doors that you hadn't seen before; this time, you are much more likely to open one or two of these doors. The message is simple—pursue opportunity and you will see more opportunity.

Six of the most common sources of high-value ideas for new ventures include customers, employees, suppliers, professional networks, trade publications, and magazines/newspapers.[14] All of these sources highlight the importance of being alert to information at your disposal and to problems that can be solved. These opportunities are often right under your nose, such as existing customers who want something the company is not offering. If these sources seem rather lame and you think there has to be more to the process of coming up with great ideas than this, consider the following three examples for a moment:

1. IKEA discovered its "flat-pack" furniture concept when an employee, Gillis Lundgren, cut the legs off a bulky table he had just purchased because it would not fit into the trunk of his car.

2. A Wal-Mart store manager in Crowley, Louisiana, tried to scare off shoplifters by introducing "store greeters" rather than security guards; this new perspective soon became a signature of Wal-Mart stores.

3. The idea behind American Express Travelers Cheques was born out of the frustration of an Amex executive who tried unsuccessfully to cash his letters of credit while on holiday in Europe.

B-I-G ideas—they are everywhere, all the time. Just keep your ears and eyes open, and you will soon realize the problem that is driving you crazy is a B-I-G business idea.

QUESTION #10: HOW DO I KNOW IT IS A "GOOD" OPPORTUNITY?

Answer: There are a number of different methods for evaluating opportunities. While some people rely on intuition or a hunch, others use rules of thumb to screen opportunities, such as those in the list shown in Table 5-1. More comprehensive analyses of the attractiveness of an opportunity, similar to methods used by venture capitalists, rely on the following set of criteria:[15]

1. Create or add significant value to a customer or end user.

2. Solve a significant problem or meet a significant need/want for which someone is willing to pay a premium.

3. Promise robust market, margin, and money-making characteristics (the 3 M's).

4. Match founders' experience and background.

5. Balance risk and reward.

TABLE 5-1   Ten Rules of Thumb for Attractive Opportunities
1. Revolutionary or evolutionary solution
2. Alleviation of massive customer pain
3. Large growing market
4. Team of industry experts
5. Feasible
6. Low capital requirement
7. Cash flow positive by year two
8. Significant payoffs
9. Clearly defined exit strategy
10. Competitive advantage (e.g., patent)

Source: Timmons, J. (1999). *New venture creation: Entrepreneurship in the 21st century.* Homewood, IL: Irwin.

CAPITALIZING ON CHANGE BY RECOGNIZING, DISCOVERING, AND CREATING OPPORTUNITIES

All entrepreneurial opportunities are not created equal. Some are obvious and more easily discovered by an enterprising agent, while others are the brainchild of imagination and fantasy, and still others are socially constructed. Having examined the different questions related to the nature of opportunity, attention now shifts to how these opportunities come into existence. Opportunities can be "recognized, discovered, or created. They involve the coming together of new or existing ideas or inventions, one or more ends (i.e., subjective aspirations and/or objective goals), beliefs about things favorable to the achievement of those ends, and possible implementation of those ends through the creation of new economic artifacts."[16] Thus, three different mechanisms come into play as opportunities are uncovered: opportunity creation, opportunity discovery, and opportunity recognition (see Figure 5-3).

In each mechanism, knowledge emerges along different paths: imagination and vision, discovery by which exploitation leads to exploration, and novel combinations of existing knowledge. These knowledge paths in turn result in different types of outcomes:

- *Land of Possibilities,* that is, an unarticulated need and no value-creating solution.

FIGURE 5-3   Three Views of Entrepreneurial Opportunity

Opportunity creation	Opportunity discovery	Opportunity recognition
Supply doesn't exist Demand doesn't exist Create supply and demand (e.g., MIR space resort, Beanie Babies)	Supply exists Demand doesn't exist Discover demand side (e.g., Laser technology) or Demand exists Supply doesn't exist Discover supply side (e.g., Cures for diseases)	Supply exists Demand exists Match supply and demand (e.g., Starbucks, Dell)
Effectuation Vision Imagination Future thinking Serendipity	Deliberate search Lead users Market development New-product development Innomediation Open innovation Scientific/technological advances	Pattern/signal detection Identifying trends Marketing research Empathic design Prior knowledge

Future is largely unpredictable → Future is largely predictable

- *Hot Spots,* that is, an articulated need but no value-creating solution, or an existing solution but unarticulated needs.

- *Cool Places,* that is, an articulated need and a novel value-creating solution.

Each mechanism in Figure 5-3 involves a different process to connect supply (value-creating solutions or means) and demand (needs or ends). Of the three mechanisms (recognition, discovery, and creation of opportunities), it is likely that creation is more general than, and precedes, recognition and discovery. Creation contains the inputs (means and ends) necessary for recognition and discovery. Before someone can *recognize* or *discover* an opportunity, it has to be *created*. Once sources of demand and supply have been created, then it becomes possible for someone to discover new sources of demand/supply, or to recognize new ways to match sources of supply with sources of demand. Each of the three mechanisms is now discussed in turn in the order they appear in Figure 5-3.

OPPORTUNITY CREATION (IN THE LAND OF POSSIBILITIES)

If neither sources of supply nor demand exist, one or both have to be *created* through a dynamic and interactive process for the opportunity to come into existence in the "land of possibilities." With uncertainty in both the source of demand (the customer need) and the supply (the value-creating method for meeting this need), a particular future is largely unpredictable and will depend mostly on human effort. This human effort requires an action orientation, coupled with a predisposal toward experimentation, and governed by the principle of affordable loss. Such a combination helps minimize investment in potential failures and helps treat lessons from early failures as a necessary platform for later successes.[17] Effectual logic is enacted through a series of experiments that leads to the creation of opportunities. Classic examples include the opportunities for U-Haul and radio frequency identification (RFID) tags. Because effectual action entails curiosity-driven ideas rather than problem-driven ideas, serendipity plays a significant role. Such serendipity was at work in the market opportunities created by Velcro, Corn Flakes, Band-Aids, Post-it Notes, Nike's waffle sole, Teflon, penicillin, and polyurethane, among a host of others.

OPPORTUNITY DISCOVERY (IN THE HOT SPOTS)

When only one side exists—demand exists, but supply does not (or vice versa)—the nonexistent side has to be *discovered*. As a case in point, the devastating effect of AIDS in Africa and in other parts of the world (demand) has resulted in a concerted effort to find a cure (supply), or at the very least to prolong the lives of those infected with the HIV virus. An example where supply exists but demand does not, is the search for new uses or applications for well-established technologies such as Hewlett-Packard's inkjet technology in Exhibit 5-3. Both instances are driven by an environment in which the future cannot be predicted and are "hot spots" of new technologies. Other examples of opportunities to be discovered in the future include nanotechnology, smart cars, iTV retailing, and

---

EXHIBIT 5-3 Supply in Search of Demand at Hewlett-Packard

Hewlett-Packard's inkjet technology is an example of a solution in search of a problem (or supply in search of demand).

Following Moore's law, HP's inkjet performance has doubled every 18 months for the past 17 years in terms of drops of ink per second. With these technology increases, HP is able to enter a number of new markets beyond printing, some of which include television and computer displays, printed electronic circuits, automotive fuel-injection systems, and even drug delivery for treatments of diseases like diabetes.

These technological advances have also found application in the American textile industry that allowed the textile industry to offer highly customized fabrics made in shorter production runs. The inkjet systems print colored patterns on all kinds of fabrics, including clothing and carpets.

Source: http://www.nytimes.com/2004/10/11/business/11inkjet.html

---

cashless wallets. Opportunities are discovered through deliberate or active searches for the missing element by an enterprising and alert individual or group. A number of different sources of opportunity are relevant here, some of which include lead users (users whose needs are far ahead of the main market), corporate and university R&D centers, innomediation,[18] and open innovation.[19]

OPPORTUNITY RECOGNITION (IN THE COOL PLACES)

When both a source of supply and a source of demand exist, then the opportunity for bringing them together has to be *recognized* by the arbitrageur. Franchises are examples of a situation in which sources of supply and demand are known, and a particular future is more predictable. The entrepreneurial marketer uses existing knowledge and the logical, rational process of causal reasoning to match means and ends in novel combinations. This process occurs through pattern detection in which the marketer "connects the dots"[20] to uncover the "cool places" where innovative consumers go in search of newness and difference, niches, or the next big thing. Situations in which potential opportunities might be recognized include efforts to solve problems, dissatisfied buyers, market/marketing research or trend analysis, and empathic design (observing how customers use a particular product or service).

VALUE CREATION: THAT'S WHAT IT'S ALL ABOUT

This brings us to the essence of opportunities and entrepreneurial behavior as it concerns the marketer: value creation. Positioned at the base of the pyramid in Figure 5-1, value creation is the foundation on which all entrepreneurial activity exists. As indicated by the earlier definition and reiterated in Figure 5-1, entrepreneurship consists of the identification and exploitation of opportunities to create *new* value, which underpins the creation of new products, new markets, new wealth, new ventures, new employment, new markets, and so forth. Without any net new value created, there has been no entrepreneurship.

FIGURE 5-4   The Two Dynamic, Overlapping, and Interacting Processes Underlying Value Creation

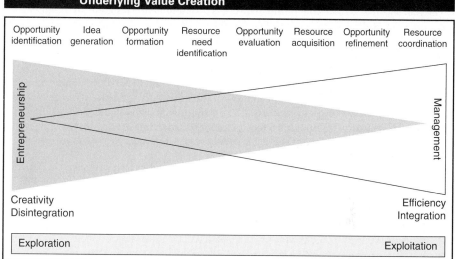

The value-creation process has a dual nature. It can be separated into two distinct processes that overlap and interact dynamically: exploration and exploitation (see Figure 5-4). Exploration is an entrepreneurial activity that addresses ambiguity and interpretation asymmetries (experimentation, search and discovery, variation). Exploitation is a managerial activity that addresses uncertainty and information asymmetries (efficiency, refinement, selection, and implementation).[21] Different stages in the exploration process include opportunity identification, idea generation, opportunity formation, opportunity evaluation, and opportunity refinement.[22] The exploitation process deals with identification of resource needs, resource acquisition, and then ongoing resource coordination.

From the perspective of the company, some of the value it has created by developing, producing, and delivering innovative products and services to the market must be captured or appropriated. Returns must be extracted from the marketplace. The entrepreneur must accomplish these two tasks (value creation and appropriation) even before the real attractiveness of the market opportunity is known.[23]

Alternatively, from the perspective of the market,[24] value without innovation offers only incremental benefits, whereas innovation without value is either too futuristic or offers benefits buyers are not willing to pay for. However, when both innovation and value are present, also called "value innovation," the potential exists for quantum-leap improvements. Value innovation overcomes the traditional value-cost trade-off requirements. For example, Southwest Airlines offers outstanding customer service and rock-bottom prices, as does JetBlue—something that defies traditional marketing logic. It is this perception of new value (i.e., the customer's response) that confers a competitive advantage to early-stage new ventures, especially where innovation results in the creation of new markets.

EXHIBIT 5-4 Value Creation of an Unusual Kind: The Mini

The fuel shortage at the time of the Suez crisis prompted Alec Issigonis to design a car for Lord Nuffield's company, BMC. Production was about to start from two lines when—disaster!—in came the market research. It revealed the small car's Achilles' heel. It wouldn't sell because people thought it looked "silly," because it had no proper, big wheels—only little 10-inch jobs. BMC was in a quandary. Should it strangle the new baby at birth? In the end there was a good old British compromise. The car went ahead, but on one line, not two. Of course, very soon after the car hit the road the nation went crazy for: the Mini. The "silly" car became the biggest selling British car in history; 5.3 million rolled off the production lines.

People loved the Mini's look. They loved the price. And they loved the cavernous space allowed by those silly small wheels.

So was the market research inaccurate? No. It captured exactly how people felt about cars as they currently understood them. But the final product changed the way they thought about cars.

Source: http://www.austin-rover.co.uk/index.htm?blogs200608f.htm

---

But customer perceptions of value and innovation are not always right. There are numerous examples of innovative products and services that were initially rejected by consumers, such as the microwave, CNN, the Sony Walkman, and Boeing's 747. An example of the paradoxical dilemma of value creation and value appropriation (from the company's perspective) and value perceptions (from the customer's perspective) can be found in the story of the Mini in Exhibit 5-4.

Value is created by meeting customers' needs better or solving a customer's problem better than competitors. It can be quantified and expressed in monetary terms. While the notion of value as it relates to pricing is covered in Chapter 11, two aspects of value are important when discussing the process of opportunity identification and exploitation: customer value and the value proposition. A simplistic conceptualization of "value" is provided in Table 5-2. Opportunities for customer value innovation[25] can be found by constructing a buyer-utility map, which is a matrix that matches six utility levers (collective productivity, simplicity, convenience, risk, fun/image, environmental friendliness) with six different stages in the buyer experience cycle (purchase, delivery, use, supplements, maintenance, disposal). Asking questions such as, "Which levers are most important for customers?", "Which levers can add competitive advantage?", "What ideas will offer greater utility to customers?", and "Which elements of the buyer cycle are most important to customers?" provide a important sources of new insight related to the discovery of new marketspace.

Not all products provide breakthrough value or are of historic importance like the space shuttle or the computer. For instance, while value has typically implied "the new and different," marketers have found ways to create value around yesteryear's nostalgia, where old products become new again:

Retro is all around: retro autos (like the P.T. Cruiser and BMW Mini Cooper), retro radios (shellac outside, digital inside), retro sneakers

TABLE 5-2   Creating and Estimating Customer Value

Seller value = Seller price − Seller cost

Total customer value = Customer benefits − Customer costs
where

Customer benefits = [Product value] + [Possession value] + [Value in use]
and

[Product value]   = Functional + Social + Emotional + Epistemic + Conditional

Therefore,

Customer benefits = [Functional + Social + Emotional + Epistemic + Conditional]
                    benefit + [Benefit in possession] = [Benefit in use]

Customer costs   = Sacrifices in terms of price paid
                   = Price + Perceived costs + Search cost + Cost of acquisition
                   + Cost of use + Cost of repair + (Non)monetary costs
                   + (Non)financial costs + Psychological costs

Source: Woodruff, R. B. (1997). Customer value: The next source of competitive advantage in the 21st century. *Academy of Marketing Science* 25(2): 139–153.

(P.F. Flyers and Chuck Taylor All Stars), retro video games (from Pacman to Doom 3), retro rock music (The Strokes, The Darkness, etc.), retro house-furnishings (courtesy of Restoration Hardware, Ralph Lauren, et al.), retro movies (remakes, comic book rip-offs, sequels of prequels of Star Wars), retro television (The Muppets are back, Kermit akimbo), retro communities (Disney's celebrated Celebration), retro celebrities (Donald Trump returns, comb-over intact), retro commercials, (Britney Spears coos "Come Alive" for Pepsi), and countless others are all the retro rag.[26]

Marketers have identified opportunities for markets around baby boomers who are longing for products with happy memories, while these same products create an entirely different kind of value that is all new for the next generation. These examples reinforce the conclusion that value perception is highly personal and subjective.

The greatest opportunities find the marketer avoiding incremental steps and creating breakthrough value. This is more likely when the marketer attempts to address unarticulated and unanswered needs in two situations: creating entirely new markets around discontinuities (e.g., Amazon.com; Apple's iPod) and creating new market spaces within an existing industry (e.g., The Body Shop with its *natural* cosmetics in attractive packaging; Southwest Airlines selling fun, on-time arrival and lower prices in the airline industry). Seeing the future first by exploring the "white space"[27] requires the entrepreneurial marketer to look beyond the obvious to (re)think everything—(re)define the need; (re)conceptualize the value proposition; (re)compose the channel; (re)label the competitors; (re)invent the industry; (re)imagine possible functionalities.

BREAKING RULES AND THE PEOPLE WHO BREAK THEM

How does the marketer (re)think everything to create this breakthrough value in the white space? Is it possible to discard previous ways of thinking? The reality is that people see the world from their own points of view; they identify opportunities based on their existing knowledge and experience. Chances are that you've heard the cliché "get out of the box" far too many times. Usually, the inference is that you must be more creative. That's all good and well, but how far can you push beyond your current perceptions of the boundaries? How do you find the edge where it becomes possible to create a breakthrough innovation rather than find a more creative solution for an existing problem? Can you break the barriers of your own mind? Is there a secret garden in your mind waiting for you to find the hidden key? One thing is certain: if you believe your mind is similar to a computer that works in a logical, rational manner and approach a problem only from your own bounded contextualized experience, chances are you will explore all the corners of the box and be able to define, measure, explain, and analyze the box with 100% accuracy, but you will never be able to break free of the self-imposed boundaries of your mind.

Thinking differently entails rejection and replacement of previous mental models, not merely making an adjustment through creative thinking. Breakthrough value requires that you create a situation in which the old rules no longer apply. All games (marketing included) are defined by their rules.[28] The first step is to discover and fully understand the constraints and the rules. Only then does it become possible to manipulate or overcome constraints—to break the rules that prohibit the creation of new perceptions, understanding, and experience. For instance, scientists discovered that ellipsoids (shaped like M&Ms) pack closer than spheres. This fundamentally altered the rules of the game—rules that had been determined by scientists who have previously proven the opposite.

If you break a rule, you have to assume there will be disadvantages; in most cases, at least. Take a soccer game, for example. An attacking player is deemed to be offside if, at the moment the ball is passed to him or her, he or she is closer to the opponent's goal line than the last-but-one player of the opposing team. (A few fine details vary and expand this rule slightly; however, for our purposes, we can safely ignore them.) If the referee blows the whistle, the ball (and thus, the advantage) goes to the opponent.

If we do not know how to play a game but want to learn it, we typically begin by studying the instructions in order to understand the rules. If we notice another player breaking the rules, we usually draw their attention to the fact. Strange as it may seem, players who break the rules are not taking the game seriously, and a game is usually only fun to play when we do take the rules seriously. A game can, of course, also get into a rut and grow boring. At this point, a time-out may be called and rule changes agreed upon. Developing new rules is itself a creative act. A set of rules works well if it ensures that the outcome of the game cannot be known in advance; this generates tension and excitement. Only under these conditions can all players compete to the best of their abilities and hope to win the game. Once the rules have been redefined, the game can start over.

—BICKHOFF & BIEGER (2006)

The limits to what can be done in any market are forever unknown and unknowable. Entrepreneurship is about new ways that are forged by the conflict between what everyone knows is the way it must be done and the vision of "what if" thinking. Can you imagine a bookstore with no books and no store? This is Amazon.com. Can you imagine glue that doesn't really stick? This discovery led to the creation of Post-it Notes. What about moving trucks without movers? This is U-Haul. How about music with no tape recorder or CD player? This is Apple's iPod. Counterfactual reasoning allows us to challenge assumptions, uncover potential underlying causes, generate useful questions, or raise provocative hypotheses about causality. Counterfactual thinkers use the "what if" compass to break free of outdated constraints and limiting means-ends frameworks. According to Karen Strauss at Ketchum, "Informed creativity emerges somewhere between emotion and reason, between wishful thinking and thinking pragmatically. Therefore, an effectively led creative session must delicately straddle unimpeded ideation *and* critical evaluation. Over-emphasize idea free-flow and you end up with a fun experience, but lots of exciting, unrealistic ideas. Overdo evaluation and you wind up with a few, well-etched ideas that reek of mediocrity."[29]

So, entrepreneurial opportunities are not created by trying to predict or control the future; creating and influencing the future requires that you determine a set of futures from among myriad possible futures that can be imagined. This is akin to mental time travel into the future[30]—projecting the self into possible future scenarios to foresee novel situations. Most people appreciate the importance of preparing for the future, but few actually pursue opportunities by taking action. Breaking rules leads to new opportunities but it also increases risk, uncertainty, and ambiguity. Risk induces a fear of failure that stifles creativity.

FIGURE 5-5   The 7 C's of an Entrepreneur's Role

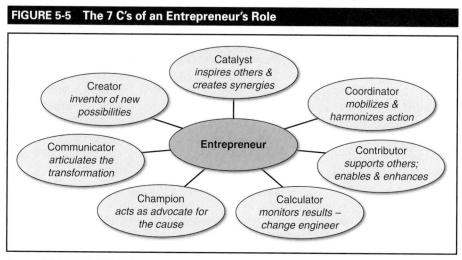

Source: Nicholls, A. (2006). *Social entrepreneurship: New models of sustainable social change.* Oxford, UK: Oxford University Press.

And yet it is only by taking action and embracing uncertainty and ambiguity that risk can be reduced. The entrepreneur must not only think, but also act. The entrepreneurial actor plays as many as seven different roles during the opportunity identification process (see Figure 5-5). For example, the role of catalyst finds the entrepreneur sparking action and accelerating things by creating more opportunities for interactions to occur. The catalyst creates the potential to trigger cycles of collective change, generates many new possibilities, and increases chances for a hit. Alternatively, as a champion, the entrepreneur keeps an idea alive in the face of resistance and serious obstacles, as well as pressures to compromise.

Summary and Conclusions

Opportunities originate from the external environment, including the marketplace. In this chapter, we have explored the nature of opportunity, where it originates, and how it can be discovered. We have focused on market opportunities, using metaphors to underscore the territorial nature of new markets. We refer to territory not in a physical sense, because markets defy any boundaries that are placed around them artificially, but in the sense of evolving areas of entrepreneurial activity. The three mechanisms for opportunity identification are characterized by the *land of promise,* in which opportunities are created; *hot spots,* where opportunities can be discovered, and *cool places,* where opportunities are recognized. Breakthrough value is created in *white spaces,* whereas markets that have outlived their usefulness due to inferior value propositions end their final days in *black holes.* This is the landscape of the new world created by entrepreneurial thinking and doing. It is not a world filled only with ideas, but also with active practice and experience.

In this world, knowledge is under active construction. It is not a picture of a preexisting world that one must respond to or make sense of. Instead, it is a world of active meaning-making by enacting opportunities, where individual actors create the world and in the process create themselves. This means that entrepreneurship is no longer something that is done at a point in time. Rather, it represents a guiding philosophy as well as an ongoing behavior. As a philosophy of business and of life, the concern is with a consciousness of, and respect for, opportunity, innovation, calculated risk-taking, and tolerance of failure. Behaviorally, there is a need for marketers to develop a personal strategy of entrepreneurial thinking, dreaming, acting, doing, and being—a kind of blueprint for the entire panorama of life's experiences. Opportunity is everywhere, if we will just see it.

Entrepreneurs have received short shrift from both the old left and the neo-liberals. The left has seen entrepreneurs as selfishly profit-driven, concerned to extract as much surplus value as possible from the labour force. Neo-liberal theory stresses the rationality of competitive markets, where decision-making is driven by market needs. Successful entrepreneurs, however, are innovators, because they spot possibilities that others miss, or take on risks that others decline, or both. A society that doesn't encourage entrepreneurial culture won't

generate the economic energy that comes from the most creative ideas. Social and civic entre-
preneurs are just as important as those working directly in a market context, since the same
drive and creativity are needed in the public sector, and in civil society, as in the economic
sphere.

—ANTHONY GIDDENS

Key Terms

- creative destruction
- entrepreneurial
  opportunity
- opportunity recognition
- opportunity evaluation
- entrepreneurial mindset
- entrepreneurial action

Questions

1. The United States is a nation of dog-lovers, and this has created enormous opportunities for new products and services. The information in the accompanying text box captures trends and facts related to pets.

   - About 31% of women and 15% of men say they spend more time with their pet than with their spouse or significant other [*Source:* Hartz's May 2005 Human-Animal Bond survey]
   - 54% of all US households own at least one pet [*Source:* American Veterinary Medical Association]
   - Here's what 901 pet owners surveyed had to say about their animal companions [*Source:* BizRate Research study for Shopzilla]:
     - Over half of the women surveyed (56%) believe that their pets are more affectionate than their partners (vs. 41% of men).
     - 45% of women think that their pets are cuter than their partners (vs. 24% of men).
     - Almost all the women (99%) said they often talk to their pets (vs. 95% of men).
     - 93% of women believe that their pets communicate with them (vs. 87% of men).
     - Almost three-quarters (73%) of female pet owners said they would be more inclined to date or marry someone who also has a pet (vs. 50% of men).
     - About 7 in 10 pet owners (68%) say their pets make them happier than their jobs. A full 72% of women feel this way, compared with 60% of men.
     - Over a third (34%) of pet owners—39% of women and 27% of men—say they would take their animal to a pet groomer, therapist, or psychic.
     - Just under a third (31%) of owners say they would consider having a pet funeral.

Answer the following questions based on the information provided here, as well as on what you know after reading the chapter:

   a. How many new ideas for products and services for people and/or their pets can you think of based on this information? Try to generate as many ideas as possible without judging them as good or bad, feasible or not. Use a standard page, and write down 5 to 10 words to describe the essence of each idea.

   b. Now look at all your ideas. How many of them already exist? A quick Google search will probably eliminate most of the ideas. Scratch those that exist (even if they are just remotely similar) and focus on the ones that are left on the page. Divide the remaining ideas into two groups: ideas for the pet and ideas for the pet owner.

   c. Choose the idea that you are most excited about. Evaluate the attractiveness of the opportunity using the criteria discussed in this chapter.

   d. Use a few creativity techniques to see if you can improve the attractiveness of the opportunity you have identified.

2. The average legal costs associated with a DUI arrest are close to $9,000, and current solutions for the problem of drunk driving have not been satisfactory (see the text box insert). NightRiders is a company that drives drunk people home in their own cars. More information related to this business venture is available at http://www.autoblog.com/2005/02/07/nightriders-drive-drunks-home-avoid-k-i-t-t-jokes/. Answer the following questions related to the NightRiders service:

   a. What is the customer need here?

   b. What is the opportunity?

   c. What is the business concept?

   d. What is the value proposition?

   e. Describe the way in which the NightRiders venture (i) solves a problem and/or (ii) takes advantage of a trend.

- Problem: drunk driving
- Cost of DUI = $8,870 (average)
- Current solutions:
  - Dedicated driver
  - Don't drink
  - Ask a friend
  - Get a taxi
- New solution: NightRiders

Resources and References

1. Amabile, T. M. (1997). Motivating creativity in organizations: On doing what you love and loving what you do. *California Management Review* 40(1): 39–58.

2. Schumpeter, J. (1975 [orig. pub. 1942]). *Capitalism, socialism and democracy*. New York: Harper.

3. Shane, S., & Venkataraman, S. (2001). Entrepreneurship as a field of research: A response to Zahra and Dess, Singh, and Erikson. *Academy of Management Review* 25(1): 217–226.
4. Schumpeter, J. A. (1934). *The theory of economic development*. Cambridge, MA: Harvard University Press.
5. Dollinger, M. J. (1994). *Entrepreneurship strategies and resources*. Burr Ridge, IL: Irwin.
6. Steyaert, C. (2000). Creating worlds: Political agendas of entrepreneurship. Paper presented at the 11th Nordic Conference on Small Business Research, Aarhus, Denmark, June 18–20, 2000.
7. Ibid.
8. Venkataraman, S., & Sarasvathy, S. D. (2001). Strategy and entrepreneurship: Outlines of an untold story. In M. Hitt, E. Freeman, and J. Harrison, eds., *Handbook of Strategic Management* (pp. 650–668). Malden, MA: Blackwell.
9. Allen, K. (2003). *Launching new ventures: An entrepreneurial approach*. Chicago: Upstart Publishing Company.
10. Sarasvathy, S., Venkataraman, S., Dew, N., & Velamuri, R. (2003). Three views of entrepreneurial opportunity. In Z. Acs, ed., *Handbook of Entrepreneurship* (pp. 141–160). Boston: Kluwer Academic Press.
11. Eckhardt, J. A., & Shane, S. A. (2003). Opportunities and entrepreneurship. *Journal of Management* 29(3): 333–349.
12. Drucker, P. (1985). *Innovation and entrepreneurship: Practice and principles*. New York: Harper & Row.
13. Ronstadt, R. (1988). The corridor principle. *Journal of Business Venturing* 3(1): 31–40.
14. Hills, G. E., & Shrader, R. C. (1998). Successful entrepreneurs' insights into opportunity recognition. In *Frontiers of entrepreneurship research* (pp. 30–43). Wellesley, MA: Babson College.
15. Timmons, J. (1999). *New venture creation: Entrepreneurship in the 21st century*. Homewood, IL: Irwin.
16. Sarasvathy, Dew, Velamuri, & Venkataraman. (2003).
17. Sarasvathy, S. (2003). Constructing corridors to economic primitives: Entrepreneurial opportunities as demand-side artefacts. In J. Butler, ed., *Opportunity identification and entrepreneurial behavior* (pp. 291–312). Greenwich, CT: Information Age Publishing.
18. Sawhney, M., Prandelli, E., & Verona, G. (2003). *The power of innomediation. MIT Sloan Management Review* 44(2): 77.
19. von Hippel. E. (2005). *Democratizing innovation*. Boston: MIT Press.
20. Baron, R. A. (2006, February). Opportunity recognition as pattern recognition: How entrepreneurs "connect the dots" to identify new business opportunities. *Academy of Management Perspectives:* 104–119.
21. March, J. (1991). Exploration and exploitation in organizational learning. *Organizational Science* 2(1): 71–87.
22. Bhave, M. P. (1994). A process model of entrepreneurial venture creation. *Journal of Business Venturing* 9: 223–242.
23. Alvarez, S. A., & Barney, J. B. (2005). How do entrepreneurs organize firms under conditions of uncertainty? *Journal of Management* 31: 776–792.
24. Kim, W. C., & Mauborgne, C. (2005). *Blue ocean strategy: How to create uncontested market space and make the competition irrelevant.* Boston: Harvard Business School Press.

25. Kim, W. C., & Mauborgne, R. (2004). Value innovation: The strategic logic of high growth. *Harvard Business Review: The Best of HBR on Strategy* 82(7/8): 172–180.
26. Brown, S. (1999). Retro-marketing: Yesterday's tomorrows, today! *Marketing Intelligence and Planning* 17(7): 363–376.
27. Hamel, G., & Prahalad, C. K. (1992). Corporate imagination and expeditionary marketing. *Harvard Business Review* 69(4): 31–43.
28. Bickhoff, N., & Bieger, T. (2006). Understanding and breaking the rules of business: Toward a systematic four-step process. *Business Horizons* 49: 369–377.
29. Strauss, K. (2002). Perspectives. *Ketchum's Online Communications Quarterly*. Accessed April 30, 2007, http://www.ketchumperspectives.com/archives/ 2002_i2/content.php?pg=global.
30. Suddendorf, T., & Corballis, M. C. (1997). Mental time travel and the evolution of the human mind. *Genetic, Social and General Psychology Monographs* 123: 133–167.

CHAPTER 6

STRATEGIC INNOVATION AND THE MARKETER
OR, WHY THE MARKETING CONCEPT IS MISCONCEPTUALIZED

IS CUSTOMER ORIENTATION ALL THAT MATTERS?

Most marketing textbooks, usually somewhere in the first chapter, argue that firms should be customer focused, customer driven, or, according to the latest marketing buzzword, customer-centric. They trace a history of the orientations that organizations have adopted and explain why each is faulty. It is wrong to be production oriented, they argue, because in times when most markets are in oversupply situations, producing enough isn't the problem; disposing of it is. It is also wrong to be sales oriented, they contend, because telling customers long and loud how badly they need your product or service is both annoying and wasteful, and usually unnecessary. And focusing on the product itself is myopic and incorrect — this ignores customer needs and wants, and results in the development and production of better mousetraps that no one wants.

Likewise, in their chapters on new-product development and product management, most marketing textbooks take a perspective that successful new products are those that customers have indicated they need, will want, and will purchase. Accordingly, no sensible firm will launch a new product without undertaking marketing research to determine customer needs and wants, and whether the new offering meets or exceeds these. In this book we take a different perspective. There is indeed a strong case to be made for customer orientation, under certain circumstances. However, there is frequently an equally compelling argument in favor of an innovation—or product—orientation. In most circumstances, it is not a simple case of "either-or"—executives need to understand the current orientation of their firms and then decide whether this is an appropriate focus. We examine both the customer and innovation orientations, and the possible blends between them, and provide a framework for strategic diagnosis and for the plotting of future direction.*

THE CUSTOMER-PRODUCT DEBATE

Recent strategic management literature has featured a debate concerning various philosophies that have competed as guiding templates for the way in which organizations conduct their business activity.[1] An *innovation orientation* asserts that customers will prefer those products and services that generate the greatest interest and provide the greatest performance, features, quality, and value for the money—in short, technological superiority.[2] Managers in firms that enact a technological innovation orientation devote their energy toward inventing and refining superior products.** A second philosophy, often identified as *customer orientation* (more commonly referred to as *market orientation*), contends that identifying the needs and wants of the target market—and delivering products and services that satisfy these needs—is key to the attainment of organizational goals.[3] Whereas discussion of the innovation philosophy generally refers to issues such as new products, innovation, and discontinuous improvement, discussion of the customer or market orientation philosophy usually concerns matters such as customer service, customer satisfaction, and customer focus.

At times there has been vigorous debate between the two schools, while on other occasions the two streams of thought have seemed to ignore each other. While some scholars have attempted to mediate between the innovation and market orientations,[4] there is a persistence of thinking that one must be right and the other flawed. What this thinking tends to overlook is that market orientation and innovation orientation might indeed be two distinct constructs that can interact in ways that can either facilitate or inhibit strategic success. In simple terms, there is no one right way for an organization to orient itself, and in reality there is no necessary conflict between market and innovation orientations.

TO SERVE OR CREATE? A REEXAMINATION OF CUSTOMER ORIENTATION

Since the time when Peter Drucker stated that the sole purpose of a firm was to create and keep customers, many managers have embraced a customer orientation philosophy.[5] As interpreted by many of his disciples, this meant that to be

---

*This chapter is largely based on Berthon, P. R., Hulbert, J. M., & Pitt, L. F. (1999). To serve or create? Strategic orientation towards technology and customers. *California Management Review* 42(1): 37–58.

**We use the term *product* to indicate any offering that an organization brings to the marketing, and rather than only in its narrow, physical, tangible sense.

successful, organizations must ascertain the customer's needs and wants and then produce the products and services that will satisfy these needs and wants. Proponents of this perspective argue that companies should be customer driven in everything they undertake, and today, more generally, customer orientation is subsumed under the idea of market orientation.[6] This latter philosophy has typically been considered to consist of three core aspects: customer orientation, organizationwide integration of effort, and clear objectives (profitability).[7]

Drucker rightly receives credit as a progenitor of customer orientation, but often forgotten is the fact that his was a concept of a business as a whole, and it embraced more than a customer orientation. Indeed, he went on to say,

> If we want to know what a business is, we have to start with its
> purpose. . . . There is only one valid definition of business purpose: to
> create a customer. . . . It is the customer who determines what a business
> is. For it is the customer, and he alone, who through being willing to pay
> for a good or service, converts economic resources into wealth, things into
> goods. What the business thinks it produces is not of first importance —
> especially not to the future of the business and its success. What the
> customer thinks he is buying, what he considers "value" is decisive. . . .
> Because it is its purpose to create a customer, any business enterprise has
> two — and only these two — basic functions: marketing and innovation.[8]

Drucker also makes it clear that when he discusses a function he is using the term broadly, not identifying a functional department:

> Marketing is so basic that it cannot be considered a separate function
> (i.e., a separate skill or work) within the business. . . . [I]t is, first, a central
> dimension of the entire business. It is the whole business seen . . . from
> the customer's point of view. Concern and responsibility for marketing
> must, therefore, permeate all areas of the enterprise. . . . Marketing alone
> does not make a business enterprise. . . . The second function of a
> business, therefore, is innovation — the provision of different economic
> satisfactions. . . . In the organization of the business enterprise innovation
> can no more be considered a separate function than marketing. It is not
> confined to engineering or research but extends across all parts of the
> business. . . . Innovation can be defined as the task of endowing human
> and material resources with new and greater wealth-producing capacity.[9]

The marketing concept has its genesis in this focus on the customer — finding out what the customer needs, wants, and values and then delivering this as expeditiously and economically as possible. The "how" (the product or service itself) is secondary in this process — a simple means to the end of a satisfied customer. The quintessential focus of a business is the customer, and marketing is the realization of this process. However, taken alone, this is an oversimplification of Drucker's philosophy. Indeed, to focus solely on this aspect is to make an implicit assumption of the simplicity of customer wants and needs. In many cases, the implicit assumption goes further, to suppose the preexistence of a customer.

Drucker spoke of creating rather than just serving a customer. A less well-articulated aspect of Drucker's vision is that which comes before the customer, enables the creation of the customer, and is concerned with innovation: the creation of innovative products and services. Reflecting on this injunction to innovate soon reveals its logic, namely, that needs, wants, and even values often arise when products are created. Product innovation has the potential to engage people's minds and imaginations, thus creating customers. For example, Disney creates the fantasy that creates the customer.[10] Over the longer term, innovation is a prerequisite for creating customers, a quite different process from attracting customers who already exist.

Drucker was not alone among pioneer thinkers in recognizing that serving customers by itself would be insufficient to ensure long-term success. As McKitterick of General Electric argued many years ago,

> A company committed to the marketing concept focuses its major
> innovative effort on enlarging the size of the market in which it
> participates by introducing new generic products and services, by
> promoting new applications for existing products, and by seeking out
> new classes of customers who heretofore have not used the existing
> products. . . . Only thinking of the customer and mere technical
> proficiency in marketing both turn out to be inferior hands when played
> against the company that couples its thought with action and actually
> comes to market with a successful innovation.[11]

Webster summarized the situation well when he wrote

> Merely being "customer oriented" in the philosophical sense was not
> enough, nor was marketing skill, narrowly defined; constant innovation
> was also necessary to deliver better value to consumers in a competitive
> marketplace.[12]

Macdonald[13] is concerned that customer focus can create confused business processes, while Christensen and Bower's[14] work suggests that firms may even lose leadership positions by listening too carefully to customers. For longer-term prosperity, the firm must not only meet the needs and wants of today's customer, but must simultaneously innovate to ensure the creation of new customers and the means of satisfying their future needs and wants—a process that has been termed "organizational ambidexterity."[15]

BEYOND CUSTOMER ORIENTATION: THE RETURN TO INNOVATION

Why has so much of the recent literature come to stress serving the customer over creating the customer? The evolution of the literature on customer orientation shows that environmental contingency played a major role. In one of the classic articles in the marketing literature, Robert J. Keith, a director of Pillsbury, suggested that the desirability of a market orientation is contingent upon condi-tions in the market environment (as we shall see, this is something that is often overlooked). In describing Pillsbury's progression from a production orientation, to a sales orientation, to a marketing orientation, and ultimately to where mar-keting permeates the whole company he points out that [i]n the early days of the company, consumer orientation didn't seem so important . . . no-one would question the availability of a market.[16]

For many years, companies found adequate solutions to their competitive problems through a well-managed functional marketing operation, typically by means of a marketing department charged with the responsibility for "market-ing." Within a time-limited paradigm, serving the customer may well suffice to bring competitive advantage. Over the longer term, however, the critical impor-tance of customer creation will surely emerge. Arguably, serving customers and creating them is an organizationwide responsibility.

Thus, as the business environment changes due to the turbulence of globaliza-tion, deregulation, rapid technological development, and unstable financial mar-kets, it becomes even more appropriate to question whether a customer orientation alone will be sufficient to ensure prosperity. In the view of a number of contempo-rary authors, the answer is that it is not. Dickson, for example, suggests that aggres-sive competition leads to oversupply, wherein customers are offered more choices and thus become more sophisticated.[17] As a consequence, achieving effective dif-ferentiation grows ever more difficult. Marketers' attempts to serve these more sophisticated consumers spur them to innovate incrementally, which in turn leads to imitation and back once more to oversupply. Paradoxically, then, while innova-tion becomes ever more essential, its advantages seem to dissipate just as rapidly.

MARKETING AND INNOVATION

Many of the studies of the benefits of a customer orientation have been short term and are therefore, by definition, unable to provide insight into the long-term importance of radical innovation and R&D. Indeed, any experienced marketer is aware that markets can mislead as well as inform. For example, Ford of Europe built the Mk4 Escort around "broad" and "deep" market research. When launched, the car was poorly received by both customers and journalists alike; sales volume had to be built through heavy discounting.[18] In some of its later ven-tures, such as the Puma Coupe, Ford deliberately avoided market-research input. Indeed, Ford went on record to state explicitly that it was now a product-led rather than market- or customer-led company.[19] Quinn[20] describes state-of-the-art technologies (such as those of Cray Research, Genentech, Hughes Electron-ics, and Kyocera) being developed in freestanding technical units not directly connected to formal marketing units.

Heads of these projects often know more about the technologies than any-one in the world, including potential customers. Thus, as long as demand in the industry to which they sell is driven solely by technical performance criteria, the lab head can essentially define the characteristics of the next generation of products. Although good timing and technical performance predominate in these cases, the project leaders no doubt possess considerable insight into the requirements of their customers.

An innovation orientation turns traditional marketing philosophy on its head: products precede needs and create their own demand by changing the way customers behave. Schumpeter[21] argues that innovations produced by companies are the engine of economic evolution and progress. Deming[22] stresses that the need for internal process innovation is central to competitive position, while Nonaka and Yamanouchi[23] view innovation as the lifeblood by which companies renew themselves. An innovation orientation can be described as having two components: what Zaltman, Duncan, and Holbek[24] call an "openness to innovation" and what Burns and Stalker[25] call a "capacity to innovate."

Sources of innovative ideas include technology, engineering and production, inventions and patents, other firms, and management and employees. An additional source of ideas for new products (and one often overlooked, as we observed in Chapter 3) is the customer. Von Hippel[26] found that in many high-tech industries, a significant percentage of innovative ideas resulted from users developing prototypes themselves. Any broad-scale survey of customers' needs and wants would likely fail to identify these breakthroughs. Innovations by consumers (as opposed to business-to-business customers) are likely to be isolated and by definition extreme outliers. A generic customer orientation would tend to aggregate customers' views and miss the potential contribution to innovation by these outlier customers. An orientation that focuses on innovation, rather than on aggregate customer needs, will more likely recognize these externally generated ideas.

The rationale for an innovation orientation is that technology has the potential to create markets and customers. It can do this by defining human needs, hence determining the nature of consumer demand. Breakthrough technologies, or "killer applications," do not merely change markets, but rather they have far-reaching effects on the way society functions and how human beings work and live, as we will also observe in Chapter 14.[27] By providing customers with new products, services, or processes, advancing technology invariably induces changes in their basic behavior, as we noted in Chapter 3—"changes that are sometimes so fundamental that before long they cannot imagine living any other way."[28] Indeed, as Hamel and Prahalad[29] have argued, being first to a market combined with continual innovation is the key to survival in a turbulent business environment.

COMPETITIVE ADVANTAGE

There is ample indication that much of the achievement in the recent past has come from anticipating and creating customer wants.[30] If one embraces a population ecology perspective,[31] then the competitors who survive will likely be ever more proficient in conventional management practice. It therefore appears quite likely that there will be dwindling opportunities to sustain competitive advantage by attempts to simply interpret and respond to existing customer wants. Although managers may perceive more inherent risk in strategies that create and target future needs and wants, accepting such risk is likely to become ever more central to competitive advantage.

CHANGING NEEDS AND ENVIRONMENTS

The pace of change raises another set of issues. If customer needs and wants continue to change rapidly, traditional customer-oriented firms will increasingly be aiming at moving targets. Given the lags inherent in even a radically reengineered product development process, by the time a firm gets its new product to market, it will be virtually impossible to avoid gambling on what customers will really desire. We therefore suggest that managers use the simple framework presented in Figure 6-1 to conceptualize and think about these issues. The matrix in the figure has been referred to as the ICON grid (innovation or customer orientation).[32]

The flow of learning between innovation and customers goes in both directions. There is the flow from customers to innovative technology, which usually involves traditional market research. It might also, however, include informal knowledge and observation of the market by managers and others, novel approaches to market research such as "spending a day in the life of the customer,"[33] and immersion with consumers or buyers.[34] Similarly, there is also a flow from the innovative technology to customers. Changes in technology have

FIGURE 6-1   The ICON Matrix

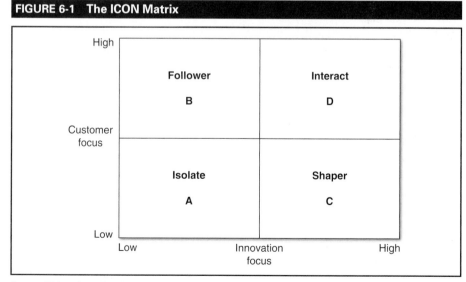

Source: Taken from Berthon, P. R., Hulbert, J. M, & Pitt, L. F. (2003). Innovation or customer orientation? An empirical investigation. *European Journal of Marketing* 38(9/10): 1065–1090; Berthon, P. R., Hulbert, J. M., & Pitt, L. F. (1999). To serve or create? Strategic orientation towards technology and customers, *California Management Review* 42(1): 37–58.

the potential to change people's perceptions, expectations, and preferences. Once commercialized, these changes may reshape the way people live, the way society is structured, and the manner in which human beings conceptualize themselves.[35] Saloner[36] has argued that Silicon Valley, a hotbed of innovative companies, "works on a 'field of dreams' business plan: if you build something, customers will come."

While this may seem extreme, anecdotal examples of new technologies that changed markets are legion. Consider, for instance, the changes wrought in working-class lives in the 19th century by the railroad; the changes in American lifestyle resulting from widespread automobile ownership in the middle part of the 20th century; or, indeed, the influence of the integrated circuit and the microprocessor on countless consumer durables, improving their convenience and functionality in ways that consumers enjoy but still do not fully comprehend. Thus, managers and their companies learn from the market, and the market (customers) learns from new technologies and the associated products. This two-way flow, or dialogue, is present in every product or service in every market.

For any one organization, the degree of focus on innovation and/or the customer can vary substantially. By dichotomizing these dimensions, we can identify four strategic orientation modes for the firm (as shown in the matrix in Figure 6-1).

ISOLATE

The organization itself becomes the focus of its own attention in the isolate mode, for there is little or no communication between innovation and the customer. Technology either stagnates or is developed for its own sake. It is not customer driven, nor is the market modified in any appreciable way by the presence of this technology. This is the classic "isolationist" mode in which either little product development occurs or, when it does, it happens without regard for customer needs or even despite them. Little or no market research happens either. Simply, there is no meaningful communication between product and market—they evolve or stagnate along separate paths.

In the isolate mode the organization becomes introverted, concerned with its own internal problems and operations at the expense of both innovation and customer focus. This mode characterized the British automobile and motorcycle industries during the late 1960s and (especially) the 1970s—remember brands like Austin, Morris, Hillman, Wolseley, and Humber? Limited product development was undertaken, and what was done was often tangential to market needs and preferences. Indeed, the industry became notorious for poor-quality, low-value products—which, while innovative, were shunned rather than adopted.

FOLLOW

The customer drives the innovation in the follow mode. To establish the parameters of products and services and to drive their development, the firm relies heavily on both formal or structured market research (using surveys) and informal or unstructured ("walking in the customer's shoes") market research. This can be done either from scratch (in the case of new-product development) or from an established position (where the product or service is refined). Examples of the former include the development by Toyota of the Lexus, where they attempted to establish exactly what the market would require of a luxury car before attempting to build it, and the development of the M5 (Miata) by Mazda, where engineers played the sounds of engines to potential customers to design the ideal sports car sound into the product. In the service environment, the Courtyard concept by Marriott Hotels, where frequent business travelers were involved in conceptualizing the ideal budget business accommodation,[37] provides another illustration. In the words of the manager who sponsored the project, "In designing the actual product, the research allowed management to focus on the items customers wanted, and we avoided focusing on things important to management but not important to the customer."

SHAPE

In this mode, innovative technology shapes the market. Indeed, potential customers may not have even been aware that they needed or wanted the benefits derived from a particular technology until it became available. Shaping suggests that technology defines human needs and hence determines the nature of customer demand by providing new products or services that induce changes in basic behavior. The product becomes essential in shaping or defining a given market. This typically occurs in two areas: the forming of expectations and the forming of prototypical preferences.

For example, Japanese auto manufacturers followed the forming of expectations route in the 1970s by loading their basic products with options not normally available as standard in their competitors' cars. Customers' expectations were raised, and they began to question why these options were not standard in other manufacturers' vehicles. As a result of these kinds of strategic moves, firms learned the hard way that they needed increasingly to distinguish between qualifying and determining attributes: as competitors become better at fulfilling the important requirements of customers, sometimes the determinants of choice are the less important (but determining) attributes.

SUVs or 4 × 4 vehicles provide an excellent example of "shaping" products. Indeed, if marketers had done research in the mid-1980s to determine whether a majority of customers would have purchased these products, the vast majority of respondents would have regarded them as crazy. Yet by the turn of the century, in countries such as the United States, Canada, and Australia, around 20% of new passenger vehicles being purchased were SUV/4 × 4s. Examples of the shaping of prototypical preference strategy in defining the four-wheel drive utility market are Jeep in the United States and Land Rover in the United Kingdom. These manufacturers shaped what consumer psychologists call the customers' category prototypes and disproportionately influenced the criteria against which customers evaluated other, later entrants to the market.

The shaping strategy also manifests itself in two distinct forms: defining and influencing (although it might be argued that the latter is but a delimited version of the former). The defining strategy is one in which entrepreneurial imagination and action combine with often-serendipitous series of events and lead to a product defining a market. In the early 1980s, for example, Chrysler forged ahead with the original minivan concept, despite market research showing that people were strongly negative toward the vehicle. The Chrysler minivan went on to create and define the minivan market.

In the influencing mode, products influence market expectations and trends, but in and of themselves do not define the market, nor necessarily capture it. For example, Apple's Macintosh defined what most customers wanted in a personal computer—a user-friendly tool with a graphic interface that did not require technical computing skills. It did not go on to dominate the PC market. Ironically, Apple seemed to think it might learn these lessons in the case of the Newton, its handheld personal digital assistant (PDA), launched in 1993. "The Newton's features were defined through one of the most thoroughly executed market research efforts in corporate history; focus groups and surveys of every type were used to determine what features consumers would want."[38] Yet the Newton failed dismally and was withdrawn by Apple in late 1996. Freddie Laker's ill-fated airline venture did not delimit the air travel market. However, it did drastically shape the expectations and perceptions of travelers concerning the price of trans-Atlantic travel and opened the way for subsequent entrants. It was no accident that Virgin's Richard Branson wanted to name his first aircraft "Spirit of Sir Freddie."[39]

Not all shaping strategies are good and necessarily productive, since a great many fail.[40] Successful shaping requires the placing of two large bets—one on technology and the other on the market. Failure rates in developing new technologies are notoriously underestimated because of their tendency to sink without a trace. The failure of shaping strategies also occurs because technological pioneers often have a poor understanding of market and customer learning processes. Much of the new research is based on the benefits of being first in the mind of the buyer. However, the technological bias of many innovative companies leads them to believe that being the first to perfect, to produce, or even to sell and distribute is enough to win the marketplace prize. By underinvesting in marketing communications (by design or default), they unwittingly cede their position to a follower. The management consulting firm A. D. Little sees an ironic symmetry to this problem:

> Technologists in fast-moving consumer goods companies—archetypes of marketing-dominated companies—tend to adopt a low profile and do what they are asked to do without much debate, so convinced are they that their companies, being market-oriented, must be marketing-driven. The reverse is equally true: in technology- or engineering-driven companies, marketers often tend to follow—and sometimes mimic—their colleagues in the technical departments (from which they themselves often come).[41]

INTERACT

A true dialogue is established between the customer and technology in the interact mode. While a dialogue is present over time in any marketplace, at any one time firms are usually engaged in a monologue. The term *dialogue* is appropriate here because it uses the metaphor of speech to underpin the market–technology relationship, providing a spectrum ranging from "conversation" to "negotiation." The term *conversation* conjures up the image of a fairly genteel, two-way flow of information—ideas offered, modified, and evolved. *Negotiation* sums up the harder image of a power play between products and markets, where there are trade-offs of values and features. Many industrial markets operate in the negotiation–interact mode: a prospective customer publishes a bid or tender and invites potential suppliers to submit their offers before moving toward the next step in the development of the product or service. In contrast, tailors have for years involved their customers in conversational dialogues concerning the product that they will in a very real sense "co-produce."

Many of the early automobile manufacturers at the upper end of the market (such as Bentley, Duesenberg, Alvis, and Bugatti) cooperated with independent coachbuilders to make cars to owners' specifications. Interestingly, Rolls Royce seemed to be moving once again in this direction in the late 1990s as a way to distinguish itself from other high-quality car producers. It announced that no two cars leaving its factory would be the same—each car being exactly tailored to the individual customer's specification.[42] The interact position is also used in highly capital-intensive purchasing situations, where the seller has to have some kind of commitment from a buyer before a new product can even be conceptualized. In the passenger jet industry, for example, Boeing worked closely with its major customers, airlines such as United Airlines and Singapore Airlines, to design and produce the Boeing 777. A more recent example is that of Airbus and the AX380, where important customers (major airlines) have been involved in the development of the product.

CHOOSING A MODE OF FOCUS

There is a temptation to be normative about which mode to pursue—devout marketers might espouse a following strategy, and engineers and technologists a shaping strategy. Even an isolation strategy might have adherents—for example, a mining company, extracting base minerals, doesn't really stand to benefit from following, shaping, or interacting. After careful thought, however, interaction would probably get the popular vote. Unfortunately, reality is seldom that simple. Dialogue and interaction may be expensive at best, and irrelevant at worst. Further, although dialogue and interaction may reduce risk, they may be less likely to consistently produce either the breakthrough product or service that characterizes the successful shaper or the devotion to true customer satisfaction that good followers are able to deliver.

A given mode of operation is as likely to emerge by default as by managerial design. Before considering a change of mode, however, managers should review the conditions that might lead them to choose one mode over another.

ENVIRONMENTAL FACTORS

The efficacy of a particular mode is partly contingent on the characteristics of a specific business environment. In a very stable environment, an *isolate* strategy might be effective and economical. In contrast, in an environment of complex and rapidly evolving customer needs and wants, a *follow* strategy would be better. In contexts of rapidly evolving technology (such as genetics), a *shaping* strategy would be most suitable. Finally, where customer needs and wants proliferate and a wide variety of substitutable technologies are present, an *interaction* approach would be appropriate.

ECONOMIC POWER OF EXISTING CUSTOMERS

Where the bargaining power of the existing customer base is considerably greater than that of suppliers, a *follow* strategy is likely to be manifest among suppliers. There is some evidence that this change occurs in the food industry, as the power of large customers like Wal-Mart in North America and Tesco in the United Kingdom grows relative to that of their manufacturer suppliers.

COMPETITIVE FACTORS

Globalization and deregulation are intensifying competition in many markets around the world. *Shape* or *interact* modes would appear to be more likely to succeed under these kinds of competitive conditions. In industries with these characteristics, such as computer hardware and software or Internet-based industries, there are countless examples of yesterday's darling being supplanted by the analyst's new love. Consider, for example, the usurpation of Psion and Newton by PalmPilot (and the latter's subsequent tumble at the hands of cell phones such as BlackBerry and Razr), the 1999 fall from grace of Compaq, the growth of SAP outstripping that of Oracle, or the emergence of Amazon.com and its effect on Barnes & Noble's superstore strategy. In such markets, stability is but a temporary illusion, and the market–technology dialogue will be ongoing.

POLITICAL FACTORS

Sometimes, strong constituencies within the firm exert dominant influence on mode choice. For years, brew masters dominated the beer industry and mill managers the steel industry, with important influences on their companies' cultures. Indeed, even where survival is evidently at risk, strong constituencies such as labor unions (consider airline pilots in various post-deregulation disputes) and top management may persist in advocating and supporting an existing mode, obdurately resisting change. Firms typically establish and embed approaches to technology and market deeply in their cultures, and this inertia renders them unlikely to change unless presented with a threat to their survival. Once a given mode is established, however, it is likely that very substantial change will be necessary to bring about a shift from one mode to another.

UNDERSTANDING STRATEGIC DYNAMICS

A given mode is neither good nor bad in and of itself; evaluation depends on how it is used. Organizations change modes over time, and valuable lessons may be learned from each mode. The potentially maligned isolation mode can be a period in which a company turns its attentions inward. This can be highly productive in phases of reflection, reassessment, and reorganization (such as during company mergers).

Despite the likely "stickiness" associated with changes of mode, it has long been recognized that organizations are in a continual state of flux.[43] Thus, there can be movement among the modes over time. For example, a *shaper* might become a *follower*, then lapse into *isolation*, and eventually become truly *interactive*.

It is possible to diagnose a firm's mode of focus. The simple checklist in Exhibit 6-1 can be used by an individual manager to identify the mode of focus mostly followed by his or her organization. Of course, the simple tool is put to even better use when it is used by a group of managers within a firm, to see whether they perceive it in the same way. Having done this, they can then decide whether the mode of focus is the appropriate one under the circumstances, and if this needs changing, what to concentrate on in the change.

EXHIBIT 6-1   The Amended ICON Scale

Instructions: Think about the organization you work for—how it views its customers and its competitors; how it thinks about technology in the form of products and services; its perceptions of the business environment in which it operates, its employees, and, of course, itself. Then complete the short questionnaire that follows. Read each of the four descriptions of an organization (A, B, C and D), and then mark a "1" next to the description that you think best fits your organization, a "2" next to the description that fits it next best, and so on, until you place a "4" next to the description that least describes your organization. In many cases of course, you may find the descriptions quite similar, so read them carefully. Also, there may be instances where you want to say, "It all depends." Don't worry too much about this— there are no "right" or "wrong" answers, so simply record your first impression.

Descriptions of Organizations

1. *Our organization views customers as:*
   A. Necessary sources of revenue for the firm _____
   B. The primary reason for the firm's existence _____
   C. People who will respond positively to innovative products and services _____
   D. Co-partners in the development of customized products and services _____

2. *Our organization views innovative products and services as:*
   A. A means to extract revenue from customers _____
   B. A means of responding to the needs and wants of customer _____

(Continue)

C. The primary reason for the firm's existence

D. As something that is co-developed with customers

3. *Our organization views the business environment (factors such as the political and legal situation, the economy, and sociocultural change) as:*

A. Of primary importance, because of its impact on the firm

B. Of primary importance, because of its impact on customers

C. Of primary importance, because of its impact on innovative products and services

D. Of primary importance, because of its impact on the interaction between customers and innovative products and services

4. *Our organization views competitors as:*

A. Rivals who attempt to take away our firm's market share and financial rewards

B. Rivals who attempt to satisfy customers' needs and wants better than we do

C. Rivals who attempt to develop innovative products and services, and who shape wants better than we do

D. Rivals who attempt to engage customers in interaction with innovative products and services better than we do

5. *Our organization views itself as:*

A. A vehicle for the creation of shareholder and employee wealth

B. A vehicle for the creation of satisfied customers

C. A vehicle for the creation of innovative products and services

D. A vehicle for the creation of interactions between customers and innovative products and services

6. *Our organization views employees as:*

A. Dedicated to the service of the firm

B. Dedicated to the service of the customer

C. Dedicated to the development of innovative products and services

D. Dedicated to the establishment of interaction between customers and innovative products and services

Instructions for Scoring

Once you have completed your impressions of all the situations, add up all your scores for "A" descriptions, and place them in the box under "Type A" firms below, then do the same for all the "B" descriptions, then the "C", and so on.

Type "A" Firm	Type "B" Firm	Type "C" Firm	Type "D" Firm

To check your calculations and scoring, you might want to remember that the largest number that could be in a box is 24, and the smallest, 6. Also, once you have completed the four boxes, the numbers in them must add up to a total of 60.

Source: Taken from Pitt, L. F., Salehi-Sangari, E., Berthon, J.-P., & Nel, D. (2007). ICON's influence: Customer and innovation orientations in South African firms. *Marketing Intelligence and Planning* 25(2): 157–174.

UNDERSTANDING THE IMPLICATIONS
OF CHANGES OF MODE

Three high-profile cases illustrate some of these transitions from one mode to another.

• *Boeing*—In the times prior to deregulation, Boeing was a *shaper*. The major U.S. airlines did not possess significant marketing capability, and Boeing stepped into the breach by acting as an ancillary marketing department for its customers, analyzing future patterns of demand and future equipment needs. As the capital costs of new airframes rose, however, evidence of movement toward the *interact* mode began to appear.[44] The 747 relied on a high degree of collaboration with PanAm, but the most dramatic example was provided by the 777, for which eight leading airlines actually provided employees to participate in Boeing's design teams on an ongoing basis.[45] With the decision to drop the development of a so-called Super-jumbo of 600 to 800 seats, however, it appears that Boeing has settled into a *follow* mode. Only British Airways and Singapore Airlines had expressed strong interest in the Super-jumbo proposal, and Boeing decided to follow the rest of the airlines in saying no to the project, at least for the time being. This left the way open for Airbus to step into the open space with the A×380, and for a time in the early years of the new century, it seemed that Boeing might even have become an *isolate*. However, its recent development of the 787 Dreamliner suggests that the firm has once again changed its mode of focus.

• *AOL*—Initially a *shaper,* America Online dominated the online provision of Internet services, shaping customer expectations of what an Internet provider should be. Others emulated AOL's strategy, with varying degrees of success. However, complacency overtook AOL; its customer base learned and expectations evolved faster than the company realized. From a *shaper* position, AOL slipped back into relative *isolation*. AOL became increasingly out of touch with customer expectations, focusing rather on the internal objective of growth. To this end, in December 1996 AOL offered an unlimited-use fee structure. It came as quite a shock when customers started to rebel at the poor response time the AOL servers were providing. Initial platitudes soon turned into panic. In the late 1990s AOL edged into a *follow* mode, with its customers dictating their requirements.[46] Then with the advent of easily available and affordable broadband Internet access, AOL seemed to slip into an *isolate* mode, with no really new ideas or services, and it does not seem to have recovered from this.

• *Microsoft*—Initially in *isolate* mode, Microsoft derided the Internet, ignored the market, and did little in the way of product development in the area of a web browser. However, seeing the exponential growth of the World Wide Web—and the explosive success of Netscape, the *shaper* of the browser software market—Microsoft was spurred into action. In a well-documented turnaround, Microsoft moved from *isolate* to *follow* mode. It developed its Explorer browser software by imitating virtually every feature of Netscape's seminal and defining Navigator product. Indeed the market that Microsoft has come to dominate is littered with *shapers* who haven't always won—Netscape lost the browser wars; it was Apple, not Microsoft, who shaped the market for the graphic user interface with its Macintosh operating system. Yet Apple has been a much smaller player for a long time.

Summary and Conclusions

The mode transitions discussed in this chapter have much in common with Schotter's perspective on economic institutions, namely, that the institution's development can be inferred from the existence of an evolutionary problem, for every evolutionary economic problem requires a social institution to solve it.[47] The history of marketing specifically, and of organizations generally, is consistent with this perspective. Vertically integrated functional organizations (such as Ford at the time of the Model T) dominated the early years of the 20th century, when relatively stable market environments, characterized by low customer purchasing power and simple customer preferences, caused the focus to be on production. Following this, organizations became multidivisional (e.g., General Motors in the Sloan years) in an attempt to be both product and market oriented. The environment of increased spending power and more sophisticated tastes both permitted and necessitated this. As this power and sophistication intensified, however, the multidivisional organizations were in turn supplanted by some form of matrix organization, often attempting to align marketing more closely with science and engineering.[48] In the 1980s, matrices gave way to networks,[49] as it became apparent that many effective organizations, such as those from Japan and Korea, owed their success to factors outside the firm.

Duncan highlights a basic contradiction in organizational structures best suited to innovation versus efficient implementation.[50] His proposal is that organizations should change shape in their transition from innovation to implementation. In Figure 6-1, changing from *shape* mode to *follow* mode might mean becoming far less organic and more mechanistic. Indeed, the *interacting* firm might require the most radical organizational form of all—one that is constantly changing shape, structure, processes, and even objectives. These types of firms have been described as "experimenting" organizations,[51] which are in a constant state of self-redesign, characterized by flexibility and adaptability. An article in *The Economist* illustrates the phenomenon:

> To an unusual degree Silicon Valley's economy relies on what Joseph
> Schumpeter, an Austrian economist, called "creative destruction." . . .
> [T]he basic idea is [that] old companies die, and new ones emerge,
> allowing capital, ideas and people to be reallocated.[52]

It would be tempting for managers to simply look at the strategic modes in the grid in Figure 6-1 and oversimplify by assuming that there is one wrong focus for an organization (the *isolate* mode) and one ideal focus (the *interact* mode, which integrates customer and innovation orientations). While this might be appropriate in an ideal world, in reality there is no such thing as an ideal or a misplaced focus per se. Rather, it is more important that the mode in which the firm operates is pertinent to the environment in which it competes. A case can even be made for the *isolation* mode under certain circumstances, such as in times of crisis in commodity markets or in the instance of a major corporate merger. The greater risk to the organization is a focus that is inappropriate to the circumstances, such as engaging customers in interaction when all that the market requires is to be served, or attempting to serve and follow customers exclusively when the market is ripe for *shaping*. Rather than merely attempting to attain a particular focus, regardless of the situation, decision makers benefit more from understanding what their current mode of focus is and determining whether this mode is appropriate to the circumstances in which the organization finds itself.

In conclusion, the issue is not one of insufficient customer focus or inadequate attention to innovation, but rather of an inappropriate overall strategic focus given the environmental circumstances. When considering customer and innovation orientations, managers must realize that they are not looking at an either/or decision, but rather they must ask which strategic posture will best help fulfill their companies' future goals and objectives.

Key Terms

- customer orientation
- market orientation
- innovation orientation
- marketing concept
- ICON
- archetypes
- mode of focus

Questions

1. How would you respond to a marketer who says, "Focusing on products is myopic and stupid? The only way to ensure business success is to determine what customers want and give it to them."
2. Identify your own examples of organizations or products/services that fit into each of the four quadrants in the ICON matrix in Figure 6-1. Describe them, and explain why you think they fit appropriately into each quadrant.
3. Under what circumstances would it be understandable and acceptable for a firm to adopt an isolate mode of focus?
4. Complete the ICON checklist in Exhibit 6-1 for the organization you work for or one with which you are familiar. What is the mode of focus this organization adopts? Is it the most appropriate mode? What do you think the best mode of focus for the organization would be?
5. How would you advise firms to use both the ICON checklist in Exhibit 6-1 and the matrix in Figure 6-1?

Resources and References

1. See, for example, Slater, S. F., & Narver, J. C. (1995). Market orientation and the learning organization. *Journal of Marketing* 59(3): 63–74; Christensen, C., & Bower, J. (1996). Customer power, strategic investment, and the failure of leading firms. *Strategic Management Journal* 17(3): 197–218.
2. See, for example, Smith, L. (1980, December 1). A miracle in search of a market. *Fortune*: 92–98; Clark, K. B., & Fujimoto, T. (1991). *Product development performance.* Boston: Harvard Business School Press; Kodama, F. (1995). *Emerging patterns of innovation: Sources of Japan's technological edge.* Boston: Harvard Business School Press; Utterback, J., Allen, T. J., Holloman, J. H., & Sirbu, M. A. Jr. (1976). The process of innovation in five industries in Europe and Japan. *IEEE Transactions on Engineering Management* 23(1): 3–9.
3. See, for example, Band, J. (1991), *Creating value for customers.* New York: John Wiley; Day, G. S. (1990). *Market driven strategy: Processes for creating value.* New York: Free Press; Day, G. S. (1994). Capabilities of market-driven organizations. *Journal of Marketing* 58(4): 37–52; Naumann, E. (1995). *Creating customer value.* Cincinnati, OH: Thompson Executive Press; Webster, F. E. Jr. (1988). The rediscovery of the marketing concept. *Business Horizons* 32(3): 29–39.
4. See, for example, Gupta, A. K., Raj, S. P., & Wilemon, D. (1986). A model for studying R&D—Marketing interface in the product innovation process. *Journal of Marketing* 50(2): 7–17; Souder, W. E. (1987). *Managing new product innovations.* Lexington, MA: Heath; Shanklin, W. L., & Ryans, J. K. Jr. (1984). Organizing for high-tech marketing. *Harvard Business Review* 62(6): 164–171.
5. Drucker, P. F. (1954). *The practice of management.* New York: Harper and Row.
6. Kohli, A. K., & Jaworski, B. J. (1990). Market orientation: The construct, research propositions, and managerial implications. *Journal of Marketing* 54(2): 1–18; Narver, J. C., & Slater, S. F. (1990). The effect of a market orientation on business profitability. *Journal of Marketing* 54(4): 20–35.
7. Kohli and Jaworski; McGee, L. W., & Spiro, R. L. (1998). The marketing concept in perspective. *Business Horizons* 31(3): 40–45.
8. Drucker, *The practice of management,* pp. 37–38.
9. Drucker, P. F. (1973). *Management: Tasks, responsibilities, practices.* New York: Harper and Row, pp. 63, 65–67.
10. Fjellman, S. M. (1992). *Vinyl leaves: Walt Disney and America.* Boulder, CO: Westview.
11. McKitterick, J. A. B. (1957). What is the marketing concept? In F. M. Bass, ed., *The frontiers of marketing thought and science.* Chicago: American Marketing Association, pp. 71–82.
12. Webster, F. E. Jr. (1994). *Market driven management: Using the new marketing concept to create a customer-driven company.* New York: John Wiley, p. 10.
13. Macdonald, S. (1995). Too close for comfort: The strategic implications of getting close to the customer. *California Management Review* 38(3): 8–27.
14. Christensen and Bower.
15. Duncan, R. B. (1976). The ambidextrous organization: Designing dual structures for innovation. In R. H. Kilman, L. R. Pondy, & D. P. Slevin, eds., *The management of organizational design,* vol. 1. New York: Elsevier; Tushman, M., & O'Reilly, C. (1996). Ambidextrous organizations: Managing evolutionary and revolutionary change. *California Management Review* 38(4): 8–30.

16. Keith, R. J. (1960). The marketing revolution. *Journal of Marketing* 24(1): 37.
17. Dickson, P. R. (1992). Toward a general theory of competitive rationality. *Journal of Marketing* 56(1): 69–83.
18. "Building a class leading platform." *Car,* April 1997, p. 10.
19. Bulgin, R. (1997). Enter the Puma. *The Daily Telegraph,* p. C3.
20. Quinn, J. B. (1992). *Intelligent enterprise.* New York: Free Press.
21. Schumpeter, J. (1934). *The theory of economic development: An inquiry into profits, capital and the business cycle.* Boston: Harvard University Press.
22. Deming, W. E. (1986). *Out of crisis: Quality, productivity and competitive position.* Cambridge: Cambridge University Press.
23. Nonaka, I., & Yamanouchi, T. (1989). Managing innovations a self-renewing process. *Journal of Business Venturing* 4(5): 299–315.
24. Zaltman, G., Duncan, R., & Holbek, J. (1973). *Innovations and organizations.* New York: Wiley.
25. Burns, T., & Stalker, G. M. (1977). *The management of innovation,* 2nd ed. London: Tavistock.
26. See von Hippel, E. (1977). Has a customer already developed your next product? *Sloan Management Review* 18(2): 63–75; von Hippel, E. (1978). Successful industrial products from consumers' ideas. *Journal of Marketing* 42(1): 9–49.
27. Downes, L., & Mui, C. (1998). *Unleashing the killer app.* Boston: Harvard Business School Press.
28. Pilzer, P. Z. (1990). *Unlimited wealth: The theory and practice of economic alchemy.* New York: Crown Publishers, pp. 53–54.
29. Hamel. G., & Prahalad, C. K. (1991). Corporate imagination and expeditionary marketing. *Harvard Business Review* 69(4): 81–92.
30. See Carpenter, G. S., & Nakamoto, K. (1989). Consumer preference formation and pioneering advantage. *Journal of Marketing Research* 26(3): 285–298; Carpenter, G. S., Glazer, R., & Nakamoto, K. (1994). Meaningful brands from meaningless differentiation: The dependence on irrelevant attributes. *Journal of Marketing Research* 31(3): 339–350.
31. See, for example, Hannan, M. T., & Freeman, J. (1977). The population ecology of organizations. *American Journal of Sociology* 82: 929–963; McKelvey, B., & Aldrich, H. (1983). Populations, natural selection and organizational science. *Administrative Science Quarterly* 28(1): 101–128.
32. Berthon, P. R., Hulbert, J. M, & Pitt, L. F. (2003). Innovation or customer orientation? An empirical investigation. *European Journal of Marketing* 38(9/10): 1065–1090.
33. Gouillart, E., & Sturdivant, E. (1994). Spend a day in the life of your customers. *Harvard Business Review* 72(1): 116–120.
34. Johansson, J., & Nonaka, I. (1987). Market research the Japanese way. *Harvard Business Review* 65(3): 16–22.
35. For example, Wiener, N. (1954). *The human use of human beings: Cybernetics and society.* New York: Doubleday; Mander, J. (1991). *In the absence of the sacred: The failure of technology and the survival of the Indian nations.* San Francisco: Sierra Club.
36. "A survey of Silicon Valley." *The Economist,* March 27, 1997, p. S-17.
37. Wind, J. Green, P. E., Shifflet, D., & Scarborough, M. (1992). Courtyard by Marriott: Designing a hotel facility with consumer-based marketing models. In C. H. Lovelock, ed., *Managing services: Marketing, operations and human resources.* Englewood Cliffs, NJ: Prentice-Hall, pp. 119–137.

38. Christensen, C. (1997). *The innovator's dilemma: When new technologies cause great firms to fail.* Boston: Harvard Business School Press, p. 134.

39. Brown, M. (1994). *Richard Branson: The inside story.* London: Headline.

40. Quinn, J. B. (1985). Managing innovation: Controlled chaos. *Harvard Business Review* 63(3): 73–84.

41. Deschamps, J.-P. (1994). Managing the marketing/R&D interface. *Prism* 4: 5–19, 11–12.

42. "No two rollers will be the same again." *Car,* February 1997, p. 10.

43. Hannan, M. T., & Freeman, J. (1984, April). Structural inertia and organizational change. *American Sociological Review* 49: 149–164.

44. W. Beeby, W. (1983). *Manufacturing information flow.* Washington, D.C.: U.S. Leadership in Manufacturing, National Academy of Engineering, p. 86.

45. Quinn, *Intelligent enterprise,* p. 180

46. "America Online." *The Economist,* February 1, 1997.

47. Schotter, A. (1981). *The economic theory of social institutions.* New York: Cambridge University Press.

48. Bartlett, C. A., & Ghoshal, S. (1990). Matrix management: Not a structure, a frame of mind. *Harvard Business Review* 68(4): 138–145.

49. See for example, Powell, W. W. (1990). Neither market nor hierarchy: Network forms of organization. In L. L. Cummings and B. M. Staw, eds., *Research in organizational behavior.* Greenwich, CT: JAI, pp. 295–336; Iacobucci, D., ed., *Networks in marketing.* Thousand Oaks, CA: Sage.

50. Duncan.

51. Hedberg, B., Nystrom, P. C., & Starbuck, W. H. (1976). Camping on seesaws: Prescriptions for a self-designing organization. *Administrative Science Quarterly,* 21(1): 41–65.

52. "A survey of Silicon Valley," p. S-7.

RUNNING A DIFFERENT RACE
FROM INNOVATIVE PRODUCTS TO REVOLUTIONARY BUSINESS MODELS

COOL BUSINESSES ARE BUILT ON UNIQUE MODELS

Companies like Starbucks, Dell Computer, Swatch, and Amazon.com are considered to be entrepreneurial success stories. While they operate in entirely different industries, these firms actually have a number of things in common. Each went beyond responding to customers in existing markets and instead created entirely new market spaces. Their basic approach was to lead customers instead of just following them. Most notably, each is a value innovator that created a sustainable business approach by challenging existing assumptions and ways of doing things. It is these sustainable business approaches, or what can be labeled the firm's "business model," that hold invaluable lessons for entrepreneurial marketers.

A business model represents one of the most important, and least understood, concepts when it comes to creating a viable, sustainable, and profitable venture. It is critical not only when starting a new firm, but in sustaining the growth of existing companies. In fact, three very common questions in contemporary organizations are the following:

"What is our business model?"
"Is our business model working?"
"Is it time to revise or replace our business model?"

Unfortunately, the term *business model* is used fairly loosely to refer to a number of different issues. No consensus exists regarding a definition, and few insights are available regarding the exact nature of a business model. Similarly, little is understood regarding how business models evolve or why they succeed or fail.

In this chapter, we clarify some of these issues. An integrative framework for capturing a firm's business model is introduced. We demonstrate how marketing issues drive each of the components of a well-constructed model. Our central argument is that the business model is a platform for innovation when designing a new business. When done properly, it can isolate a firm from competitors, in effect allowing innovators to define the rules of the competitive game.

PRODUCTS, CONCEPTS, AND MODELS

When creating new ventures, either from scratch or within an existing company, the entrepreneur or manager faces three sequential challenges:

- Come up with a new product or service.
- Translate these products or services into a unique business concept.
- Develop an original business model around the innovative concept.

Let us consider each of these challenges and how they affect one another.

THE PRODUCT OR SERVICE

We start with a new product or service, which can be defined as any unique item sold to customers on an ongoing basis. Products are tangible; services are not—but both represent solutions to customer needs. The great challenge with any product or service is to build in enough uniqueness such that the item can be differentiated from the offerings of competitors. Creative marketers tend to view their product or service differently than others do. A company like Apple is more likely to see a computer as an artistic tool to facilitate a person's creative potential than as a box full of components; a company like Snap-on Tools might view a wrench not as a tool made of metal but as an extension of the hand of an auto mechanic. Hence, from a marketing standpoint, a *product* is defined in terms of what it does for the customer. Customers are less concerned with particular physical features, ingredients, or components and more concerned with solving a problem or need. They do not really care about the seller's state-of-the-art equipment, modern facilities, or intricate processes. Accordingly, a product should be thought of as a bundle of problem-solving attributes or a package of benefits.

A valuable framework for viewing products differently, and ultimately for achieving differentiation, can be found in Figure 7-1. Here, the marketer sees a product as existing on four levels, each of which is a source of potential innovation.[1] At the *core*, or most basic level, the product is defined in terms of the primary benefit sought by a customer. Consider the example of Rolls Royce jet aircraft engines, which power a large proportion of the world's jet aircraft fleet,

FIGURE 7-1 Seeing Products as Creative Variables

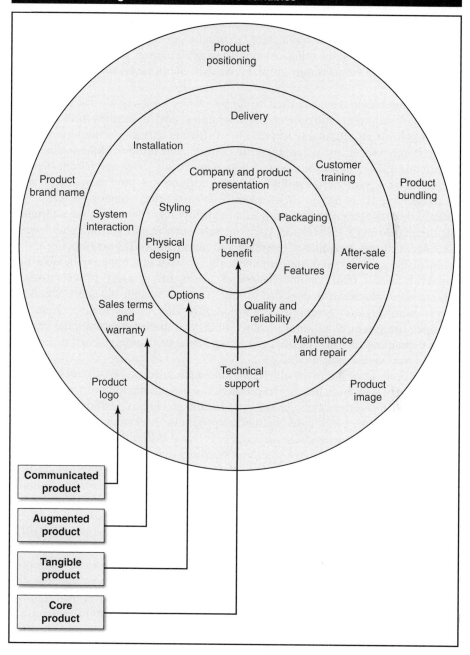

including many Boeing 767s. The core benefit for such a product might be superb power and reliability.

The *tangible* product refers to any and all aspects of the item itself. At this level, products can be distinguished by quality levels, features, sizes, options, styling, colors, and packaging. Again using jet engines, a distinctive feature (power-to-weight ratio) can produce, in the customer's view, an entirely different product.

The tangible offering can then be *augmented* by a variety of support services, including installation, delivery, credit, warranties, advice, training, and post-sale servicing. Rolls Royce is able to provide worldwide servicing, maintenance, and replacement backup for its engines, thus minimizing the downtime airlines will experience if their aircraft are powered by Rolls Royce. Such services or benefits are an integral part of the total value the customer is purchasing. This post-purchase support is an excellent example of a product dimension frequently ignored by managers. Product support covers anything that contributes to maximizing a customer's satisfaction after the sale, such as parts availability, equipment loans during downtimes, operator and maintenance training, serviceability engineering, and warranty performance. These programs must be flexible and require frequent modification. Customer needs for product support usually become more sophisticated as the product moves through the life cycle. Also, expectations regarding support will frequently vary by market segment. For example, the tolerable amount of downtime for a malfunctioning machine will differ depending on the type of customer and time of year (e.g., peak order time versus a period of slack demand).

The final level involves the *communicated* product, which includes the assignment of a brand name to the product, the design of a logo or trademark to convey product identity, the manner in which the product is positioned, and ways in which the product is bundled with other products or services.

The value of this four-circle perspective is that it brings the product or service alive for the entrepreneurial marketer. It becomes apparent that a product is not a fixed thing—it is a variable that can be manipulated creatively in hundreds of ways. In fact, with the same basic product, it becomes possible to construct unique product packages for one market segment compared with another. Thinking of a product or service as a platform for innovation, and one that can be defined differently for different target audiences, opens entirely new opportunity doors for the marketer.

Finally, it is vital to note that entrepreneurial marketers do not view a product (or service) simply as an object to be sold. Instead, they personally identify with their products. They internalize the product and what it stands for, such that the product takes on certain values and captures certain beliefs—and the marketer shares these values and beliefs. This sort of product identification is critical not only for believing in one's products and what they stand for, but also for ensuring that the marketer her- or himself is believable in the mind of the customer. Great marketers have a passion for their products, no matter what it is they are selling. They emotionally connect with, and tend to see themselves in, their products.

THE BUSINESS CONCEPT

Entrepreneurial behavior is about venture creation. To create a new venture, the entrepreneur or manager needs more than a product or service—he or she needs a business concept. Stated differently, a marketer must redefine the product or service into a *core value proposition*. The business concept captures the fact that the core value of the firm may come from the product, but it might also be defined by the way the product is sold, how it is distributed, or the manner in which it is priced or the customer makes payments. Starbucks sells coffee, muffins, and CDs, among other things. But their core value proposition is defined more by the environment and experience they create than just by these products. Similarly, the business concept of a company like Proactiv, which sells acne and related skin treatment products, includes the fact that they sell directly to customers, in this case through infomercials on television and kiosks in malls.

Business concepts should be concise statements that center on what is really being done for a customer. Consider two examples. The casual observer might argue that CNN offers various products, such as *Larry King Live* or *Anderson Cooper 360*. Yet, the more astute observer will recognize that CNN's core value proposition goes beyond these products, and is more focused on an underlying customer need. One might define the business concept at CNN as "instant information, anytime, from anywhere." In that sense, regardless of what products it adds or deletes, it is really all about instantaneousness, timeliness, and total connectivity to a global environment. Similarly, a business that sells high-end desserts should not define itself in terms of the cheesecakes, chocolate pies, or tiramisus that it sells. The entrepreneur goes deeper, and addresses the needs being served and the benefits being delivered. In this spirit, an entrepreneur with a successful dessert bar in the Midwest concluded simply that "we sell indulgent experiences."

THE BUSINESS MODEL

Creating a venture requires that we think through not just a core value proposition, but a logical set of decisions that will produce a sustainable business. This brings us to the notion of a business model. A model is a simplified abstraction of a real situation. It is a structure that purports to represent something else. Thus, when the entrepreneur develops a business model, he or she is attempting to design a structure that captures key aspects of a sustainable new venture.

A business model is more than a business concept but less than a business plan. It captures the essence of how the business system will be focused. Specifically, we can define it as a concise representation of how an interrelated set of decision variables in the areas of venture strategy, venture architecture, and venture economics will be addressed to create sustainable competitive advantage in defined markets.

To illustrate the distinction between a business model and related concepts, consider the case of Dell. Started in 1984, the firm has grown to more than $35 billion in annual sales, placing it among the largest U.S. corporations. The company's *products* include a mix of PCs, notebooks, workstations, servers, and software products. Their *business concept* involves direct selling of customized information technology solutions at competitive prices. However, the Dell *business model* integrates strategic considerations, operational processes, and decisions related to the firm's economics. It is a model designed around elimination of intermediaries; systems built to order; highly responsive customer service; moderate margins; rapid inventory turnover; speedy integration of new technologies; and a highly efficient procurement, manufacturing, and distribution process. Adherence to these elements guides not only operational decision making, but the ongoing strategic direction of the firm. When deviating from the model, such as selling through retailers, the results for the company have been problematic.

As we can see from this example, the business model serves a number of purposes:

1. It can help ensure that the entrepreneur brings a fairly logical and internally consistent approach to the design and operations of a new venture and that the entrepreneur communicates this approach to employees.
2. It represents the architecture for identifying key variables that can be combined in unique ways, and hence is a platform for innovation.
3. The business model can serve as a vehicle for demonstrating the economic attractiveness of the venture, thereby attracting investors and other resource providers.
4. It provides a guide to ongoing company operations, in that it provides parameters for determining the appropriateness of various strategic or tactical actions that management might be considering. The model represents a kind of filter through which a company looks at the world.
5. Once a model is in place, mapping it can help facilitate necessary modifications as conditions change over time.

BREAKING IT DOWN: ELEMENTS THAT DEFINE A BUSINESS MODEL

How do we design a business model that captures the essence of a new venture? Here, we present a standard framework developed by Morris, Schindehutte, and Allen.[2] It is a reasonably simple, logical, and measurable approach, while being at the same time comprehensive and operationally meaningful. Importantly, it can be argued that the elements that make up this framework are fundamentally marketing issues, highlighting the importance of an entrepreneurial marketing perspective.

At its essence, a well-formulated business model must address six key questions. These questions include the value proposition, the customer, internal processes and competencies, competitive strategy, how the venture will make money, and the growth and time objectives for the venture. Let us examine each of these components in more detail (see also Table 7-1).

TABLE 7-1   The Core Components of a Business Model

Component 1

How do we create value?   (select from each set)   *(factors related to the offering)*
- Offering: primarily products/primarily services/heavy mix
- Offering: standardized/some customization/high customization
- Offering: broad line/medium breadth/narrow line
- Offering: deep lines/medium depth/shallow lines
- Offering: access to product/product itself/product bundled with other firm's product/service
- Offering: internal manufacturing or service delivery/outsourcing/licensing/reselling/value-added reselling
- Offering: direct distribution/indirect distribution (if indirect: single or multichannel)

Component 2

Who do we create value for?   (select from each set)   *(market factors)*
- Type of organization: B2B/B2C/both/other
- Local/regional/national/international
- Where customer is in value chain: upstream supplier/downstream supplier/government/institutional/wholesaler/retailer/service provider/final consumer
- Broad or general market/multiple segment/niche market
- Transactional/relational

Component 3

What is our source of competence?   (select one or more)   *(internal capability factors)*
- Production/operating systems
- Selling/marketing
- Information management/mining/packaging
- Technology/R&D/creative or innovative capability/intellectual
- Financial transactions/arbitrage
- Supply chain management
- Networking/resource leveraging

Component 4

How do we competitively position ourselves?   (select one or more)   *(competitive strategy factors)*
- Image of operational excellence/consistency/dependability/speed
- Product or service quality/selection/features/availability
- Innovation leadership
- Low cost/efficiency
- Intimate customer relationship/experience

Component 5

How we make money?   (select from each set)   *(economic factors)*
- Pricing and revenue sources: fixed/mixed/flexible
- Operating leverage: high/medium/low
- Volumes: high/medium/low
- Margins: high/medium/low

Component 6

What are our time, scope, and size ambitions?   (select one)   *(personal/investor factors)*
- Subsistence model
- Income model
- Growth model
- Speculative model

1. *How will the firm create value?* This first question is concerned with the value offering of the firm. It includes the particular products or services being sold, the nature of the product/service mix, and the relative depth (number of lines) and breadth (number of items or variations within each line) of this mix. In addition, the value proposition is defined by whether the firm provides access to the product or service, sells the actual product or service by itself, or sells the product or service as part of a bundle or total system. Other issues include whether the firm makes the product or service, outsources product manufacturing or service delivery, licenses others to make and sell, acquires the product and resells it, or acquires the product and then modifies and resells it. Finally, the value proposition is affected by whether the product or service is sold directly by the firm or through an intermediary or middleman.

2. *For whom will the firm create value?* This question focuses on the nature and scope of the market in which the firm will compete. Of importance is whether the firm will principally sell to consumers (B2C), businesses or organizations (B2B), or both, and where the customer falls in the value chain. When selling to businesses, the entrepreneur must further distinguish where in the value chain the firm's customers will be, such as upstream (mining, agriculture, basic manufacturing), midstream (final manufacturing, assembling), downstream (wholesaling, retailing), or some combination. The geographic scope of the market should also be specified, such as local, regional, national, or international. Ventures also vary in the extent to which their success is driven by a focus on discrete transactions with a wide range of customers or deeper relationships with particular accounts.

3. *What is the firm's internal source of advantage?* The term *core competency* is used to capture an internal capability or set of skills that enables the firm to provide a particular benefit to customers. Hence, Federal Express delivers a benefit of on-time delivery based on its competency in logistics management, while Wal-Mart achieves low prices based on its superior supply chain management skills. While a company might attempt to build operations around any number of competencies, sources of advantage can be organized into seven general areas. These include the firm's production/operating system, capabilities in technology development or innovation, selling or marketing expertise, information management/mining/packaging prowess, competence in financial management/arbitrage, mastery of supply chain management, and skills at managing networks and leveraging resources.

4. *How will the firm differentiate itself?* Depending on how they are applied, core competencies can enable the firm to differentiate itself from direct and indirect competitors. Differentiation involves creating something perceived to be truly unique in the marketplace. The challenge of differentiation is to identify salient points of difference that can be maintained over time. Given the ability of companies to quickly imitate one another, the entrepreneur seeks bases for differentiation that are more than cosmetic or transitory. Sustainable strategic positions tend to be designed around one of the following five bases of differentiation: operational excellence, product quality/selection/availability/features, innovation leadership, low cost, or intimate customer relationships/experiences.

5. *How will the firm make money?* A core element of the firm's business model is its economic model. The economic model provides a consistent vehicle for earning profits. It has four subcomponents. The first of these is the firm's operating leverage, or the extent to which the underlying cost structure is dominated by fixed costs or is driven more by variable costs. The second subcomponent is volumes, and whether the firm is organized for high, medium, or low volumes in terms of both the market opportunity and internal capacity. The third consideration is whether the firm will be able to charge high, medium, or low margins on its products and services. Finally, the economic model considers how many revenue drivers (major sources of revenue or product lines) the firm has and whether their prices are fixed or flexible. At one extreme would be a company that is dependent on a single product that it sells for a fixed price. Alternatively, a very different economic model might find a firm selling three complementary product lines plus a number of value-added services at varying prices, depending on the customer segment and market conditions. This second firm has much more flexibility in terms of its revenue drivers. Flexible revenue drivers are the source of many of the creative business models found in dot-com ventures such as Amazon.com.

6. *What are the entrepreneur's time, scope and size ambitions?* The business model must also capture the entrepreneur's objectives and ambitions. As such, it is helpful to view a new venture in terms of an investment model. Four such models can be used to characterize most ventures: subsistence, income, growth, and speculative. With the subsistence model, the goal is to survive and meet basic financial obligations. When employing an income model, the entrepreneur invests to the point that the business is able to generate an ongoing, healthy income stream for the principals. These are often called lifestyle or "mom and pop" ventures. A growth model finds not only significant initial investment, but substantial reinvestment in an attempt to grow the value of the firm to the point that it eventually generates a major capital gain for the initial investors. The speculative model is employed when the entrepreneur's time frame is shorter, and the objective is typically to demonstrate the potential of the venture and then sell it.

BEYOND THE BASICS: MAKING DECISIONS AT THREE LEVELS

The business model framework goes a step further, and considers these six decision variables at three levels—the *foundation, proprietary,* and *rules* levels. There is, at the foundation level, a need to make very basic or generic decisions regarding what the business is and is not and to ensure such decisions are internally consistent. Thus, fundamental decisions are made regarding what is being sold, to whom, and so forth. At the proprietary level, the purpose of the model is to innovate. That is, the model enables the creation of unique combinations among decision variables that result in marketplace advantage. Decisions made at the foundation level are relatively easy to replicate, whereas proprietary-level decisions are unique to the venture and allow for innovations that impose competitive barriers. At this point, the framework becomes a customizable tool that encourages the entrepreneur to focus on how value can be created in each of the six decision areas. The usefulness of any model is limited, however, unless it provides specific guidance and discipline to the operations of a business. The need to consider implementation issues necessitates a third level of decision making. The rules level of the framework delineates guiding principles that govern execution of the decisions made at the foundation and proprietary levels.

EXPLORING THE PROPRIETARY LEVEL: CREATING UNIQUE COMBINATIONS

While the foundation level is adequate to capture the essence of many firms' business models, sustainable advantage is ultimately dependent on the ability of the entrepreneur to apply unique approaches to one or more of the foundation components. Having determined the firm will sell some combination of goods directly to businesses, or that it will sell in consumer markets at high margins and low volumes, the entrepreneur identifies ways to implement such decisions in a novel manner. This is the proprietary level of the model because it entails innovation that is unique to a particular venture. It is going well beyond doing what competitors do. Entrepreneurial marketers focus on doing different things than other firms are doing or doing the same things in entirely different ways. At the proprietary level, conventional assumptions about how business must be done are challenged.

While the foundation level is more generic, the proprietary level becomes strategy specific. The foundation level model is fairly easily replicable by competitors, whereas the proprietary level is not. Replication is especially difficult because of the interactions *among* the proprietary-level components of the model. Consider the earlier example of Dell. At the foundation level, the company sells a mix of products and services, with a heavier product focus. The product offering is customizable and is sold through a direct channel in both business and consumer markets. However, competitive advantage derives from unique approaches that are applied to two of the foundation-level components. The so-called *Dell Direct Method* is the result of proprietary approaches both to defining the value proposition and to organizing internal logistical flows. It is these proprietary concepts that enable the firm to consistently deliver speed and customization at a moderate price, which translates into a sustainable marketplace position.

UNDERSTANDING THE RULES LEVEL: ESTABLISHING GUIDING PRINCIPLES

When a business model is implemented, its success is often tied to a basic set of operating rules. These are guidelines that ensure the model's foundation and proprietary elements are implemented in a disciplined manner. Eisenhardt and Sull refer to a similar idea in discussing "strategy as simple rules."[3] As examples, they discuss "priority rules" that determine how Intel allocates manufacturing capacity and "boundary rules" that govern the types of movies that Miramax decides to make. Girotto and Rivkin, in a case study of Excite and Yahoo!, observe that Yahoo! adheres to a set of guiding rules in the formation of partnerships, a critical part of the firm's business model, including "Put the product first; Do a deal only if it enhances the customer experience; And enter no joint venture that limits Yahoo!'s evolvability."[4] In our earlier Dell example, such rules might include turning inventory in 4 days or less or delivering replacement parts to the customer by the next business day. Rules are important at the level of execution. Consistent adherence to basic principles can make the difference between two companies that otherwise have identical business models.

APPLYING THE FRAMEWORK IN A MAINSTREAM INDUSTRY

Table 7-2 illustrates the application of the framework to Southwest Airlines. Southwest has a unique business model that has sustained the company's growth for more than 30 years. Not only has the company achieved profitability every year since 1972, but it is consistently ranked among the top 10 most desired companies to work for by *Fortune* magazine and has won a number of industry awards for efficiency and service. The robustness of the firm's model is evidenced in the firm's sustained levels of performance in the aftermath of the 9/11 terrorist tragedy that devastated the industry. Not surprisingly, the Southwest model has been copied in whole or in part by others (e.g., JetBlue, Ryanair, Continental "Light"). While there are notable success stories among them, none of these firms has achieved the level of success as Southwest, and none has competed successfully on a head-to-head basis with Southwest. The superiority of Southwest in exploiting this model makes it clear that a well-conceived and well-implemented business model both affects and is affected by such organizational variables as culture and quality leadership.

The Southwest model is first captured at the foundation level. Here, the focus is on *what* the firm is doing, as opposed to *how*. This level gets at the basics of the firm's approach and represents a standardized set of questions that can be easily quantified. At the proprietary level, Southwest has innovated in a manner that has changed the ways in which other airlines operate, and yet, is a manner that others have been unable to replicate. From Table 7-2 it can be seen how each of the basic components of the model is tailored and how each element is intertwined and internally consistent with the others. Arguably, Southwest's model centers on the firm's core competency: its production/operating system. This unique operating system (e.g., employee policies, airport and route selection, no code sharing, independent baggage handling, standardization of aircraft) makes possible a unique value proposition (short-haul, low-fare, direct service that is on time and "fun"). Finally, it would be easy to deviate from this model, especially given competitive and regulatory pressures. However, a number of rules help ensure that strategic or

TABLE 7-2 Characterizing the Business Model of Southwest Airlines

	Foundation Level	Proprietary Level	Rules
Component 1 (factors related to offering)	• Sell services only • Standardized offering • Narrow breadth • Shallow lines • Sell the service by itself • Internal service delivery • Direct distribution	• Short haul, low-fare, high-frequency, point-to-point service • Deliver fun • Serve only drinks/snacks • Assign no seats/no first class • Do not use travel agents/intermediaries • Fully refundable fares, no advance purchase requirement	• Maximum one-way fare should not exceed $___ • Maximum food cost per person should be less than $___
Component 2 (market factors)	• B2C and B2B (individual travelers and corporate travel depts.) • National • Retail • Broad market • Transactional	• Managed evolution from regional airline to providing service to 59 airports in 30 states • Careful selection of cities based on fit with underlying operating model	• Specific guidelines for selecting cities to be serviced • 85% penetration of local markets
Component 3 (internal capability factors)	• Production/operating systems	• Highly selective hiring of employees that fit profile; intense focus on frontline employees. • Do not operate a hub-and-spoke route system. • Fly into uncongested airports of small cities, less congested airports of large cities • Innovative ground operations approach • Independent baggage handling system • Use of Boeing 737 aircraft • No code sharing with other airlines	• At least 20 departures per day from airport • Maximum flight distance should be less than ___ miles • Maximum flight time should be less than ___ minutes • Turnaround of flights should be 20 minutes or fewer
Component 4 (competitive strategy factors)	• Image of operational excellence/consistency/dependability	• Differentiation is achieved by stressing on-time arrival, lowest possible fares, and passengers having a good time (a spirit of fun) • Airline that love built	• Achieve best on-time record in industry

(continued)

Table 7-2 (continued)			
	Foundation Level	*Proprietary Level*	*Rules*
Component 5 (economic factors)	• Fixed revenue source • High operating leverage • High volumes • Low margins	• Short-haul routes and high frequency of flights combined with consistently low prices and internal efficiencies result in annual profitability regardless of industry trends	• Maintain cost per passenger mile below $___
Component 6 (personal/ investor factors)	• Growth model	• Emphasis on growth opportunities that are consistent with business model	• Managed rate of growth

tactical moves that are inconsistent with the business model are not made. Rules regarding maximum fares, flight turnaround times, and on-time performance effectively delimit courses of action management might consider, while also reinforcing in the minds of operating personnel the strategic intent of the firm.

As can be seen with this example, the framework is reasonably simple to apply, and each element is measurable. In addition, the framework is comprehensive in nature, capturing the essence of a sustainable business in terms of strategy, operations, and economic performance. Further, it should be noted that the framework applies to ventures of all types and sizes and allows for the possibility that firms with multiple divisions or strategic business units may have different models for different divisions.

THE IMPORTANCE OF INTERNAL AND EXTERNAL FIT

Sustainability requires that the components of the model demonstrate consistency, as in the Southwest example. Consistency has been described in terms of "fit," both internal and external.

Internal fit includes both consistency and reinforcement within and between the six subcomponents of the model. Hence, an economic model with high operating leverage, low margins, moderate volumes, and fixed revenue sources may, by itself, be untenable. Further, the economics must fit with the other five components of the model. Thus, a given economic model might not be workable when selling in a regional B2B market where significant investment in customer relationships is required, or when selling a value offering that involves high levels of customization. If the economic model calls for penetration pricing with low margins and relatively high fixed costs, this may imply a value proposition that centers on medium- to lower-end quality, a target market that is fairly broad and relatively price elastic, competitive positioning based on cost leadership, and a long-term growth investment model.

Ultimately, each component affects and is affected by every other component. And while each is vital, the firm's investment model effectively delimits decisions made in each of the other component areas. For instance, a speculative business, with its shorter time horizon before the venture is sold, may require a cost structure with lower operating leverage and a customer focus that is not predicated on long-term customer relationships. Alternatively, if building a lifestyle business, the firm is apt to have a more narrowly defined product and market focus, may be more dependent on customer relationships, and is likely to require an economic model that includes medium to low volumes. Further, with the lifestyle venture, it may not be necessary to invest as much at the proprietary level of the business model.

External fit is concerned with consistency between choices in each of the six areas of the model and conditions in the external environment. As environmental conditions change, the model may require adaptation or wholesale change. An example can be found in the work of Rindova and Kotha, who describe the evolution of Yahoo!'s business model from provider of search functions to supplier of content to source of interactive services.[5] As firms increasingly confront a set of environmental conditions that are highly turbulent, a strong internal fit can undermine adaptability in the face of a poor external fit. It may be that over time, companies must work to disrupt their own advantages as well as those of competitors through continuous business model innovation. Adaptability may require regular introduction of new elements that change the dynamics among existing elements.

HOW BUSINESS MODELS EMERGE

Although some entrepreneurs have a clearly formulated model when undertaking a venture, many start with partially formed models and incomplete strategies. Even the existence of a written business plan does not ensure that a well-formulated business model exists. Whether or not a formal model has been specified, core elements and supporting activities are usually in place. The likelihood is that the entrepreneur initially has an intuitive sense of how the firm must operate to make money. What may be a mental model at this point is likely to include some aspects and assumptions that are relatively specific and others that are more tenuous or vague.

A process of trial and error may be involved as the business model emerges. Lessons are being learned regarding what is required to make money on a sustainable basis. As competencies are developed within the venture, keener insights may result regarding sources of innovation or competitive advantage as they relate to those competencies. The entrepreneur is also likely to become more strategic in his or her view of business operations over time, while he or she may also find time becomes available to focus attention on issues that initially did not receive priority.

In terms of the framework, a firm's business model might be expected to evolve from the foundation level toward a more complete articulation of the proprietary and rules levels. Initially, the entrepreneur may have a fair picture of the foundation level, along with limited notions about some components at the proprietary level. As the firm develops and learns, it is able to flesh out more components at the proprietary level, furthering its advantage, and to develop rules that guide operations and ongoing development. Model evolution can also be linked to the type of venture being pursued. Models for lifestyle versus high-growth ventures might be expected to vary in formality, sophistication, and uniqueness. For instance, the proprietor of a lifestyle business may have an implicit model in mind when the venture starts, and the model may never develop beyond basic decisions at the foundation level. He or she might develop a set of rules of thumb that support the basic model, such as how much inventory must move at certain times of the year. This entrepreneur might also periodically deviate from the model, introducing elements that are inconsistent with existing elements. Alternatively, a more formal, comprehensive, and potent model is needed to provide direction and attract resources to a high-growth venture. Decisions at the proprietary level become vital for sustainable competitive advantage.

Summary and Conclusions

It has been argued in this chapter that the business model represents a strategic framework for conceptualizing a value-based venture. The framework provided herein allows the user to design, describe, categorize, critique, and analyze a business model for any type of new venture. It provides a useful backdrop for strategically adapting and changing fundamental elements of a business.

With the framework, each of six components is evaluated at three levels. The first of these, the foundation level, finds the model defined in terms of a standardized set of decisions regarding the new venture. At the proprietary level, considerable scope for innovation exists within each of these same decision areas. Thus, the model becomes an innovation platform or form of intellectual property. The business model also has the potential to serve as a focusing device for the entrepreneur, managers, and employees, especially when it is supported by a set of rules or guidelines that derive from decisions made at the proprietary level. Rules provide a clearer sense of the firm's value proposition and are a source of guidance regarding the types of actions that might compromise the value equation.

Entrepreneurs and managers vary considerably in the extent to which they make the right strategic choices, focus on the correct activities and activity sets, and determine appropriate levels and combinations among activities. The business model encourages them to (1) conceptualize a new venture as an interrelated set of strategic choices; (2) seek complementary relationships among elements through unique combinations; (3) develop business activities around a logical framework; and (4) ensure consistency among elements of strategy, architecture, economics, growth, and exit intentions.

Entrepreneurs make many strategic choices by intent, but a number of others are made by default. The business model framework makes the major choices explicit. The framework is a relatively simple way to delimit and organize the key sets of decisions that an entrepreneur or manager must make at the outset of a venture. It sets out critical decision variables that must be addressed in an internally consistent manner. As such, the framework helps ensure that these decisions reflect strategic intent or are purposeful. Stated differently, the model provides a framework for deciding what *not* to do (e.g., what services not to offer or what prices not to charge). Further, it assists the entrepreneur in assessing consistencies and recognizing trade-offs required in strategic decision making.

Key Terms

- business concept
- business model
- core competency
- differentiation
- economic model
- proprietary approaches

Questions

1. What is the difference between a business concept and a business model? How might the business concept influence the design of the business model?
2. In what sense is a business model a "platform for innovation"? How might an entrepreneur use this framework to be more innovative in designing a company?
3. Think about the six major elements or decision areas that make up the foundation level of a business model. Why can it be argued that each of these is fundamentally concerned with marketing decisions?
4. Think about the business model for a company like Starbucks. Do you think any one of the six decision areas is more critical for explaining their success over time?
5. Why do you think the Southwest Airlines business model has not been successfully copied by other firms in the airline industry? Do you think it is a business model that can sustain the company for decades to come, or at some point will it have to be radically changed?

Resources and References

1. Levitt, T. (1991). *Levitt on marketing.* Boston: Harvard Business Review Publishing.
2. Morris, M., Schindehutte, M., & Allen, J. (2005). The entrepreneur's business model: Toward a unified perspective. *Journal of Business Research* 58(6): 726–735.
3. Eisenhardt, K. M., & Sull, D. (2001). Strategy as simple rules. *Harvard Business Review* 79(1): 107–116.
4. Girotto, J., & Rivkin, J. (2000). *Yahoo!: Business on Internet time.* Harvard Business School Case 9-700-013. Boston: Harvard Business School Press.
5. Rindova, V. P., & Kotha, S. (2001). Continuous morphing: Competing through dynamic capabilities, form, and function. *Academy of Management Journal* 44(6): 1283–1280.

CHAPTER

TRENDS IN CUSTOMER COMMUNICATION PRACTICES

A few thousand years ago there was a marketplace. . . . Traders returned from far seas with spices, silks, and precious, magical stones. Caravans arrived across burning deserts bringing dates and figs, snakes, parrots, monkeys, strange music, stranger tales. The marketplace was the heart of the city, the kernel, the hub, the omphalos. Like past and future, it stood at the crossroads.

People woke early and went there for coffee and vegetables, eggs and wine, for pots and carpets, rings and necklaces, for toys and sweets, for love, for rope, for soap, for wagons and carts, for bleating goats and evil-tempered camels. They went there to look and listen and to marvel, to buy and be amused. But mostly they went to meet each other. And to talk.

—CLUETRAIN MANIFESTO

LESSONS FROM THE MARKETPLACE

Throughout history, the market's relevance to everyday life has been undeniable, not only for necessities, but also for its social value. "Markets are conversations."[1] Markets are spaces allocated to the exchange of goods (products and/or services) as well as information. These markets are filled with people—a place buzzing with conversations.

Today, however, most transactions do not occur in the type of marketplace described in the quotation from Cluetrain Manifesto. While goods and services are still available around the corner, at a farmers' market, or at the click of a finger, the conversations and social value of the marketplace have changed throughout the ages. In truth, the conversations are still out there—in coffee shops, at book club meetings, over the garden fence, at the corner store. Millions of conversations are going on about hundreds of topics relevant to your company every day. People haven't changed—they still like to talk. The basic need is still the same—connecting buyers with sellers. However, the *market* (a physical place filled with people and interesting things) has changed to a *marketspace* (a conceptual place) that is the responsibility of *marketing* and *marketers* (i.e., companies that sell brands instead of items, using marketing communications instead of personal conversations).

Marketing communication in the post-World War II era was a rather simple process. The firm's communication with the customer was typically grouped into four categories of a communications mix: advertising, sales promotion, personal selling, and public relations (and publicity). This communications mix was orchestrated by a marketing professional or an advertising firm in an effort to walk the customer through the hierarchy of effects by matching the marketer's selling process with the customer's buying process—from awareness, to interest, to desire, and finally to action (purchase). The marketer's concern here was how to best optimize the communications mix; marketing became almost synonymous with advertising in the battle for eyeballs on the google-box (a.k.a., television) in the living rooms of target households. With only three major television networks in the United States during the mid-1960s, reaching the vast majority of consumers on a regular basis was as simple as advertising Tide in the daytime and Pepto-Bismol during the evening news—supplemented by advertisements in a handful of broadly targeted magazines with huge circulation numbers.

But a proliferation of television channels and media options in the new millennium, combined with the power of remote control units, quickly changed this picture of a homogeneous media environment. In the pre-digital era with a limited number of competing product and media options, the marketing race was a marathon. Carried aloft by the Internet and reinforced by the echo chamber of a million always-on consumers, the marketer's world changed from a marathon into a sprint with the blink of an eye. Suddenly marketing budgets must be s-t-r-e-t-c-h-e-d across a vastly greater number of activities. This requires new levels of flexibility and responsiveness from marketers who face consumers with increasingly shorter attention spans. In the world of fast-moving windows of opportunities and hotly competitive, ever-shifting market spaces, understanding *who* is communicating and *how* communication is happening has become all-important.

Fast forward to today. Going, going, gone . . . is the stream of advertising-laden programming on TV—thanks to TiVo and other digital video recorders (DVRs) in a consumer-editor era. No longer confined to a solitary unit in the hub of each home, TV sets in every room of a home now serve multifunctional niches. They are used for playing video games, surfing the Internet, listening to music, or shopping—in addition to being the trusted source of information and entertainment. Progression of economic value, emergence of the emotive consumer, and the consumer's backlash against advertising have resulted in explosive growth in new media, entertainmentization of marketing, and numerous innovative marketing practices—fundamentally altering the communications landscape, and the marketers' role in it, forever.

Even more change is under way: the consumers are reinventing marketing communications. They like to talk and hear what others (like them) have to say about products they might be interested in buying. They are not interested in sterile, politically correct company propaganda manufactured by a creative advertising agency or public relations company. They want to get behind the lies marketers tell.[2] Moreover, where and how people get information keeps changing—they are no longer relying on the static and predictable world of newspapers, magazines, and TV. Jim Stengel at Procter & Gamble sees the situation as follows:

> The consumer is gaining control over territory formerly owned by manufacturers like the Procter & Gamble Company. She is empowered with new technologies that let her determine when, how, and if she receives our brand messages. She's becoming aware of our brands in ways we can't possibly anticipate. She has more choices than ever yet craves simplicity, which drives her to have higher expectations for product performance, price competitiveness, and brand relevance.[3]

Change occurs unabatedly, resulting in new challenges and opportunities for marketers. Yet, there are several enduring characteristics of successful marketing efforts in the contemporary environment: efficiency in marketing expenditures by leveraging resources, creative and alternative approaches for managing marketing variables, ongoing product and process innovation, customer intensity, and an ability to effect change in the environment. These commonalities address some of the criticisms of contemporary marketing which are covered in Chapter 2 where the focus is on how the customer—not the marketer—creates products, communicates about products, sets prices, and dictates where a product should be sold. In this chapter we explore specific trends and dynamics affecting marketers' communication efforts with the customer.

EFFECTS OF THESE CHANGES—NEW DEVELOPMENTS IN MARKETING PRACTICE

A number of alternative marketing approaches have been introduced over the past decade, each of which is intended to provide a prescription for success in the new environments within which firms must compete. Some of the more prominent new marketing practices are summarized in Table 8-1, with extensive sources for additional information. Although many of the new marketing practices have become quite popular, none of the individual marketing approaches presents a framework comprehensive enough to guide marketing practice in the future. Moreover, in assessing the common themes among the emergent forms of marketing (e.g., expeditionary, disruptive, radical) as summarized in Table 8-1, several of the dimensions of entrepreneurial marketing (see Chapter 2) can be detected. Resource leveraging is perhaps the single most emphasized element in these emergent practices, and is especially prominent in guerrilla marketing and radical marketing.

The chronological order in which the new tools in the marketing practices toolbox appear in Table 8-1 reflect two important shifts: the increased popularity

TABLE 8-1	Perspectives on the Emerging Nature of Marketing	
Term/Date/ Source	**Underlying Dimensions/Characteristics**	**Examples[4]**
Relationship marketing (1983)[5]	Identifying, establishing, maintaining, enhancing, and terminating relationships with customers and other stakeholders, at a profit; achieving objectives of both parties	Garnier Delta Airlines
Expeditionary marketing (1992)[6]	Creating markets before competitors; continuous search for innovative product concepts; overturning price/performance assumptions; lead rather than follow customers; tolerate failure	Skype Starbucks
Guerrilla marketing (1993)[7]	Low-cost, effective communications; cooperative efforts and networking; leveraging resources, using energy and imagination	McCain Crescendo Rising Crust Pizza Breathe Right
One-to-one marketing (1993)[8]	Marketing based on knowing the customer through collaborative interactions (dialogue and feedback) to tailor individualized marketing mix on a one-to-one basis; product-centric	New Zealand Dairy Foods
Real-time marketing (1995)[9]	Technology-facilitated, real-time dialogues with interactive services	Television New Zealand
Subversive marketing (1995)[10]	Marketing that doesn't look like marketing; champion outrageous ways to penetrate consumer indifference; also known as stealth, ambush, roach-bait, and undercover marketing	Pot Noodle MTV Red Bull
Disruptive marketing (1996)[11]	Shattering culturally embedded biases and conventions; setting creativity free to forge a radical new vision of a product, brand, or service	Swatch
Viral marketing (1997)[12]	Self-replicating promotion fanning out over community webs and spreading like a virus, multiplying and mutating as like-minded people market to each other	Hotmail Snickers
Digital marketing (1998)[13]	New forms of interaction lead to deeper relationships and greater personalization	Volkswagen DIRECTV
Permission marketing (1999)[14]	A prospect explicitly agrees in advance to receive marketing information	Amazon.com American Express
Experiential marketing (1999)[15]	Elicits a powerful sensory/cognitive consumer response through sensory (sense), affective (feel), creative cognitive (think), physical/lifestyle (act), and social-identity (relate) experiences	Visit London BMW (The Hire)
Radical marketing (1999)[16]	Redefines competitive rules; challenges conventional wisdom of the industry; strong visceral ties with target audience; maximal exploitation of limited budget	National Basketball Association Grateful Dead

(continued)

TABLE 8-1 (continued)		
Term/Date/ Source	*Underlying Dimensions/Characteristics*	*Examples*
Buzz marketing (2000)[17]	Consumer-generated information dispersal through individual network hubs by generating excitement, infatuation, and missionary zeal	The Blair Witch Project Rheingold Brewery
Customer-centric marketing (2000)[18]	Seeks to fulfill needs and wants of each individual customer; focuses on the needs, wants, and resources of customers as starting point in planning process	O2 (cellular services)
Convergence marketing (2002)[19]	Fusion of different technologies to create new possibilities for the hybrid consumer; convergence on customerization, choices, communities, channels, and competitive value	Western Wireless
Neuro-marketing (2002)[20]	Uses MRI (magnetic resonance imaging) to map brain patterns in response to a particular advertisement or product to determine drivers behind consumer choices	DaimlerChrysler
Search marketing (2003)[21]	Increases visibility of a website in search engine results through search engine optimization, pay-per-click, and paid inclusion	Monster.com Virgin Trains
Pay-to-say marketing (2005)	Monetary compensation for posting comments on blogs; compensation rates determined by the amount of exposure, advertisers, or a blogger's Alexa ranking	PayPerPost LoudLaunch.com
Duct tape marketing (2007)[22]	Small business marketing roadmap; to be effective, approach marketing must be approached as a system—not an event; composed of simple, effective, and affordable techniques	Various small businesses

of face-to-face or P2P (peer-to-peer) methods and a move away from the broadcast-based model of one-to-many communications (company to mass market) to a one-to-one model (company to customer). These shifts coincide with a move toward segmentation and customization during the 1990s when personalization became fashionable. Deemed more effective and efficient, permission marketing campaigns (pseudo-personalized e-mail messages sent to selected individuals) suddenly became an all-important tool in the marketer's toolkit—trust, loyalty, and customer relationship management replaced talk about media buying and cost per thousand impressions (CPM) rates around the office watercooler. These changes were accompanied by a shift of advertising dollars away from mass media toward sales promotions and direct marketing.

Some of these practices are more strategic in nature (e.g., radical and expeditionary marketing), more centered on technology (e.g., convergence and neuro-marketing) or more tactical (e.g., permission and guerrilla marketing) in nature.

They also vary in terms of their emphasis on promotion versus the entire marketing mix, and the extent to which they focus on smaller ventures versus established firms. Although new buzzwords are becoming adjectives applied to *marketing* on a daily basis, it is possible to organize these terms into four representative categories based on common elements in the underlying principles and practices of each group:

1. Bootstrap or grassroots (e.g., guerrilla, subversive, street, and duct tape marketing).
2. Conversation starter (e.g., word of mouth, buzz, and viral marketing).
3. Technology facilitated (e.g., relationship, permission, digital, and neuro-marketing, etc.).
4. Visionary (e.g., radical, experiential and expeditionary marketing).

1. BOOTSTRAP/GRASSROOTS METHODS

Marketing activities in this category are typically tactical in nature, unconventional, low cost, not by-the-book, nontraditional, and extremely flexible. The creative possibilities with bootstrap or grassroots methods are limited only by the imagination of the marketer who invests time, energy, and creativity—instead of money. Bootstrap methods rely on resource leveraging and stretching (doing more with less and using resources you don't necessarily own or control). Although grassroots methods are often used by new or small firms that are strapped for cash, firms of all sizes and in most industries rely on grassroots marketing as an important element in their communication activities. These methods are most effective and efficient when marketing occurs in short bursts or surgical strikes and when it is fun, unexpected, in-your-face, and offbeat—all of which depend on how appropriate it is for the intended audience. Examples in this category include unusual direct mail, flags and banners, T-shirts, unique business cards, using fax forms as mini-advertisements, tattoos, personal letters with a twist, seminars or demonstrations, and freebies (e.g., matchbooks, pens, and calendars). Bootstrap marketing is, therefore the tactical use of low-cost, unconventional tactics to get your message out to the intended audience. Out-thinking, not out-spending your competitor! Additional examples for each of the different methods in this category (e.g., guerrilla, subversive, street, and duct tape marketing) can be found in the various sources listed in Table 8-1.

Street marketing (e.g., truck-side ads; car, building, or airplane wraps; street teams; barricades; orange traffic cones; fences; sidewalk drawings; and many others) has become an especially popular activity. For example, Sony hired 60 actors and actresses to walk in busy areas and ask passersby to take a snapshot of them using their new camera phone, hoping that picture takers would be impressed enough to tell others about the new camera phone. Using nonevasive conversation tactics, Sony's street marketing took place in 10 different cities as part of an undercover campaign called "fake tourists." Also known as subversive or stealth marketing, this is a subset of guerrilla marketing in which the target audience is unaware that they have been marketed to. Potential ethical issues that might arise as a result of undercover marketing activity (in which the identity of the marketer is not disclosed) are discussed in detail in Chapter 16.

2. CONVERSATION-STARTER METHODS

Word of mouth (WOM) is essentially a linear process with information passing from one individual to another, then to another—the oldest method of marketing in a snail-mail world. Revival of WOM in the new millennium has resulted in a highly intense and interactive form of WOM—buzz (think of bees in a beehive, literally and figuratively). Buzz is created when interactions are so intense that WOM moves in a matrix pattern. It is very different from linear WOM. Whereas WOM is typically initiated by a customer who spontaneously tells others about a product or service, the marketer is able to create buzz by generating excitement and a kind of missionary zeal around product releases with local market influencers and trendsetters. The message spreads vigorously through self-reinforcing cycles of WOM across individuals' preexisting social networks as individuals pass along a message that resonates with them.

Buzz is the aggregate of all these conversations, both online and offline. It is important to give people a reason to talk (i.e., give them something that can be passed along)—something tangible (e.g., a sticker) or intangible (e.g., word of a secret sale). For example, Enterprise Rent-A-Car takes boxes of donuts and "friendly smiles" to auto repair shops, and this is known to result in a burst of new referrals. Or a restaurant owner has a big party and invites every hairdresser in town for a free meal, leading to lots of talking the next day.

In some instances, information dispersal occurs through the individual network hubs of talk show hosts such as Howard Stern and Oprah Winfrey. In other instances, self-replicating promotion fans out over community webs with potential for exponential growth in the message's exposure and influence. When the message spreads like a virus, multiplying and mutating rapidly as large numbers of like-minded people market to each other via "word of mouse" (via the Internet), it is referred to as viral marketing. Well-known examples of viral marketing include Hotmail, eBay, and Google's Gmail. In 2007, Google was ranked as the world's top brand—it has become an everyday name despite using relatively little advertising and instead relying on word-of-mouth.

Success in this category depends on the marketer's ability to capture the attention of consumers (and the press!) to the point where talking about a brand becomes entertaining, fascinating, and newsworthy. According to Mark Hughes[23] there are six surefire ways to push consumers' "buzz buttons":

1. The taboo—sex, lies, and bathroom humor
2. The unusual
3. The outrageous
4. The hilarious
5. The remarkable
6. The secret—both the revealed and the unrevealed

Marketing's new role is encouraging people to talk about a brand. Getting customers to tell friends, family, and co-workers about a brand can potentially translate into new sales leads, new customers, increased sales, and improved brand awareness—as well as get the brand noticed by the media. This is no small feat to accomplish and it requires "a product or service that is remarkable, is worth talking about, exceptional, interesting, and most importantly, a Purple Cow. In a busy marketplace, not standing out is the same as being invisible."[24] Quite clearly, the product has to be phenomenal, counterintuitive, exciting, and unbelievable to become buzz-worthy.

A great example of buzz is the Lance Armstrong Foundation campaign to raise cancer awareness, made visible through the yellow LiveStrong bracelet that generated conversations and increased donations. The buzz created resulted in unprecedented publicity—which started more conversations, and so forth. A truly self-reinforcing spiral of WOM—infused with buzz and viral marketing! The opposite effect is unfortunately more often the rule than the exception. For instance, General Motors won a Media Lion at the Cannes Lions in 2005 for getting $100 million in free publicity by giving away 276 cars on *Oprah*. Talk about letting your media ROAR! Just months after this sales promotion, though, no one was buying. GM slashed prices, but still no one was buying. Think about the cost involved in this sales promotion effort. This is the antithesis of effective and efficient marketing—without sales, even months after this event, has any marketing occurred? When a tree falls in the woods and nobody is there to hear it fall, does it make a sound?

3. TECHNOLOGY-FACILITATED METHODS

In this category, different technologies are used to manipulate information from, about, and to the customer. Relationship marketing relies on customer relationship management (CRM) software and databases to collect customer information for ongoing campaigns, such as Delta Airlines' frequent flyer program, in which loyal customers earn air miles. The opposite of traditional interruption marketing, which has resulted in communication overload and consumer backlash, permission marketing encourages the customer to share personal information that enables the marketer to refine the company's segmentation and targeting efforts. With a commitment to respect privacy concerns, the marketer gains permission to engage in a dialogue that the customer actually wants. In return, the customer receives information from the company based on previously stated preferences and tailored to time, location, and personal characteristics— over time the relationship strengthens and deepens.

Another method in this category is pay-to-say marketing in which third-party bloggers diffuse brand information on the Internet. Search marketing uses technology-enhanced methods that allow potential buyers to find them, and the information they want, faster. Neuro-marketing is a new method in which functional magnetic resonance imaging (fMRI) technology is used to detect information that the customer is not cognitively aware of, but that affects the purchasing decision-making process. It is used as a marketing research method to under-stand the brain's responses while being exposed to marketing communication messages. Additional information about the specific technologies on which the various marketing practices rely can be found in Table 8-1.

4. VISIONARY METHODS

Marketing practices in this category are more strategic and typically involve cor-porate imagination to create and dominate new markets. For example, Fidelity Investments unlocked a vast new market by packaging sophisticated investment vehicles for middle-income investors, thereby overturning traditional assump-tions and leading customers rather than simply following them. A radical market-ing genius, Sir Richard Branson continues to achieve radical results for Virgin by using adventure and counterculture to create publicity when he takes on the big players. The secret with radical marketing lies in a carefully crafted and consis-tent strategy that integrates across all marketing efforts. Visionary methods differ significantly from the on-off periodic tactics in the other categories—these are strategic tools that require careful planning and execution. Marketing efforts in this category are supported by the organizational philosophy and strategic orien-tation. The strategic value of experiential marketing and its importance in brand management are discussed in Chapter 9.

Each of the three practices—radical (e.g., the Grateful Dead, Harley-Davidson, and Harvard Business School), expeditionary (e.g., Amazon and eBay), and experiential (e.g., Nike and Starbucks)—have one or more of the seven components associated with entrepreneurial marketing (see Chapter 2) in common. In some instances (e.g., Harley-Davidson, Amazon, Starbucks), charac-teristics associated with market-driving behavior are also present. Most notably, marketers in this category are customer informed, but idea led. Instead of merely aiming to satisfy current needs, these companies surprise, delight, and amaze customers by spotting the opportunities overlooked by others, creating a future guided by their own original and visionary ideas; in the process, they transform customers' perceptions (e.g., of motorcycles, bookstores, and coffee).

EVOLUTION OF THE INTERNET: FROM INFORMATION TO INTERACTION

It wasn't long before the one-to-one models of the late 1990s changed again—this time due to the globe-shrinking system of communications technologies. Over the past 10 years, there has been a noticeable shift from information (a push model) to interaction (a pull model) in marketing communication.[25] This shift has been accompanied by a move away from one-to-one, company-customer monologues toward many-to-many customer-customer dialogues. The customer has taken charge. In effect, the marketer has become an agent of the customer, in-stead of acting as an agent for the company. The Internet continues to evolve, and users are discovering new sources of power as a result of being interconnected through a click of the mouse—increasingly this means that consumers are finding ways to bypass marketers' propaganda. This shift was not foreseen by marketers and, of course, happened without their permission—and it happened at lightning speed, catching them unaware!

A powerful inter-galactic conversation has begun. Through the Internet, people are discovering and inventing new ways to waste time at work, download naughty pictures, and build pipe bombs. As a direct result, things are getting really weird—and getting weird faster than the parking lot at a Grateful Dead concert.

—CLUETRAIN MANIFESTO

Evolution of the Internet is constantly confronting marketing communications in unexpected ways—causing some very successful companies to make a transition from the conventional real world to an imaginary virtual world. More specifically, they have moved their "place of business" to Second Life—a virtual world where millions of dollars are being spent. Conquering these virtual realms is both appealing and necessary because the virtual world is fast becoming a marketing test bed for corporate marketers such as Sony, Nissan Motor, Adidas, Toyota Motor, and Starwood Hotels. Virtual-world proponents, the likes of Amazon.com founder Jeffrey Bezos and eBay co-founder Pierre Omidyar, believe, "the entire Internet is moving toward being a three-dimensional experience that will become more realistic as computing technology advances."[26] The Internet is the great equalizer, commoditizing products and services on a global scale—it has given consumers a voice, a publishing platform, and a forum where their collective voices can be heard, shared, and strengthened (also see Chapter 14). No longer a domain belonging to trained specialists exclusively, the Internet puts information technology within reach of the general population comprised of people of all ages, interests, and backgrounds.

Up to this point we have examined new trends in isolation. However, when we take a look at the intersections of the many emerging trends, we start to appreciate their long-term implications for marketing communications. The intersection of three trends is especially noteworthy: ongoing evolution of personal communication devices, changing customer behavior, and continued morphing of media and channels. The confluence of these emerging trends has resulted in four new phenomena in customer communications—advertisement, the emergence of new media, consumer-generated media (CGM), and mobile marketing. These communication methods promise to alter the future marketing landscape in unprecedented ways. Importantly, these four practices are outside the direct control of the marketer; they can be influenced, but not controlled, by marketers, quite unlike viral, guerrilla, buzz, and street marketing. Let us take a closer look at these four new phenomena.

1. FROM ADVERTAINMENT TO IN-GAME ADVERTISING

Apart from the defection of audiences to other forms of entertainment—DVDs, the Internet, video games, and cable—potential customers are blocking ads with TiVo or simply do something else when advertisements appear on TV. Intent on not being defeated, advertising agencies responded by introducing a new weapon—advertainment!—which combines traditional advertising with an entertainment component. During the early years of advertainment, major companies relied on product placement in movies or television programs as a rich source of co-branding. Some examples include Reese's Pieces candy, which was featured in *E.T.: The Extra-Terrestrial,* or prominent displays of Coca-Cola tumblers on the judges' table in *American Idol.* Later developments in branded entertainment involved featuring a company's product or brand name directly in the script of a show or a movie—a window cleaner, Windex, became part of the storyline as a solution for all kinds of ailments in the movie *My Big Fat Greek Wedding.* BMW launched its branded entertainment activities on the silver screen with James Bond (007) driving around in the newly released BMW Z3, flashing an Omega watch, and using an Ericsson cell phone. Not willing to let the brand play second fiddle to other stars, BMW later sponsored entertaining short films for the Internet in which a BMW automobile is the main feature (see Table 8-1, The Hire).

Branded entertainment deals typically involve product placement, joint promotion of the movie or television program, and online or mobile phone marketing campaigns—with an eye toward attracting better press coverage and improving brand engagement with potential customers. In some instances, advertisers contribute toward production costs, most notably in the 2006 film *Akeelah and the Bee,* which was partly financed by coffee giant Starbucks Corporation. In the reality television show *The Apprentice,* wanna-be Donald Trumps develop new products for the toy company Mattel or design marketing brochures for the Pontiac Solstice (a new General Motors model)—making the show appear more like an hour-long infomercial for its corporate sponsors. Another format that has gained prominence is advergaming. For example, as part of a subversive (also known as stealth) marketing campaign, Toyota and other car manufacturers embedded their brands and logos in Sony's Gran Turismo electronic video game.

But product placement on TV, in movies, and in electronic video games is fast being replaced by the next frontier—advertising and product placement in online video games. Marketers in companies of all sizes have recently discovered Second Life—considered by many a truly unique and cutting-edge business platform. What started as a virtual world inhabited by digital alter egos (avatars) has attracted real money from big business in what seems to be a digital utopia. Companies that have made a foray into the parallel universe of Second Life include retailers (e.g., Reebok, Nike, Amazon, and American Apparel) that sell digital as well as real-world versions of their products; Sun Microsystems, which unveiled a new pavilion to promote its products; and IBM alumni, who held a virtual reunion. Meanwhile, Nissan allows Second Lifers to drive around in their own digital versions of the Sentra (a car they can purchase from a gigantic vending machine). This move has led to coverage by real-world news outlets CNET and Reuters—both of which have reporters embedded full time in the virtual realm. Chapters 1 and 14 present a more detailed discussion of the features and applications of Second Life.

2. Emergence of New Media

As traditional mass media lose their footing, their replacements—the Internet and new media formats—are rising in prominence in the marketer's toolkit. Popular new online media forms include chat rooms, video games, online stores, user-generated content sites (e.g., YouTube), social networking sites (e.g., MySpace and Facebook), and community-supported information services (e.g., Wikipedia and craigslist). Perhaps the most fascinating story of 2006 was the website created by a 21-year-old college student who sold advertising space for $1 per pixel. More than half of its revenue was made within the first month. Needless to say, with all the media attention it received once word got out, Internet pixel-selling rose to frenetic levels, but none of the copycats achieved even remotely the same success as the pioneer.

But new media are not limited to the Internet. Other new media include video projection billboards (such as three-dimensional, movement-enhanced versions of the traditional outdoor billboard), an interactive urinal communicator, and LED (light-emitting diode) screens on the London Underground. The number of offline guerrilla media keeps expanding—they range from moving billboard wraps on vehicles, trucks, and planes to postcards in ATM machines; from advertisements on coffee lids to entirely branded toilets in bars; from banks that narrowcast ads on their ATM screens to gas stations selling ad space on their gas pump screens.

With the resurgence of buzz marketing mentioned earlier in this chapter, marketers are looking for novel and unconventional ways to get conversations started, which means the search is on for high-consumer-involvement media. In many instances, this involves getting up-close and personal. Media such as ass-vertising, dog-vertising, pregnant belly advertising, and foreheADs are all hard-to-miss spots for a message. For example, in various foreheADs campaigns, college students agreed to paste Dunkin' Donuts logos on their foreheads during a National College Athletic Association basketball tournament or to shave the Apple logo or Firestone tire tracks into their hair.

Increased international travel has attracted attention to airplane trays and airsickness bags as convenient new media to attract the attention of captive passengers who are overjoyed by the arrival of a snack to break the boredom of a long flight without food service. And with the advent of ads on snack packs, a new era of brand-in-hand marketing is heralded in: a throwback to the days of reading the information off the cereal box.

3. Consumer-Generated Media: Complement, Substitute, or Threat?

Whether you call it consumer-generated media, online consumer word-of-mouth/buzz, user-generated content, consumer-generated marketing, or consumer-generated advertising, the consumer is undeniably an important force to be reckoned with in all communications—especially the consumer's new media of choice. CGM "encompasses the millions of consumer-generated comments, opinions, and personal experiences posted in publicly available online sources on a wide range of issues, topics, products, and brands."[27] CGM originates from blogs, message boards and forums, public discussions (Usenet newsgroups), discussions and forums on large e-mail portals (Yahoo!, AOL, MSN), online opinion/review sites and services, and online feedback/complaint sites.

Pete Blackshaw of Nielsen BuzzMetrics, asserts, "CGM delivers high-impact, targeted ad impressions well outside the scope of conversation among 'familiars,' a big reason it bears an important distinction from word of mouth. Search in particular magnifies CGM's reach and effect by matching those who create it ('speakers') with curious, information-hungry pre-shoppers ('seekers')."[28] The first CGM wave was more static and was organized around third-party information exchange (e.g., online discussion forms, membership groups, boards, and Usenet newsgroups). The impact of recent developments—blogs and online videos that consumers create and share among themselves—is more dramatic because it is interactive, inexpensive, influential, and immediate. The driving force behind this creative energy of social networking is a need to create social currency. Ideas, images, concepts, words, and other constructs that can be exchanged online serve as proxies that function in a similar manner to other forms of social currency such as jokes or water-cooler topics (e.g., in *The Sopranos* on HBO).

Using various publishing tools such as blogs, wikis, social networking profiles, and messaging, consumers have exclusive say in *who* is talked about and *what* to say—all the marketer can hope for is that the consumer would have positive things to say (ideally they would "digg this" or think it is "del.icio.us"). This raises an interesting question: Is the consumer becoming the marketer (or perhaps agency) of the future? For example, large social networking sites, such as MySpace, generate most of their income from advertising revenues. Another question: Why is CGM important to the marketer if it is so difficult to influence something controlled by consumers? Think about this for a moment. The concept of "information from a trusted source" has taken on an entirely new meaning. Because the message is created by consumers for other consumers, it is trusted implicitly. Fellow consumers, who are unknown to each other except for their respective online presence, accomplish in an instant what corporate marketers have struggled to achieve despite long-standing and expensive relationship marketing efforts.

Here is another thought. Verbal terrorists are rising to new levels of activity—on average they speak to twice as many people than advocates of a brand and potentially reach millions of people through blogs and online communities. One example is that of "Dell Hell" from the *Buzz Machine*.[29] Blogging pioneer Jeff Jarvis explained problems he was experiencing with his Dell computer and associated difficulties with customer service in a letter to Michael Dell (CEO of Dell), which he posted on his blog *Buzz Machine*. In short succession, 398 unhappy Dell customers added their complaints about Dell's customer service. This online buzz penetrated the mainstream press when the *New York Times* reported on the "Dell Hell" story. Apart from the exceedingly bad PR for Dell, the worst was still to come. Shortly after the New York Times article appeared, and for the first time ever, Dell announced it was not able to achieve its earnings forecasts. Simply a coincidence? Vonage is another example. Just before going public, its poor customer service made headline news in *The Wall Street Journal*, causing its stock price to fall by 13% on the first day of trading. People-power through the Internet, combined with the snowball effect of negative publicity, is a nightmare that keeps companies walking on eggs.

This brings us to the proverbial "chicken and egg" situation that lies at the heart of the marketer's problem. Research findings[30] from studies on total WOM conducted in 2006 show that a large majority (90%) of WOM conversations take place *offline*—face-to-face interaction and phone conversations account for 72% and 18%, respectively. When it comes to *online* WOM, e-mail/instant and text messages each garner 3%, while chat rooms and blogs each account for 1%. This means only 7% of total WOM takes place through the various *online* channels. How is this possible when CGM is so prevalent?

While some argue that measurement techniques for online WOM are faulty, Doug Rushkoff asserts, "It's the simplest lesson of the Internet: it's the people, stupid. We don't have computers because we want to interact with machines; we have them because they allow us to communicate more effectively with other people."[31] Online interaction shapes offline conversations—but doesn't replace it. For example, people submit pictures and videos of news items and disasters via camera phones *online;* the media report on these stories, which then shape offline conversations. WOM results from CGM—in many instances, CGM is the catalyst, and therefore CGM is quite often the difference between site traffic that resembles a waterfall and traffic that resembles a trickle. On the other hand, CGM can be the crucible that provides a platform for ongoing interaction, long after WOM on the street has simmered down.

Thanks to the coming of age of streaming video and the high penetration of broadband, video blogging (better known as vlogging) is fast becoming the latest hot new trend in the post-and-share world (also see the fish tank phenomenon in Chapter 14). The unprecedented success of video-sharing web service YouTube is evidence of the appetite of people for a service that aggregates user-generated content, as well as provides a filter mechanism for the piles of junk out there. The evolution of user-generated content has created user celebrities who "have built and sustained large, persistent audiences through the creation of engaging videos, their content has become attractive for advertisers, which has helped them earn the opportunity to participate on YouTube as a partner."[32] YouTube announced in May 2007 that between 20 and 40 users with the most popular content will receive advertising revenues similar to professional partnership agreements with CNN and CBS. Other reliable and high-quality filter systems like the Converse Gallery are fast becoming an indispensable service. Consumers want to see and be seen; this means they must be able to find things of interest to them. They also want to hear and be heard—where and when it matters to them, not according to a fixed scheduling of a TV show or news broadcast.

Some are quicker than others to catch on to this important trend. Following the YouTube model of "aggregator and filter" and CNN's *I-report*, BBC News launched a new TV program based entirely on user-generated content—called

Your News. The new program draws on the thousands of daily e-mail messages from the public in which they share story suggestions, comments, and pictures on the BBC News website. In a slightly different approach that combines a complimentary magazine, social networking, streaming video, and web TV, Savvy.com has created a very popular online lifestyle site for men (also referred to as the "Yahoo! for men"). Its male-oriented news, sports, and entertainment content attracts heavy traffic from a mostly young and male demographic on a daily basis — encouraged by community-building activities and its fan clubs.

However, all is not what it seems. The time has come to rethink social networking. Social networks have been pigeonholed as a web-page paradigm — analogous to a virtual Rolodex that grows so big that it lacks context, and hence relevance. What if social networking becomes part of a larger "experience" — one that blends the best of online and offline worlds? That social networking experience is what Joost (a.k.a., the Venice Project)[33] is trying to mimic in its service. Imagine a personalized TV channel that provides you with only shows your friends are literally talking about. What if the *Lost* characters didn't do their next "Alternative Reality Game" on the web, but in Joost itself, allowing you to collaborate with your friends to collect clues while watching the show? Watching television together online, chatting about it, and talking about what you are watching in real time could be part of everyday life in the very near future. The best part is that you can control your network. Think about the ways in which this could transform programming itself — a metadata framework that might just revolutionize the way you watch television. But more importantly, think of the ways in which this transforms marketing communications such as product placement and advertisements. Joost is the brainchild of Niklas Zennström (the founder of Kazaa and Skype) and Janus Friss. It will launch with commitments from more than 30 advertisers such as Hewlett-Packard, Coca-Cola, Nike, Microsoft, the U.S. Army, and General Motors. This Internet TV platform will enable weblike targeting and measurement of advertisements, many of which would test new ways to target a specific market.

4. THE MOBILE MARKETING ECOSYSTEM

Just imagine this: there are 1.3 billion landline phones, 1.5 billion television sets, 1.4 billion credit cards, 850 million PC users, 1.1 billion Internet users, 1.5 billion e-mail boxes used by 800 million people, all of which are dwarfed by the 2.7 billion mobile subscribers — two-thirds of whom (1.8 billion) are active text-messaging users.[34] Findings from a 2007 study by ABI Research indicate the value of the global mobile marketing and advertising market will increase from about $3 billion by the end of 2007 to $19 billion by 2011 because of developments in mobile search and video advertising. In addition, interactive voice response (IVR), multimedia, gaming, mobile micro-sites, and related mobile services are experiencing rapid growth in demand. Moreover, the mobile phone is fast becoming a platform that complements traditional media such as television, print, radio, outdoor, and the Internet — in addition to changing them in significant ways. Mobile video is expected to surpass the short message system (SMS) as it attracts attention from mobile marketers, accounting for $9 billion in spending by 2011 as numerous companies turn to the mobile channel to engage their audience with products, content, and services. The advent of the era of mobile marketing has arrived in full force!

Now let us take a look at the other side of this coin—the mobile phone user. The social consumer is increasingly a mobile consumer, which increases the likelihood that he or she is using mobile technologies. The era of the BlackBerry—also referred to as "crackberry" due to its addictive nature—is everywhere thanks to third-generation technology (3G), Bluetooth, and multimedia messaging systems (MMS), or video messaging. As a unique new medium, the versatile mobile phone has a distinct role in consumers' lives. Whereas Starbucks is the "third place"—the mobile phone is the "third screen." Despite its much smaller screen size and lower processing power compared with a personal computer or television, the mobile phone's essential features—it's personal, it's portable, and it's used every day[35]—has led some to believe it will be the ultimate tool for "brand-in-the-hand marketing." Moreover, unlike other media, the relatively low cost of a mobile phone has put it within reach of a large portion of the world's population, and it is fast becoming "man's best friend"—and an indelible part of everyday existence. The television program *American Idol* was the first to demonstrate the mobile phone's versatile nature beyond a personal communication device in which the ease of information availability truly empowers its user—who would have thought of using it as a voting machine for your favorite contestant? The mobile phone is used for voice communications, messaging, information gathering, entertainment, shopping, and commerce; it is also a safety device that can be used in emergencies or as a global positioning system (GPS) tracking device if you get lost in the mountains.

Initially, mobile services (in the United States) were exclusively bundled within the "walled garden" of a mobile operator's technology network, significantly limiting its potential. Unbundling of the mobile operator's value chain[36] has opened mobile marketing to corporate brands, content owners, and marketers, who are now able to use mobile networks to distribute services and content through the channel, in addition to direct customer engagement for raising brand awareness, prospecting, and customer acquisition and customer retention purposes. This creates fertile ground for exciting new services and opportunities from existing and new industry players such as mobile ASPs (application service providers and application solution providers), aggregators (who provide single-point connectivity within different mobile operator networks), and enablers (who provide foundation technology, processes, regulations, and related support to the value activities within each sphere). Relying on a variety of technological platforms such as wireless application protocol (WAP), SMS, and MMS, *mobile marketing* is defined quite broadly as "using interactive wireless media to provide customers with time- and location-sensitive, personalized information that promotes goods, services, and ideas, thereby generating value for all stakeholders."[37] Mobile marketing has an enormous array of vertical segments: common short codes (integral to the SMS experience), chat marketing, loyalty programs, mobile storefronts, mobile advertising, premium SMS, mobile sweepstakes, mobile couponing, Txt n' Win, interactive TV voting, content downloads, iRadio, podcasting, gaming, mobile search, mobile TV/mobisodes, TXT2Screen, P2P (e.g., mBlox, m365), and IVR. The Mobile Marketing Association (MMA) (**www.mmaglobal. com**) has brought together the mobile marketing ecosystem, which includes global operators, brands, technology enablers, and agencies, in the face of exponential growth projections for mobile technologies in the United States.

Few marketers have figured out how to best harness the full power of this medium in what has become the mobile era for the mobile consumer, despite realizing its potential as a new and visible marketing tool for services beyond voice. Unlike the PC and most social media, a mobile device offers a uniquely personalized communications channel. Even more compelling are recent findings that indicate mobile advertising campaigns generate responses as high as 40%, compared with average response rates of only 3% with direct mail and 1% with Internet banner ads. Key success criteria for using the mobile phone as a marketing and advertising platform include meeting consumer's expectations of secure and error-free user interactions, which are in turn underpinned by user permission, wireless service provider (WSP) control, and brand trust. Consumers are especially wary of SMS mobile advertising and high levels of spam, elevating the importance of user permission, similar to permission marketing via e-mail.

And that's just the start! All these possibilities can be overwhelming—however, from the perspective of a marketing practitioner, it is possible to group the different options into four categories: access web, see TV/video, sweeps via SMS, and mobile content as premiums to drive sales. Applications that represent best practices in the mobile content industry were singled out as winners of the 2006 FierceMobileContent "Top App Award"[38]—the list includes the Sprint Music Store, Disney Mobile's Family Alerts, Comedy Central's "Take Out," MySpace Mobile on Helio, JumpTap's mobile search platform, and SeeMeTV, among others. These winners span the value chain and include some of the industry's biggest players (carriers included); as a group, the winners offer applications for sharing mobile games and other content easily with friends, a mobile TV solution that simplifies navigation to content, and a user-generated content service that actually makes the carrier money (in addition to the user). By leveraging multiple strategic partners throughout the mobile marketing ecosystem network, Counts Media created a new genre of service—a "mixed reality entertainment experience"—thus turning the world into a canvas and making the mobile phone its brush. The "Yellow Arrow" campaign is an interesting example of experiential marketing filled with "theatrical moments." Users were invited to create a mobile experience by placing Yellow Arrow stickers (with a unique keyword) locations, on objects of interest, places of cultural importance, or just for fun; the arrow is then "programmed" via SMS with a text story or information to explain its significance. When someone text messages this keyword to a short code, it results in a reply text message that contains the story.

The versatility of the mobile phone has resulted in three developments that are especially noteworthy. News Group Newspapers, a division of the Rupert

Murdoch-owned British print media conglomerate News International, launched ".mobi site" in April 2007. This new mobile advertising solution combines newspaper and mobile platforms—facilitating and enhancing the notion of brand-in-hand marketing. So-called smart ads have keywords and "shortcodes" inserted into print advertisements, enabling readers to receive additional information via WAP links mailed to their mobile handsets. The range of media options available to advertisers includes streaming video, mobile vouchers, call-back options, and data collection. Meanwhile, Time Warner's AOL has acquired Third Screen Media (a mobile advertising firm), which combines online and mobile platforms. In a different move that features next-generation interactivity, Internet giant Yahoo! announced a partnership with MobiTV (a mobile broadcast service provider) to launch a new mobile advertising alliance. Yahoo! will serve as the ad network partner for MobiTV's mobile video ad sales and delivery efforts—advertisers are offered a fully integrated service across all mobile advertising platforms, including video, text, and banner ads.

Summary and Conclusions

A combination of the Internet, new digital technologies, and reality TV programming has caused a "tidal wave of brand democratization"[39]—resulting in a global transformation of marketing. Entertainment has moved online to social networking sites like MySpace and Facebook; so have the reference library and dictionaries (e.g., Wikipedia). A multilingual blogosphere renders every person a potential reporter, advocate, or critic. New digital technologies and access to broadband, powerful computers, search engines, open source software, and easy-to-use tools enable everyone to develop creative expressions through a combination of text, pictures, sound, and video—now you can be a journalist, filmmaker, or film star, too! All indications are that user content creation will only get easier. Newspapers are facing a calamity; the traditional local content model is obsolete. Newspapers are scrambling to find new relevance in an online world that is global, with content created by anyone amid a convergence of different media (e.g., TV, radio, and newspapers).

Consider the implications. Realities of the new viral world of instantaneous information in an age of social media mandate that marketers continually evolve. The model has changed from push to pull, which means the message content as well as the mode of delivery (experiential marketing, search marketing, or buzz marketing) has to change. This requires a deep understanding of what is meaningful to today's empowered, and increasingly vocal consumer. It also requires internal/external synergy: holistic integration that ignites external expression and facilitates internal expression. The most recent buzzwords in marketing circles are *people-powered marketing* and *third-screen marketing,* which means the new marketing mantras are social currency (e.g., on YouTube and thousands of other blogs), emotional resonance (through authenticity and storytelling), and "Google Juice" (i.e., a very wide search funnel).

The marketer must become a WOM catalyst—leveraging social currency through pass-along and forwarding of viral marketing messages. Marketers such as Mary Kay and Tupperware rely on social networks to sell their goods—and in so doing, social networks become active participants in effecting social change in addition to improving the economic well-being of the marketers. The same holds true for the online environment. People demand an attitude of openness, authenticity, trust, and responsiveness—from other consumers and marketers alike; messages should be intense, deep, and sincere. The consumer must be engaged, not merely informed. Because the new model is built on trust, messages might need to undergo quantified assessment and certification by third parties such as TRUSTe or authentication/accreditation/validation by whoever is transmitting it.

A word of caution: Social media (blogs, chats, text messaging, podcasts, vlogs) provide a wealth of raw conversations. The main thing to remember as a marketer is that social networking is about people expressing themselves and connecting with like-minded others on their terms—at hubs they own. Marketers who try to set up blogs as a forum for advertising are doomed to fail because it undermines the consumer's sense of importance, self-control, and ownership. Additionally, there is widespread concern that advertiser-prompted blog posts will increase clutter and diminish the persuasive value of commercial references in blogs—eroding the social currency of a trusted blogger. When using one of the many mobile marketing tools, it is all too easy to bombard consumers with excessive or irrelevant messages. As communication channels multiply, it becomes increasingly important that marketers think harder about which media will elicit the right kind of response—and then consolidate messages that stir interest, generate buzz, and influence behavior, without contributing to more clutter instead of less. Instead of coaxing, cajoling, and enticing the consumer into share of mind (SOM) of brands, the emphasis should be on increasing consumers' share of voice (SOV) to affect the shape, size, velocity, and effect of conversations about the brand.

Whereas user-generated content or CGM shifts power from marketer to consumer, mobile marketing seems poised to maintain marketers' control via a new medium that is evolving in interesting and new ways. Marketers view mobile marketing as a source of potential enhancement of CRM efforts due to more effective targeting and tailoring of messages. However, although CGM, mobile marketing, and other new media are treated as separate phenomena for the sake of our discussion of new developments, there are already indications that these new media are morphing and emerging into something entirely different. In March 2007, Italian-based social networking and mobile community services provider Dada.net announced a partnership with search giant Google to launch "friend$." Based on Google's AdSense platform, friend$ is an affiliation program that enables subscribers to earn fees in return for user-generated content—primarily from text advertisements placed on their own web pages, as well as from ads on pages of friends they've invited into the Dada service. This blending of web advertising and the viral nature of social networking with user-generated content like blogs and video clips reinforces the extent to which marketing activities are shifting from marketer to consumers, who can now generate interest in their own sites and, by extension, earn revenue. And this is only the beginning of what promises to be a rollercoaster ride as marketers are frantically trying to capitalize on the plethora of marketing opportunities that are opening up overnight.

Some have called for marketing to be viewed as a system, or more specifically as an ecosystem that considers the whole marketing "supply chain"—the complex interconnections among all the parties involved in planning, creating, reviewing, managing, producing, and distributing marketing communication materials related to a specific brand. This intricate web of relationships includes advertising agencies, creative teams, copy writers, direct marketing channels, fulfillment houses, corporate communications, brand managers, sales teams, intermediaries, public relations firms, and a host of other subcontracted groups— each with a specific role to play and each dependent on others for direction and approval. To achieve coordination and avoid a branding nightmare, the interconnections among parties must operate as a well-designed and seamless system to ensure control over marketing content that preserves brand consistency, but also to increase a competitive advantage through marketing activities.

Key Terms

- guerrilla marketing
- buzz marketing
- viral marketing
- consumer-generated media
- mobile marketing
- social networking
- social media
- social currency

Questions

1. What are the most recent innovations in marketing practices? See how many new marketing practices you can identify in the popular press or your everyday life that are not covered in this chapter.
2. Neuro-marketing is a controversial new field of marketing that uses medical technologies such as functional magnetic resonance imaging (fMRI)—not to diagnose or heal patients, but to sell products. What do you think are the potential dangers of neuro-marketing in the following instances?
   a. Political campaigns
   b. Fast food, alcohol, or potentially harmful products
   c. Products aimed at young children or teenagers
3. What do you think of the methods used by Sony to promote its new camera phone as discussed in the example about street marketing? Would you feel deceived (and perhaps angry) if you discovered you were being "duped" into believing the charade by the actors and ended up buying a Sony camera phone? Would the Sony street marketing campaign have worked if people knew up-front that it was advertiser sponsored? Is there a difference between techniques that disclose the identity of the marketer and those that do not?
4. Do you agree or disagree with the following statement? "Stealth marketing is unethical but buzz marketing isn't." Explain your answer. This topic is discussed in more detail in Chapter 16.

5. These are indeed interesting times for the marketer. Some doomsayers predict that consumer-generated marketing will counteract company-generated marketing and that the latter will eventually disappear. Think back to the arrival of Napster and how it has changed the music industry. Do you believe CGM is here to stay, or will it disappear and be replaced with something else? What are your predictions for the following:

   a. Will CGM evolve as time goes by?

   b. How will CGM affect the way companies do marketing in the future?

6. There is concern that advertiser-prompted blog posts will results in more clutter and erode the social currency of trusted bloggers. Do you think the blogosphere will become corrupted as a result of pay-to-blog services?

7. Have you (or will you) buy something based on a recommendation from someone who is "paid-to-say" in face-to-face conversations or on a pay-to-post blog? Why or why not?

8. Mobile marketing in the United States has been trailing developments in the rest of the world, but that might soon change. In April 2007, Vodafone announced a partnership with Internet giants Google and Yahoo! to launch a suite of ad-supported mobile services in mid-2007. How might this partnership change mobile marketing in Europe and the United States?

9. In a pioneering move, mobile marketing service provider VoiceIndigo announced a worldwide partnership with Samsung. Advertising-supported podcasting service by VoiceIndigo, beginning with the music-centric dual-face device UpStage, which is currently available from Sprint, will be preloaded and shipped bundled on a Samsung handset.

   a. The VoiceIndigo CEO believes this move puts the customer in control. Do you agree?

   b. How does this partnership offer the customer increased value?

   c. In your opinion, will this feature increase the sales of Samsung mobile phones? Why or why not?

Resources and References

1. Locke, C., Levine, D., Searls, D., & Weinberger, D. (1999). *The Cluetrain Manifesto: The end of business as usual.* New York: Perseus Publishing.
2. Godin, S. (2005). *All marketers are liars: The power of telling authentic stories in a low-trust world.* New York: Portfolio.
3. Vollmer, C., Frelinghuysen, J., & Rothenberg, R. Special Report. The Future of Advertising is Now. Strategy + Business. http://www.strategy-business.com/freearticle/06204?pg=all&tid=230, Accessed on November 2, 2007.
4. For these and other examples, see World Advertising Research Center. (2007). *Search marketing.* Available at http://www.warc.com/Search/WordSearch/Results.asp.
5. Grönroos, C. (1994). From marketing mix to relationship marketing: Towards a paradigm shift in marketing. *Management Decision* 32(2): 4–20.
6. Hamel, G., & Prahalad, C. K. (1992). Corporate imagination and expeditionary marketing. *Harvard Business Review* 69(4): 31–43.

7. Levinson, C. (1993), *Guerrilla marketing: Secrets for making big profits from your small business*. Boston: Houghton Mifflin.
8. Peppers, D., & Rogers, M. (1993). The new marketing paradigm: One to one. *American Advertising* 9: 4.
9. McKenna, R. (1997). Real-time: Preparing for the age of the never-satisfied customer. *Upside* 9(10): 138–143.
10. Rushkoff, D. (2005, January, 30). *The merchants of cool.* http://www.pbs.org/wgbh/pages/frontline/shows/cool/view/.
11. Dru, J. M. (2002). *Beyond disruption*. New York: John Wiley.
12. Jurvetson, S., & Draper, T. (1997). Viral marketing. Netscape M-Files (original version). Edited version published in *Business 2.0,* November 1998.
13. Parsons, A., Zeisser, M., & Waitman, R. (1998). Organizing today for the digital marketing of tomorrow. *Journal of Interactive Marketing* 12(1): 31–46.
14. Godin, S. (1999). *Permission marketing: Turning strangers into friends and friends into customers.* New York: Simon and Schuster.
15. Schmitt, B. H. (1999). *Experiential marketing: How to get customers to sense, feel, think, act, relate.* New York: The Free Press.
16. Hill, S., & Rifkin, G. (1999). *Radical marketing: From Harvard to Harley. Lessons from ten that broke the rules and made it big.* New York: Harper Collins.
17. Rosen, E. (2000). *The anatomy of buzz: How to create word of mouth marketing.* New York: Doubleday.
18. Sheth, J. N., Sisodia, R. S., & Sharma, A. (2000). The antecedents and consequences of customer-centric marketing. *Academy of Marketing Science Journal* 28(1): 55–66.
19. Wind, Y. J., Mahajan, V., & Gunther, R. E. (2002). *Convergence marketing: Strategies for reaching the new hybrid consumer.* Upper Saddle River, NJ: Prentice Hall.
20. Kelly, M. (2002). The science of shopping: What is neuromarketing. http://www.cbc.ca/consumers/market/files/money/science_shopping/.
21. WARC Report.
22. Jantsch, J. (2007). *Duct tape marketing: The world's most practical small business marketing guide.* Nashville, TN: Thomas Nelson.
23. Hughes, M. (2005). *Buzzmarketing: Get people to talk about your stuff.* New York: Portfolio.
24. Godin, S. (2003). *Purple cow: Transform your business by being remarkable.* New York: Portfolio.
25. Hughes.
26. Siklos, R. (2006, October 18). Virtual worlds are moving toward commercial reality. *New York Times,* http://www.iht.com/articles/2006/10/18/business/virtual.php.
27. Blackshaw, P. (2007, March 14) *CGM overview,* http://www.nielsenbuzzmetrics.com/cgm.asp.
28. Blackshaw, P. *The pocket guide to consumer-generated media,* http://www.clickz.com/showPage.html?page=3515576.
29. "Measuring the influence of bloggers on corporate reputations" (2005). *Market Sentinel,* Onalytica, ImmediateFuture.com.
30. Keller, E., & Berry, J. (2006). Word-of-mouth: The real action is offline. *Advertising Age* 77(49): 20.
31. Rushkoff, D. (2007). *Get back in the box: How being great at what you do is great for business.* New York: Harper Collins.
32. http://www.cnn.com/2007/BUSINESS/05/04/you.tube/index.html?eref=rss_topstories.
33. "Top You Tube contributors can become partners." (2007, May 4). http://gigaom.com/tag/Joost.

34. Ahonen, T., & Moore, A. (2007). Putting 2.7 billion in context: Mobile phone users. http://communities-dominate.blogs.com/brands/2007/01/putting_27_bill.html.
35. Ito, M., et al. (2005). *Personal, portable, pedestrian: Mobile phones in Japanese life.* Boston: MIT Press.
36. Anderson, J., & Williams, B. (2004). Unbundling the mobile value chain. *Business Strategy Review* 15(3): 51–57.
37. Dickinger, A., Haghirian, P., & Murphy, J. S. (2004). An investigation and conceptual model of SMS marketing. *Proceedings of the 37th Hawaii International Conference on System Sciences: IEEE.*
38. Top Mobile Applications 2006, http://www.fiercemobilecontent.com/top-mobile-applications-2006.
39. Neisser, D. (2006, May 29). Tidal wave of democratization: Vital speeches of the day. Delivered at the International Advertising Association, Jordan Chapter, Amman, Jordan.

CHAPTER 9

THE MAGIC OF
MARKETING JUJU

THE CHANGING ROLE OF BRANDS

It is a jungle out there! The product choices facing people today can be overwhelming: 26 kinds of Coca-Cola include Diet Coke, Cherry Coke, Diet Cherry Coke, Caffeine-Free Diet Coke, and others; 39 flavors in Ben & Jerry's flavor world, plus you can create your own with the flavor generator; 66 sub-brands of GM cars; hundreds of cereal options to kick-start your day; 40,000 SKUs (or stock-keeping units) in a typical supermarket has become commonplace. And these numbers keep growing—especially in an online world, where Amazon.com offers shoppers almost anything they can think of. Unlimited choice is good, right?

Unfortunately, sometimes more is less, and less is more. This is the paradox of choice[1]—as the options to choose from increase, so do the unfortunate complications associated with making choices: decisions require more effort and the probability of making mistakes or being disappointed increases. Amid this sea of choices facing buyers, brands effectively serve a reduction function:[2] they reduce search costs related to finding the product and making product comparisons, reduce perceived risks of regret due to poor quality, and reduce potential social or psychological risks associated with buying the "wrong" product.

Each product is associated with a brand name, logo, and/or slogan. According to the American Marketing Association (AMA),[3] a *brand* is "a name, terms, sign, symbol, or design, or a combination of them intended to identity the goods and services of one seller or group of sellers and to differentiate them from those of competition." A brand offers a complex blend of functional, symbolic, and emotional values and benefits, regardless of the simplicity or complexity of the product itself.

But what is a brand *really?* A brand starts as a product and a name, but "a brand is not a product. It is a product's essence, its meaning, its direction and it defines its identity in time and in space. A product is something made in a factory. A brand is something bought by a consumer. A product can be copied by a competitor, a brand is unique. A product can be outdated. A brand is timeless. A product has a lifecycle; a brand is eternal."[4] Brands have histories. A brand embodies stories constructed over time by the brand organization and its user. A brand is alive—it resonates in the heart of its beholder through dynamic relationships that its creator (or owner) attempts to nurture and maintain with relentless and painstaking effort. Some brands seem to breathe with eternal life, while other well-known brands die a sudden and untimely death (e.g., energy provider Enron, the accounting firm Arthur Andersen, and MCI in telecommunications). Some brands ooze with transformational energy (i.e., marketing juju), while others merely have the sizzle without the steak.

Tracing a brief history of brands and branding concepts enables us to understand what a brand is from the perspective of the company; understand why consumers' perceptions about its role might change; and gain some insight into why some brands, having remained prominent during successive iterations of a brand's role, are seemingly timeless and endure for generations. The different stages depicted in Figure 9-1 serve as convenient demarcations that facilitate more in-depth discussion of brands and branding in this chapter; these stages are not intended to suggest stable or distinct shifts in the branding landscape. Let us first examine some of the factors that have led to the transitions in Figure 9-1 before considering the impact of these transitions from the respective viewpoints of the marketer (in terms of his or her role) and the consumer, as well as concomitant changes in the perceived role of the brand.

The value-added ladder of forward-thinking marketers changed from goods and raw materials (stuff and things) to services (stuff and transactions) with a realization in the 1990s of the importance of a relationship with customers. The way in which companies could get ahead amid fierce competition was to create

FIGURE 9-1 The Changing Role of Brands

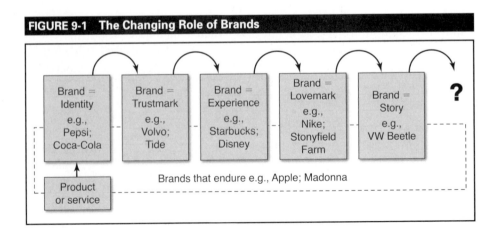

game-changing solutions for new and existing customer problems. The different principles underlying this opportunity-seeking and advantage-seeking approach are discussed in more detail in Chapter 10. The advent of the experience economy prompted companies to stage spell-binding and transformational experiences as a source of differentiation that could create entirely new ways of adding value in the face of increased commoditization of goods and services. The experience economy was soon eclipsed by a shift from the attention economy to the attraction economy.[5] In an increasingly digital world that is cold, calculating, and scientific, the language of emotion has moved center stage. Instead of rational appeals using factual information, matters of the heart reign supreme.

It is clear from Figure 9-1 that the functional role of brands has changed significantly, much of which can be ascribed to the recent shift from 4 P's to 4 C's (see Chapter 2) in a world where the consumer is king of the jungle, not the organization that owns the brand. These changes occurred in waves, and they overlap each other with no clear beginning or ending points except for the stages during which marketing practitioners, consultants, and various authors popularized a particular approach that reflected a fundamental shift in the reality underlying each new economy.

The remainder of this chapter is organized around the underlying tenets of dominant views regarding the role of brands in the organization as well as in people's lives. In view of the distinct perspectives indicated in Figure 9-1, the first section is devoted to six specific roles played by the brand in terms of its primary function as a source of value creation for the firm: the brand as identity, trustmark, relationship builder, experience, lovemark, and story. This section is followed by insights from the evolution of branding activities through the eyes of a brand management master: Procter & Gamble (P&G). The third section examines the relatively recent phenomenon in which company and brand user share ownership of the brand—it serves as a bridge between the view of a brand's role solely through the eyes of its creator and a perspective dedicated to that of the brand's beholder. In the fourth section the focus shifts to the multiplicity of meanings a brand can have in people's lives. Finally, we turn our attention in the fifth section of this chapter to the set of brands that have endured trends while staying relevant for more than 20 years. Considered by many as the most loved and respected (e.g., Apple), these brands have transcended product categories, markets, time, and space. It is this set we are most interested in; the entrepreneurial nature of their marketing activities reveals the source of "marketing juju."

THE BRAND IN THE EYES OF ITS CREATOR

As a potential source of value for the company, a brand shapes a wealth of perceptions, beliefs, attitudes, and experiences in the consumer's world. Brand value is created and appropriated from its various roles, some of which are briefly discussed here. First, the brand is considered as a differentiating identifier that acts as a signal of origin used by consumers to decide between competing products. Second, the brand is viewed as a trustmark, a mark of quality. Its third role is that of a source of relationship building. The fourth major platform for brands, especially in the services and retail sectors, involves the brand as an experience provider. During the early 2000s, the importance of emotion in consumer decision-making processes resurfaced and changed the brand from acting an identifier or trustmark to that of a lovemark — its fifth role. Finally, the sixth role is that of a character with personality as part of the history and culture of the company. In today's marketplace, a brand could have all six roles (and more), but not all brands do, nor should they.

1. THE BRAND AS A PRODUCT/COMPANY IDENTITY

By itself the brand name has little significance or value, yet it serves as the foundation stone for an elaborate edifice — it is an identifier, an ownership symbol of the producer/seller, a seal of authenticity, a source of differentiation from competing products, a guarantee of quality, and a mark of distinction. In combination, the various symbolizations constitute the brand as an intangible asset composed of expectations that are developed and reinforced over time. Attributed and anticipated benefits associated with the brand name become powerful decision-making tools for consumers. Moreover, in the absence of a direct interface between seller and buyer, the brand name represents the unfamiliar manufacturer at some distant location in a type of surrogate relationship with the consumer.

What is in a name? Originally, products were associated with tangible features and functional benefits. Over time product attributes (i.e., features, functions, and benefits) were associated with trademarks, which required protection of its intellectual property value. Soon a trademark alone wasn't enough because every supplier had one — the supplier also had to augment the product with services and guarantees beyond the physical product. The change from trademark to brand required that its essential characteristics (i.e., differentiation, identity, and uniqueness) were communicated to potential consumers. It might be useful at this stage to refer back to Figure 7-1 in Chapter 7, which shows how a product can be differentiated at the level of the core benefit, tangible product, augmented product, communicated product, and potential product, that results from product development efforts.

The new brand world became infused with -*er* words: cleaner, stronger, whiter, brighter, and so forth — each brand proclaiming its virtues, which are supposedly better in some way relative to a competitor's offering because consumers will pay more for better design, better performance, better quality, and better value. The brand message is repeated in the mass media to capture potential buyers' attention. This message is reinforced with sales incentives to convince the consumer that the product/service is *really* different and has a distinct identity (which include notion of the brand-as-person, brand-as-organization, brand-as-symbol, and brand-as-product). However, the main objective of the brand message is to ensure that it is top-of-mind and considered the only option (not merely the better option) when it is time to make the purchasing decision. In this scenario, the watchword for marketers is the unique selling/value proposition (USP), which is associated with functional, emotional, and self-expressive benefits. Thus, the brand is positioned in the mind of the consumer—although communication of a brand's positioning is done by marketers, consumers' perceptions of the brand are subjective and personal. Ultimately, the brand's actual positioning in the consumer's mind might not coincide with the combination of core brand associations or brand mantra assigned by the marketer based on points of parity and points of difference within a competitive set.

2. Increasing Brand Relevance: From Product Identity to Trustmark

Soon there was a rumble in the jungle. With every brand claiming to be the better, best, or the only choice, consumers needed reassurance created by consistent identity, positioning, and communication over time to be convinced of making the "right" purchasing decision. This meant an identity, slogan, or catchy promotional jingle was no longer enough—the brand had to become a symbol of trust. But trustworthiness has a price tag associated with it: gaining affinity as part of an evolving relationship in which the company becomes a trusted friend costs money. Long-term visibility and credibility require deep pockets for relentless promotion that echoes the brand promise and keeps it top-of-mind for the consumer—just ask Coca-Cola and Pepsi!

The brand's owner quickly realized that speaking in a clearly identifiable voice required ongoing and expensive brand communications. Some sort of return on this substantial investment can be found only if consumers indeed develop loyalty toward the brand, which in turn can be leveraged to multiple product categories. For instance, someone buys an iPod and then decides to buy Apple products in future because he or she starts to trust the brand. Consequently, key differentiating factors moved from -er words that were derived from the products to words that provide psychological benefits such as comfort, convenience, simplicity, timeliness, and so forth. Once formed, the brand-consumer relationship could be strengthened through a strong, continuous feedback loop that reinforces a level of trust as opposed to disconnected, periodic brand communications.

As a trustmark, the brand provides the necessary reassurance to alleviate choice fatigue from copious and time-consuming evaluation of other brands or nonbranded products during every purchasing decision. In the sea of choices and multiple new offerings, from numerous new and existing companies, consumers instinctively turn to brands they know and trust. But trust is a fragile thing. One misstep and all the years of carefully controlling the brand's image and millions of dollars spent to keep consumers informed are gone with the blink of an eye—compromising what has become a company's most precious competitive asset. Beyond the ever-present internal challenges related to interfunctional coordination, brands also face ongoing threats from external forces. A marketplace shift from surplus demand to surplus supply—together with increasingly fragmented and dispersed markets, proliferation of media options amid declining mass media popularity, and complicated segmentation efforts—increased costs dramatically. However, it was the power shift from company (4 P's) to customer (4 C's) and the significant decline in brand loyalty that finally forced companies to reexamine the role of trustmarks and relationships in the late 1990s.

3. The Brand as a Relationship Builder

The customer can have a relationship with the brand as an object (via the product/service) or with the company. A relationship with the brand is based on three components: liking, yearning, and decision/commitment. Presence or absence of these three components in various combinations can result in eight possible customer-brand relationships:[6] nonliking, liking, infatuation, functionalism, inhibited desire, utilitarianism, succumbed desire, and loyalty. The nature of the company–customer relationship is an important topic and Chapter 15 is dedicated to an in-depth discussion of relationship management. Relationships are typically built around a mutual exchange of information to increase customer satisfaction, trust, respect, loyalty, and customer lifetime value. But what if the relationship between company and customer becomes more interactive and goes beyond merely exchanging information with each other? This might mean that customers also interact with each other—not only with the company—strengthening the customer-brand bond even further. Rather than manipulating the customer into buying a brand, the consumer can participate in a way that is meaningful to him or her—in the creation, pricing, promotion, and delivery of the product/service. This could result in the type of relationship a customer might actually want, rather than being locked in on the marketer's terms. If the customer is involved with the brand in this manner, she or he may have a new sense of commitment and loyalty as a stakeholder in the future of the relationship. Attention now turns to an approach that involves this type of interactive value exchange instead of passive information exchange between the customer and the company.

4. Improved Customer Interactions: From Identity to Experience

No more monkey business. There is a new call in the jungle, and it is saying "Me-Me-Me-Me-Me!" One day without warning, the lion realized he was no longer the trusted king of the jungle. No longer content with their assigned roles, the animals raised their voices in dissent and claimed a say in who, why, when, where, how, and what should happen—regardless of the size or perceived importance to the former king. Apart from a willingness of the king of the jungle to relinquish the tight rein, it requires reverse thinking—from CRM to MRC. To remain king in a reconceptualized brand jungle, customer relationship management (CRM) had to change to managing relationships to develop customers (MRC). More specifically, in this new interactive brand jungle, the brand is viewed as an experience provider and a source of interaction within a customer community—not as a relationship builder. Gone are the days in which quality, service, style, and selection, combined with the right price, get the marketer a foot in the door. Instead, holistic customer experiences that transform and rejuvenate have become the new foundation for competitive differentiation, value creation, and brand equity. It is this shift from the brand-as-trustmark to the brand-as-experience-provider that we turn our attention to next.

The strategic experiential marketing (SEM) framework[7] consists of five types of customer experiences that are organized as follows:

1. *Sense:* create sensory experiences that are dynamic through sight, sound, touch, taste, and smell. Examples of *Sense* marketers include Nokia mobile phones, Hennessy cognac, and Procter & Gamble's Tide Mountain Fresh detergent.

2. *Feel:* appeal to customers' inner feelings and emotions to create affective experiences that range from mildly positive moods to strong emotions during consumption that encourage the formation of new perspectives and empathy. Examples of marketers who have used a *Feel* approach include Hallmark, Campbell's Soup, and Häagen Dazs Cafés.

3. *Think:* appeal to the intellect to engage customers in rational problem-solving experiences involving convergent and divergent thinking through surprise, intrigue, and provocation. Examples of *Think* marketing include Microsoft's "Where Do You Want to Go Today?" campaign, Apple Computer's revival, Genesis ElderCare, and Siemens.

4. *Act:* aim to induce bodily experiences in response to motivational and inspirational content by illustrating alternative lifestyles and ways of doing things that would enhance customers' well-being provided that they change their behavior. Examples of *Act* marketing include Gillette's Mach3, the Milk Mustache campaign, and Martha Stewart Living.

5. *Relate:* integrate aspects of sense, feel, think, and act marketing that go beyond the individual by relating the individual to his or her future "ideal self" or to other people in a broader socila system or in different cultures. *Relate* marketers include Harley-Davidson, Tommy Hilfiger, and Wonderbra.

Successful marketers typically employ experiential hybrids that combine two or more SEMs to broaden the experiential appeal. For instance, when drinking Red Bull, the consumer becomes aware of a rush of energy beyond the physical effect of the drink that touches the senses and emotions and affects motivation based on expectations formed around the brand.

5. LOYALTY BEYOND REASON: FROM TRUSTMARK TO LOVEMARK

> *. . . 80% of our life is emotion, and only 20% is intellect. I am much more interested in how you feel than how you think. I can change how you think, but how you feel is something deeper and stronger, and it's something that's inside you. How you think is on the outside, how you feel is on the inside, so that's what I need to understand . . . It's all emotion. But there's nothing wrong with emotion. When we are in love, we are not rational; we are emotional. When we are on vacation, we are not rational; we are emotional. When we are happy, we are not [rational]. In fact, in more cases than not, when we are rational, we're actually unhappy. Emotion is good; passion is good.*
>
> —GERALD ZALTMAN

Just imagine that! Only 20% of our lives revolve around our minds and yet we often allow rational decision making to trump our emotions, viewing them as irrational or somehow inferior. How we feel about something runs deep—it is associated with beliefs and complex response tendencies of a psychological, neurological, and physiological nature. However, changing your mind, for instance, during an argument while reasoning about something cognitively is relatively simple. Emotion provides the motivational energy to act and to commit. If the brand experience resonates within a person's heart, a lasting emotional connection is formed. Emotions are engaged more effectively when all five senses are engaged: arresting smells, sensuous touch, interesting tastes, and the sound of music, in addition to visual impressions. Even more involvement is possible when the person makes physical movements by interacting with the brand (or something else). Multiple experiential touch points increase the likelihood of attracting attention and engaging the whole person in the experience.

The conclusion is a straightforward one: love is what it's all about! "The most powerful and lasting benefit you can give a customer is an emotional one. Physical benefits are the necessary currency of exchange. . . . That by themselves [sic] can be quite unremarkable and pedestrian no matter how great your products are. Great brands transcend great products."[8] The Nike story is an especially powerful example; a running shoe with a swoosh overnight turned from trustmark into lovemark when Nike found an emotional connection with consumers through its association with Michael Jordan. What is a lovemark?

In the words of the creator of the lovemark concept, Kevin Roberts (CEO, Saatchi & Saatchi Worldwide) of the lovemark concept, "A Lovemark is a brand that has *created loyalty beyond reason;* it is infused with *mystery, sensuality, and intimacy,* and that you recognize immediately as having some kind of iconic place in your heart."[9] Whereas trustmarks operate at a brand level, a lovemark acts at a human level—the brand is no longer part of the product's identity but has become transformed as part of the individual's identity. Brands like Harley-Davidson, Saturn, JetBlue, and Nike make their customers feel unique, important, and part of an exclusive group—this leads to long-term relationships between a brand and its users. Another company that has created a lovemark is Stonyfield Farm, as shown in Exhibit 9-1. Its organic dairy products from "happy cows" that could be adopted by kids as part of a campaign fused consumer education and promotion stirred the hearts of the younger and older generations alike.

6. THE BRAND AS A CHARACTER IN A STORY

In a competitive, product-saturated marketplace, a product needs something beyond the brand—an added value, an idea, mythic images—a "story" that is real and enticing about the origin, history, or potential use of the item. Metaphors endow brands with connotations beyond literal meanings because they are able to capture "the entire teleology of meaning, which . . . coordinates metaphor with the manifestations of truth."[10] Beyond its characteristics as an entity, the brand

---

EXHIBIT 9-1   Moosletters from Stonyfield Farm's Happy Cows

Stonyfield Farm has also created a unique kind of culture for consumers. Here, people are not just buying Stonyfield yogurt for the product attributes alone, but they are also buying into the emotional appeal of the brand as well. To its customers, Stonyfield Farm is a company that represents integrity, quality, and even a sense of humor. Stonyfield has many layers of linked, "real" experiences that customers can explore as they delve deeper and deeper into the brand. This includes contributions to grassroots nonprofits that support women, children, and the environment; an active company tour and gift store at the company's headquarters in New Hampshire; live farm "Moosletters" from a dairy farmer on the Stonyfield website; and the extension of the brand into the restaurant space with "O'naturals" restaurants. The wholesome values that this "simple" yogurt represents are instilled in a cultural brand that is representative of the shifting values that people "feel good" about. Consumers wouldn't buy the product if it didn't taste good, but they will continue to repeat their purchases and are much more loyal to it because of the cultural infrastructure of the brand.

Source: www.stonyfieldfarm.com

also has mental associations in the minds of consumers such as brand image, personality, identity, and life cycle. Marketers use the informational and transformational abilities of advertising to create a compelling image, identity, and personality that give the brand its meaning and appeal. As seen in point 5 where the brand acts as experience provider, consumer emotions play a defining role in shaping perception, experience, and memory of the brand—a story facilitates the quest for an emotional connection with the consumer because it has the power to unlock feelings and recollections. People of all ages love stories, whether telling or listening to them. In his book *All Marketers Are Liars,* Seth Godin[11] advocates that marketers should start telling authentic stories in the low-trust world of marketing. An authentic story can provide powerful emotional connections that maintain and reinforce brand identity and personality by imbuing the corporate brand with human characteristics, values, words, and action. Metaphors and stories also play a critical role in marketing juju, as we'll see later in this chapter.

EVOLUTION OF BRANDS AND BRANDING: THE STORY OF PROCTER & GAMBLE

The fundamental changes in marketing communications during the different eras of branding as shown in Exhibit 9-2 are reflected in the branding activities of the inventor of brands, Procter and Gamble (P&G).[12] Voted as the best marketer of the 20th century by *Advertising Age* magazine, P&G is traditionally known for spending billions of dollars a year "shouting" its brands' messages through persistent advertising: P&G's Pantene is the best shampoo for your hair, its Tide ensures whiter, brighter laundry; and its Pringles is just what your stomach craves. But brand management has changed considerably since its inception. On May 13,

---

EXHIBIT 9-2   The Story of the Wizard of Brands—P&G

From trustmark to lovemark and beyond

Tide has been used by families for more than 50 years. Some consumers were actually bathed in Tide as children. But we don't just use Tide because Mom and her mother used it.

Tide is no longer a laundry detergent. The days of buying a washing powder are over. It is not about getting clothes clean anymore. Any detergents will get your clothes clean. We don't use tide just because it cleans well. It is about everyone in the family wearing clothes that look good and that last for a long time—Tide plays a role in family harmony, not just in washday.

Think about that for a moment. Tide has moved from the heart of the laundry to the heart of the family. Tide is about much more than a detergent—it has a deeper meaning than that: it's an enabler; it's a liberator. Instead, we have come to see Tide as being like us. We assign (or accept) some sort of personality to a brand, and then we start seeing that personality as being similar to our own. The laundry detergent's trusted name and its red-and-yellow bull's-eye logo has become a Pop Art icon.

The brand's formidable aura draws people to the Tide.com website, which offers fabric-care advice and handy features like the Stain Detective—a digital tip sheet on how to remove almost any substance from almost any fabric. Consumers can even download the Stain Detective to a Palm computing device.

Source: www.pg.com

1931, the classic memo of Neil McElroy at P&G that led to the "invention" of the modern brand that was more than a mere trademark—Ivory Soap. Exhibit 9-2 gives an overview of some of these changes and the concomitant shift of advertising dollars to new media such as blogs and video games.

The focus in the story about P&G revolves around changes made by consumers of fast-moving consumer packaged-goods. Clearly products such as toothpaste and washing powder do not have the potential to become cultural icons or answer the primal call that brands such as Apple, VW, and Harley-Davidson seem to do. Yet P&G, with its portfolio of low-cost, low-involvement products, has found a way to connect with the everyday problems and needs of the consumer. Consumers might not necessarily want to *buy* P&G's products when they go online. In the case of Tide, their problem is stain removal, and their interest is information related to different remedies. Whereas before the company's main concern was selling the product with an eye toward highest possible return on investment (ROI), P&G now has to think about things from the consumer's point of view: What is the consumer's return on involvement? And not, What *not* what is the company's return on investment?

The changes in P&G's approach to brand management reflect the shift from an attention economy to an attraction economy[13] mentioned at the beginning of this chapter. The attention economy is characterized by interruption techniques (e.g., 30-second ads every 15 minutes on TV) in which companies that are larger than life shout their unidirectional, high-powered messages that make big promises about what consumers need. In this reactive and highly repetitive approach, the consumer is informed, educated, and persuaded. As demonstrated in the P&G example, in an attraction economy the focus shifts to consumer engagement. Instead of the one-to-many model of before, the company has to find ways in which it can facilitate many-to-one interactions by enticing consumers with engaging content about elements of importance in their lives. Apart from the changes in brand communications, finding connections with consumers means that the primary source of ideas, products, and technologies at P&G are no longer within the sole domain of the company, a particular division within the company, or a specific product category. Instead, design of new products is derived from a better understanding of the customer ecosystem as a result of rethinking ideas around the consumer's desired experience.

With an increase in customer involvement, mass customization has become the next natural extension of consumer products. Three examples illustrate the different forays P&G has made in that direction—these are discussed in the order of increasing collaboration between company and consumer facilitated in an online environment. The first two examples relate to online communications directed at teenage girls. First-timers shopping for feminine hygiene products often feel uncomfortable. To alleviate potential discomfort at the nearest shopping mall, P&G's Femcare division created an interactive site, BeingGirl, where teenagers have easy access to answers to questions they might have. In the second example, a blog created for P&G's range of products in the antiperspirant/deodorant market, SparkleBodySpray.com, features four teenage authors under identities of Vanilla, Tropical, Peach, and Rose. Information on the site covers topics that are top-of-mind—music, fashion, sports, dating, and parties—rather than product features and company advertisements. Girls can also create a dream date with choices provided online and share this with friends. The final example is Reflect.com, which goes beyond brand communications—it lets the customer shape the brand by combining personalization with a strong brand identity. Customers create and recreate their own versions of makeup, perfume, and other beauty care products using interactive software to mix and match colors, scents, and other options. Once the product is "made," the customer "brands" it by choosing an original package design that contains the Reflect logo, the customer's name, and the customer's selection from several jewel-shaped emblems.

FROM BRAND AS SOURCE OF VALUE TO VALUE CO-CREATION AND VALUE EXCHANGE

A power shift from company (brand identity) to consumer (brand experience) has implications for value creation and value appropriation. For instance, with the company in control of the brand, the business model is based on opportunity-seeking and advantage-seeking activities through distinctive core competencies such as technology-securing patents (e.g., Priceline.com), design and innovation (e.g., 3M), or excellent customer service (e.g., Southwest Airlines). With the brand as its center, the company relies on costly internal processes to secure competitive and positional advantages based on added value (see Chapter 7 for more information related to business models). The marketer's thinking is a one-way street—my company, my brands, and my customer. From a traditionally closed perspective, the company "produces a brand's physical embodiment, exclusively narrates the brand's text, unilaterally directs the brand experience, and broadcasts the brand's meaning."[14]

However, with the customer at the epicenter in experiential environments, the company is no longer a brand's sole proprietor; customers become active participants in ongoing discourse as well as co-owners of the brand as they "create the physical offering, author the text, generate the experience, and evolve the brand meaning. In this process, control shifts from directed to emergent, and coordination passes from hierarchy to heterarchy."[15] In this case, the brand is a fusion of formal company-initiated marketing activities and consumer-generated content, buzz marketing, community activities, or other social media (see Chapter 8). Consumers are motivated to contribute their efforts for a variety of reasons: status, fun, connection, access, devotion to the brand, and so forth. A value-exchange model that revolves around three different co-creators of value changes the dynamics involved in value creation and appropriation: the company and its network, the customer, and the customer community—each of which we now discuss in turn.

THE COMPANY AND ITS NETWORK AS CO-CREATOR OF VALUE

The company with its marketing network is a natural source of value creation. On one end of the spectrum, marketers with shallow pockets use events, or a series of events, to create a memorable and emotional connection with customers. Special events don't end up in the clutter and are often more effective and less expensive than media advertising. One example is the creation of an "Irish Village" for Guinness Fleadh events in New York, San Francisco, and Chicago—pre-event point-of-purchase campaigns from retailers are followed with lots of beer sampling during the event. Another example of an innovative campaign was launched by a U.K. gallery, Tate Britain, in an attempt to heighten the museum experience. Tate Britain invited people to develop a mini-collection of paintings around a theme, similar to the gallery's own selection for its "Rainy Day" collection. The museum experience was further enhanced through new technology that added an extra dimension of interactivity with the brand.

A different form of value co-creation occurs when the company's network is the source of service experiences. Retail outlets (such as Gap, Sephora, or Victoria's Secret) are emotion-evoking because of the shopping experience itself. It could also result from an unexpected customer service moment that is built into a shopping experience to surprise and delight shoppers. This might be as simple as an unsolicited bonus item when the shopper completes the transaction at the cash register, or it might be a more substantial retail experience in a destination store such as Niketown, the Apple Store, or Nintendo World, where major brand organizations allow brand users to become immersed in the brands they love.

On the other end of the spectrum lies the more advanced form of a comprehensive branded experience through theme parks such as Legoland, Hersheypark, and VW Autostadt. For instance, Disney creates the magic of a fantasy world that is magnified on the silver screen and brought to life with nostalgic walks down memory lane in their theme parks and through holidays on cruise ships. Consider this for a moment: at Celebration, consumers are moving *inside* the Disney brand—from the moment they arrive until they leave. Full vertical integration, no competition, and the undivided attention of consumers mean there is no need for overt marketing. Bliss for consumers? Brand nirvana for Disney?

THE CUSTOMER AS CO-CREATOR OF VALUE

Value can be uniquely co-created by the customer based on personal meaning derived from interactions with the brand. Customers might act as collaborators, competitors, and/or co-developers. An example in which the customer acts as collaborator is that of TiVo, which acts as an intelligent digital video recorder that analyzes the user's tastes and interests based on a personal viewing history. These results are then used to evaluate the programming available on accessible channels, select programs the user will most probably enjoy, and record these when they are broadcast without the need for any user intervention. This adaptive learning process with the experience network is the basis for real-time action. Other examples include Sony's PlayStation (PS2) and Nintendo's Wii.

Customers also act as competitors of other customers when they are price-setters, as is the case of products purchased on Priceline and eBay. An experience scenario that is becoming increasingly popular involves customers as co-developers of products (e.g., Build-a-Bear Workshops, NIKEiD) or co-producers of the service experience (e.g., Southwest Airlines and Café TuTu Tango [see what's waiting at **www.cafetututango.com**]). Another example is the cable/satellite network, Current TV, in which 30% of the content is "viewer-generated." In this scenario, the company and customer(s) are participants in the experience—the company provides the physical resources, while the customer makes the experience happen as a result of engaging the resources provided. The example in Exhibit 9-3 describes a novel dining experience at the restaurant Dans le Noir? in France, where the blind are feeding the blind—literally. This co-created experience is a source of unrivalled value.

THE CUSTOMER COMMUNITY AS CO-CREATOR OF VALUE

Think back to the last ballgame you attended—people might have been in two camps, each cheering for their favorite team, but for participants in the crowd, the value co-created by the spectators and derived from the game experience far surpasses the value of watching the same game at home. Now imagine how magnificent it would be if you could bring the anticipation and excitement related to the game experience into your own home. Impossible? Fantasy football

---

EXHIBIT 9-3   The Blind Feeding the Blind at Dans le Noir?

Dans le Noir? offers a unique sensory experience of a very different kind—a restaurant where attention shifts from food to a sense of adventure and the focus shifts from vanity to practicality. This is a restaurant where everything happens in total darkness—thick, velvet blackout curtains ensure you can't see at all. The waiters are blind, and therefore you are in quite capable hands.

The experience involves maximum participation of four of the five senses: touch, smell, hearing, taste. Sight is strictly not allowed. Other rules regarding what is prohibited include no mobile phones (they emit light), no smoking (or cigarette lighters), no watches (a potential source of illumination), no loud talking, no moving around without the help of a waiter, no gesticulating with cutlery, no offense taken when someone touches you unexpectedly.

As a matter of fact, physical contact is a requirement; patrons move around with their hands on the shoulders of the person in front, so as not to trip and fall. As for eating with a knife and fork—it makes a lot more sense to figure out what's on your plate with your fingers (i.e., what does it feel like?) before you taste it, and of course to transport whatever it is in the direction of your mouth, because it is difficult to get or keep it on a spoon. Refilling everyone's wine glasses is another intriguing challenge in dexterity. Even conversations take on a different meaning in the absence of facial clues.

In the absence of sight, taste becomes much more potent and is further enhanced through the tactile experience. The very brave can opt for the surprise menu; this means you find out what you've had for dinner only after the meal.

This doesn't sound like a great evening out to you? The room seats 58 and is full most nights—its popularity is spreading internationally beyond Paris, London, and Moscow through franchising.

Source: http://www.danslenoir.com/

---

enables sports fanatics to celebrate and share their common interest by providing them with an online area for interaction (see Exhibit 9-4). Apart from inducing fantasy football team participants to watch NFL games regularly, it also reaffirms the relationship between players and fans.

The customer community can also serve as a co-creator of value by acting as customer evangelists; for example, the Harley-Davidson ownership groups (also known as HOGs) actively recruit others to the Harley community and lifestyle—persuading them in the process to purchase one of the many Harley products beyond the actual motorcycles. The manufacturer of the motorcycle has little to do with the brand message when Harley-Davidson's weekend warriors hit the road. Outside of formal events sponsored and organized by the manufacturer, the owners of the Harleys control the image and community around the brand. Other companies that have created outspoken evangelists for the brand include Southwest Airlines, Krispy Kreme, and the Dallas Mavericks. These companies now have a small army of unpaid, but passionate, missionaries who act as a surrogate marketing team for the brand.

Significant potential value can be derived if companies go beyond *giving* customers the tools to manage the relationship with the company—the marketer must

EXHIBIT 9-4   **Fantasy Doesn't Get Any Better Than This**
FantasyFootball.com is an innovative and in-depth fantasy football website where football fanatics can celebrate their passion for the game with others just like them. Devoted fans spread the word and feel compelled to pass information on to others.
The service aggregates information about the NFL from the media, player-agent contacts, and a number of other sources, which is updated 24 hours a day, 7 days a week for the purpose of giving NFL fans an edge in their fantasy football league. The information includes player analysis, up-to-the-minute player projections, pre-season and weekly player rankings, drafting, real-time cheat sheets, and breaking news updates. Different services are included in the three packages: silver, gold, and platinum.
On this FantasyPlanet, NFL devotees can truly live, and share, their fantasy. Fantasy football owners acquire their players through auctions, trade, or other forms of payment. For example, auction dollar values based on a typical 12-team auction league utilize a $200 salary cap (budget).

Source: www.fantasyfootball.com

give customers access to information that allows them to make informed, empowered choices as well as manage the actual experience, thus providing customized value. Smart companies are encouraging participation in their brands—even if that means relinquishing control to some extent. For example, Lucasfilm allowed fans to create their own *Star Wars* videos instead of hitting them with copyright violations.[16] The company actually contributed to fans' efforts by posting sounds (like Darth Vader breathing) and other digital material on its website for fans to share.

THE BRAND IN THE EYES OF ITS BEHOLDER

In 2007 the top five global brands were Google, General Electric, Microsoft, Coca-Cola, and China Mobile (the only non-American company). When impact of the brand on people's lives is considered, the top-five list features Google, Apple, YouTube, Wikipedia, and Starbucks. In Europe the top five brands are IKEA, Skype, Nokia, Zara, and Adidas, while the most loved brands are Disney, Nike, and BMW. Interestingly, the least loved brands are American Express and Citibank—people may use credit cards, but they definitely don't love the brand or the companies who extort high interest rates and fees from them! These rankings are based on a combination of publicly available financial data and interviews with a million consumers worldwide. The brands in the various lists highlight two of the many perplexing questions about brands: What draws us in? What alienates us?

In considering these questions, it is important to remember that people do not view themselves as "consumers." People participate in different experiences as part of daily life; they are not consumers of things! People's lives are multidimensional: they belong to multiple social networks in which they have relationships with friends, family members, colleagues at work, a sexual partner, and so forth. They also have richly textured associations with others based on gender, religion, neighborhood, politics, ethnicity, and common interests (e.g., sport or leisure activities). Behavior and decision making derive from a kaleidoscope of thoughts and emotions that spill over from one context to the next—multiple rationalities[17] blur distinctions between decisions that are economically or noneconomically motivated and consequences of decisions that might have social, political, psychological, or other outcomes associated with them.

When viewed through the prism of the daily life of a person, brands have a certain purpose; they are simply means to achieve ends. The individual doesn't care about the brand itself—at a basic level it fulfills a personal need, want, wish, or desire. For instance, people "buy products because they need them, e.g., an inexpensive Chevy simply to go back and forth. They buy products because they want them, e.g., a BMW because it makes a strong statement about their success. They buy products they wish for, e.g., a Porsche because it is a symbol of automobile perfection. They buy products they desire, e.g., a PT Cruiser because it takes them back to their childhood."[18] Along this continuum of wants, needs, wishes, and desires, people's interest in brands are threefold: (1) they seek brands that make the humdrum of everyday existence more meaningful; (2) they long for memorable experiences that captivate them in sensory, affective, and creative ways; and (3) they look for brands to connect them with others in different spheres of their lives.

To marketers, a brand that is "loved" leads to brand loyalty, which makes their job easier: loyalty leads to repeat purchase, which in turn enhances corporate financial performance.[19] However, despite marketers' best efforts to carve out a brand personality and brand personas, people don't perceive brands as being humanlike. Emotions cannot be glued to them; instead emotions are aroused when the brand serves its intended purpose and meets/exceeds expectations. This section explores the repurposing of the brand from the individual's perspective. The shift in purpose that demarcates transitions in Figure 9-1 involves a change from a mark on the product (i.e., an identity, trust, or solution) to a mark in the minds and hearts of people (idea, story, or emotion), from something related to the product's functionality to something that is personally meaningful. People's perceptions of brands result from a sense of self and possibilities that moves the individual further up Maslow's hierarchy of needs toward self-actualization. The brand is a source of upliftment, relaxation, excitement, and entertainment as it becomes intimately connected with the psyche of society (culture and icons) and human beings (dreams, aspirations, sense of belonging)—a cultural property to be shared, (re)mixed, and (re)constituted.

Thus, regardless of the brand's specific utility value or purpose, the brand is a source of potential functional, interpersonal, experiential, emotional, psychological, and sociocultural value, all of which are associated with its instrumental value in terms of personal needs, wants, wishes, and desires. But values are not static. People are active creatures with constantly changing demands, values, and experiences during a lifetime. These changes are reflected in the way they live and in what, where, and how they buy. The brand's meaning cannot be assigned by the

FIGURE 9-2 The Lived Space of Individuals' Interactions with Brands

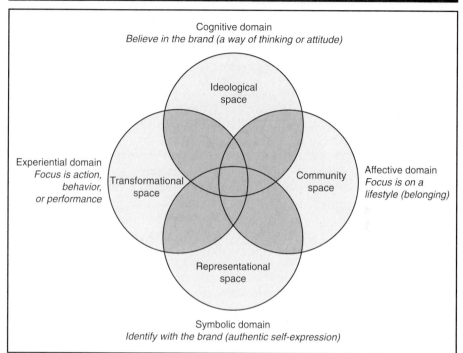

brand owner; it is uniquely crafted by the brand's beholder as part of any number of touch points in his or her life. Figure 9-2 depicts four different spaces in an individual's life: representational space; transformational space; ideological space; and reciprocal space. Together, these four spaces contribute to an individual's directly lived space—an in-between space that is a hybrid environment around the people involved. The four spaces form two opposite pairs: the first pair refers to conception and perception (i.e., ideological space and community space); the second pair contrasts structure and agency (i.e., representational space and transformational space).

The brand's *place* has changed from being positioned in our minds as a trustmark, a place in our hearts as a lovemark, as a sensation in our bodies, as an experience in our daily existence, to a hybrid of four multidimensional *spaces*. Whereas *place* refers to something (somewhere) fixed, *space* is something we can explore, seemingly forever—new exciting experiences, the unknown, and the not-yet-meaningful.[20] Spatial metaphors are used here to facilitate the discussion of how people dynamically generate meaningful spaces to inhabit.[21] The four spaces do not represent either-or propositions. These spaces morph as people move between them based on the most salient aspects of life (always in a process of becoming): in between the different life worlds that are imposed institutionally and the lived space. It underscores the fact that people transform information into action in an enactive, emerging process driven by feelings that interact with thoughts and actions. The remainder of this section is organized around these four spaces to illustrate the complexity and dynamics underlying a brand's potential roles in people's lives.

REPRESENTATIONAL SPACE (SYMBOLIC DOMAIN)

People constantly seek a sense of identity to reaffirm their individuality. Self-narratives play an interesting role in the ongoing (re)construction of identities in search of a consistency of self-conception and "the self-telling of life narratives achieve the power to structure perceptual experience, to organize memory, to segment and purpose-build the very events of a life, in the end, we become the autobiographical narratives by which we 'tell about' our lives."[22] The narrative provided by the brand is a way in which people "construct themselves"—brand narratives imitate their experiences, and in turn their experiences start to imitate the brand narratives, giving life a sense of meaning and direction. For instance, brands can suggest traits such as being passionate and compassionate (properties of the heart), creativity and discipline (aspects of the mind), and agility (properties of the body).

Our dreams and desires are no longer articulated by JFK nor generated through personal epiphanies—they are now the intellectual currency of Pepsi and Diesel.
—SCOTT NEWBURY

The brand moves beyond being a product identifier to become a personal signifier and social text—a "symbol of who I am"—with a meaning that is easily understood by others. Brands like Diesel and Adidas have become a means of self-expression through personalization and exist as symbols in popular culture with their meanings contingent on a particular cultural context. People experience themselves as being provocative through Diesel's association with provocation as symbolized in its advertising campaigns. In the case of the MG brand subculture, MG owners gain a sense of authenticity via the object, its ownership, driving experiences, and interactions with others in the MG community. The social context of this representational space is an important part of gaining acceptance and validation in social networks. The brand is, therefore, a creator of lifestyle worlds—they represent who you are.

IDEOLOGICAL SPACE (COGNITIVE DOMAIN)

Increasingly, people make a cultural and political statement with the brands they purchase, often in opposition to the dominant order—a kind of philosophy on social life. For example, people strive to impart subversive views and unseat the establishment when they purchase an Apple computer instead of a Dell PC or Microsoft's software. Similarly, the act of driving a Toyota Prius instead of a Ford Expedition is viewed as an ideological gesture. From the sneakers on your feet to the toaster in your kitchen to the vodka in your martini to the carrier for your flight to London—Reebok (*not* Nike), Philips (*not* Braun), Absolut Vodka (*not* Smirnoff), Virgin Atlantic (*not* British Airways)—the brands you choose make a statement about what you think. The binding glue in these ideational *memes,* or "self-replicating patterns of information" in which ideas are communicated in memes, is this: "just as genes propagate themselves in the gene pool by leaping from body to body via sperm or eggs, so memes propagate themselves in the meme pool by leaping from brain to brain via a process which, in the broad sense, can be called imitation."[23] The brand is therefore a powerful conveyor of ideas.

The great brands of this end of the century are those that have succeeded in conveying their vision by questioning certain conventions, whether it's Apple's humanist vision, which reverses the relationship between people and machines; Benetton's libertarian vision, which overthrows communication conventions; Microsoft's progressive vision, which topples bureaucratic barriers; or Virgin's anticonformist vision, which rebels against the powers that be.

—JEAN-MARIE DRU

In her book[24] Naomi Klein protests the colonization of public spaces by branding processes that insidiously saturate and ultimately dominate cultural production. Iconic brands such as Coca-Cola, Madonna, Mountain Dew, the VW Beetle, and Corona have social lives and cultural significance that are similar to icons such as Nelson Mandela, Steve Jobs, Sam Walton, Oprah Winfrey, Martha Stewart, Michael Jordan, Muhammad Ali, Andy Warhol, Bruce Springsteen, John Wayne, and Woody Allen. Cultural icons dominate our world. The iconic brand acts as a social or cultural authority that creates and/or reflects its values. The example of Snapple[25] in Exhibit 9-5 shows how a brand inserts itself into the social rituals of everyday life.

EXHIBIT 9-5   Snapple's Critique of the Establishment

By 1994, Snapple had generated plenty of buzz, was considered by many to be a cool trendsetting brand, and had even attracted a hardy band of followers who formed an occasional Snapple community. But these viral effects were artifacts of the brand's success, not causes. Snapple earned these desirable qualities because the brand pushed a compelling new identity myth. Snapple's company of amateurs championed a fantastic populist alternative to the growing disgust with the new-economy labor market and the elites in government and business who were installing it. Consumers loved Snapple for acting this way, talked about the brand, considered it ahead of its time compared with conventional soft drinks, and even enjoyed gathering sporadically with people who felt the same.

The buzz that Snapple generated was the consequence of the power of its myth. Simply getting people to talk about something—say, repeat a catch phrase from an ad—is not a particularly noteworthy event. Most such talk quickly fades from memory and, regardless, becomes detached from the meaning of the story. What sticks are stories that affect how people think about themselves in the world. The problem with the viral model is that it assumes that any communication is good as long as it's retold. Much more important, however, is what people remember and use symbolically in their everyday lives. Snapple didn't just get people talking. Instead, the brand served as a role model, a rather absurd one, which provided a silly but meaningful critique of corporate life in the early 1990s.

Source: Holt, D. B. (2004). *How brands become icons: The principles of cultural branding.* Boston: Harvard Business School Press.

TRANSFORMATIONAL SPACE (EXPERIENTIAL DOMAIN)

Within the representational space mentioned earlier, the individual celebrates being him- or herself. In the transformational space, people engage in experiential encounters that have a life-transforming effect on their personal and social wellness. People make lasting changes to something of importance to them at a physical, emotional, or mental level. They view brands as a means to an end. However, if the brand facilitates achievement of aspirations in the quest for self-actualization, rather than merely offering the means to do so, its value increases substantially. Nowhere is the need for changes in behavior more prominent than in the nourishment of our bodies. Food is a fundamental part of our well-being, but the definition of what constitutes healthy eating habits keeps changing, making it difficult to keep up. Whole Foods aims to change this. The Whole Foods brand makes it easy to feel good about what you eat amid all the pressures of today's fast-paced life that adversely affect people's ability to eat balanced meals on a regular basis. By giving people convenient access to foods high in nutritional value, Whole Foods closes that gap between people's aspirations and their lifestyles.

Another dimension of the transformational space relates to fantasies—or an alternative reality. These fantasies might be the result of people seeking notoriety, success, a sense of importance, or an adrenaline rush. For example, people fantasize about an alternate reality such as irresistible sex appeal, omnipotence, dominance, and so forth—characteristics reminiscent of the special powers that superheroes are endowed with. These fantasies are no longer restricted to the two-dimensional world of a Hollywood movie. Nor are they the selling points of advertisements. People now have various options for transformational experiences that make these fantasies a reality through interactive video games and virtual worlds like Second Life—offering people the power to transform reality.

RECIPROCAL SPACE (AFFECTIVE DOMAIN)

The reciprocal space is set up through interactions, connections, and encounters within a social niche of like-minded others through voluntary associations or communal relationships where perspectives are negotiated and translated. Additionally, interactive gathering spaces that are formed around self-interests in associative relationships play an important role in honing particular skills through peer-to-peer forums that connect and inspire them. The meaning and purpose of reciprocal spaces are derived from a sense of belonging to a community that shares similar lifestyle and common patterns of behavior such as being in a band, being a skateboarder, or being in the group of people who fly with JetBlue. For example, when speaking to a Saturn dealer or owner, both will tell you without a hint of irony that they belong together: "we are the Saturn family." A group formed around a specific cause based on certain values also falls in this space.

A brand can become part of a social network if it resonates with its members' preferences and shared values. Exhibit 9-6 provides some details about the community formed around the Starbucks brand—a *third place*—a place that is not work or home but where people gather as part of an everyday ritual of drinking

---

EXHIBIT 9-6   The Starbucks Fix

We have identified a "third place".
And I really believe that sets us apart.
The third place is that place that's not work or home.
It's the place our customers come for refuge.
                                         —NANCY ORSOLINI (DISTRICT MANAGER, STARBUCKS)

Starbucks transformed coffee from its traditional role as a daily habit to a "luxury" ritual of personal significance—and the rise of a coffee culture at $3 per cup. Interestingly, it did this by creating a coffee shop in which the coffee being sold is of secondary importance. Instead people see it as social place between home and work where one goes to relax or refresh—the Starbucks fix. Coffee shops now come in two flavors: the local and Starbucks.

The experience of the Starbucks brand includes its own community, language, and culture. Although coffee is at the center of this experience, Starbucks' brand equity is derived from its black-aproned employees who love coffee and what they do, and its loyal customers—its philosophy of "everything matters" has created a context in which the company can sell products beyond coffee such as music. Starbucks has shunned mass media advertising and instead relies on "coffee shop" talk to spread the word, together with synergy of the brand, its logo, and its story all over the world.

Source: www.starbucks.com

---

coffee. There is very little logic behind the "coffeehouse" community: the service is not quick, location is not the most convenient, nor is it the best-tasting coffee despite being rather expensive. Yet Starbucks has not only survived, but prospered, because of a unique set of values that exceeds its coffee offering.

This poses an interesting question. What do Apple, Nike, and Harley-Davidson have in common with the Hell's Angels and the Unification Church? These organizations all exemplify the characteristics of a tight community or cult; they consider themselves to be different from mainstream society in some fundamental way. A cult brand is one "for which a group of customers exhibit a great devotion or dedication. Its ideology is distinctive and it has a well-defined and committed community. It enjoys exclusive devotion (i.e., not shared with another brand in the same category), and its members often become voluntary advocates."[26] Other examples of very successful cult brands include *Star Trek,* Oprah Winfrey, Volkswagen Beetle, Jimmy Buffett, Vans Shoes, and Linux. The dynamic underlying these tribal-like communities is kinship—a sense of belonging.

THE MAGIC OF MARKETING JUJU[27]

Finally, we get to the question that started our discussion. What is marketing juju—and how do we get it? Marketing juju is the holy grail of marketing—the elusive and much-sought-after elixir that promises the brand everlasting vitality. Marketing juju will protect the brand against the marketing vampire that wants to suck the life out of it on behalf of the competitor. The good news is that marketing juju doesn't cost a lot of moola—all you need is plenty of creative mojo! This juju is derived from a brand that has a radiant sense, motivational qualities, and a deeply mythic allure that touches the human spirit. People associate this juju with a philosophical or ideological ideal that creates a spirit of camaraderie and celebration and a feeling of unity. Juju operates at the ideational level around ideals such as egalitarianism, collective responsibility, sharing, and group solidarity, very much in the spirit of the 19th-century French author Alexandre Dumas's *The Three Musketeers*, with their motto: "all for one, and one for all."

The not-so-good news is that there is no secret formula; there is no pixie dust and no magic wand for getting the special marketing juju associated with the world's most enduring brands. While there are some common threads in terms of principles underlying their success, there are many more differences. Moreover, as discussed in this chapter, brand management just isn't what it used to be. People buy things because they are driven by feelings of happiness and a sense of accomplishment, not because of brand identities and personalities or award-winning advertisements. Value is uniquely co-created by people based on personal meaning derived from the experience of the brand. These values relate to outcomes such as self-expression in a representational space, association with social groups in a reciprocal space, hybrid experiences in a transformational space, and political and cultural statements as part of an ideological space. So what is a marketer to do?

Samuel Koch, founder of Boston Beer, asserts that[28] the answers have to come from the part of you that is governed by spirit and metaphor and imagery and mythology. Instead of sitting down with Newton's laws and looking for gaps he could fill, Einstein dreamed of time, space and movement in new ways. This statement makes three important points about the branding challenge facing marketers:

1. The desire to make meaning out of something is universal. People search for patterns, looking for personal insight or a revelation. However, not everything is important enough, memorable enough or valuable enough to spend time making sense or meaning of it.

2. Despite all its rigor and quantification, no marketing research study will identify the gaps between what people have and what they really would like to have. That is only possible by being part of people's lived space—where they work, live, love, learn, and play.

3. The language of emotion is associated with myth, metaphor, mystery, magic, meaning, and memory. When people are moved, they act. People make decisions with their hearts, but to reach their hearts you have to go through their minds to make new connections to facts and feelings that lie beneath the surface. This requires imagination, inspiration, intuition, and inspiring ideas.

Brands must address needs, wants, wishes, and desires. Powerful and imaginative ideas matter—ideas that are "made to stick."[29] These ideas are simple, unexpected, concrete, credible, and emotional, and they tell stories.

The entrepreneurial imperative requires that marketers view their brands and people differently than others do. Think about Apple's spirit of liberty regained. Exhibit 9-7 elaborates on the philosophy that underlies Apple's "Think Different" attitude. This slogan gives expression to something in the collective psyche; a universal truth—something everyone can identify with.[30] The idea embedded in the

---

EXHIBIT 9-7   Apple's "Think Different" Universe

In the 30 years since its founding, the Apple brand has transcended each of the transitions in Figure 9-1—it is a trustmark, experience, lovemark, cultural icon, cult, story, and more—in a transformation from a tiny niche PC maker into a high-end consumer electronics and services company. In so doing, it has become an important part of people's lives—it promises fulfillment of ideals and fantasies. The brand exudes emotions associated with paradox, elevating it to cultural icon status. Successfully navigating its struggle against dominant and oppressive forces (e.g., Microsoft), Apple acts as a role model of behaviors that leads to self-actualization.

Apple's marketing juju revolves around a vibrant idea: Think Different. This purposeful mindset underpins everything the company does: advertising campaigns (ordinary people can become extraordinary and creative), the types of hardware it makes (stimulating tools associated with self-expression through sounds and images), the way it communicates with internal and external audiences (ownership of the brand that can be shared with others), and the way Apple brings its products to market (radical new retail experiences). Apple does what its slogan promises—Think Different.

During the pioneering years of the personal computer, the Macintosh was a rebel of the industry that refused to bow to the growing power of Microsoft Windows. It was preferred and loved by highly demanding graphic designers, who relished in its leading-edge features.

Much later, the iMac appeared on the scene, now compatible with Windows, proving the PCs don't have to be grey and boring like all the other beige boxes on the market. Instead, it offered user-friendly designs that were also aesthetically pleasing to the user's operation. The iMac was positioned as a tool for creative minds, not a computer. In sharp contrast to Microsoft, Apple nurtures it relationships with customers, which has resulted in a fiercely loyal community of evangelical users (i.e., the Apple-heads, Mac-heads, and Mac-faithfuls).

A few years after the iMac's success, the iPod ushered in a new millennium living by a new set of rules. The iPod and its complementary iTunes download website became the industry leader, and a cultural phenomenon, at a time when digital music formats were struggling to move beyond a CD that is sold through retailers in the old physical world. While traditional players in the music industry were battling Napster's free but illegal downloads, Apple's iPod became the top-selling portable MP3 player, despite not being the first digital music player on the market. Apple's iPod community creates their own advertisements for the product to demonstrate their devotion. A website allows iPod owners to transform their photos into iPod ads, which can then be printed onto T-shirts, greeting cards, and other novelty items. No longer subjected to the play lists of major corporations, the spaces of culture were reclaimed as a largely private and mobile experience in which the entire digital world is in your hand—giving the Apple brand its magical quality and marketing juju.

Sources: www.apple.com; www.lovemarks.com

"Think Different" slogan has a multitude of potential interpretations and possibilities; it stays constant through its emotional connection with people and changes with emergent properties of products; it reinforces the brand's past and present meaning, while realizing its future potential. This is the creative mojo that keeps the Apple brand oozing with marketing juju. The abstract ideal behind Apple's campaign is a promise to transform the status quo on behalf of all.

Summary and Conclusions

The changes in realities discussed in this section prompt a reexamination of the role of a marketer and a repurposing of marketing activities. Whereas product-centric managers consider cost, efficiency, quality and product variety as the primary sources of value, brand-centric managers treat their brands as intellectual property that needs to be controlled, communicated, and leveraged to optimize brand equity by gaining the trust and affinity of consumers. In an era of customized solutions, accumulated company expertise supplemented and complemented by product features and functions have become the core source of value added. The marketer's concern here is customer management—customers are viewed as investments, and the customer base is an asset that can be valued similar to any other financial asset. In experience-based marketing, the emphasis is on interactivity, connectivity, creativity, integration, personalization, and adaptability. The marketer is no longer a brand manager or chief marketing officer (CMO), but the chief experience officer (CXO) involved in community experience development. In the marketing theater, the CXO uses company offerings as props to orchestrate memorable events for customers—memory of the experience itself becomes both the expression of the brand and a tool for marketing it.[31] When the customer participates in an experience that is transformational (e.g., education), the value created far exceeds the direct inputs. The next stage puts the marketer in charge of the emotion transportation business as brands become tools for attraction, intimacy, and seduction.

This brings us to the current situation, where brands are being "hijacked" by consumers and marketers are no longer sole authors of brand image or message content. To aggravate the situation, proliferation of media options and bouts of anti-consumption continue unabated. Moreover, societal needs in the developing world do not share the first world's appreciation of brand value. To make things worse, American brands are suffering from low-priced made-in-China alternatives that are flooding the market and severely eroding existing brand equity. As players in an increasingly global market, verbal and nonverbal language differences are affecting the marketing of products. Apart from different meanings in other cultures, changing norms are affecting meaning and values within people's own cultures. Some brands have embraced the ambiguity: "Red Bull soda combines hedonism and health, energy and enervation, and the injurious and the innocuous. Prada's recently launched perfume is predicated on a plurality of personalized appeals ('I am the first and the last. I am the honored one and the scorned one. I am the wife and the virgin'). Madonna, meanwhile, adopts and abandons every image imaginable, from sexually ambiguous virago to Kabala-espousing supermom."[32]

Functional excellence and instrumental utility are fast becoming necessary, albeit, not sufficient, attributes of a successful brand. In this new and ever-evolving brand world, marketers must do far more than develop a unique, vivid, and meaningful identity for the brand. People are not interested in companies' efforts to position their products/services as authentic—they don't want to have their perceptions "managed." In this era of brand democratization, consumers co-produce brand meanings. Yet, as brand guru Wally Olins asserts, "[g]reat brands are like amoebae or plasticine. They can be shaped, twisted, and turned in all sorts of ways yet still remain recognizable."[33] Marketers must harness, rather than challenge, consumer power. If marketers and brands are to be part of people's lives, then it behooves marketers to find wisdom—not emotion, sensuality, and mystery, but meaning derived from eternal truths.

When meaning is transformed to the symbolic, its potential broadens because it can be (re)interpreted in different contexts that draw on archetypal stories, characters, beliefs, and values that exist in the collective unconscious. A brand archetype that can transform into an icon is important, especially in global brand management. Marketers are realizing that finding suitable and respected in-crowd influentials[34] for different niches must replace the one-size-fits-all model of before. A human brand offers significant potential as an endorser by enhancing personal feelings of autonomy and relatedness. Like people, "brands have not only a genetic code but also karma."[35] The entrepreneurial imperative is more than just a new way of thinking about marketing; it is a way of doing marketing that requires affective capital and creative leverage. It requires care, advocacy, persistence, respect, and dedication. Think of Richard Branson (Virgin), who is on a self-imposed Robin Hood mission to look after the little guys by taking on the big guys. Entrepreneurial marketers understand how to build a family of strangers, and realize that it is about community building, not brand management.

Key Terms

- trustmark
- brand experience management
- lovemark
- cult brands
- iconic brands
- customer evangelists
- cultural icons
- marketing juju

Questions

1. Why is branding important when brand loyalty is now nearly nonexistent?
2. What is the relevance of positioning in the contemporary brand world, which revolves around creating an unforgettable customer experience?
3. How does the co-creation experience in a Build-a-Bear Workshop or on a Southwest Airlines flight differ from the self-help service transaction such as

online banking through Bank of America or Citibank? Both of these involve the consumer as a co-producer of the transaction, yet there are fundamental differences between the two.

4. Are marketers overestimating the powers of branding? Do you believe brands have the powers ascribed to them in this chapter (e.g., as experience provider or as a lovemark)? Can brands create social and/or cultural values?

   a. If your answer is yes to either of these questions, explain your answer(s) by giving examples of brands that have managed to do this.

   b. If your answer is no to either of these questions, explain why you believe brands fail to achieve this particular outcome.

   c. Regardless of whether your answer is yes or no, do you think brands *should* shape social and/or cultural values? Why or why not?

5. People's affection for brands seems to have grown, despite warnings by Naomi Klein (an activist) and others that consumers would rise up in protest against corporations whose brands had infiltrated their homes, their schools, and their public spaces.

   a. Where do you personally stand on the prevalence of marketing activities intruding in your personal space?

   b. Can you explain why consumers remain willing to tolerate marketers' intrusions in their private spaces?

   c. Assuming you are interested in becoming a successful marketer yourself, what is the ideal approach for brand communications that respects consumers' call for less intrusion yet still maintain a meaningful connection with current and potential customers?

6. There is an ironic paradox in marketing: the same people who create brands and their advertisements are paying not to be marketed to—in effect creating unbranded spaces in which to spend their private and leisure time. Would you be willing to pay extra if that meant you would not be advertised to?

Resources and References

1. Swartz, B. (2004). *The paradox of choice: Why less is more.* New York: HarperCollins.
2. Pitt, L. F., Watson, R. T., Berthon, P., Wynn, D., & Zinkhan, G. (2006). The penguin's window: Corporate brands from an open-source perspective. *Journal of the Academy of Marketing Science* 3(2): 115–127.
3. Macrae, C., & Uncles, M. D. (1997). Rethinking brand management: The role of "brand chartering." *Journal of Product & Brand Management* 6(1): 64–77.
4. Source unknown.
5. Roberts, K. (2007). *The lovemarks effect: Winning in the consumer revolution.* New York: PowerHouse Books.
6. Shimp, T. A., & Madden, T. J. (1988). Consumer-object relations: A conceptual framework based analogously on Sternberg's triangular theory of love. In M. J. Houston, ed., *Advances in consumer research*, vol. 15 (pp. 163–168). Provo, UT: Association for Consumer Research.
7. Schmitt, B. H. (1999). *Experiential marketing: How to get customers to sense, feel, think, act, relate.* New York: Free Press.

8. Roberts.
9. Ibid.
10. Derrida, J. (1982). *White mythology: Metaphor in the text of philosophy*. Trans. A. Bass. Chicago: University of Chicago Press (Original work published 1972).
11. Godin, S. (2006). *All marketers are liars: The power of telling authentic stories in a low-trust world.* New York: Portfolio.
12. Warner, F. (2001, July). Don't shout, listen. *Fast Company* (49): 130. Accessed November 14, 2007, http://www.fastcompany.com/magazine/49/bestpractice.html.
13. Roberts, p. 34.
14. Pitt et al.
15. Ibid.
16. Ibid.
17. Ettlinger, N. (2003). Cultural economic geography and a relational and microspace approach to trusts, rationalities, networks and change in collaborative workplaces. *Journal of Economic Geography* 3: 145–172.
18. Kaden, B. (2006, March 20). Can you tap into customers' desires to give your brand a purpose? Accessed November 14, 2007, http://www.customerthink.com/article/give_your_brand_purpose_ tap_into_customer_desire.
19. Aaker, D., & Jacobson, R. (2001). The value relevance of brand attitude in high-technology markets. *Journal of Marketing Research* 38(4): 485–494.
20. Tuan, Y. F. (1977). *Space and place: The perspective of experience.* London: Edward Arnold.
21. Lefebvre, H. (1991). *The production of space.* Cambridge, MA: Blackwell.
22. Bruner, J. (1987). Life as narrative. *Social Research* 54(1): 11–32.
23. Dawkins, R. (1989). *The selfish gene.* New York: Oxford University Press, p. 192.
24. Klein, N. (2002). *No logo: No space, no choice, no jobs.* New York: Picador.
25. Holt, D. B. (2004). *How brands become icons: The principles of cultural branding.* Boston: Harvard Business School Press.
26. Atkin, D. (2004). *The culting of brands: When customers become true believers.* New York: Portfolio.
27. The word *juju* is associated with an aura, energy, karma, or some other magical property. It originates from West Africa. See http://www.randomhouse.com/wotd/index.pperl?date=20010510 for background information.
28. Hill, S., & Rifkin, G. (1999). Radical marketing: From Harvard to Harley, lessons from ten that broke the rules and made it big. New York: Harper Collins
29. Heath, C., & Heath, D. (2007). *Made to stick: Why some ideas survive and others die.* New York: Random House.
30. Roberts.
31. Pine, J., & Gilmore, J. (1999). *The experience economy.* Boston: Harvard Business School Press.
32. Brown, S. (1999). Retro-marketing: Yesterday's tomorrows, today! *Marketing Intelligence and Planning* 17(7): 363–376.
33. Brown, S. (2005). Fail better! Samuel Beckett's secrets of business and branding success. *Business Horizons* 49(2): 161–169.
34. Weimann, G. (1994). *The influentials: People who influence people.* Albany: State University of New York Press.
35. Bedbury, S. (2002). *A new brand world: Eight principles for achieving brand leadership in the 21st century.* New York: Viking.

CHAPTER 10

LESSONS FROM THE RED QUEEN

"Well, in our country," said Alice, still panting a little "you'd generally get to somewhere else—if you run very fast for a long time, as we've been doing."

"A slow sort of country!" said the Queen. "Now, here, you see, it takes all the running you can do, to keep in the same place. If you want to get somewhere else, you must run at least twice as fast as that."

—LEWIS CARROLL (IN *THROUGH THE LOOKING GLASS*)

THE RED QUEEN EFFECT

The contest for survival[1] is often referred to as the "Red Queen's race," named after a character in Lewis Carroll's *Through the Looking Glass*[2] (a sequel to *Alice's Adventures in Wonderland*). In this novel, Alice comes across the Red Queen—a life-size, animated chess piece—who relentlessly runs faster and faster, never stopping. There is a moment when Alice breathlessly comments that everyone in the domain of the Red Queen seems to be perpetually running, and yet the faster she runs, the more she tends to stay in the same place relative to other fast-moving and uncertain activities in her environment.

Foxes and rabbits (i.e., predators and prey) provide a simple illustration of the Red Queen effect. The race for survival of these two unrelated species will likely be asymmetric.[3] The fox wants to catch the rabbit, but the rabbit in turn needs to escape and clearly has more motivation for this outcome than the fox. The faster the rabbit runs, the faster the fox runs. Rabbits and foxes are competing for the same resource (rabbit flesh) in a zero-sum game according to game theory. The sum of resources that can be gained or lost is constant; what is lost by the rabbit is gained by the fox, and vice versa. Is it possible for the rabbit and the fox to ever escape the Red Queen effect? We will return to the plight of the fox and the rabbit later when we consider the different options open to each of them.

The Red Queen runs and runs and runs—relentlessly. Chances are you can identify with this feeling. Like the Red Queen, we live in a world of breathtaking change as a result of ever faster cycles of innovation and competition. In fact, according to Klaus Schwab (head of the World Economic Forum),[4] "we are moving from a world in which the big eat the small to a world in which the fast eat the slow." Let us consider for a moment what the implications of the Red Queen effect are for the marketing world, especially in a time of increasing velocity of innovation and knowledge generation. Margins are shrinking; competition is becoming ever more fierce; more nimble competitors are entering markets; the nature of competition keeps changing; new technologies are appearing unabatedly; and amid all this, new business models are emerging, mutating, and becoming dominant. Red Queen competition is "an ongoing process wherein competition triggers adaptive learning among organizations, making them more viable so that they compete more strongly, which in turn triggers adaptive learning in their rivals."[5]

The Red Queen effect can be especially deleterious when new rivals enter the market. While incumbents struggle to improve efficiencies, upstarts and new entrants capture a niche in existing markets or create new ones. For example, the MP3 phenomenon changed the music industry by enabling people to download songs or entire albums over the Internet. Peer-to-peer file sharing cost the music industry billions of dollars, and the long-term impact left the incumbents in the music industry in shambles. The rules of the game were changed irrevocably. Competition did not emanate from a traditional counterpart, but a new rival (this is also discussed as part of the "fish tank phenomenon" in Chapter 14). Moreover, the established companies failed to respond to technology changes—at the time they deemed the new competitors to be mere imposters and the initial customers as irrelevant, not realizing the significance of the shifts. Then Apple entered the music industry! Not one music company executive had foreseen this move from a "computer company."

Falling behind means you have to adapt in creative ways to keep up with the faster runners who shape your world. Marketers must continually evolve—whether to create change or to respond to it. As the old adage has it, "innovate or die." But how? The remainder of this chapter attempts to answer the question of how to overcome the Red Queen effect—in which improving your situation merely increases the competition, rather than giving you an advantage. The Red Queen problem is addressed metaphorically as it opens up possibilities that are not limited by rational or literal interpretations.

CRAFTING A STRATEGY IS AN EXERCISE IN ENTREPRENEURSHIP

The Red Queen just keeps running faster. To better understand how to escape the Red Queen effect, let us examine some basic questions of strategy. What is *strategy?* The word is often used broadly to refer to a plan, concept, course of

TABLE 10-1 The Means, Ends, and Ways Triumvirate of Strategy

$$\text{Strategy} = f\,(\text{Ends} + \text{Ways} + \text{Means})$$

where

f = function

Ends = objective (the desired end state or goal)

Ways = courses of action (options, methods, or approaches to reach the ends)

Means = the resources (people, money, equipment) to be utilized in the way to achieve the ends

action, or some "idea" of a direction in which to proceed. The essence of strategy is the creation and exercise of choice based on a preference for a particular future state or condition.[6] What does success look like? As indicated in Table 10-1, strategy addresses the ends, means, and ways triumvirate:[7] What are the ends you are trying to achieve? What means can help you achieve your ends? What are the different ways to achieve your ends? Strategy is about how (the way) leadership will use the power (the means or resources) available to it to exercise control over sets of circumstances and geographic locations to achieve specified objectives (the ends, goals, or desired outcome).

Although strategy is conveniently expressed as an equation in Table 10-1, it is not simple or clear-cut—it is a constantly moving target, dynamic and emergent. Strategy aims to manage the present, while creating the future. Strategy provides direction—it is by nature proactive and anticipatory; it attempts to control rather than react to the environment. It starts with the end in mind; analysis of the end state yields objectives that will lead to the desired end state. Strategy is risky because of the many unknowns and the potential for failure, either by failing to achieve objectives or failing to secure an advantage over adversaries. The strategist attempts to create strategic degrees of freedom and mitigate risk by balancing the objectives sought (ends), the methods to pursue the objectives (ways), and the resources available (means). Objectives are expressed as verbs and provide purpose, focus, and justification for the actions embodied in a strategy. Objectives must be SMART: specific, measurable, achievable, realistic, and time-stamped.

The three overarching objectives[8] of strategy are to create value (why), avert imitation (how), and determine size and scope ambitions (what). Value creation and appropriation lie at the core of the *why* question of strategy, which requires a balance between shareholder interests (i.e., profit maximization) and those of other stakeholders (e.g., customers, community, environment, etc.). Issues related to value creation and performance metrics are addressed in considerable detail in Chapter 16. The *how* question of strategy centers on preventing imitation by others and confers a competitive advantage, whether through differentiation, core competencies, or other mechanisms. Competitive advantage is defined as the ability of a business to derive abnormal profits in a competitive industry based on a value-creating strategy not simultaneously implemented by any current or future competitor. The *what* question of strategy considers organizational size and scope decisions related to two fundamental concerns: the mission or purpose of the organization (what business are we in) and the firm's position in the value network of the industry. A superior market position correlates with superior customer and social value and/or the achievement of lower costs. It is one that resists imitation and results in market dominance and an industry leadership position.

If you get too caught up in the production of information, you drown in the data. . . . You disaggregate everything and tear it apart, but you are never able to synthesize the whole.
—MALCOLM GLADWELL (IN *BLINK*)

In the 1980s the watchwords in strategy were portfolio planning, the experience curve, Porter's five forces, the value chain, and generic strategies that revolved around tools like SWOT (strengths, weaknesses, opportunities, threats) analysis that focused on the impact of external (industry) factors and the internal situation (strategy) of the company. According to Porter's three generic strategies, competitive advantages are derived from differentiation, cost leadership, or focus (cost/differentiation). Strategy formulation represented a conscious act of formulating a strategy (thinking first) and then implementing it (by acting), using factual data and extrapolating from historical trends. The standard solution offered to alleviate the disadvantages of competing on price with products customers perceive as similar is to engage in differentiation strategies. In this case, all firms have an incentive to differentiate with associated price increases, yet because everyone is doing this, the price premium vanishes quickly as everyone gets dragged into the war of attrition. This cycle of differentiation and price fluctuation continues until a competitor attains an exclusive point of differentiation that is difficult to copy or until a new product is introduced. An example of a lasting point of differentiation is the exclusivity agreements Pepsi has with its distributors: if you sell Pepsi, you can't sell Coke, which effectively eliminates Coca-Cola from that part of the market.

The strategic landscape changed dramatically in the 1990s, with the onset of increased turbulence, hypercompetition, radical innovations, new technologies, evolution of the Internet and other related technologies, and increased globalization, among other factors. In a more frenetic world, the classic approach to strategic planning was questioned for not being dynamic enough. A new wave of tools and perspectives dominated strategy: total quality management, reengineering, core competence, competing on capabilities, resource leveraging, learning organizations, innovation, and business models. According to the resource-based view (RBV)[9] that became popular during the 1990s, a company is a collection of tangible and intangible resources (assets and capabilities). These resources do not only refer to money and people but also cover a wide range, which is represented by the PROF-IT acronym in Table 10-2. The strategic imperative of a firm is sustained, superior financial performance,[10] which can be achieved through a sustainable competitive advantage (SCA) from having heterogeneous resources, or resources in combination, that are valuable, rare, and difficult to imitate or substitute.

TABLE 10-2   Sources of and Criteria for Obtaining an SCA

IF		ARE		THEN		IS	
Physical resources (e.g., buildings, equipment, land)							
Relational resources (e.g., customers, suppliers, alliances)		Valuable		COMPETITIVE ADVANTAGE		SUSTAINABLE	
Organizational resources (e.g., policies, culture, databases)		Rare					
Financial resources (e.g., cash, bonds, investments)		Inimitable					
Intellectual & human resources (e.g., employees, sales force prowess)		Organized for exploitation					
Technological resources (e.g., proprietary processes, patents)							

A competitive advantage is sustainable when the advantage resists erosion by a competitor who is unable to duplicate the benefits of the strategy—it must be a unique, rare, difficult-to-copy value-creating strategy. The acronym VRIO in Table 10-2 represents the criteria a resource must adhere to. It should be *valuable* in the sense of potentially contributing to an SCA,[11] *rare* (i.e., few others possess this), *inimitable* (i.e., difficult and costly to copy), and *organized* for exploitation. Imitation can affect value and rarity. Three factors assist in protection against imitation: path dependency (unique historical path), social complexity (complex interaction of factors), and causal ambiguity (difficulty in understanding how something is done).

Conventional strategy making is inconsistent with the discontinuities that have taken, and are taking place. Whereas the traditional marketer considers existing resources when planning strategies that will conserve and maximize use of these resources, in the entrepreneurial world of strategy, the marketer looks for opportunities (ends) first and then searches for resources (means) in pursuit of these opportunities (ends). As shown in Table 10-3, the organizational strategies required to be successful in the 21st century are very different from those required in the 1980s and 1990s. Coping in a rapidly changing world requires increased flexibility, an ability to reduce uncertainty, rapid experimentation, and an ability to improvise. Companies that are locked in a Red Queen race must radically change their business model to stay ahead (see Chapter 7). The answer lies in discovering new ideas, innovating relentlessly, co-evolving collaboratively, and anticipating what customers want and competitors might do. Revolutionary thinking enables organizations to use novel insights to create successful innovations, while topsight (i.e., the ability to see the whole system) and foresight lead to early discovery of patterns that secures first-mover advantages. The nontraditional strategies for achieving an SCA all involve an entrepreneurial mindset and actions that shape the facts of the present into possibilities for the future. Strategic entrepreneurship is currently conceptualized as entrepreneurial action with a

TABLE 10-3 Comparison of Strategies for Creating an SCA	
Traditional Strategies for an SCA	*Entrepreneurial Ways toward an SCA*
• Continued innovation	• Relentless innovation
• Lowest cost producer	• Flexibility/adaptability/speed
• Best made product	• Revolution, renewal, and resilience
• Operational excellence	• Market ownership
• Excellent customer service	• Customer value co-creation
• Enhanced performance	• Entrepreneurial mindset and action
• More convenient locations	• Opportunity obsession
• Most reliable/durable product	• Foresight and topsight
• Product leadership, etc.	

strategic perspective and strategic action with an entrepreneurial mindset such that it "is the integration of entrepreneurial (i.e., opportunity-seeking behavior) and strategic (i.e., advantage-seeking) perspectives in developing and taking actions designed to create wealth."[12]

ESCAPING THE RED QUEEN EFFECT: FIVE LESSONS

The Red Queen keeps running—ever faster. Just to stay in place you have to run very, very fast—and to get anywhere else you have to run even faster. The race between SBC and Verizon, who were running so fast to beat one another in the broadband communications race[13] that neither of them got ahead—provides a timely recent illustration of this effect. In 2005, they spent billions of dollars battling cable companies and new market entrants such as Vonage, Google, Yahoo!, and Skype Technologies. All to no avail. In 2007, any home user can make inexpensive calls through Vonage, using a broadband modem, for half the price of regular landline telephone service. Better still, Skype users can make free phone calls to other Skype users using a simple computer, headset/microphone, and the Skype software program.

Ultimately, the only way out of the Red Queen's race is to run a different one or to play another game. You must know when to break the rules, when to bend the rules, and when to follow the rules; but most importantly, you must know when to change the rules.[14] IKEA broke the rules by challenging the status quo and altering who it was and what it did. Google broke the rules by defining itself as a provider of information and not as a search engine. Other companies have questioned industry orthodoxy and traditional practices, including Dell (built-to-order manufacturing and direct selling without middlemen) and Amazon.com (virtual stores that offer millions of new, used, and collectible items). The marketer must approach strategy with a questioning mind—thinking the unthinkable can nullify the Red Queen effect. When Alice asserts that "one can't believe impossible things," the Queen simply replies, "I daresay you haven't had much practice. When I was your age, I always did it for half an hour a day. Why, sometimes I've believed as many as six impossible things before breakfast."[15] A rational, analytical approach might suggest that it is impossible to triumph, but not if you reverse the thinking—think with your heart and follow with your mind. Be the alternative: turn left, when everyone else is turning right.[16]

[T]he disruption stage is about all-out questioning, about developing new hypotheses and unexpected ideas. It is a journey into uncharted territory, a quest for angles of attack that have never been used before.

—JEAN-MARIE DRU (IN *DISRUPTION*)

The Red Queen will not be ignored and must be confronted. There are multiple ways in which marketers can play a different game that disrupts markets to create the next competitive advantage. In the next section, we consider the lessons marketers can learn to escape the disastrous effect of falling into the trap of a Red Queen race. Five strategies for escaping the Red Queen effect each of which fundamentally alters the basis of competition are shown in Figure 10-1 and discussed in turn. Each of the lessons has a different metaphor from which it derives principles for its strategy: lesson #1 draws on military strategy and guerrilla warfare; lesson #2 draws on principles from judo, such as "push when pulled," as part of a resource leveraging strategy; lesson #3 employs the creativity and improvisational nature of jazz; lesson #4 builds on the principles of co-opetition as it applies to NASCAR, which has become a very popular venue for marketers; and lastly, lesson #5 contrasts shark-infested, red oceans with blue oceans of uncontested potential in new markets that are created using a value innovation strategy.

LESSON #1: EVERY BATTLE IS WON BEFORE IT IS EVER FOUGHT

故曰：知彼知己，百戰不殆；不知彼而知己，一勝一負；不知彼，不知己，每 戰必敗

So it is said that if you know your enemies and know yourself, you will win a hundred times in a hundred battles.
If you only know yourself, but not your opponent, you win one and lose the next.
If you do not know yourself or your enemy, you will always lose.

—SUN-TZU

FIGURE 10-1   Overview of the Five Lessons from the Red Queen

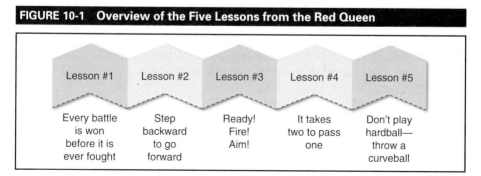

Lesson #1	Lesson #2	Lesson #3	Lesson #4	Lesson #5
Every battle is won before it is ever fought	Step backward to go forward	Ready! Fire! Aim!	It takes two to pass one	Don't play hardball— throw a curveball

The word *strategy* is derived from the Greek word *stratēgos*, which means "general." A famous general who lived in northeastern China about 2,500 years ago, Sun-Tzu was considered an expert in military strategy due to his many victories on the battlefield. His book, *The Art of War*, is a classic and is considered by many to be the authoritative work on strategies and tactics. Sun-Tzu[17] proposes 13 general principles for strategists to follow (not strategy *du jour*). Some of these principles are especially appropriate for crafting a strategy with which to counteract the Red Queen effect. For instance, one of Sun-Tzu's proscriptions is this: "all warfare is based on deception. If your enemy is superior, evade him. If angry, irritate him. If equally matched, fight and if not, split and re-evaluate." This statement refers to 3 of his 13 principles—developing tactics and maneuvers, attacking weak points and leveraging strengths, and using reconnaissance and spies (at least metaphorically for our purposes). It is the combination of the tactical side of strategy in Sun-Tzu's *Art of War* and the principles of guerrilla warfare in *The Little Red Book* by another military strategist, Mao Tse-Tung,[18] that offers very powerful ideas for beating the odds in the game of entrepreneurial strategy.

So what lessons can we learn about strategy from the generals who use unconventional methods to defeat their enemies? Guerrilla warfare marketing strategies are designed to circumvent the need for direct frontal attack such as that engaged in by Pepsi and Coca-Cola in their battle for market share leadership in cola drinks. Instead, the guerrilla strategists use various tactics to wear the opponent down over multiple rounds of attack. The aim is not to conquer but to outlast the opponent—guerrilla forces never win wars, but their adversaries often lose them. This type of strategy entails a series of sporadic attacks in short intensive bursts (i.e., surgical strikes), all of which involve five principles:

1. A guerrilla force is divided into small groups that attack the target at its weak points.

2. They use manifold moves in terms of multiple surge-strike-retreat-hide sequences, with the guerrilla teams disappearing between each strike by blending in with the general population or retreating to a remote place, remaining under the radar to the extent possible.

3. They preserve their resources—they never attack the enemy's main force, but form short-term alliances to gain an edge and never act like a market leader, regardless of the level of success achieved.

4. They use unorthodox methods that are flexible and can adapt to unforeseen situations, whether on the offensive or defensive.

5. They are willing to withdraw quickly and completely. "Know your enemy and know yourself and victory will always be yours" is their dictum.

As with everything else in life, there are upsides and downsides to this type of strategy. One of the disadvantages of a guerrilla approach is that being this ingenious takes time, energy, and creativity. Additionally, some of the guerrilla marketing tactics used by companies involve playing dirty, using deception, or worse, using unethical practices in a dog-eat-dog fight.[19] However, this should not overshadow the many more practical and ethical aspects of guerrilla marketing strategies such as choosing a niche and not making your foray into this chosen market segment known until you are embedded. This is a critical strategy for a new startup or a small business with limited resources that faces a strong competitor. Many large companies apply similar strategies with new-product introductions or when adding a new geographic territory during market development. The weaker company uses small, intermittent assaults on different market segments held by the stronger competitor, typically through special sales promotions (i.e., often more tactical in nature). Instead of trying to outspend the opposition in head-on competition, the weaker company out-thinks the competitor by crafting a value proposition that hits the sweet spot for a specific target market in a focused, high-impact marketing effort.

LESSON #2: STEP BACKWARD TO GO FORWARD

To raise new questions, new possibilities, to regard old problems from a new angle, requires creative imagination and marks real advance in science.

—ALBERT EINSTEIN

The world went from being flat to round and now "the world is flat"[20] again. In a shrinking world where competition happens on Internet time, the margin for error is much smaller than before—a couple of seconds can make the difference between a bumper quarter and a death spiral. Yet timing and tempo are often neglected variables in the marketer's arsenal. The lesson from the Red Queen is clear: rather than trying to run faster, think about pace and rhythm—the moment, and the duration between the moments.[21] Act early. Act quickly. The greatest danger is standing still. Timing really is everything![22]

The second approach for securing an advantage in the Red Queen race is therefore to speed up the rate of response. The takeaway in lesson #1 was that you should know yourself and your enemy so you are able to surprise your opponent and attack when, and where, it is least expected using unorthodox methods in surgical strikes. Lesson #2 builds on this foundation and involves using speed as a strategy. For the marketer, this means making decisions faster to get the right product, to the right customer, with the right price, in the right condition, at the right place, at the right time. It has been noted that market opportunities "have an expiration date, just like a carton of milk. Markets change, and if data are not used within a certain time, the information might go sour. The consequences of going to market based on information past its 'use by' date are low response rates, wasted money."[23] But it isn't merely about being *faster*. Speed as a strategy can also involve active waiting. For instance, you can buy time and space by using the "puppy dog ploy" to avoid provoking an attack that could be fatal.

There are three principles of competition in judo strategy[24] that are extremely insightful when crafting a strategy around speed: rapid movement, balance, and leverage.

1. Rapid movement: Follow through quickly using your smaller size and the ability to move quickly to secure a lead over potential rivals. It is possible to seize

an edge by using agility and speed to undercut a stronger opponent's ability to compete on the basis of size and strength.

2. Balance: Preserve balance is central to avoiding defeat. Balance entails more than just staying on one's feet. In mastering the principle of balance, the marketer must "push when pulled," not by meeting force with force, but by using the opponent's momentum. At first give way, then redirect the force, and use it on your terms to stay on the offensive.

3. Leverage: Understand your opponent's vulnerabilities — the competitor's most important and critical resources — and then force your opponent into a position where the choice is between losing valuable resources and responding to your initiatives. One approach to exercising leverage involves entering into an alliance with the opponent's competitors to avert the possibility of any retaliation.

Another military strategist, Napoleon, understood the importance of combining lesson #1 (element of surprise) and lesson #2 (speed). He brought a number of innovations to the battlefield, three of which are relevant to our discussion: securing a lead over rivals by increasing the army's marching rate and implementing tactics faster than the enemy; organizing his army into self-contained units that could act quickly, each with specialized skills; and attacking the opponent's lines of supply to establish a strong stable position by avoiding a head-on fight. It was important to make the most of any advantage gained because, even here, the Red Queen interfered. As soon as the enemy caught on to Napoleon's strategy, they made adjustments to increase their pace or changed the nature of their approach. This problem brings us to lesson #3.

LESSON #3: READY! FIRE! AIM!

[E]xperimentation . . . in hopes of finding alternatives that improve on old ones . . . thrives on serendipity, risk taking, novelty, free association, madness, loose discipline, and relaxed control.

—J. MARCH

How can we make good decisions with imperfect information? Strategists often don't have the luxury of historical data to guide decisions during the process of exploration and exploitation,[25] especially not when entering new markets or when radical innovations and new technologies are involved. Even when the world seems knowable, there is a wide range of possible outcomes that cannot be predicted. The challenge is to make the best possible strategic decisions despite the reality of living with imperfect information, uncertainty, and ambiguity. Figure 10-2 summarizes the characteristics of three different modes of strategic decisions,[26] each of which is appropriate under different circumstances: analysis, intuition, and improvisation.

Contrary to popular belief, not all decisions are made using a "think first" approach that proceeds in a rational, analytical manner. This is the approach that begins with definition of the problem, then diagnosis of its causes, followed by

FIGURE 10-2 A Comparison of Three Strategic Decision-Making Modes

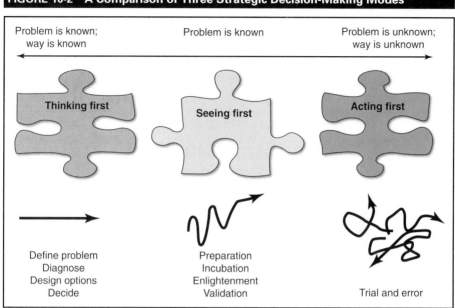

designing possible solutions, choosing a recommended strategy, and finally imple-menting the preferred strategy. It is the typical process involved in case analysis, where the issues are clear and the pros and cons of strategic alternatives can be weighed.

However, it is more likely in the contemporary environment that the prob-lem is known, but too complex, which makes it impossible to analyze and quantify all the potential strategic alternatives. Sometimes when ideas are untested and raw, there is very little to guide decisions apart from an inner voice that proclaims that the information "just doesn't feel right." In a "seeing first" approach, the strategist relies on intuition and uses visualization to create a picture of the fu-ture from a combination of different solutions. The strategist has a vague sense of knowing without being able to verbalize it clearly. This gut instinct is interspersed with moments of illumination that lead to unexpected discoveries along the way to facilitate decision making. A strategist's ability to imagine, synthesize, and in-terpret cannot be replaced by a spreadsheet full of numbers.

The third approach, "doing first," is the improvisational mode where the strategist tries out several things and keeps what works. When the situation is novel, ambiguous, and complex, the strategist relies on a process of "enlightened experimentation"[27] at the edges of understanding and action or practice. Compa-nies favoring an action-oriented approach to strategy facilitate serendipitous dis-covery as they act out the future and then make sense of things retrospectively in a three-step approach to learning: enactment, selection, and retention. This ap-proach is illustrated in Figure 10-3.

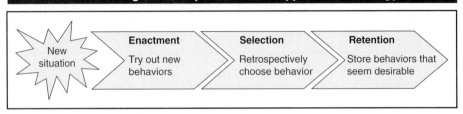

FIGURE 10-3 The Enlightened Experimentation Approach to Strategy

Approaching strategy as improvisation[28] helps companies overcome early misjudgments by having multiple experiments that allow them to take risks without sacrificing everything. In an approach that values action over analysis, "pacesetter companies tended to act before they had a complete plan. . . . [T]hey created the plan by acting. In short, they improvised." The company learns through trial and error in parallel experiments that breed bold action.

In an improvisational setting, actors must shed attitudes and behaviors that stop the action. People cannot be rigid about the right way to do something—'this is how it's always been done.' They have to avoid knee-jerk 'no's' when a particular idea can't be articulated well until it has been demonstrated in action.

Instead of following a rational, analytical approach, "effective improvisation requires dynamic visionaries whose belief is unwavering" in an approach that is proactive, inquisitive, venturesome, and persistent.

Strategy as improvisation reflects many of the characteristics found in jazz: it strives against the status quo and "business as usual" mentality; it reinvents, recreates, and rejuvenates; it encourages imagination and freedom within a set of established guidelines; and it embraces the paradoxes that stimulate creative tensions. Jazz orchestras are exemplars of the interplay between structure and freedom inherent in improvisation as part of coordinated action in an effort to manage the unexpected and unpredictable in complex environments.[29]

Creative work needs the ethos of jazz. . . . A leader will pick the tune, set the tempo, and start the music, define a style. After that it is up to the ensemble to be disciplined and free, wild and restrained, leaders and followers, focused and wide-ranging. . . . to integrate the "voices" in the band without diminishing their uniqueness. The individuals are expected to play solo and together.

—MAX DEPREE (IN *LEADERSHIP JAZZ*)

The underlying premise in the "Ready! Fire! Aim!" approach is entrepreneurial enactment—rational, analytical, causal reasoning is combined with effectual action. Effectual action describes a situation in which known means are used to create innovative alternatives (i.e., "Given my knowledge, my skills and my community, what kinds of actions can I effect?").[30] The entrepreneur's knowledge is enacted with the express purpose of expanding the range of alternatives from the given set of means through novel adaptation that resists existing structural conditions. It stresses the importance of playfulness, experimentation, and intuition in strategic action. Although prompted by an event, action is emergent, not a conscious decision to act.[31] Strategy as improvisation involves acting first and thinking later such that "execution is analysis and implementation is formulation."[32] This is also considered a grassroots model of strategy formation, with strategies emerging from actions rather than plans.[33]

LESSON #4: IT TAKES TWO TO PASS ONE

Run as fast as you can and then even faster in the Red Queen race—or is there another way? For lesson #4 we return to the story of the fox and the rabbit. Recall that the rabbit's flesh was the sought-after resource for both players in a zero-sum game. What are the alternatives open to the fox and the rabbit *beyond* the strategies suggested in lessons #1, #2, and #3 (i.e., the use of unconventional tactics, speed, and improvisation, respectively)? Let us first consider the resource options each of them has: the energy stored in grass is a resource, but it is incompatible with the fox's digestive system; rabbits might survive on fox flesh, but this is a highly unlikely scenario. Consequently, the competition between the two of them is limited to a single shared resource (rabbit flesh) until one of them has developed either the digestive mechanism or hunting strategies required for access to new resources. In the Red Queen race of predator and prey, successful competition requires that both competitors increase their only competitive advantage (i.e., both rabbit and fox must learn to run more efficiently). Can you forsee an alternate ending to the scenario presented, or do they simply never escape the cycle? What happens when the situation doesn't involve a predator (e.g., Microsoft) and prey (many companies in different industries), but competitors from the same species such as trees in a forest (e.g., competitors in the same industry)? Is it possible that the trees' competition for sunlight (i.e., faster growth) could result in an overall decrease in fitness to the disadvantage of all the trees and the sustainability of the forest (e.g., the entire industry)?

Let us replace the trees with cars competing in NASCAR[34] for the moment—*Fortune* 500 meets Daytona 500. In a sport that combines physics with game theory, the stock cars' performance, the driver's athletic ability, and overall team strength are not sufficient for success. The NASCAR axiom is "It takes two to pass one." Instead of relying on your own skills or team members' support, winning depends on cooperation between competitors in a series of temporary allegiances and defections. During a process known as "drafting," which involves cars following each other very closely, drivers in cooperating cars can each increase speed due to a drop in air resistance—the lead car from the vacuum created at its rear and the second car from protection against the wind. When "a racer in a line wants to break out and get ahead, he needs at least one partner. If he swings out alone, he is bound to lose momentum," which partially explains the reason behind the rows of tight-fitting stock cars around the track. Other techniques for gaining even the slightest bit of extra momentum involve a slingshot or "fan the tail" approach, where the driver attempts to create havoc in the aerodynamics for other drivers. Ultimately, a racer must defect and pass opponents to earn victory, but this requires extreme skill in managing the tension between competition and cooperation in which "it takes two to pass one."

Run faster and faster in the Red Queen race or compete by *not* competing—compete by cooperating. The gamesmanship in NASCAR is similar to the dynamics in the "drafting lines" that Microsoft and Cisco have developed with potential competitors such as Intel, Compaq, and Dell. These strategies have left nonparticipating drivers like Apple who tried to go it alone out in the cold unable to keep up with the synergistic effects of drafting partnerships during the 1990s. Co-opetition[35] is fast becoming a necessary strategy for long-term sustainability. Independent parties achieve mutual goals through cooperation, which aligns critical activities and processes, while at the same time competing with each other as well as with other firms. This is a pragmatic strategy that creates dynamic opportunities by facilitating radical innovation that can be brought to market quickly. By partnering with opponents and adhering to the rules of the co-opetition game, each competitor strengthens its overall competitive position. At the same time, the competitors limit the room for maneuvering, and preempt head-to-head competition. Not surprisingly, it didn't take Apple long to catch up and "think different," or to do the unthinkable, as can be seen in its partnerships with IBM and Motorola to ensure uninterrupted supply of Apple's computer chips. Another example of competitors who've agreed to compete by cooperating are the Swedish glass and crystal manufacturer, Orrefors Kosta Boda, and its Danish competitor, Royal Copenhagen.

LESSON #5: DON'T PLAY HARDBALL—THROW A CURVEBALL

The best swordsman in the world doesn't need to fear the second best swordsman in the world; no, the person for him to be afraid of is some ignorant antagonist who has never had a sword in his hand before; he doesn't do the thing he ought to do, and so the expert isn't prepared for him; he does the thing he ought not to do and often it catches the expert out and ends him on the spot.

—MARK TWAIN

During the dot-com frenzy in the late 1990s and early 2000s, strategy seemed to revolve around innovative business models that could monetize eyeballs during the process of replacing bricks with clicks. While disintermediation didn't quite turn out to be the silver bullet everyone was predicting and anticipating, the notion of innovative business models had staying power, especially when they disrupted the market and (re)defined the competitive space. It became clear that differentiation was not an effective long-term strategy—a revolutionary business model is a more likely source of sustainable competitive advantage (see Chapter 7).

However, even with a novel business model, the future is not secure because new market forces and entrants can potentially destroy the most promising business model. Take, for example, Google: it has become synonymous with continuous and radical innovation. Almost no industry is off-limits to this search giant—it has added capabilities to search for airline flights (competing with Expedia), built an online classified advertisement site (previously craigslist territory), and created a Wi-Fi service in San Francisco (taking on large telecommunication companies). What is next? Known for its simplified homepage, Google is introducing features that offer users greater scope for personalization. This innovator's objective is to develop a more user-centric web that will allow users to publish their own content on a personalized Google homepage. Google is an example of a competitor emerging from nowhere to redefine the current industry, reinvent value propositions, disrupt markets, and obliterate existing business models.

Ideally, a firm would like to have no competitors, especially not giants like Google. But can strategists make the competition irrelevant? In today's complex environment, the strategist has to remove the blinders imposed by the present. While it is important to manage today's business, it is critical to be part of the future, not only by trying to predict it but also by creating the future to the extent possible. The market universe consists of two sorts of oceans[36]—violent *red oceans* of bloody competition for the same group of customers using comparable value propositions and calm *blue oceans* of uncharted territory filled with untapped market potential. Companies in red oceans are stuck within perceived industry boundaries where they attempt to outperform competitors through low cost or differentiation strategies built around incremental innovations that keep shrinking profit pools.

Unlike red ocean competitors that accept industry norms and rules as a given, blue ocean strategists avoid head-to-head competition by challenging the industry's strategic logic and taken-for-granted assumptions. They ask *what-if?* questions such as the following: What if we reduced or eliminated certain factors on the cost side? What if we raised or created certain factors on the revenue side? What if we combined all four factors (reducing, eliminating, raising, creating) as part of value innovation? These three questions are part of an action framework—one that provides the basic building blocks for developing new value curves and new business models to create new markets that are uncontested. Kim and Mauborgne, the originators of the value innovation concept, explain, "Value without innovation tends to focus on value creation on an incremental scale. Innovation without value tends to be technology driven, market pioneering, or futuristic, often overshooting what buyers are willing to accept and pay for."[37] Value innovation integrates differentiation and low-cost strategies to create blue oceans that offer quantum-leap increases in value built around buyer utility, price, cost positions, and adoption.

The radical changes that have occurred over the history of the high jump event at the Olympics are a good illustration of the type of paradigm shift involved in blue ocean strategies.[38] There have been four discrete stages of improvement in high jump, each of which consists of incremental changes over a period of time, interspersed with non-linear, discontinuous or quantum jumps:[39]

- Initially, all high jumpers used the Scissors technique, which was similar to jumping hurdles. Efforts to jump higher involved launching from one foot, alternating legs over the bar while keeping the body in an upright position.

- The first breakthrough came when the Western Roll was introduced. Instead of alternating legs in the approach, high jumpers launched and landed on the same foot, facing the bar. The Western Roll was the dominant style for 25 years, until the rules of the game changed again.

- The second reinvention was known as the Eastern Roll (also known as the Straddle), in which high jumpers launched and landed on opposite feet, facing the bar.

- The third quantum change occurred in 1968 when Dick Fosbury, a former gymnast, broke the Olympic record by three inches. The Fosbury Flop involved a straight approach, jumping with both feet, backward (head first) while keeping the back facing the bar (face-up away from the bar). This was made possible by using better technology (foam under the bar) and a new mental model about jumping gleaned from gymnastics (i.e., a different industry).

Each breakthrough change in performance is associated with a new technique (analogous to a new business model) that transformed high jump (the industry).

As seen in the high jump example, the strategic curveball of a blue ocean strategy makes proven models of success obsolete by going beyond classic strategy formulas. For example, Southwest Airlines created a blue ocean instead of joining the price warring competitors in the red ocean by using two synergistic and complementary strategies. First, the company changed the dominant paradigm of air travel by introducing a new business model that abandoned the traditional hub-and-spokes model, maximized utilization rates of airplanes through faster airport turnaround time, and changed dominant labor approaches. Second, the company used strategic pricing imbedded in value innovation to give customers more for less. Strategic pricing enabled the company to set prices low enough to attract customers away from the red ocean and even attract previously non-existent customers. Competitors in the red ocean retaliated by trying to imitate Southwest Airlines, but quickly found themselves on the brink of bankruptcy, as seen with the woes of United Airlines, Delta Airlines, and others. By making airline travel not just cheaper, but an effective substitute for driving or traveling by bus, Southwest Airlines successfully made the competition irrelevant. This is the ultimate goal of a blue ocean strategy: to own the market by gaining market share as quickly as possible, making it tough for competitors to enter. Microsoft, Dell, and Wal-Mart have business models that various competitors have tried to emulate unsuccessfully.

Summary and Conclusions

The Red Queen runs and runs and runs—ever faster. In this chapter, we considered some of the potential strategies marketers can implement to survive as the external environment speeds up. Moving at ever higher tempos, organizations reach a point of persistent co-evolution, where no one has a competitive advantage for very long. Instead, competitive advantage consists of a series of comparative advantages—that is, until someone does something that changes the dynamics. Like the Red Queen, marketers live in a turbulent and uncertain world characterized by ever faster changes in markets, technologies, competitors, society, and people's behavior that require companies to run as fast as they can just to stay in the same place. The problem in this scenario is that companies typically try to run faster or try harder. They focus on improving current practices, performing benchmarking exercises, and improving efficiencies in efforts to adapt to changes. However, tangible resources, explicit competences, International Organization for Standardization (ISO) standards, Six Sigma procedures, and relationship management solutions are no longer distinctive best practices—they have become threshold requirements or, in simple terms, costs of doing business. While doing more of the same seems less risky, it is fatal in the long term because a few companies will realize they have to run a different race. When they alter their business models or customer-value propositions, the rules change, leaving the rest out in left field. To make matters worse, in a hypercompetitive environment, the better an idea, the shorter its life. Therefore, rather than trying to avoid or do away with the escalating Red Queen effect of competition, marketers have to craft strategies that get them ahead of the curve[40]—strategies that jump curves or create the next curve.

The days of comparing strategic decision making with strategic moves in a chess game are over. In chess, the players are known, the chess pieces are limited to predefined moves, and the rules of the game are fixed. The chess player can plan multiple moves ahead, and the solution to the problem is a preset algorithm (which is why supercomputers are now able to regularly defeat grand masters). The dynamics of 21st-century competition defy the old logic. Today's strategy game is an emergent process that is being redefined as the game is played. The players keep changing, and existing players keep modifying their behavior, adding to the complexity. The players cannot rely on historical data analysis and traditional planning to guide future actions. They have to go beyond making sense of the information at their disposal. They learn through trial and error. Improvisation, insight, intuition, and imagination are key skills, as are "creative abrasion" and "creative conflict."[41] The players do not comply with the rules of the game; they don't break the rules either. Rather, they play a completely different game in which they create new rules. Instead of an information processing perspective that assumes a problem as given, the players define the problem "from the knowledge available at a certain point in time and context."[42] They create knowledge and act at a faster rate based on the new knowledge. Playfulness become vital, as it helps to create a work environment conducive to new aspects of knowledge creation, sense making, and "interpretative flexibility."[43]

Moreover, successful strategists apply the five lessons from the Red Queen to become market drivers. As discussed in Chapter 2 and again in this chapter, a market driver is able to "own" the market. To own is to know—it is to lead, to create, to conquer, and to be first in the mind of the target market (e.g., Intel).[44] Market ownership leads to a powerful competitive position and substantial earnings (Amazon.com). This becomes a self-reinforcing spiral—because you own the market you dominate. Because you dominate, you deepen ownership (e.g., Microsoft).

If you can't be number one in the market you're in, find a market in which you can be number one (e.g., Apple). Find your niche and own it (e.g., Jones Soda). You can own the market by redefining the market. For example, Cirque du Soleil reinvented the notion of a circus and created a radically new form of entertainment modeled around theatrical performances. Become a champion of ideas. Starbucks recreated the Italian espresso-bar experience by designing a customer-value proposition around freshly brewed espressos, cappuccinos, and lattes served by baristas in the neighborhood café. Start your own curve instead of merely staying ahead of the curve (e.g., Southwest Airlines). The marketer doesn't always have to predict the future or even create it. Instead, he or she can redefine the present (e.g., Harley-Davidson). Leopards never change their spots, but people do—and marketers must. Doing so requires an entrepreneurial mindset that constantly challenges and rethinks the value proposition and continually questions where people and other resources fit in a picture of the company's future.

Key Terms

- Red Queen effect
- blue ocean strategy
- hypercompetition
- competitive advantage
- improvisation
- co-opetition

Questions

During the first quarter of 2007, Sony and Nintendo, two of the world's most popular video game makers, battled over a pool of consumers that could ultimately make or break each company's short-term success. Sony's new PlayStation 3, which was released during the last quarter of 2006, fell short of expectations with a reported 5.3% drop in net income in the third quarter (from October 1, 2006, to December 31, 2006) compared with the same period the previous year. Meanwhile, Nintendo's new Wii focuses on game play with a unique motion sensor controller, which was embraced enthusiastically by consumers, resulting in a net income that exceeded that of the previous year by 43.1%.

1. Are Sony, Nintendo, and Microsoft engaged in a Red Queen race in the video game industry? Explain why (or why not) you think this is the case.
2. Does Sony's PS3 have a sustainable competitive advantage? Explain your answer.
3. Does Nintendo's Wii have a sustainable competitive advantage? Explain your answer.
4. Which of the following statements do you agree with? Explain your answer from a strategic standpoint.
   a. More people are buying the Wii because of its lower price, not because of any specific feature. The Wii costs $249.99 while the PS3 is sold in two different models, which can be bought for $499 and $599, respectively. With the PS3, the consumer must pay for the extra features whether they like it or not.

    b. Nintendo became the new video game industry superpower, ahead of Sony and Microsoft, when it introduced Wii.

    c. Whereas Sony and Microsoft focused on improving the video game itself, Nintendo improved the game console. Because of the emphasis on the gaming experience, the Wii created a blue ocean strategy that effectively put it in a class of its own. Nintendo's Wii effectively owns this new market space in which it makes the rules.

5. When Nintendo introduced the Wii, did it apply any of the five lessons from the Red Queen discussed in this chapter?

6. Google is clearly a phenomenal contender to keep in mind as a potential competitor and new entrant in multiple industries.

    a. Given Google's history of entering markets with high potential and the attractiveness of the video gaming industry, do you think it would be a good idea for this innovator to take on giants like Nintendo, Sony, and Microsoft? Why or why not?

    b. Google uses all of the five lessons from the Red Queen. Can you identify examples where this search giant has used each of these lessons?

    c. Using Google as a case in point, are there other entrepreneurial strategies not mentioned in this chapter that you believe contribute to the company's meteoric rise in prominence and extraordinary financial performance?

Resources and References

1. Van Valen, L. (1973). A new evolutionary law. *Evolutionary Theory* 1: 1–30.
2. Carroll, L. (Pseudonym of C. L. Dodgson). (1871). *Through the looking glass and what Alice found there.* Oxford: The Millenium Fulcrum Edition.
3. Heylighen, F., & Campbell, D. T. (1995). Selection of organization at the social level: Obstacles and facilitators of metasystem transitions. *World Futures: The Journal of General Evolution* 45: 181–212. (Special issue on The Quantum of Evolution: Toward a theory of metasystem transitions, F. Heylighen, C. Joslyn, & V. Turchin (eds.).)
4. Barnett, W. (2007). *Red Queen competition among organizations.* Princeton, NJ: Princeton University Press.
5. David W. Rajeski. (n.d.). S&T Challenges in the 21st century: Strategy & Tempo. Accessed on November 2, 2007, http://www.wilsoncenter.org/does/staff/Rajeski_stratempo.pdf.
6. Ohmae, K. (1982). The mind of the strategist: The art of Japanese business. Burr Ridge, IL: McGraw Hill Professional Book Group.
7. Yarger, R. H. Towards a theory of strategy: Art Lykke and the Army war college strategy model. Accessed April 30, 2007, http://dde.carlisle.army.mil/authors/stratpap.htm.
8. Frery, F. (2006). The fundamental dimensions of strategy. *Sloan Management Review* 48(1): 71.
9. Barney, J. (1991). Firm resources and sustained competitive advantage. *Journal of Management* 17(1): 99–120.
10. Collis, D. J., & Montgomery, C. A. (1995). Competing on resources: Strategy in the 1990s. *Harvard Business Review* 73(4): 118–128.

11. Peteraf, M. A. (1993). The cornerstones of competitive advantage: A resource-based view. *Strategic Management Journal* 14(3): 179.

12. Ireland, R. D., Hitt, M. A., & Sirmon, D. G. (2003). A model of strategic entrepreneurship: The construct and its dimensions. *Journal of Management* 29(6): 963–989.

13. "Rewired and ready for combat." (2005, November). *BusinessWeek.* Accessed November 14, 2007, http://www.businessweek.com/magazine/content/05_45/b3958089.htm.

14. Hill, S., & Rifkin, G. (1999). *Radical marketing: From Harvard to Harley. Lessons from ten that broke the rules and made it big.* New York: Harper Collins.

15. Carroll, L. (1989). *Alice's adventures in Wonderland.* The Ultimate Illustrated Edition. Compiled & arranged by C. Edens. New York: Bantam Books. (Original publication date 1865.)

16. Hill & Rifkin.

17. Sun-Tzu. (2003). *The art of war plus the ancient Chinese revealed.* Trans. G. Gagliardi. Seattle, WA: Clearbridge Publishing.

18. Chairman Mao Zedong. Better known in the west as "The Little Red Book". Published by the Government of the People's RTepublic of China since April 1964.

19. Stalk, G. Jr., & Lachenauer, R. (2004). Hardball: Five killer strategies for trouncing the competition. *Harvard Business Review* 82(4): 62–73.

20. Friedman, T. L. (2005). *The world is flat: A brief history of the 21st century.* New York: Farrar, Straus and Giroux.

21. Brown, S. L., & Eisenhardt, K. M. (1998). *Competing on the edge: Strategy as structured chaos.* Boston: Harvard Business School Press.

22. Ibid.

23. Courtney, H. (2001). Making the most of uncertainty. *McKinsey Quarterly* 4: 38–47.

24. Yoffie, D. B., & Kwak, M. (2001). How to compete like a judo strategist. Boston: Harvard Business School Press.

25. March, J. G. (2001). Exploration and exploitation in organizational learning. *Organization Science* 2: 71–87.

26. Mintzberg, H., & Westley, F. (2001). Decision making: It's not what you think. *Sloan Management Review* 42(3): 89–93.

27. Thomke, S. (2001). Enlightened experimentation: The new imperative for innovation. *Harvard Business Review* 79(2): 66.

28. All quoted material in this paragraph is taken from Kanter, R. M. (2002). Strategy as improvisational theater. *Sloan Management Review* 43(2): 76–81.

29. Weick, K. E., Gilfillan, D. P., & Keith, T. (1973). The effect of composer credibility on orchestra performance. *Sociometry* 36: 435–462.

30. Sarasvathy, S. (2003). Constructing corridors to economic primitives: Entrepreneurial opportunities as demand-side artefacts. In J. Butler (ed.), *Opportunity identification and entrepreneurial behavior,* pp. 291–312. Greenwich, CT: Information Age Publishing.

31. Starbuck, W. (1983). Organizations as action generators. *American Sociological Review* 48: 91–102.

32. Weick, K. E. (1987). Organizational culture as a source of high reliability. *California Management Review* 29(2): 112–127.

33. Mintzberg, H. (1994). Rethinking strategic planning, Part I: Pitfalls and fallacies. *Long Range Planning* 27(3): 12–22.

34. All quoted material in this paragraph is taken from Duhigg, C. (2003, February 17). Fortune 500, meet Daytona 500: What NASCAR can teach us about business. Accessed November 14, 2007, http://www.slate.com/id/2078672.

35. Zineldin, M. (1998). Towards an ecological collaborative relationship management. *European Journal of Marketing* 32(11/12): 1138–1164.

36. Kim, W. C., & Mauborgne, R. (2005). *Blue ocean strategy.* Boston: Harvard Business School Press.

37. Ibid., p. 29.

38. Webber, A. M. (2001). How business is a lot like life. *FastCompany* 45: 130130. Accessed [DATE], http://www.fastcompany.com/magazine/45/pascale.html.

39. "High jump." *Wikipedia.* Accessed October 19, 2007, http://en.wikipedia.org/wiki/High_jump.

40. Barnett.

41. Eisenhardt, K. M., Kahwajy, J. L., & Bourgeois, L. J. III. (1997). How management teams can have a good fight. *Harvard Business Review* 75(4): 78–85.

42. Nonaka, I., & Takeuchi, H. (1995). *The knowledge creating company.* New York: Oxford University Press.

43. Ibid.

44. McKenna, R. (1991). Marketing is everything. *Harvard Business Review* (69)1: 65–79.

CHAPTER

11

PRICING SECRETS OF MARKET SHAPERS

THE MAGIC OF PRICING

Conventional pricing is being turned on its head. Consider some of the ways the status quo has been challenged in recent years:

- Netscape decides to compete by making its browser source code available for *free*.
- Glaxo takes over a pharmaceutical market by charging *more* than the competition for a comparable product.
- Bally Total Fitness Centers offers *more than 20 different pricing arrangements* for the basic opportunity to perspire while working hard.
- Where the *Encyclopedia Britannica* used to sell for $1,500 or more, its content becomes available for *no direct fee* on the Internet.
- Priceline.com creates *negotiated* prices for almost any product or service imaginable.
- The online Pricesearch service makes it possible to *instantly compare* prices on just about anything. And when using this service for an American Airlines ticket, the traveler will find the rates for a trip between point A and point B *change by the hour* as the company refines its use of yield management software.

Deciding what prices to charge represents one of the more visible decision variables confronting entrepreneurs and managers. The prices of products send clear messages regarding customer value and company objectives. Few business decision areas can have a more rapid or dramatic impact on profitability than improved price management. And yet, pricing has historically been one of the least emphasized of strategic issues, and one that people in business are hesitant to critique or discuss. We might call this tendency "price avoidance."

Historically, entrepreneurs and managers in general have taken price for granted, concluding its principal function is to cover costs and generate a reasonable rate of return. Some assumed that most firms charge about the same or that legal and regulatory constraints limit their ability to use price as a strategic weapon. However, a more fundamental explanation for price avoidance is the fact that many business leaders do not really understand how to price, and are insecure about the adequacy of the pricing approach they employ. As a result, they rely on overly simplistic rules of thumb and place an exaggerated emphasis on cost-based formulas.

There is evidence to suggest that this state of affairs may be changing. Firms are beginning to adopt more sophisticated and creative approaches to price management and are coming to appreciate the strategic importance of the price variable. As we shall see in this chapter, some are now managing prices in a truly proactive and value-based manner. In general, firms are developing more complex price structures (e.g., banks and financial institutions), initiating more frequent price changes (e.g., car rental agencies), and customizing their prices to individual market segments (e.g., telecommunications companies, magazine publishers, universities).

These changes do not represent isolated events or random occurrences. Firms are being forced to change their approaches to prices, and the pressures for these changes are driven by the competitive, customer, social, economic, and technological environments. As the external environments of firms become less predictable and more uncontrollable, entrepreneurs find they must be more strategic in their pricing behaviors to survive, much less prosper. More to the point, environmental conditions that are increasingly dynamic, hostile, and complex create a need for opportunistic or entrepreneurial pricing.

WHAT IS A PRICE?

A price is ultimately a number. For many entrepreneurs and managers, it is a number that, more than anything, captures the costs involved in providing a product or service to a customer. These costs can differ significantly, though, depending on the firm. The determination of average unit cost can also be a bit arbitrary. The reality is that the costs of making or providing a good should have relatively little to do with what is actually charged by the firm. Instead, costs indicate only what the firm *must* charge to achieve breakeven (and in some instances, exceeding breakeven is not even the objective). Consider any five people on a given airline flight. The strong likelihood is that each is paying a different amount to get from point A to point B, and this has relatively little to do with the airline's costs of providing that particular flight to a given person.

Those who understand the real creative potential of pricing tend to see things differently. That is, they view prices in fundamentally different ways than most people view them. They recognize five key characteristics of the price charged by a firm for a particular product or service:

- *Price is value:* The amount a customer is willing to pay is, in the final analysis, a statement of the amount of value they perceive in the product or service. The customer who pays $9.50 for a garden salad in one restaurant and $3.00 for the same salad in another restaurant is, in each instance, making a statement regarding the value he or she sees himself or herself getting.

- *Price is variable:* What any one customer actually spends to acquire a given product or service can be varied or manipulated in myriad ways. Examples include varying the absolute amount of payment, the components of payment, what is actually being paid for, the time of payment, the form of payment, the terms of payment, and the person doing some or all of the paying.

- *Price is variety:* Firms typically sell multiple products and services, and they may be attempting to use price to accomplish different things for different items. For instance, they may use the price of some items to influence the sales of others, attempt to bundle (or unbundle) sets of items when setting prices, or price in a manner that pushes items with higher versus lower profit margins.

- *Price is visible:* Customers see and are aware of the prices of most things that they buy, although they do not always consider all components of the actual price they are paying. Because of their visibility, prices send signals to the customer about value, image, product availability, demand conditions, exclusivity, and related characteristics of the transaction.

- *Price is virtual:* Among marketing decision variables, an item's price is arguably the easiest and quickest to change, with many companies able to make adjustments to their price schedules instantaneously in response to market conditions, especially in an electronic age. Technology is one way to achieve real-time pricing, but there are many examples of long-standing pricing practices that result in prices that are set at the time of purchase and can be quickly changed (e.g., negotiated pricing, spot markets, and black markets).

Many entrepreneurs fail to recognize and capitalize on these characteristics of a price. Instead, they rely on relatively inflexible and reactive pricing methods. The beginning point in changing this state of affairs is to adopt a more comprehensive view of a company's pricing decisions.

A STRATEGIC PERSPECTIVE ON PRICING

Price is both a noun and a verb. While a price is something a firm or person charges, to price is to determine how much, when, where, and how one will pay. Indeed, price management actually includes a large number of decisions. The challenge is to organize these decisions in a systematic way. Although some entrepreneurs focus solely on determining the level at which to fix a price for each item in the company's product mix, a more strategic approach recognizes the need for decisions in five key areas:

- *Price objectives*—what the firm is trying to accomplish with the prices customers are charged for a product. These objectives should be measurable levels of performance and can range from a specific profit level the firm wants to achieve to a desired image the firm is trying to project in the marketplace to discouraging market entry by a potential competitor.
- *Price strategy*—the theme or direction of a firm's pricing efforts. The strategy provides the glue that holds together all of the individual pricing decisions; examples include skimming, parity, penetration, or price leadership strategies.
- *Price structure*—the architecture around which the firm's mix of prices is designed and perhaps the area with the greatest room for creativity. The structure specifies how prices will vary based on aspects of the product/ service (e.g., bundling/unbundling), the type of customer (e.g., price differences by market segment), and time and form of payment (e.g., the discount structure).
- *Price levels*—the establishment of actual prices for individual products and services (including odd-pricing); the determination of specific price gaps among items in a given line.
- *Price promotions*—the situational employment of various types of price promotions and special discounts, such as a cents-off coupon, a two-for-the-price-of-one deal, or a rebate.

A whole host of creative options exist within each of these areas, as we shall discuss. The key to strategic pricing is that the decisions be made in a systematic fashion, reflecting the company's overall marketing strategy, competitive positioning, and target markets. Further, there is a logical order to these decisions. Price objectives should first be set, then a pricing strategy is determined, followed by structural decisions, and so forth. Just as important is the need to ensure internal consistency among these five decision areas.

THE UNDERLYING PRICING ORIENTATION OF A COMPANY: TOWARD ENTREPRENEURIAL PRICING

The overall approach managers bring to making and implementing price-related decisions, including their underlying attitudes and assumptions, can be considered the firm's "pricing orientation." Thus, there is a guiding philosophy regarding the firm's pricing behavior, and it drives the decisions made regarding the various options in each of the five areas outlined earlier. In some companies, the elements of this orientation can be explicitly stated, formalized, and planned. However, in many firms, they are implicit in pricing decisions and emerge over time.

Little is known regarding company pricing orientations. However, we believe that a firm's pricing actions have at least four key underlying dimensions. The first of these is the extent to which pricing decisions are *cost based* versus *market based*. Cost-based pricing finds management placing far more emphasis on covering its own costs than on other determinants of price (e.g., demand conditions, competitive market structures, company marketing strategy). It typically involves a reliance on some sort of cost-plus, keystone, or target-return formula. Market-based pricing is more customer centered, wherein the principal purpose of price is to reflect the amount of value of customer is getting from the firm's total product offering. There is a recognition that different customer groups perceive different amounts of value in a given purchase.

The second component is whether pricing is more *risk aversive* or *risk assumptive*. Risk-aversive pricing represents a conservative approach. Prices are modified only when absolutely necessary, price levels are kept in close proximity to those of competitors, the focus is on covering costs, and the price structure is kept as simple as possible. Risk-assumptive pricing finds entrepreneurs employing pricing schemes that are novel; are untested; and have the potential of producing revenue losses, confusing or alienating customers, or other ill-effects.

The third component emphasizes whether a firm's pricing is done in a *reactive* or *proactive* manner. Reactive pricing involves mimicking the price moves of competitors, responding after the fact to signals from customers, or adjusting prices only after a change in regulations or a new technological breakthrough radically affects costs. Proactive pricing comes into play when the firm takes a leadership role not only in changing price, but in being the first to introduce innovative pricing structures and payment schemes. It also reflects more aggressiveness in pricing, and more speed in adjusting prices to reflect new opportunities.

The fourth underlying component is the extent to which management emphasizes *standardization* versus *flexibility* in pricing. Standardization is reflected in a tendency to charge a universal price for a product or service regardless of the user, the buying situation, or environmental (including competitive) contingencies. Flexibility, alternatively, finds the company varying prices based on segment or user elasticities and time and place of purchase, as well as in response to opportunities for product or service unbundling or bundling or anticipated or actual moves by competitors, among other factors.

While there may be other dimensions which characterize a firm's pricing behavior (e.g., an ethical dimension), we believe that these are the dominant ones. Further, while each of these dimensions captures an important aspect of pricing behavior, they clearly interact with one another. For instance, being more proactive with pricing actions may entail greater risk. Similarly, employing flexible pricing is likely to be correlated with being more market based.

The success of firms in virtually all industries is increasingly dependent on their ability to engage in pricing that is market based, risk assumptive, proactive, and flexible. We refer to this combination of elements as opportunistic or *entrepreneurial* pricing. Examples of this type of approach can be found with growing frequency in a wide range of industries. Let us consider some examples and explore the underlying need for such an approach.

THE NEW PRICING: EXAMPLES OF EMERGING PRACTICES

Entrepreneurial pricing manifests itself in a variety of ways. As with any type of innovation, and especially with a decision area that is not only visible but has significant implications for financial performance, the new pricing methods frequently take the form of experimentation, trials, and limited-scale tests. The diversity of approaches can be seen in an examination of developments in eight industries.

- *Software:* Companies are moving away from the traditional reliance on a one-time payment for software, instead relying on leasing, yearly licensing, and usage-based pricing. Another novel approach involves a point system, where points are assigned based on what the software is managing (e.g., a desktop versus a server), with prices set for various point ranges.
- *Communications:* Some firms are basing their prices on the expected return to the customer. Using inputs regarding customer expectations of the network and its financial impact on the organization, unique prices are determined for different communications systems.
- *Chemicals:* Firms are concentrating on total economic value to the customer in their pricing methods. One example involves the pricing of pipe-sealing gaskets based on the cleanup costs and potential liabilities that buyers could avoid.
- *Public utilities:* Utilities are unbundling the offering to create product and service packages of different values. This can include removing some element of the product/service for customers insisting on low price points. They parade a menu of offerings and prices to different customer segments and attempt to shift the focus to customer energy management.
- *Financial services:* Similar to offering different mortgage products to different borrowers, lenders are starting to adopt risk-based pricing, where loans are priced individually based on a borrower's risk.
- *Construction:* Firms are enabling buyer choice by reducing standard features on new homes in favor of options and upgrades, each of which is prepriced and has a profit margin that is often greater than it would be as a standard item. Another approach involves systematic increases in prices for changes to plans the closer the project comes to completion.
- *Services:* Adoption of new yield management systems by service providers with capacity constraints (e.g., ski resorts, airlines, theme parks) permits efficient management of time-based pricing, early discounts, limited early sales, demand allocating, and so forth.

The pervasiveness of these emerging approaches suggests that cost-based methodologies and fixed-list prices may soon become relics of a fading industrial age.[1] Replacing an era in which standardized prices were necessary to support scale economies, mass production, product standardization, mass marketing, and intensive distribution, a new set of forces is driving contemporary pricing efforts.

WHY ENTREPRENEURIAL PRICING HAS COME OF AGE

Corporate strategy experts have written extensively on the need for companies to design strategies and make structural changes to counter threats and capitalize on opportunities in the external environment.[2] The external environment consists of everything outside the company (e.g., competitive conditions, customer demands, technological developments, economic conditions, etc.) As we have noted in other chapters, environments confronting most industries are generally becoming more turbulent. A turbulent environment is one that is experiencing rapid rates of change, is threatening or hostile, and is growing in heterogeneity and complexity.

Environmental turbulence has important managerial implications. A faster pace of change means the company's products move through their life cycles more quickly, new market segments with distinct needs continually emerge, new forms of competition regularly appear, and managerial decision windows get shorter. A more hostile environment is characterized, in part, by more aggressiveness on the part of competitors. Firms encounter more difficulty in differentiating their offerings, and there is downward pressure on margins. Higher rates of product innovation occur, which means higher rates of product failure. With increases in the complexity of the environment, we find firms engaging in more product and market specialization and "nichemanship." Mass markets disappear in favor of markets that are more fragmented and segmented.

Faced with circumstances such as these, successful firms tend to be those that demonstrate more adaptability and flexibility, and higher levels of innovation and entrepreneurship, than their less successful counterparts. Marketing activities (including pricing) become especially critical under such conditions. For instance, a faster changing and more complex environment is resulting in a greater emphasis by companies on niche marketing, relationship marketing, customization of marketing programs, the obsolescence of mass advertising, the use of speed as strategy, and a general pervasiveness of marketing throughout the organization.

At the same time, scholars have devoted relatively little attention to determining the specific implications environmental dynamics hold for pricing strategy.[3] There has been some recognition that pressures from the external environment make pricing decisions more delicate, complex, and important in companies. Environmental turbulence elicits fear, uncertainty, and doubt among sellers and buyers alike when it comes to making price-related decisions, but it also forces firms to make faster and more frequent price decisions. Beyond these fairly general observations, few systematic insights have been provided.

However, consideration of some of the more pervasive environmental developments leads to some fairly clear pricing implications. Market fragmentation is resulting in more price differentiation, with prices set based on the market segment. A blurring of industry definitions is leading to experimentation where effective pricing approaches used in one industry are being adapted for use in a different industry. Competitive intensity is forcing greater emphasis on customer relationships, and price becomes a potential indicator of the quality of the relationship. Technological change is producing software that makes activity-based costing, data-mining, yield management systems, and revenue optimization much easier for the typical firm. Smart cards are transforming the basic nature of transactions by not only empowering the buyer, but also placing a wealth of customer-specific intelligence at the fingertips of the manager. The speed wrought by new information and telecommunications technologies supports the emergence of new business models, where some or all of the core offering of companies can be given to customers for no charge.

Evidence of how developments in the external environment encourage innovative pricing can be seen with the example of Netflix provided in Exhibit 11-1. Not only was the firm's initial positioning in the marketplace driven by clever

---

EXHIBIT 11-1 How the External Environment Defines the Pricing Challenge: Netflix

The pricing challenge posed by today's competitive environment is well-illustrated by the experiences of Netflix, the video-rental-by-mail pioneer. The company successfully penetrated the video rental business at the same time that the industry had matured and markets were fairly saturated. As a price innovator, it chose to structure prices based on a monthly membership fee, with five different price plans available. Its most popular plan involves three movies at a time for $16.99 per month. Its pricing also reflects the elimination of late fees (a potential source of revenue) and free shipping both ways. In effect, customers can pay less for more, depending on the number of videos they choose to rent at a time. While Netflix successfully penetrated the market, and built a loyal customer base, it has found the environment becoming even more turbulent.

Consider some of the emerging threats. Blockbuster launched a competing service, where customers could order DVDs on the Internet for delivery by mail, while also using the Blockbuster stores to return or pick up movies. The company also eliminated late fees in its stores, which was one of the main factors that drove many customers to Netflix in the first place. Meanwhile, retail giant Wal-Mart, who has offered online DVD rentals since 2003, seeks to undercut Netflix on price. Amazon.com, a company that well knows electronic commerce, introduced a rival online DVD rental service in particular markets. With these new players in the market, how should Netflix respond? The challenge for Netflix is to avoid price wars with large competitors who have deep pockets, especially as margins are being squeezed as the cost to acquire a new subscriber continues to rise. It is a challenge that centers not on price cutting, but instead on continued innovation with the price structure.

Source: Authors.

pricing, but ongoing changes in the external environment posed significant threats which tempted the company to cut prices, but in fact challenged the company to be even more innovative in how it sets prices.

A vivid picture of how environmental influences will change pricing in the coming years can be seen by considering the impact of just one influence, the Internet. Table 11-1 groups some of the more significant changes in how prices are set based on whether they are likely to represent threats or opportunities (or, more typically, both) to entrepreneurs and managers. The Internet is making price the determining issue for many transactions, in effect commoditizing the business. Consumers can do more—and faster—product and price searches, they can propose and negotiate prices, and they are able to transact whenever they want. For their part, companies can more easily modify their prices based on what is purchased, when, and by whom. They can collect data in real time on purchase patterns and demand conditions, leading to revenue-optimizing price adjustments. The Internet can also be used to stage buying experiences in ways that allow the entrepreneur to sell more and charge more. Transaction costs are markedly reduced through the efficiencies created via electronic commerce. It is only a matter of time before developments such as these influence all firms, regardless of what is being purchased or through which channel.

In the final analysis, a more turbulent environment creates a need for fundamental changes in the way firms determine and manage their prices. More specifically, companies are likely to find that their long-term success is dependent on a move to entrepreneurial pricing. Entrepreneurs are forced to abandon conservative, risk-aversive pricing approaches when faced with rapidly maturing products, demands from customer groups for unique product/service packages, and aggressive competitor forays into their markets. Firms are likely to turn to market-based pricing as they find cost-based approaches are failing to provide the

TABLE 11-1   How e-Commerce Is Changing Pricing

New Opportunities for the Entrepreneur	New Challenges for the Entrepreneur
1. Differentiated pricing by time of day, week, or month, or type of customer	1. Technology facilitates rapid customer search for competitive options
2. Using customer data to optimize pricing by creating customer switching barriers	2. Customers make (rather than take) prices
3. Using technology to de-menu pricing	3. Customers have more control over transactions
4. Being much better at differentiation—such as by staging experiences on the web	4. Return to one-to-one negotiation
5. Finding customers willing to pay higher prices than expected	5. Products and services become more commoditized, markets more efficient
6. Establishing electronic exchanges	6. Marketers must invest more time and effort in price setting
7. Employing efficient ways to negotiate prices	
8. Maximizing revenue and price	

adaptability necessary to keep abreast of customer expectations, to take advantage of opportunities created by niche markets, and to respond quickly to competitor initiatives.

Firms will also be more comfortable taking the lead in initiating price actions as rapid environmental change undermines the stability of traditional market positions. Competitor hostility is apt to create more price-based than non-price-based competition, but this does not mean simple price cutting. Rather, it is likely to result in more creativity in manipulating the whole range of price variables. Environments that are more complex allow firms to act independently (or undetected) on price within a given niche.

Finally, new opportunities will emerge for capitalizing on the different price/value perceptions found in various parts of the marketplace when environments are changing rapidly and to reflect differences in price elasticity among the numerous niche markets that appear. These opportunities will be coupled with competitive pressures for differential treatment of key accounts. The ability to address such opportunities will require that prices become more flexible and less standardized.

APPLYING AN ENTREPRENEURIAL ORIENTATION TO THE FIRM'S PRICING PROGRAM

The four key components of a firm's pricing orientation can be applied to the formulation of objectives, strategies, structure, levels, and price promotions, as illustrated in Figure 11-1. For example, in terms of price objectives, price can be used for much more than generating an acceptable, or even a relatively high, rate of return. Objectives that focus on the use of price to encourage a particular behavior on the part of buyers, establish a foothold in a new market, speed the exit of marginal competitors, take advantage of the learning curve, disincentivize certain groups of customers, or use one product line in the firm's portfolio to generate sales of another line reflect a more entrepreneurial perspective.

Similarly, entrepreneurial pricing is reflected in strategies that are value based, capturing the total value proposition as perceived by individual segments and customers. Firms may need to develop multiple strategies, depending on the market context. Both premium and parity pricing strategies might be used by the same firm operating in different markets, and the firm may serve as price leader or price taker depending on the product context.

Price structure is the decision area that invites the greatest amount of innovation and creativity. Structure is concerned first with which aspects of each product or service have a price attached. Sample pricing approaches might include bundling (a bank charges one price, for which a customer receives check-writing privileges, a savings account, use of an ATM for deposits/withdrawals/transfers/inquiries, a statement each month, returned checks, and traveler's checks at no additional charge) and/or unbundling (the same bank charges individual prices for each of these services). It could entail value-added services that are provided

FIGURE 11-1   Integrative Framework for Entrepreneurial Pricing

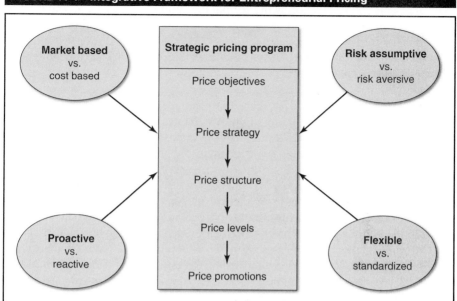

to the customer without raising price. Alternatively, the marketer could sell its basic offering at a very low price and then make money on higher margin consumables or add-ons. Selling the same product under different brand names for different prices is a further variation. Time-period pricing, where the product (or aspects of it) is priced differently at particular times, such as peak or low-capacity utilization periods, also represents a structural option. Two other variations might be unlimited use of a given product or service for a set fee or an initial base price followed by a variable charge once usage exceeds some threshold. The price might also be tied to the performance of the product or service such that the customer pays in direct proportion to the benefits he or she receives.

The second aspect of structure concerns how prices will vary for different customers and usage situations. The principal focus is charging price differentials based on the market segment or individual account. This is arguably the most significant trend in pricing today, where segments having different price elasticities are charged accordingly (e.g., airlines and business versus leisure travelers), although many firms remain fairly naïve in the way they implement segment differentials (e.g., senior citizen discounts). Other alternatives could include loyalty schemes for repeat or heavy users and establishing price differences for users who can consume only at certain time periods. Tying price to some variable aspect of customers—such as the size of their feet if operating a shoe store or the size of their car if operating a car wash—is another possibility. Current technology allows firms to take price differentials even further, making one-to-one pricing a practical reality.

Price structure is also concerned with the conditions, time, and form of payment. The chief consideration is the formal discount structure, including cash or early payment discounts, volume discounts (cumulative or noncumulative), and functional or trade discounts (e.g., for distribution or logistical services, cooperative advertising, and so forth). Also included here are various time payment schemes and trade-in allowances.

In a similar vein, price levels and tactics lend themselves to a more entrepreneurial approach. Price levels (or the actual amounts charged for each product or service and the actual level of any discounts given) require creativity in deciding on such issues as the use of odd prices ($9.95 instead of $10.00), the use of price to convey a level of quality in a product, and the size of the price gap to allow between items in a given line (e.g., the low-end, middle-of-the-road, and high-end versions of the same product).

Finally, the use of short-term tactics, such as rebates, coupons, cents-off deals, and price promotions, represents an ongoing means for achieving market-oriented flexibility and proactiveness in pricing. Such tactics can be quick, precisely targeted, and relatively inexpensive. Further, any number of guerrilla tactics can be employed in the pricing arena. For instance, a jewelry store offers diamonds at 75% off if it snows on Groundhog Day, a copying company invents a reusable coupon that increases in value with each use, or a price promotion is done jointly between a movie theatre and a restaurant.

There is ample room for experimentation in each of these areas, and conventional rules need not apply. Thus, a restaurant might charge different amounts for a meal depending on the table at which one is seated, a college might charge higher prices depending on how many credit hours a student has completed, and an industrial manufacturer may set prices today based on the accuracy of the industrial buyer's demand forecasts over the past 18 months. The challenge is to identify and find inventive ways to capitalize on the creative variables that can have important profit impacts over time and that contribute to the customer-value equation. Answering this challenge requires not only an intimate understanding of the customer, but a willingness to lead customers rather than simply follow them or take them for granted.

Summary and Conclusions

Price is the most neglected variable in the marketing efforts of companies. Entrepreneurs have tended to view price simplistically in terms of margins and costs, not as a strategic marketing variable or as a core part of corporate strategy. Thus, the mindset is often to compete on a price basis when absolutely necessary, but otherwise focus on nonprice forms of competition (e.g., sales promotions, product quality, after-sale service, relationship building).

Such an orientation may be increasingly untenable. In fact, formulaic and cost-based approaches to price determination are becoming a liability in companies.[4] In turbulent times, organizations find that sustainable competitive advantage lies in flexibility, adaptability, speed, aggressiveness, and innovation. Pricing can play a key role in achieving such advantage, but only if entrepreneurs develop a better understanding of the multiple dimensions and component decisions that come under the general banner of "pricing"; address these components in a systematic and integrated fashion; and ensure that these efforts are driven by a consistent, underlying corporate philosophy toward pricing. In terms of the latter issue, our recommendation is that companies adopt a philosophy of entrepreneurial pricing.

More specifically, entrepreneurs should consider pricing approaches that are more market based and reflective of a willingness to assume calculated risks, be proactive, and be flexible. Thus, those responsible for company pricing actions should regularly apply the following key questions to business operations:

- How novel is our pricing approach? Are we creating value for the customer in the ways that we price? What sorts of assumptions are our prices predicated upon, and do those assumptions reflect the contemporary and emerging marketplace and technology?

- Are we sufficiently proactive in terms of price increases, decreases, or changes in the various components of price? Proactiveness implies a willingness to act quickly and to take the lead in instituting price moves relative to competitors. It implies a preference to undo competitors rather than cooperate with them.

- Do we pursue pricing actions that entail a degree of calculated risk in terms of customer response, distributor receptivity, and competitor reaction? Such risk-taking does not imply single, dramatic pricing actions. Instead, efforts must be managed in the sense that the firm pursues a number of different price moves and is continually experimenting with the components of price and conducting pricing test markets in various market niches.

- Are we sufficiently flexible in tailoring prices to different markets, segments, and key accounts? Does this flexibility enable the firm to get much closer to its customers in terms of understanding the sources of value a given customer realizes from the company's offerings, and the trade-offs customers will make between price and various product attributes?

From a managerial standpoint, price must be a strategic-level decision variable, which means developing programs that take full advantage of various components of price. There is a danger, of course, that firms will develop pricing programs that are too managerially cumbersome or confusing to customers. Too many choices may confuse company staff and exasperate customers.[5] In addition, complexity can result in customers who are not as price sensitive paying less than they might otherwise have paid. Weigand also warns of a need for creative tactics for dealing with customers angered at discovering they are paying more than others for items that represent a meaningful proportion of their budgets. This problem can be minimized if managers carefully and consistently segment their markets, develop reliable indicators of segment price sensitivity, and effectively communicate price policies to key decision makers within segments. Further, the administration of the price structure must appear seamless, because this helps counter the perception that the price a given customer is being asked to pay is arbitrary.

Just as important is the need for entrepreneurs to move their focus away from variables and events inside the company. Pricing must be externally focused, with formal and ongoing environmental monitoring efforts. The ability to anticipate variability in rates of change, movements toward greater market heterogeneity, or intensification of competitor aggressiveness, and to quickly adapt price strategy, would seem paramount.

It should also be noted that the underlying dimensions of price identified here are likely to be interrelated. Thus, entrepreneurs may find that risk-taking in pricing may lead to more flexibility, which in turn permits price proactiveness within segments. Moreover, the underlying pricing dimensions are likely to interact with other elements of the marketing mix. As an example, it might be that advertising expenditures will be positively associated with pricing that is more flexible or more proactive, given the need to communicate such pricing efforts to the correct audiences on a timely basis.

In the final analysis, the time has come for companies to redefine the role of price as a strategic variable. Price must become an innovative means for adapting to and capitalizing on the increasingly complex changes in the external environment. This is the essence of entrepreneurial pricing—and the key to a turbulent future. Ironically, it is by bringing a more disciplined approach to price management that firms will be able to realize the potential of an entrepreneurial approach.

Key Terms

- customized pricing
- price flexibility
- price strategy
- price structure
- proactive pricing
- risk-assumptive pricing
- value-based pricing

Questions

1. Why should price be a reflection of value, not the firm's costs? In what way does cost-based pricing limit the marketer's creativity?
2. Explain the concept of "price structure." Why is it an area that especially lends itself to imagination and creativity? Assume you were selling advertising space on your website. What might be 10 ways to play with the price structure?
3. In what way might a company's pricing approach be "risk assumptive"? Provide an example of a pricing approach that involves taking some calculated risks. In what sense are the risks "calculated"?
4. What do you see as some of the challenges or complexities in running a business where you are changing prices every week and even every day, and charging different prices for the same products or services sold to different customers?
5. In what sense does the Internet lead to more empowered customers? How does selling over the Internet lead to radical changes in how prices are managed?

Resources and References

1. Desiraju, R., & Shugan, S. (1999). Strategic service pricing and yield management. *Journal of Marketing* 63(1): 44–56.
2. Sirmon, D., Hitt, M. A., & Ireland, R. D. (2007). Managing firm resources in dynamic environments to create value: Looking inside the black box. *Academy of Management Review* 32(1): 273–291.
3. Davidow, E. (2000). The dynamics of pricing. *Home Textiles Today:* 42; Dolan, R. J. (1995). How do you know when the price is right? *Harvard Business Review* 73(5): 174–183; Matsukawa, I., Asano, H., & Kakimoto, H. (1999). Engineering the price-value relationship. *Marketing Management* 8(1): 48–53.
4. Euster, C. C., Kakkar, J. N., & Roegner, E. V. (2000). Bringing discipline to pricing. *McKinsey Quarterly* 14(1): 132–139; Matson, E. (1995). Customizing prices. *Harvard Business Review* 73(6): 13–14.
5. Weigand, R. E. (1999). Yield management: Filling buckets, papering the house. *Business Horizons* 42(5): 55–64.

CHAPTER

CHANGING CHANNELS
REDEFINING DISTRIBUTION
STRATEGY

IN TIMES OF CHANGE...NOTHING CHANGES

In the late 1980s, Ford Motor Company implemented a project called "Project Olympus,"[1] which was aimed at addressing the major problems caused by a distribution system that had remained largely unchanged for more than a hundred years. Since the company's foundation by Henry Ford in the early 1900s, the firm had distributed its products through a network of franchised Ford dealers. Anyone wishing to purchase a new Ford car had to do so through one of these dealers, and Ford products still under warranty had to be serviced and repaired through these dealers. Dealers were bound by contract not to carry the products of other manufacturers, and Ford was compelled to supply them with new products and suitable offerings. It was very difficult for Ford to fire a dealer, and even poor performance by a dealer was no grounds for breaking the franchise contract.

No one was happy with the way in which automobiles were distributed. Customers regarded buying a new car as on a par with visiting a dentist on the list of unpleasant consumption experiences. They hated the haggling that always seemed to accompany a new-car purchase and resented the attempts of pushy salespeople to coerce them into buying products that they really didn't want. They always felt that they could have gotten a better deal. Women especially felt that they were talked down to by insensitive male salespeople who didn't have their best interests at heart. Many automobile purchasers actually preferred to do their shopping at night when dealers were closed to avoid encountering pushy salespeople, and most said that they were prepared to drive long distances to get something that they really wanted. When it came to service, customers hated the fact that there were always surprises—work done that wasn't quoted, hidden charges, and surprise bills. Work was often not performed right the first time, and the operating hours of service providers were inconvenient and unacceptable. When the warranty on their cars expired, many customers preferred to shop around and have their cars serviced by independent operators.

Dealers were also unhappy about the franchise system. Many felt that the financial returns to be made from operating a dealer franchise were well below what equivalent other businesses were able to achieve. The mark-ups on new cars were very low indeed, and many dealers reported losing money on service provisions. They complained that they were seldom able to get the exciting new products that customers wanted and that would sell easily, and instead found themselves being overwhelmed with less popular products that Ford's factories were churning out in a way that was insensitive to customer demands.

Ford found itself between the proverbial "rock and a hard place." It was contractually difficult to eliminate underperforming dealers, and the company's reputation with customers suffered as a result of the poor service and aggressive selling techniques of its dealers. Customers didn't blame just the dealer for the unpleasant experiences, Ford claimed, they blamed the company, because they perceived that Ford and its dealer network were one entity.

SEARCHING FOR A WAY OUT— AND BEING CREATIVE

In the late 1980s and early 1990s, Ford began to explore a number of alternative business models to address the shortcomings of a distribution strategy that had remained largely unchanged throughout its existence. One of the alternatives to a traditional dealer was the notion of an "auto theme park," probably located in a rural area, that would provide a huge selection of products to customers. Customers would be able to visit these venues, test drive new products on special tracks, and avail themselves of all the necessary information without being accosted by pushy salespeople. There would be restaurant facilities and entertainment for adults and children alike. Not surprisingly, this concept was given the code name of "DisneyFord"! Likewise, Ford considered that the ideal place to have a regular maintenance service had more in common with a fast-food restaurant than an auto dealer. These facilities would offer "menu pricing," hence avoiding unpleasant surprises, and operate around the clock to offer convenient hours. Because customers were willing to shop around to get the best deal, there would have to be lots of these types of operation, and they would all have a similar generic feel to them. This business model got the code nickname of "McFord." The ideal place to have major repairs done to a car turned out to have much more in common with an academic teaching hospital than a traditional auto dealer. Here, specialists would solve the customers' problems and provide the comfort and reassurance that a major repair would necessitate. While the company itself did not give a code name to this business model project, industry observers jokingly referred to it as "St Ford's" or "MayoFord" (or as one wag said, "Anything but Betty Ford").

THE MASSIVE CHALLENGE OF CHANNEL INERTIA

Almost 20 years later, little has changed. The franchised dealer system is still well entrenched; dealers still complain about the margins; Ford still has huge problems with its dealers; and customers still complain about pushy dealers, poor service, and inadequate product choice. The distribution problem is not unique to Ford; the majority of other motor manufacturers have attempted to change the distribution model, most with only limited success. The problem is that distribution channels build up huge inertia, and change often comes slowly and painfully.

ARE CHANNELS OF DISTRIBUTION
WHAT THE TEXTBOOKS SAY?

Almost 50 years ago, Philip McVey asked, in a very prescient article in the *Journal of Marketing,* whether channels of distribution were as simple as marketing textbooks seemed to say, or as ordered and logical as Department of Census statistics made them out to be.[2] He contended that the reality of distribution and distribution channels was very different. It would seem that little has changed. To this day, most marketing textbooks would have us believe that marketing executives make only conscious and objective decisions about distribution channels and distribution strategy. Supposedly, marketing executives can decide on how distribution objectives fit into overall strategic marketing objectives and then make the best choices that will allow those objectives to be met. The reality is very often far removed from this: marketing executives can't always make the best decisions when it comes to distribution; they simply have to accept the reality of what is already there and adapt as best they can. Rather than you choosing a distribution channel, the channel chooses you. Once choices are made, managers are reluctant to mess with success or to fix something that, while not broken, isn't always ideal. Rather than maximize when it comes to distribution, marketing executives are usually happy to satisfice.

In simple markets of old, producers of goods or services dealt directly with the consumers of those offerings. In some modern business-to-business (B2B) markets, suppliers also interact on a face-to-face basis with their customers. In most contemporary markets, however, mass production and consumption have lured intermediaries into the junction between buyer and seller. These intermediaries have either taken title to the goods or services during the flow from producer to customer, or in some way facilitated this by specializing in one or more of the functions that must be performed for such movement to occur. These flows of title and functions, and the intermediaries who have facilitated them, have generally come to be known as distribution channels.

For most marketing decision makers, dealing with the channel for a product or service ranks as one of the key marketing quandaries. In many cases, despite what the textbooks suggest, there is frequently no real decision as to *who* should constitute the channel; rather, the question is how best to deal with the incumbent channel. In addition, marketing channel decisions are critical because they intimately affect all other marketing and overall strategic decisions. Distribution channels generally involve relatively long-term commitments, but if managed effectively over time, they create a key external resource. Small wonder, then, that they exhibit powerful inertial tendencies: once they are in place and working well, managers are reluctant to fix what is not broken.

SO . . . IS ANYTHING HAPPENING?

While channels do tend to take on lives of their own, and while distribution inertia is still a fact of life for many firms, recent years have in fact witnessed significant changes in the way many products and services are distributed. These changes have come about as the result of major shifts in the environment of business—changes in legislation that have freed channels and broken restrictive trading practices; changes in economic circumstances; changes in cultural and social values; and perhaps more than anything else, changes in technology. Without doubt, the Internet has changed distribution like no other environmental force since the Industrial Revolution. Not only has it modified many of the assumptions on which distribution channel structure is based, in many cases it has transformed and even obliterated channels themselves. As a result, many traditional intermediaries have died (or are at least very ill), while new channels and new intermediaries have evolved and taken their places.

BACK TO BASICS: WHAT IS THE PURPOSE OF A DISTRIBUTION STRATEGY?

In 1958, Wroe Alderson summarized the importance of distribution, stating that the "goal of marketing is the matching of segments of supply and demand."[3] A half-century later, a distribution channel has been defined as "sets of independent organizations involved in the process of making a product or service available for use or consumption."[4] Quite simply, the purpose of a distribution channel is to make the right quantities of the right product or service available at the right place and at the right time. What makes distribution strategy unique vis-à-vis other marketing mix decisions is that it has depended, in the case of all goods, and for most services, almost entirely on physical location. The old saying among retailers is that the three keys to success are the "3 L's": location, location, location.

Alderson also argued that intermediaries provide economies of distribution by increasing the efficiency of the process.[5] They do this by creating time, place, and possession utility—right product, right place, right time. He maintained that intermediaries fulfill three basic functions, which Stern and El-Ansary[6] have distilled into the following three essential purposes of distribution channels:

1. Intermediaries support economies of scope by adjusting the discrepancy of assortments. Producers supply large quantities of a relatively small assortment of products or services, while customers require relatively small quantities of a large assortment of products and services. Through the process of exchange, intermediaries create possession utility, in addition to creating utility of time and place. Such activities, referred to as *reassortment*/sorting, comprise the following:

- Sorting, which consists of arranging products or services according to class, kind, or size.
- Sorting out, which refines sorting by, for example, grading products or output.
- Accumulation, which involves aggregating stocks from different suppliers, such as household equipment manufacturers or book publishers.
- Allocation, which is really distribution according to a plan—who will get what the producer has produced. This typically involves an activity such as "breaking bulk."
- Assorting, which means putting an appropriate "package" together. Thus, a men's outfitter might provide an assortment of suitable clothing—shirts, ties, trousers, socks, shoes, underwear.

2. Intermediaries routinize transactions so that the cost of distribution can be minimized. Because of this, transactions do not need to be bargained on an individual basis, which would tend to be inefficient in most markets. *Routinization* facilitates exchange by leading to standardization and automation. Standardizing products and services enables comparison and assessment, which in turn abet the production of the most highly valued items. By standardizing issues such as lot size, delivery frequency, payment, and communication, a routine is created to make the exchange relationship between buyers and sellers both effective and efficient. In channels where it has been possible to automate activities, the costs of such tasks as reordering can be minimized—an order is placed automatically when inventories reach a certain minimum level. In essence, automation involves machines or systems performing tasks previously performed by humans, thereby eliminating errors and reducing labor costs.

3. Intermediaries facilitate the *searching* processes of both producers and customers by structuring the information essential to both parties. Sellers are searching for buyers and buyers are searching for sellers; at the simplest level, intermediaries provide a place for these parties to find each other. Producers are not sure about customers' needs, and customers are not sure their needs can be satisfied. Intermediaries reduce this uncertainty for both parties.

These three basic functions can be used to construct a grid called the Internet distribution matrix.[7] With this matrix, we can pinpoint the effects of technology on changing distribution functions.

WHAT DOES TECHNOLOGY DO TO DISTRIBUTION?

In the early days of the World Wide Web and the Internet, much of the excitement, and certainly most of the speculation on the effects that the technology would have on marketing, centered on how it would change the ways firms communicated with their customers. While these effects have been quite remarkable, with the benefit of hindsight we now know that the most profound effects have been on distribution and distribution channels.

Internet technologies have had three major effects on distribution. They have killed distance, homogenized time, and made location largely irrelevant in the case of a significant number of industries, markets, products, and services.

THE DEATH OF DISTANCE

In the mid-1960s, an Australian named Geoffrey Blainey wrote a classic study of the impact of geographic isolation on his homeland entitled *The Tyranny of Distance*.[8] He argued that Australia and its neighbors (the case is also true for far-flung countries in the southern hemisphere such as Argentina, Chile, and South Africa) would find it far more difficult to succeed in terms of international trade because of the vast physical distances between the country and the world markets. In 1997, journalist Frances Cairncross wrote a study on the convergence of three technologies—telephone, television, and computer—and chose to recast Blainey's title by calling her book *The Death of Distance*.[9] She contends that "distance will no longer determine the cost of communicating electronically." For the distribution of many products—those that can be digitized, such as pictures, video, sound, and words—distance will thus have no effect on costs. The same is true for services. And for most products, distance will have substantially less effect on distribution costs.

THE HOMOGENIZATION OF TIME

In the physical market, time and season predominate trading and, by definition, distribution. We see evidence of this in the form of hours of operation—activities that occur by time of day and in social and climatic seasonality. The virtual marketplace is atemporal; a website is always open. The seller need not be awake to serve the buyer. Often, the buyer need not be awake, or even physically present, to be served by the seller. The web is independent of season. In fact, it can even create seasonality, such as in the case of Thanksgiving web browsers, or Google's celebration of special times such as Valentine's Day, Easter, and Halloween. Time can thus be homogenized—made uniformly consistent for all buyers and sellers. This is akin to what McKenna has called "real time": "our sense of ultra-compressed time and foreshortened horizons . . . [that] occurs when time and distance vanish, when action and response are simultaneous."[10]

THE IRRELEVANCE OF LOCATION

Any screen-based activity can be operated any place on earth. The original Internet bookstore, Amazon.com, supplies books to customers located anywhere from book suppliers located anywhere. The location of Amazon.com matters neither to book buyers nor to book publishers.

No longer is location key to most business decisions. Indeed, we can dispute whether the term even has meaning in the case of Internet pure-plays (or firms who are to all intents and purposes solely Internet based), because defining location itself becomes onerous. Is it the address where the firm is officially registered? Is it where most of the people employed by the firm work? Or is it where the server is physically situated? None of these alternatives really answers the question; the very necessity for an answer itself is questioned.

Rayport and Sviokla characterize this phenomenon as a move from marketplace to "marketspace."[11] They point out that to compare marketspace-based firms with their traditional marketplace alternatives, we need to contrast three issues: content (what the buyer purchases), context (the circumstances in which the purchase occurs), and infrastructure (simply what the firm needs in order to do business). The best way to understand a firm like Amazon.com* as a marketspace firm is simply to compare it with a conventional bookstore on the basis of these five criteria:

1. Conventional bookstores sell books; Amazon.com sells information about books, with a vast selection and a delivery system.

2. The interface in a conventional bookstore situation is in a shop with books on the shelves; in the case of Amazon.com, it is through a screen.

3. Conventional bookstores require a building with shelves, people to serve, a convenient location, and most of all, a large stock of books; Amazon.com requires a fast, efficient server and a big database.

4. Try as they might, conventional bookstores can never stock all the books in print; Amazon.com stocks only those books that sell in great numbers, yet paradoxically stocks all books.

5. The location of a conventional bookstore matters a great deal—convenient spot, high traffic, pleasant surroundings; Amazon.com's location is immaterial (while headquartered in Seattle it could indeed be anywhere), at least from a distribution perspective.

Technology is creating many marketspace firms. In doing so, cynics may observe, it is enacting three new rules of retailing: location is irrelevant, irrelevant, irrelevant.

---

*Obviously, since its inception, Amazon has moved far beyond books as its principal offerings, and today sells a vast array of merchandise. However, as a book vendor, the firm still provides an excellent, simple example and illustration of the marketspace concept.

FILLING IN THE BLOCKS: THE EFFECTS OF TECHNOLOGICAL CHANGES ON THE FUNCTION OF DISTRIBUTION CHANNELS

Contrasting the three effects of technology vertically with the three basic functions of distribution channels horizontally permits the construction of a three-by-three grid, which has been called the Internet distribution matrix[12] (shown in Figure 12-1). The matrix can be a powerful tool for managers who wish to identify opportunities for using Internet technology to improve or change distribution strategy. It can also assist in identifying competitive threats by allowing managers to concentrate on areas where other actors might use technology to perform distribution functions more effectively. Often, competition may not be from acknowledged, existing competitors, but from upstarts and players in entirely different industries (a concept that is further explored in Chapter 14).

Each cell in the matrix permits the identification of an effect of technology on a distribution function. A manager can ask, for example, what effect the death of distance will have on the function of reassortment and sorting in a company or what effect the irrelevance of location will have on the activity of searching.

To stimulate thought in this regard, and to aid what Bandura[13] calls "vicarious learning," or learning from observing others, we now consider several examples of organizations using the Internet to exploit the effects of technology on distribution functions. It should be borne in mind that neither the technological effects nor the distribution functions are entirely discrete—that is, uniquely identifiable in and of themselves. In other words, it is not possible to say that a particular website is only about the death of distance and not about time homogenization or location irrelevance. Nor is it possible to say that just because a website changes reassortment and sorting, it does not affect routinization and

FIGURE 12-1 The Internet-Distribution Matrix

	Reassortment	Routinization	Searching
Death of distance	?	?	?
Homogenization of time	?	?	?
Irrelevance of location	?	?	?

searching. Like most complex organizational phenomena, the forces all interact with each other in reality.

THE DEATH OF DISTANCE AND REASSORTMENT/SORTING

Apple's iTunes allows customers anywhere to assemble music collections of their own for playing on their computers, iPods, or other devices by sorting through vast lists of recordings by various artists of every genre and selecting just the songs they want. The service charges per song, rather than requiring a customer to purchase an entire album. Rather than compiling a collection of music for the average listener, as traditional recording companies have done in the past, or attempting to carry an acceptable and adequate inventory, like a conventional music stores, the service lets customers perform reassortment and sorting for themselves, regardless of where they are. A customer who wants Beethoven's Fifth and Guns N' Roses in the same collection, and on the same device, can have them.

THE DEATH OF DISTANCE AND ROUTINIZATION

A problem frequently encountered, particularly by B2B marketers with large product ranges, is that of routinely updating their catalogs. A catalog must accurately reflect the availability of new products and features, modifications to existing products, and price changes. Once all these changes have been made, the catalog must be made available to customers in some ways. Historically, this meant that it had to be printed and physically delivered to customers who might be located quite far away, with all the inconvenience and cost such activity incurs. The problem is compounded by a need for frequent updates, product complexities, and the potentially large number of geographically dispersed customers.

The office supplies retailer Staples carries a vast range of products, particularly in items like bulk stationary, including various kinds of paper, printer cartridges, adhesives, and the like. The Internet has proved to be a boon to the firm, which uses its website as a catalog (**www.staples.com**), thus enabling it to serve a wide range of customers, some of whom are physically distant from their nearest Staples store. The firm can also regularly update its website, rather than producing printed catalogs, and customers can use this online products directory to order supplies and replacements.

THE DEATH OF DISTANCE AND SEARCHING

Anyone who has experienced being a traveler in country A who wants to purchase an air ticket to travel from country B to country C remembers the frustration of being at the mercy of travel agents and airlines, both at home and abroad. Prices of such tickets verge on extortion, and the customer is virtually powerless in trying to deal with parties in foreign countries, especially when unable to shop on the ground locally and obtain the best deal.

Now of course, travelers have access to the local websites of online travel agents such as Expedia and Travelocity (which have websites in most major countries), as well as being able to shop on the websites of discount airlines outside of their own country. A traveler in Canada for example, who wishes to fly from Leeds in the United Kingdom to Nice in France can book this through a local travel agent and pay a full fare, or use the website of a discount airline such as Jet2 (**www.jet2.com**) and purchase a ticket for as little as £9.99.

THE HOMOGENIZATION OF TIME AND REASSORTMENT/SORTING

In a conventional setting, students who wish to complete a degree need to be in class to take the courses they want. The faculty who teach the classes and the other students who attend must also be there, all at the same time. When the time slots of two desired courses conflict or the classes are taught one after the other at opposite ends of the campus, students generally cannot attend more than one at a time.

This problem was particularly prevalent in many MBA programs when it came to elective courses and students having to choose among appealing offerings in a way that generally resulted in satisficing rather than optimizing. Traditional distance-learning programs attempted to overcome these problems, but they were only partly successful. Students missed the live interaction real-time classes provide.

Currently, it is almost possible to have the best of both worlds, as education has moved online. Some excellent traditional university business schools, such as the University of Baltimore or Colorado State University, offer MBA programs that are entirely virtual. The Internet has also created opportunities for entrepreneurial institutions to enter the education market—for example, Jones International University (**http://jonesinternational.edu/**) is an entirely online university owned by a for-profit firm that offers a wide range of high-quality courses to potential students anywhere. Its business school has even earned the accreditation of the Association of Accredited Collegiate Schools of Business (AACSB), placing it in the same ranks as high-quality, traditional schools around the world.

THE HOMOGENIZATION OF TIME AND ROUTINIZATION

Technology has made it possible for customers to complete tasks that used to be entirely dependent on time, when it suits them and not when it suits a firm or a service provider. For example, there was a time when a customer had to wait for a bank to open before he or she could obtain service. Members of airline frequent flyer schemes had to wait for the airline to assess their miles, print a report, and mail it to them. Stock traders had to wait for a brokerage to open before placing a buy or sell order. Now, a customer simply logs on to his or her banking website to check account balances, make payments, and transfer funds between accounts. A member of an air miles rewards scheme can check up-to-the minute balances and request tickets or upgrades whenever he or she wants to. A stock trader can receive up-to-the-minute market information and then buy or sell accordingly.

Thus, time has become homogenized and transactions routinized because customers can perform activities when it suits them, without having to wait for reports to be mailed or for offices to open. What were once highly customized activities have been reduced to routines by systems.

THE HOMOGENIZATION OF TIME AND SEARCHING

In many markets, the need to reduce uncertainty by searching is compounded by the problem that buyer and seller operate in different time zones or at different hours of the day or week. Even simple activities such as routine communication among parties are problematic. Employee recruitment presents a good example of these issues—companies search for employees and individuals search for jobs. Both parties often rely on recruitment agencies to enter the channel as intermediaries, not only to simplify the search processes but also to manage their time, such as setting up interviews convenient for both.

A number of enterprising sites for recruitment have been established online. One of the largest of these, Monster (**www.monster.com**), lists many thousands of jobs all over the world. The company keeps potential employees informed by providing customized e-mail updates for job seekers. Meanwhile, potential employers can access details and even résumés of suitable candidates online, at any time.

The recruitment market also provides excellent examples of "getting it wrong" and "getting it right" on the Internet as a distribution medium. For many years, the Higher Education Supplement of the *London Times* has offered the greatest market for jobs in higher education in the United Kingdom and the British Commonwealth. Almost all senior positions and many lower level jobs in universities and tertiary institutions are advertised. In 1996, the *Times Higher* set up a website (**www.THES.co.uk**) on which job seekers could conveniently browse and sort through all the available positions. This apparently affected sales, for within a short time the site began to require registration and subscription, probably in an attempt to shore up revenues affected by a decline in circulation.

As Schwartz has pointed out, knowing what to charge for and how on the web are issues with which most managers are still grappling.[14] Web surfers, perhaps enamored of the fact that most Internet content is free, seem unwilling to pay for it unless it produces real, tangible, immediate, and direct benefits. Universities in the United Kingdom may have begun to sense that their recruiting was less effective, or someone may have had a bright idea. At any rate, at the same time the *Times Higher* was attempting to charge surfers for access to its job pages, a consortium of universities set up a site (**www.jobs.ac.uk**) to which they all posted available positions. Not only are job seekers able to specify and search by criteria, but once a potential position is found, they can link directly to the home page of the institution to obtain further information on such issues as the student body, research, facilities, and faculty.

Jobs.ac.uk did not need to run at a profit, as did the *Times Higher.* The benefits to the institutions came in the form of reduced advertising costs and being on a site where job seekers would obviously come to look for positions. This is similar to the way shoppers reduce their search in the real world by shopping in malls that have more than one store of the type they intend to patronize. In the end, the *Times Higher* reverted to making the jobs search section of its website free to all, but there is no doubt that the original desire to charge for content led to the reintermediation of a competitor who hasn't gone away.

THE IRRELEVANCE OF LOCATION AND REASSORTMENT/SORTING

Conventional PC vendors have attempted to serve the average customer by offering a range of standard products from computer manufacturers. Most manufacturers have relied on these intermediaries to tell them what the average customer requires; they then produce an average product for this market. The customer travels to a nearby store to purchase the product. In this market, location matters; the store must be easily accessible to customers and large enough to carry a reasonable selection of goods, as well as provide access and parking.

Dell (**www.dell.com**) has proven to be one of the real success stories of electronic commerce. The company has become the number-one vendor of PCs in the world, and most of its accomplishment has been achieved online. Customers use Dell's website to customize their own computers by clicking on such attributes as processor speed, RAM size, hard drive, CD-ROM, and other features. A handy calculator instantly updates customers on the cost of what they are specifying, so they can adjust their budgets accordingly.

Once a customer is satisfied with the specified package, he or she can place an order and pay online. Then the finished product can be delivered to the customer anywhere, regardless of location. Indeed, location is irrelevant to customers; the company is where they want it to be. Meanwhile, customers actually do some of Dell's work by getting to do the reassortment and sorting themselves.

THE IRRELEVANCE OF LOCATION AND ROUTINIZATION

Typically, location has been vital to the establishment of routines, efforts to standardize, and automation. It was easier and less costly for major buyers to set up purchasing procedures with suppliers who were nearby if not local, particularly when the purchasing process required lengthy face-to-face negotiation over such issues as price, quality, and specification. Examples of major B2B purchasing off websites, however, has tended to negate this conventional wisdom.

Caterpillar made its first attempt at serious online purchasing in June 1997, when it invited preapproved suppliers to bid on a $2.4 million order for hydraulic fittings—simple plastic parts that cost under a dollar but can bring a $2 million bulldozer to a standstill when they go wrong. Twenty-three suppliers elected to make bids in an online process on Caterpillar's website. The first bids came in high, but by lunchtime only nine were still left revising offers. By the time the session closed at the end of the day, the low bid was 22 cents. The previous low price paid on the component by Caterpillar was 30 cents. The company now attains an average savings of 6 percent through its website supplier bidding system. Many large firms in B2B markets are now making use of and participating in B2B exchanges, and the growth of this phenomenon has been significant.[15]

THE IRRELEVANCE OF LOCATION AND SEARCHING

In the past, most buyers have patronized proximal suppliers because the costs of searching further afield generally outweigh the benefits of a possible lower price. This also creates opportunities for intermediaries to enter the channel. They serve local markets by searching for suppliers on their behalf, while at the same time serving producers by giving them access to more distant and disparate markets. Travel agents and insurance brokers have been typical examples of this phenomenon: they search for suitable offerings for customers from a large range of potential suppliers, while finding customers for these suppliers whom the latter would not have been able to reach directly in an economical fashion. As a result, the intermediary "owns" the customer and commands the power in the channel.

Some years ago, Blattberg and Deighton suggested presciently that interactive marketing would enable suppliers to win back power from the channel.[16] This has occurred in a number of industries. Many airlines cut the commission they traditionally offered to travel agents as they encouraged passengers to book directly online; the same phenomenon occurred in the hotel and rental car industries. Technology enables customers to fulfill the search function previously performed by travel agents. Similarly, suppliers in the travel industry do not need to rely on agents to find their customers any more. Similar effects are being seen in markets ranging from insurance services to real estate.[17]

LONG-TERM EFFECTS OF THE IMPACT OF TECHNOLOGY ON DISTRIBUTION CHANNELS

The long-term effects of the death of distance, homogenization of time, and irrelevance of location on the evolution of distribution channels will be manifold and complex. However, three effects have become apparent, and they will undoubtedly continue to affect distribution as we know it in profound ways.

First, in the future, we may talk of distribution media rather than distribution channels for most services and many products. A medium can variously be defined as follows:

- Something, such as an intermediate course of action, that occupies a position or represents a condition midway between extremes.
- An agency by which something is accomplished, conveyed, or transferred.
- A surrounding environment in which something functions and thrives.

The key distinction between a channel and a medium in this context concerns the notion of interactivity. Electronic media such as the Internet and devices such as cell phones, PDAs, and music devices such as iPods are intrinsically interactive. Thus, whereas channels were typically conduits for products, these technologies have the potential to go beyond passive distribution of products and services, to become an active (and central) creative element in the production of the product or service. They can create virtual markets (Betfair.com), virtual communities (NuNomad.com and LaptopHobo.com), or virtual worlds (Second Life). The medium is thus the central element that allows consumers to co-create a market (in the case of Betfair), their own service and product (in NuNomad), and their own virtual world (in Second Life). Critically, in each instance the primary relationship is not between customers, but rather with the mediated environment with which they mutually interact. In the case of interactive electronic media, McLuhan's well-known adage "the medium is the message"[18] can be complemented with the addendum that, in some cases, the medium is the product.

A second effect of these forces on channel functions may be a rise in commoditization because channels have a diminished effect on marketers' ability to differentiate the product or service. Commoditization can be seen as a process by which the complex and the difficult become so simple and easy that anyone can do them. It may be a natural outcome of competition and technological advances, with prices plunging and essential differences vanishing. Commoditization will be accelerated by the evolution of distribution media that will speed information flow and thus make markets more efficient. The only antidotes to it will be to identify a niche market too small to be attractive to others, an innovation sufficiently rapid to stay ahead of the pack, or a monopoly. No one needs to be reminded that the last option is even more difficult to establish than the first two. However, as much as these forces impel commoditization, they are paradoxically permitting—indeed, driving—mass customization, which is the very antithesis of commoditization.

Dell lets customers build their own computers (albeit with commoditized components); Priceline allows customers to pay the price they want to pay (albeit for a commoditized air ticket); Second Life gives customers the opportunity to create their own alter personae. Although commoditization may present a gloomy picture, there may be a fortuitous flipside to electronic media as they become the ultimate tools for mass customization, or personalization.

Disintermediation and reintermediation comprise the third effect we discern. As networks connect everybody to everybody else, they increase the opportunities for shortcuts. So when a buyer can connect straight from the computer on his desk to the computer of an insurance company or an airline, insurance brokers and travel agents begin to seem slow, inconvenient, and overpriced. The marketing of products, as opposed to more intangible services, is also being driven by cheap, convenient, and increasingly universal distribution networks such as FedEx and UPS. No longer does a consumer have to wait for a retailer (who doesn't carry a good inventory of the latest products) to open, drive there, attempt to find a salesperson (who is generally ill-informed), and then pay more than expected to purchase a product. Products and prices can be compared online, and lots of information can be gleaned. If one supplier is out of stock or too expensive, there is no need to drive miles to a competitor. Competitors abound, and all are equidistant—a mere mouse click away.

All of these opportunities can lead to disintermediation, whereby traditional intermediaries are squeezed out of channels. As networks become increasingly mass market, there is a continuous contest of disintermediation. However, these technologies also create opportunities for reintermediation, whereby intermediaries may enter channels facilitated electronically. This could occur when an intermediary performs one of the three fundamental channel functions of reassortment/sorting, routinization, and searching more effectively than anyone else. Thus, intermediaries have entered channels to facilitate search—in the auto market, for example, Autobytel (**www.autobytel.com**) entered the channel for new and used cars, a channel that had previously been unchanged for about a hundred years. Similarly, sites such as Woot (**www.woot.com**) enable over-stocked vendors to routinely dispose of excess inventory by hosting fire sales of one item a day at bargain prices. Lastminute.com facilitates a meeting place between vendors of perishable services (such as hotel rooms, flights, and theater tickets) and customers who want to do something at a bargain price "at the last minute," thus providing a very valuable reassortment service.

The Internet distribution matrix can be used by existing firms and entrepreneurs to identify at least three things:

1. How might electronic technology offer opportunities to a company to perform its existing distribution functions of reassortment/sorting, routinization, and searching more efficiently and effectively? Cases of other organizations using the medium to perform these activities, such as those we have identified, can stimulate thinking.

2. The matrix can enable the identification of competitors poised to use the media to change distribution in the industry and the market.

3. It may enable managers to brainstorm ways in which an industry can be vulnerable.

Neither a company nor its immediate competitors may be contemplating using technology to achieve radical change. However, that does not mean a small start-up is not doing so. And the problem with such small startups (as we will explore in Chapter 14) is that they do not operate in a visible way or at the same time. In many cases, they might not even take an industry by storm. But they might very well deprive a market of its most valuable customers as they exploit technology to change the basic functions of distribution.

Key Terms

- distribution
- search
- routinization

- reassortment
- death of distance
- homogenization of time

- irrelevance of location

Questions

1. Explain in your own words what is meant by "distribution channel inertia."
2. Does the "death of distance" principle operate in all markets and for all products and services?
3. What is meant by the "homogenization of time"?
4. Identify examples of innovative distribution strategies for any four of the nine cells in the matrix in Figure 12-1 not already identified in the text, and explain them.
5. Explain to executives in a firm how the matrix in Figure 12-1 can help them identify opportunities and threats that might face their current distribution strategy.

Resources and References

1. For an excellent description of this, see Schlesinger, L. A., & Pelofsky, M. (1989). *Ford Motor Co.: Dealer sales and service,* Case study 690030. Soldiers Field, MA: Harvard Business School Press.
2. McVey, P. (1960). Are channels of distribution what the textbooks say? *Journal of Marketing* 24(3): 61–65.
3. Alderson, W. (1954). Factors governing the development of marketing channels, in R. M. Clewett (ed.), *Marketing channels for manufactured products* (pp. 34–43). Homewood, IL: Richard D. Irwin.
4. Coughlan, A., Anderson, E., Stern, L. W., & El-Ansary, A. (2005). *Marketing channels.* Englewood Cliffs, NJ: Prentice-Hall.
5. Alderson.
6. Stern, L. & El-Ansary, A. (1988). *Marketing channels,* 3rd ed. Englewood Cliffs, NJ: Prentice-Hall.
7. Pitt, L. F., Berthon, P. R., & Berthon, J. P. (1999). Changing channels: The impact of the Internet on distribution strategy. *Business Horizons*, 42(2): 19–28.
8. Blainey, G. (1966). *The tyranny of distance.* Sydney: Pan MacMillan.
9. Cairncross, F. (1997). *The death of distance: How the communications revolution will change our lives.* London: Orion Business Books.
10. McKenna, R. (1997). *Real time: Preparing for the age of the never satisfied customer.* Boston: Harvard Business School Press.
11. Rayport, J. F., & Sviokla, J. J. (1994). Managing in the marketspace. *Harvard Business Review* 72(6): 141–150.
12. Stern & El-Ansary.
13. Bandura, A. (1977). *Social learning theory.* Englewood Cliffs, NJ: Prentice-Hall.
14. Schwartz, E. (L. Marino, ed.). (1999). *Digital Darwinism: Seven breakthrough business strategies for surviving in the cutthroat web economy.* New York: Broadway Books.
15. Gatti. J. (2003, September). B2B exchanges hanging tough. *Direct Marketing:* 1.
16. Blattberg, R. C., & Deighton, J. (1991). Interactive marketing: Exploiting the age of addressability. *Sloan Management Review* 33(1): 5–14.
17. Gallaugher, J. M. (2002). E-commerce and the UNDULATING distribution channel. *Communications of the ACM* 45(7): 89–95.
18. McLuhan, M. (1964). *Understanding media.* New York: McGraw-Hill.

CHAPTER

REAL GOLD GOES TO THE BOLD
THE ENTREPRENEURIAL SALES FORCE

THE NEED FOR A NEW MINDSET

This chapter is about the sales function, and the role it can and should play in 21st-century companies.[1] This is a role that is very different from the way in which sales has traditionally been approached. It is a simple truth that the majority of companies fail to realize the potential of their sales managers and salespeople. The tendency in many firms is to view sales as a mechanical set of activities, where salespeople are routinely hired and trained, territories are defined, quotas are set, incentives are offered, and performance is closely monitored and either rewarded or punished. All too often, salespeople are treated as replaceable objects, where the trick is simply one of putting together the right combination of "carrots and sticks," or incentives and sanctions, to motivate employees to sell. Management is preoccupied with making sure the salespeople are making the right number of calls, calling on the right accounts, pushing the right products, selling at the right price, and closing the right number of deals.

Today's competitive environment demands a radically different approach. The ability of firms to exploit the true potential of its sales organization requires that company executives adopt a whole new mindset about the role of the selling function within the firm, how the sales force is managed, and what salespeople are expected to produce. We believe that the sales function must serve as a dynamic source of value creation and innovation within the firm. This new mindset is centered on a number of core principles:

- The sales function must become a source of competitive advantage in companies.
- Great sales organizations are run strategically and with strategic intent.
- Sales managers and salespeople must see themselves as entrepreneurs, and the sales department should be the most entrepreneurial area within companies.
- Sales must be an opportunity-driven, rather than a resource-constrained, activity.
- Innovation is a major responsibility of those in sales.
- The ability to create, develop, and manage relationships with customers is the single biggest way in which salespeople create value in the marketplace.
- The sales function is not separate from the marketing function.
- Peak performance in sales is most likely when organizations have dynamic management systems to support the sales force.

These principles are the foundation for a redefinition of modern selling. To appreciate the relevance of each principle, we have to recognize the fundamental changes taking place in the contemporary business environment. The changes are dramatic, and they undermine many of the basic assumptions regarding what it takes to succeed in sales.

DOMINANT FORCES OF CHANGE

The 21st century is a time of amazing change. It is a basic truism within organizations that "external change forces internal change." What is happening outside the company has significant implications for how things are organized and managed inside the company. These implications are especially meaningful for the sales force. Figure 13-1 illustrates some of the key external changes affecting how a sales force operates.

A beginning in understanding these changes is to recognize that the mass market is dead. Today's markets are highly fragmented and can be expected to become only more so. Terms like *relationship marketing* and *one-to-one marketing* have been introduced to describe an environment in which not only is the market segmented into dozens and even hundreds of very narrowly defined segments (and narrow niches), but also individual customers must be approached as unique market segments. Meanwhile, customer expectations continue to ratchet upward. As a result, much more emphasis is placed on customized solutions for customers.

Those in sales must have much more knowledge at their fingertips. Not only must they understand their own products and services, but also customers expect them to know much more about the buying organization. Pre-call preparation has

FIGURE 13-1   Environmental Conditions and the Sales Force

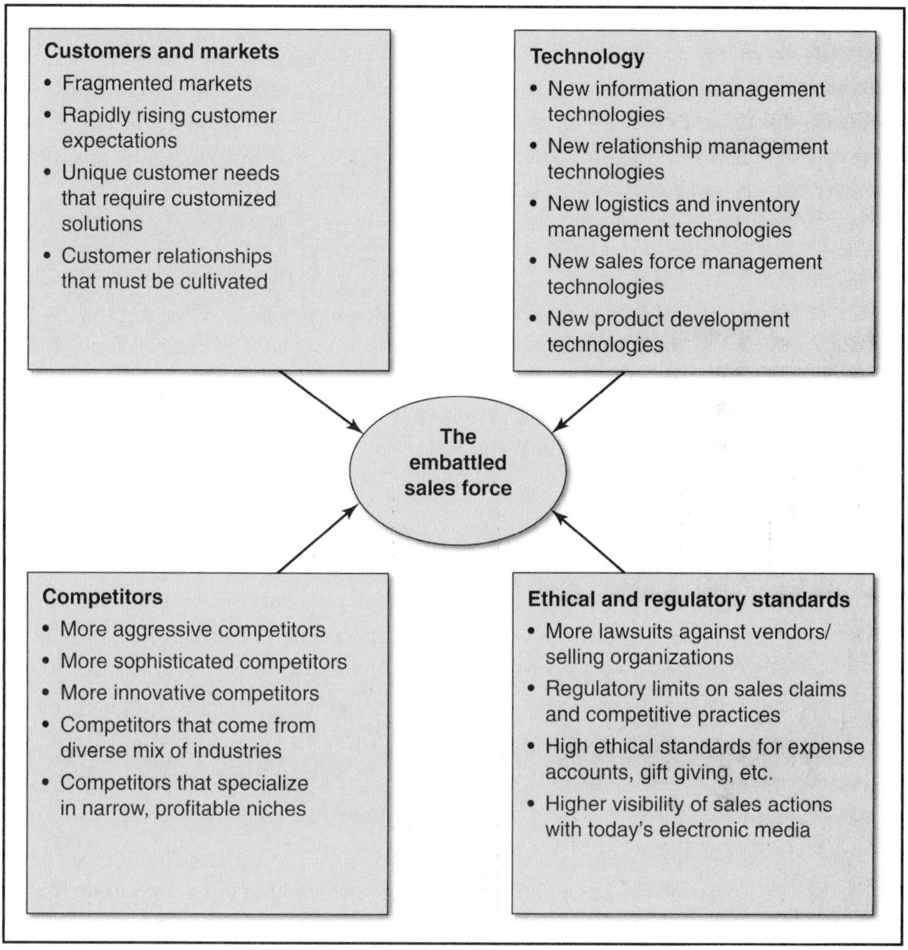

Customers and markets
- Fragmented markets
- Rapidly rising customer expectations
- Unique customer needs that require customized solutions
- Customer relationships that must be cultivated

Technology
- New information management technologies
- New relationship management technologies
- New logistics and inventory management technologies
- New sales force management technologies
- New product development technologies

The embattled sales force

Competitors
- More aggressive competitors
- More sophisticated competitors
- More innovative competitors
- Competitors that come from diverse mix of industries
- Competitors that specialize in narrow, profitable niches

Ethical and regulatory standards
- More lawsuits against vendors/ selling organizations
- Regulatory limits on sales claims and competitive practices
- High ethical standards for expense accounts, gift giving, etc.
- Higher visibility of sales actions with today's electronic media

taken on new meaning. New priorities are being placed on the sales organization's ability to collect and store the right kinds of customer data, analyze these data, and make specific recommendations that reflect the unique requirements of a given account.

Speed has become a key source of competitive advantage for companies; those that cannot keep up the pace quickly fall behind. As a result, customer expectations are on the rise regarding response time to their questions and demands. Collectively, customer demands for quick response can overwhelm salespeople, who must simultaneously balance a multiplicity of other responsibilities. Thus, in addition to information overload, salespeople can experience role overload (burnout) as they struggle to fill all the different roles they are expected to play.

To effectively serve customers' needs, salespeople must become "leveragers" of organizational resources. That is, they must be adept at tapping into a variety of resources within their own firms on behalf of customers. They must be able to appeal to and coordinate the efforts of people in production, customer service, product development, credit and finance, senior management, and other areas—all in an attempt to serve the needs of a particular customer. As these needs continually change, it becomes vital to elicit renewed support and leverage new resources from within the selling organization. Thus, salespeople must not simply build relationships with customers, they must build them with key members of their own firm.

To establish and maintain strong customer relationships, especially when selling in business-to-business markets, salespeople must also deal with a greater number and variety of individuals within client organizations. Understanding the dynamics of how people influence decision-making processes has become significantly more challenging as these processes center more around teams and networks (rather than around one or two individuals) embedded within the buying organization. The growing reliance on strategic alliances between companies makes things even more complex. Executives argue that such alliances better enable their companies to package "total solutions" for their customers. Salespeople need to be capable of analyzing lines of power and influence across blurring boundaries between firms.

Many markets today can be described as hypercompetitive. It is not simply that there are more competitors, or that these competitors are more aggressive; it is the rate at which new forms of competition emerge and old ones fall away. Companies today find themselves competing with firms not just in their own industry. These types of competitors are often the most threatening, as their assumptions about how to compete are very different. They often play by a different set of rules and are not constrained by the traditional assumptions made by existing competitors.

Competition is also changing the economics of selling. Performance expectations can be extreme as salespeople find they are squeezed between tougher revenue and profit targets, higher costs of serving customers, and greater pressure to be more efficient. As product life cycles get shorter, competitors must leapfrog one another with new products and features and new support services. For their part, salespeople struggle to manage their time, keep their market knowledge up to date, meet demanding performance metrics, maintain happy customers, and generate new business.

Another implication of the modern selling environment is that firms increasingly worry less about making a single sale to a given account and more about customer lifetime value (CLV). That is, the real goal is to capture a certain percentage of what a customer will spend on a given product category over a number of years. Effective market strategies differentiate customers based on their lifetime value. The CLV concept has critical implications for how the sales organization allocates resources to market segments and individual accounts. It forces the salespeople to approach client prospecting and account management in completely different ways.

Meanwhile, technologies are enabling salespeople to (1) find and qualify prospects with much greater sophistication; (2) interact with customers in unique ways at every stage of the selling process; (3) know customers intimately; (4) allocate time much more efficiently; (5) be instantaneously on top of changes in customer requirements; (6) identify emerging patterns in the marketplace; and (7) continuously assess the profitability of products, customers, territories, and distributors. Some of the major innovations in selling, such as customer relationship management (CRM) and sale force automation (SFA) systems, are predicated on continually changing technologies. In short, technology enables the ability of the sales force to customize, adds speed to the sales organization, and makes salespeople smarter and more efficient.

The legal and ethical environment plays a growing role in defining acceptable sales behavior. We live in a highly litigious age, where the sales efforts of companies are an increasingly popular target of lawyers and lawsuits. As a result, sales organizations are placing limitations on the claims that can be made to customers and establishing standards that must be upheld in sales transactions. Salespeople are becoming more careful about the arguments used and inducements offered when attempting to win customers. Alternatively, long-term relationships with customers can encourage compromises of a different kind. Members of the buying and selling organization become so close that they engage in compromising behaviors in the name of the overall relationship. Sales managers are being held more accountable for ensuring that their salespeople are vigilant in behaving in a manner that reflects acceptable ethical standards. Salespeople also have to be more judicious when managing expense accounts, giving gifts, addressing unethical demands from buyers, making promises about product performance and delivery, and selling products that can be perceived as unnecessary. The challenges become all the more complex when operating internationally.

A NEW CONCEPT OF THE SALES FORCE

The dramatic changes in the modern selling environment have led skeptics to question whether the sales force as we know it is becoming obsolete. In fact, in response to these environmental changes, some firms have attempted to eliminate, cut back, or outsource the selling function.[2] Others have experimented with modifications to the structure, composition, objectives, and procedures of their sales forces. For example, key account and ad hoc selling teams are replacing "lone wolf" salespeople, and a focus on building and maintaining profitable long-term customer relationships is replacing an emphasis on short-term revenue goals. Firms are also beginning to recognize a need for changes in the sales culture and ingrained behaviors of salespeople, both of which can take considerable time.

We believe that the sales force can avoid obsolescence and can actually become a significant source of sustainable competitive advantage in 21st-century companies. However, this cannot happen if companies simply make incremental modifications to sales operations. Instead, a new model of the sales force is needed.

FIGURE 13-2 A New Model of the Sales Force

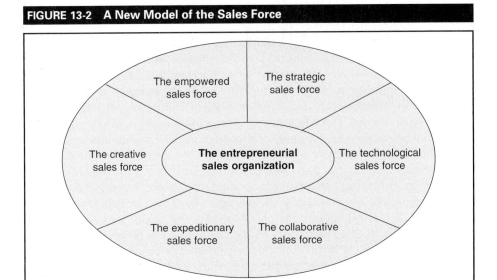

We believe that this new model should be built around six key elements that, when combined, produce what we call "the entrepreneurial sales organization" (see Figure 13-2). Let's look at each of these elements in turn.

THE CREATIVE SALES FORCE

Creativity must be the soul of the sales organization. It can be defined as the act of relating previously unrelated things. Creative thinking is vital in every facet of sales management and personal selling. To appreciate its role, let's consider creativity at the level of the sales organization as well as the individual salesperson.

Creativity in sales organizations is about destruction and construction. It requires the abandonment of certain assumptions, the rejection of accepted precepts, and a willingness to challenge established methods. It also results in concepts or solutions that can disrupt the work lives of people in companies, making them break out of patterns and comfort zones. But creativity also brings with it a fresh start, a new way, a freedom from the constraints of what was, and a path to what can be. It is a manifestation of the human spirit, such that the act of successful creativity is, by itself, a tremendous source of employee motivation and pride. To create is to matter, to count, to make a difference, to have an impact, and to be a source of value.

Sales organizations tend to be insensitive to the nuances and idiosyncrasies of the individual attempting to be creative. They typically are intolerant of failure, penalize rule-breaking, insist that people approach things from a logical point of view, discourage ambiguity, and assign people to jobs with narrow job descriptions. While sales managers routinely encourage employees to "think outside the box," they can be rigid enforcers of the rules of the box, allocating resources only to things inside the box and evaluating employees based on contributions to the box.

Although creativity will always be an art, sales organizations need not view it as unmanageable. On one level, creativity is messy, random, and unscientific. On another level, structure plays a role in creativity, and organizations that approach creativity from a more systematic perspective tend to come up with a lot more great ideas. Sales managers must emphasize practices that result in employees being challenged, provide them with freedom, and give them access to resources. Similarly, practices that result in well-designed, mutually supportive, and diverse work teams are likely to spur creativity. Also valuable is encouragement for creative outputs and reinforcement in terms of the values, systems, and structures of the sales organization.

Fostering creative problem solving also requires that sales managers figure out how to get different approaches and perspectives to grate against one another in a process called "creative abrasion." The point is not to create situations where colliding ideas battle one another, with one winning out and the other losing. Nor is the objective to encourage compromise, alignment of positions, or watering down of one or both positions so as to achieve unity of direction. Creative abrasion serves to facilitate divergence, and it must be complemented by leadership styles that ultimately produce convergence. Abrasion involves highlighting differences that are natural and that increase the level of stimulation and variety in the organization. Examples of efforts to take advantage of abrasion could include hiring salespeople who are not like current employees; putting together interfunctional sales teams (salespeople, design engineers, procurement managers, accounting personnel); giving a sales team two seemingly incompatible goals; introducing a perspective that threatens the current positions and assumptions of those in the sales group; blurring responsibilities among departments or functions; and bringing in consultants, temporary staff, or speakers who hold very different points of view.

THE EXPEDITIONARY (OR INNOVATING) SALES FORCE

When applied within the sales organization, creativity can result in innovation. Sales innovations can take many forms—from novel methods for qualifying leads to unusual solutions that solve vexing customer problems. Innovation must become a core competency in sales. This competency consists of an ability to come up with meaningful innovations and then champion them to the point that they are adopted by senior management, by other departments within the sales professional's own firm, and/or by customers.

Innovation is dynamic. It represents a moving target. New approaches have short lives and are inevitably replaced by newer approaches. Accordingly, companies must create what we call an *expeditionary* sales force, meaning a sales organization that moves quickly in recognizing opportunity and acting on it; one that is continually discovering new realms of possibility. Moreover, an expeditionary sales force *leads* its customers, *leads* its competitors, and ultimately *leads* its own firm.

Let's begin with customers. A traditional perspective on innovation is that firms should ask customers what they want and then find a way to give it to them.

In a sense, then, the sales organization is following the customer. A problem comes into play, though, when customers don't know exactly what they want or are too busy and focused on their own problems to convey a clear sense of what sort of innovations might address their needs. The term *expeditionary* describes a sales force that leads customers instead of following them. Leading customers means taking them in new directions and producing modifications in how they buy.

The ability to lead customers implies that the sales professional knows the customer intimately. This awareness extends well beyond current and upcoming product needs. It includes an understanding of the core strategies being pursued by, the current and emerging capabilities and competencies of, and the competitive and other environmental challenges faced by the customer organization.

This leadership also applies to competitors. The expeditionary sales force does not mimic the moves of its adversaries. Rather, it learns from competitor successes (and failures), improves upon them, and ultimately displaces them. Sales organizations have a tendency to believe that whatever the competition is doing must be right, and they tend to overreact to any new competitive action. While an organization cannot afford to ignore competing firms, those firms' circumstances differ, including their resources, their capabilities and constraints, and the opportunities open to them. The expeditionary sales organization effectively competes with itself. Rather than play a game of one-upsmanship with competitors, the expeditionary firm is continually trying to outdo its own achievements. A sense of "healthy dissatisfaction" pervades the organization, where managers are always seeking better ways to do everything.

Finally, the expeditionary sales force leads its own company. With changes in the business environment occurring so rapidly, one of the most important and increasingly difficult tasks confronting the sales function involves monitoring the external environment, deciphering patterns and trends, predicting how things might change, and developing strategies and plans that exploit and even modify environmental conditions. From its position on the front line of the organization, the sales force has the best perspective from which to observe and respond to market turbulence and to inform the organization about developments in the marketplace. The sales force becomes an instrumental source of guidance and direction in organizational efforts to adapt.

THE EMPOWERED SALES FORCE

Management control is vital in sales organizations. Without a variety of controls over budgets and sales personnel, it would be impossible to determine what is going on, distinguish high from low performers, satisfy customers on a consistent basis, or find ways to continually improve. And yet, too much control limits the ability of salespeople to demonstrate imagination and creativity in their jobs. The challenge is to find a balance between the tightness and the looseness of control.

The approach in many sales organizations tends to be top-down as opposed to bottom-up. In top-down organizations, territories are defined, quotas are set, selling methods are prescribed, compensation approaches are put in place, and other operating decisions are made by senior management; salespeople are then expected to implement the directives. With this approach, the salesperson is recognized as having selling talent, and management's role is to ensure the holder of this talent is properly motivated, allocates his or her time in an optimal fashion, and sells enough of the right products to the right customers.

We believe that sales managers and salespeople must be viewed as entrepreneurs. They should be opportunity identifiers, creative problem solvers, and organizational value creators. The key to this perspective is the empowerment of the sales force. *Empowerment* is an overused and frequently abused term in today's organizations. The popularity of this term suggests a general recognition that employees should be given more responsibility and authority in performing their jobs. However, in spite of this recognition, organizations fail to empower because (1) they don't really believe in it, (2) they don't understand the complexities and commitment involved in accomplishing it, or (3) their managers lack the requisite skills and are not especially good at it.

One approach to empowerment is simply to set high performance standards and let salespeople do whatever it takes to meet them. This approach is extremely short-sighted. It encourages expedient behavior and can produce outcomes that are inconsistent with the core strategies of the firm. It also ignores the fact that sustainable innovation in companies requires discipline, team collaboration, and ongoing learning. Another faulty approach to empowerment is "tokenism," where managers allow employees the occasional freedom to make decisions for themselves but then quickly withdraw that freedom when something goes wrong.

Empowerment involves risk and requires trust. It must be built into the design of sales jobs. Further, jobs themselves must be defined more broadly, with significant discretion to try new approaches and create novel solutions for customers. The salesperson in effect becomes responsible for tailoring elements of the entire marketing mix to serve an account, including the product configuration, pricing, customer communication, and logistics. He or she becomes accountable for value creation for customers and for innovating on behalf of the firm.

Empowerment does not mean that anything goes. A guiding principle of empowerment is "giving up control to gain control." By this we mean that the sales manager must be good at delegation, but it must be enlightened delegation. When a manager gives up control of some activity or area of responsibility (e.g., setting sales quotas, negotiating prices) and instead allows employees to handle it, control is being given up. And yet, if the empowered employee responds by being more conscientious, more creative, or harder working, then control is actually being gained. The control is not over the intermediate actions of the employee, but over the employee's final output, as well as the employee's sense of accomplishment and job satisfaction. Hence, giving the salesperson more discretion over some activity or decision variable must be coupled with a very clear sense of the larger objective.

THE STRATEGIC SALES FORCE

There is a tendency among sales organizations to focus heavily on tactical maneuvers and operational considerations instead of thinking and acting strategically. Considerable time and effort are spent hiring salespeople, designing sales incentives, developing sales appeals, and so forth, and these organizations try to ensure such day-to-day decisions are accomplished in a manner that ensures resources are being used efficiently. But efficiency does not imply effectiveness. Efficiency means that the actions that are being pursued are performed in the right way. Effectiveness means that the right opportunities are being exploited, the right activities are being pursued, and the right results are being achieved. Both efficiency and effectiveness are important with a sales force, and a *strategic* orientation helps ensure that both are achieved.

There are two dimensions to a strategic orientation in selling. The first of these dimensions involves the connection between the company as a whole and the sales force. The second dimension involves the connection between the overall role, direction, and priorities of the sales organization and the day-to-day operational decisions made by sales managers and salespeople. Let's consider each in turn.

The job of selling should not be managed in isolation. The strategic sales unit or department is one that is closely aligned with the strategic intent of the organization. Corporate strategy provides a clear sense of where the firm is going and the path for getting there. Overall strategy defines the firm's core value proposition; how the firm intends to position and differentiate itself; and the relative importance of existing versus new markets, existing versus new customers, and existing versus new products. The decisions in these areas should permeate every aspect of sales management and personal selling, from the types of objectives set for the sales force to the types of people hired for sales positions and from the way the sales force is organized to the determination of sales force call patterns.

Linking the sales unit or department to the overall strategies of the firm is a two-way street. Thus, the sales department should play a meaningful role in the formulation of a company's overall strategic direction. The goals of the sales function must be central to the overall goals and strategies of the firm. Salespeople should drive company innovation efforts as much as these innovation efforts drive the way salespeople are approaching their jobs.

A related aspect of a company-level strategic orientation is the need to closely align the sales function with other areas of the firm. Sales must be integrated with production, marketing, logistics, and other core functions and units within a company. Customers will invest in relationships only when the selling firm is making meaningful investments and the investments are ongoing. The selling firm must be able to continually create new sources of value for the customer. A sales force cannot achieve this type of value creation in isolation. Salespeople must be able to speak the language, understand the resources and budgets, and appreciate the operational problems of other functions and departments in their own firms.

Earlier we discussed how the sales department must become an important source of innovation and value creation within companies. However, it is important to keep in mind a caveat. As sales managers and salespeople discover and act on new opportunities, develop unique solutions for customers, or come up with whole new approaches to ways in which sales tasks are accomplished, they should not pursue new initiatives just because those initiatives are interesting, different, or expedient. Innovation that is random and unfocused can do more harm than good. It is vital that the creative efforts of those in sales be consistent with the strategic direction and the core capabilities of the firm.

The second dimension of a strategic approach concerns what happens within the sales organization itself and the manner in which sales-related activities are accomplished. Sales management involves hundreds of decisions. Life inside a sales unit or department is filled with deadlines, daily pressures to perform, and periodic crises. These realities lead managers to make decisions in isolation, on the spur of the moment, and/or expediently. While some of this expediency cannot be avoided, in the strategic sales organization there is an attempt to "connect the dots" when making decisions. This means the sales force itself has a clear sense of strategic direction. Decisions regarding who and what type of people to hire, how their jobs are defined, the manner in which their performance is assessed and they are compensated, and so forth, are made in a manner that is consistent with the strategic direction of the overall sales function.

THE TECHNOLOGICAL SALES FORCE

More than any other single factor, *technology* is transforming the capabilities of the company sales force. As a result, failure to embrace technology within sales undermines the firm's fundamental ability to compete. The integration of technology must happen both in sales management and in personal selling.

In sales management, new information technologies allow leading-edge companies to identify more and better candidates for sales positions, train salespeople continually and virtually, define sales territories in ways that optimize performance, and reward salespeople in creative ways and on a real-time basis. The sales manager is better able to estimate the lifetime value of a customer and to group accounts based on their relative attractiveness. New systems for managing customer relationships find technology bringing sellers and buyers much closer together. Other technologies also contribute to this closeness, such as electronic data interchange systems that place buyers and sellers online with one another and just-in-time inventory systems that connect the operations of buying and selling organizations. Finally, the enlightened sales manager uses technology to better understand his or her sales force. Internal research is conducted regularly to identify patterns and relationships among a large number of sales force–related variables. Such research helps the manager anticipate salesperson failure before it happens, determine optimal call patterns, identify characteristics of top-performing salespeople, understand factors that drive the turnover of salespeople, and much more.

The impact is just as significant in personal selling. Technology is helping salespeople "sell smarter," while also greatly enhancing their efficiency. Keep in mind that, to a salesperson, the three most valuable resources are time, time, and time. Technology empowers the salesperson to do more with less and to do things that heretofore she or he was unable to do. Specific tools exist for improving the salesperson's ability to generate, manage, and prioritize leads; conduct background research on customers and competitors; organize sales calls; design sales presentations; and rapidly respond to customer inquiries and requests. Just as important is the fact that customers are becoming more technologically sophisticated—salespeople have no choice but to keep up.

THE COLLABORATIVE SALES FORCE

Collaboration is a prime requirement within the modern sales organization. It is vital for encouraging individuals to work together in coming up with inventive solutions, for enhancing the speed of the organization, and for supporting the growing emphasis on team selling. Internal collaboration also enhances the firm's ability to collaborate with and create value for customers. The implications of greater collaboration can be seen at the level of the senior manager, the field sales manager, and the individual salesperson.

At the senior leadership level, moving to a more collaborative culture may mean culture change. It also implies a clash of the old with the new in terms of systems and structures. Sales executives must understand that organizational change starts with value and belief change. Organizational and individual values must be aligned.

A collaborative sales force results in a redefined role for the field sales manager. A blunt way of describing the change is captured by the phrase *the boss is dead.* Under the boss model, a person of authority emphasizes the maximization of self and the tendency to control. Authority, commands, and even fear are used to drive people in the organization with little concern for trust, empowerment, honesty, and the long-range impact of today's actions. In contrast, the collaborative sales environment emphasizes the need for coaching, plain talk, sharing authority and credit, inquiry instead of advocacy, and mutual respect of team members.

Implementing changes in culture and cross-functional processes requires new skills. Change processes must be well communicated and led from the top. Salespeople and sales teams must be brought into a new world that values team-building dimensions such as cohesiveness, helping behavior, courtesy, conflict management, and loyalty. The field sales manager plays a critical role in creating a preferred future for his or her organization. Relevant challenges center around an individual's ability to start a personal learning journey, adopt new mindsets, and pursue behaviors consistent with new cultural norms.

At the salesperson level, the challenge is multiplied. As sales organizations increasingly stress internal and external collaboration, salespeople must come to embrace their new roles and learn to trust the process of change. The notion of putting team goals ahead of self-interests requires that trust in both the senior leaders and field sales managers be developed. It also becomes important for salespeople to acquire and apply conflict resolution strategies and skills to work effectively within the organization, as well as greater expertise in problem-solving and partnering skills.

PUTTING IT ALL TOGETHER: SALES AS THE HOME FOR ENTREPRENEURSHIP

When we combine the creative, expeditionary, empowered, strategic, technological, and collaborative approaches, the result is an entrepreneurial sales force. If anything, the sales organization is a natural home for entrepreneurship. Let's consider some of the reasons.

The job of selling has much in common with entrepreneurship. First, consider the nature of the work that must be done. The sales profession can be characterized as involving ample opportunities for personal initiative, moderate freedom of action, periods of high pressure and stress, a variety of challenging job-related tasks, a strong "results" orientation, significant potential for career development, and the possibility of large financial rewards. Each of these is also a core characteristic of the task facing entrepreneurs as they create and grow new ventures.

The similarities can also be seen if we look at the people involved in these two activities. When compared with their less successful counterparts, those who achieve success in sales tend to be more confident, independent, socially satisfied, adaptive, and aggressive. The also tend to be better educated, to be more adept at planning, to have stronger leadership qualities, and to demonstrate a stronger preference for commission-based compensation programs. Such descriptors would appear to have a certain commonality with characteristics traditionally associated with the entrepreneur. For instance, the entrepreneurial personality has been described as independent, achievement motivated, tolerant of ambiguity, a calculated risk-taker, having a strong internal focus of control, and being well-organized. This commonality has led some to conclude that selling is one of the more entrepreneurial of occupations.

Management of the sales function has the potential to be an entrepreneurial pursuit as well. In fact, sales management should represent one of the most entrepreneurial areas within any company. Many of the activities that comprise the sales manager's job (e.g., defining territories, recruitment and training of the sales force, designing compensation systems, motivating sales personnel, establishing quotas, determining overall sales strategies) demand a degree of innovation and calculated risk-taking. Sales managers are in a position to give salespeople a sense of territorial proprietorship, granting authority and responsibility in a number of decision areas, encouraging experimentation while not punishing failure, and implementing creative methods for evaluating and rewarding individual performance. They can also influence the amount of paperwork and the number of bureaucratic obstacles facing a salesperson, including the nature of the relationship between sales and other areas within the firm.

Finally, individual sales territories are very much like entrepreneurial ventures. In this sense, every salesperson is defined as an entrepreneur and is expected

---

TABLE 13-1 How a Sales Territory Is Similar to an Entrepreneurial Venture

1. The territory is a self-contained unit, and a value can be placed on it.
2. The salesperson negotiates and structures deals that determine the value of the territory.
3. Performance is measured in terms of sales and profits over time.
4. Success or failure is tied to the salesperson's performance.
5. The salesperson must out-compete others to sustain the territory.
6. The salesperson allocates resources to different activities in attempting to manage the territory.
7. The salesperson seeks investments (from the sales manager) into the territory.
8. To get things done, the salesperson leverages resources from other departments within his or her company and from the external environment.
9. The possibility exists for expansion of territory potential through innovation.
10. The salesperson works with customers to develop innovative solutions to their needs.

---

to exploit the opportunity contained within his or her territory. Table 13-1 delineates 10 of the ways in which territories and ventures are similar. Chief among these is the notion that a territory represents an opportunity to be exploited; that it has a value; and that realizing this value depends on the salesperson's innovativeness, calculated risk-taking, and proactiveness.

A salesperson managing her or his territory deals with a fair amount of ambiguity, much like the entrepreneur. Sales may or may not happen, while customer requirements and buying behaviors can be difficult to decipher and continually change. A potential deal may fall apart after months of effort and significant commitment, suggesting a degree of risk, whereas another deal may close with only a modicum of work. Many leads and sales approaches prove to be dead-ends, while being well organized in terms of time management, account prioritization, call planning, and follow-up activity is a key to success. The salesperson is constantly jumping from activity to activity, such that a given day might include some prospecting, first-time calls, paperwork, a follow-up call on an unclosed account, a service call to a current customer, direct mail correspondence, complaint handling, and so forth.

Approaching a territory as a venture encourages a mentality of ownership on the part of the salesperson, while also getting him or her to think more strategically. The salesperson supports his or her venture by leveraging resources from the company, such as by collaborating with those in production, logistics, information technology, marketing, and customer service. He or she allocates resources (e.g., field sales calls, product samples, design of customized solutions, customer incentives) across accounts within the territory.

As the person responsible for an entrepreneurial venture, the salesperson should be evaluated based on how well she or he successfully grows the territory. The sales manager becomes somewhat like a venture capitalist with a portfolio of ventures in which she of he invests. The overall sales budget is approached as a type of venture capital fund, and money is invested in territories based on their potential and the ongoing efforts of the salesperson. The salesperson regularly comes up with innovative ideas and pitches these ideas to the manager. A periodic valuation of each territory is performed, with rewards tied to appreciation of the territory's value.

HOW MUCH ENTREPRENEURSHIP IS ENOUGH?

At the same time, companies and the sales organizations within them can be expected to vary in terms of how entrepreneurial they are. To fully appreciate this point, it is important to remember that entrepreneurship has three underlying dimensions or components: innovativeness, risk-taking, and proactiveness. *Innovativeness* refers to the seeking of creative, unusual, or novel solutions to problems and needs. It includes the development of new products and services, as well as new processes for performing organizational functions. In sales, such process innovation might include new approaches to territory design, goal and quota setting, prospecting, customer service, sales promotions, or sales administration, among many other possibilities. *Risk-taking* involves the willingness of managers to commit resources to opportunities having a reasonable chance of costly failure. The risks are not extreme and uncontrollable but instead are moderate, calculated, and manageable. *Proactiveness* is concerned with implementation and making events happen through whatever means are necessary. It frequently entails breaking with established ways of accomplishing a task and requires a hands-on management style. It usually implies considerable perseverance, adaptability, and a willingness to assume responsibility for failure.

Entrepreneurial activities within sales will reflect different degrees of innovativeness, riskiness, and proactiveness. Further, any number of entrepreneurial events can be produced by a sales organization in a given time period. Accordingly, all sales organizations demonstrate some level of entrepreneurship, but they differ in terms of degree (how much) and frequency (how often). The combination of degree and frequency can be referred to as *entrepreneurial intensity*. Figure 13-3 illustrates how sales organizations can be characterized in terms of their entrepreneurial intensity and includes the following four sample profiles:

- *Sales organization A:* Relatively low in both degree and frequency, this organization innovates very little, and the new approaches it does develop tend to be incremental changes from the status quo.

- *Sales organization B:* This is a sales organization that is continually experimenting with new approaches to a range of different sales activities, but the changes tend to be fairly incremental.

- *Sales organization C:* This organization does not innovate very often in terms of sales management, but when it does, the new approaches represent fairly radical change.

- *Sales organization D:* This dynamic organization is continually innovating, with a portfolio of new approaches at any given time, some of which are major breakthroughs and others of which represent incremental changes.

FIGURE 13-3 Rating Sales Organizations on Entrepreneurial Intensity

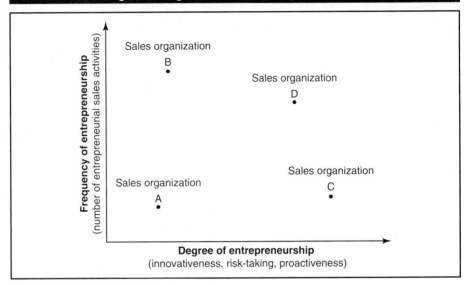

The relevance of a given approach depends on the industry, markets, and competitive environment within which the firm operates. For instance, in situations where the product sells itself, or the firm is alone in the marketplace and has a product that the customer views as a necessity, there is less need for innovative, risk-taking, proactive behaviors. As a result, sales organization A can be expected to perform reasonably well. Alternatively, when operating in a competitive market that is relatively saturated, where ongoing relationships with existing accounts constitute the core of a firm's business, the ongoing but incremental innovation of sales organization B might be more effective. If we assume that the market is quite volatile, with continual changes in technologies and product offerings, aggressive competitors, and ongoing changes in buyer organizations, then sales organization D is likely to be the winner.

Researchers have uncovered two key relationships when studying entrepreneurial intensity. First, companies that demonstrate stronger levels of entrepreneurial intensity also score higher in terms of how customer driven they are. The firm's entrepreneurial orientation may be the key to achieving a true customer orientation. The entrepreneurial firm is able to produce innovative solutions in response to customer needs, but it also capable of leading customers in new value-creating directions. Second, entrepreneurial intensity has a positive relationship with a number of measures of financial performance.[3] Quite simply, highly entrepreneurial companies tend to perform better. This second relationship appears to be most marked under conditions of environmental turbulence. When things in the competitive environment are especially challenging, the winners tend to be those that are best able to tap into the entrepreneurial spirit.

EXAMPLES OF ENTREPRENEURSHIP IN SALES

Some notable companies have come to appreciate the importance of achieving high levels of entrepreneurship in their sales organizations. Consider these examples.

• **Cisco Systems** prides itself on a highly empowered sales force, giving salespeople high stature within the company.[4] Compensation reflects this stature, with pay plans that allow for some salespeople to earn more than $1 million. Innovative selling approaches are stressed. Salespeople are expected to work closely with customers to produce innovative solutions that enhance a customer's operations. A number of creative approaches are employed in managing the sales force. One example is the manner in which they use technology in sales. Customized web pages are created for each member of the sales team from which they can manage relationships with customers, conduct all their travel and 401(k) transactions, monitor their current performance levels, access sales training videos and texts, communicate with internal departments, and more. Internal competition is encouraged between the sales force and other operating departments to find the best ways to leverage the Internet in the ways they do business.

• **IBM** has found that sales force innovation comes from freeing up salespeople to spend more time with customers.[5] By organizing the sales force into teams that serve focused clusters of customers, creating a universal reporting system that brings consistency to performance numbers, having every salesperson follow the same selling process, and mandating a dramatic reduction in internal sales meetings (to a single 30-minute meeting per week with the salesperson's direct manager), salespeople have more time on their hands, and they are expected to spend it inside customer organizations. The result is that they are much more on top of customer problems and opportunities as they emerge, and they can develop innovative solutions in real time.

• **AT&T** has developed entrepreneurial approaches to dealing with specific problems in sales force performance.[6] A case in point is the negotiation skills of their salespeople, a major problem area within the company. In addition to introducing classroom and online training that emphasizes the fact that successful negotiation involves counterintuitive skills and approaches, the company launched an online planning and knowledge management tool call "Dealmaker." The salesperson inputs information regarding a customer and then receives support in terms of how to approach the negotiation and finalize a deal. The assistance helps the salesperson creatively identify unmet customer needs and requirements, think of ways to respond to difficult issues raised by customers, formulate concession strategies, and, ultimately, put together a plan of attack for a negotiation. The salesperson can also access case studies on best practices in similar negotiations. Finally, salespeople are encouraged to document their own experiences so that others in the sales force can benefit.

Other interesting initiatives include the "sales force in reserve" program at PSS/World Medical, where 5% of the current sales force does other jobs in the company, waiting in reserve (and getting ongoing sales training). The result is that the company can move amazingly fast when a given territory needs extra help, a new territory is opened, or a field rep leaves the company or is promoted. When they hit the field, these reserve salespeople are better qualified, more confident, and more productive than would otherwise be the case.[7] Entrepreneurial initiatives can also include simple tactical moves, such as the sales team at a major rental car company that delivered complementary boxes of donuts early in the morning to car repair shops, significantly increasing client referrals. At a large company with dozens of product divisions having distinct sales forces, mini trade shows were organized at customer sites to demonstrate a wide range of company capabilities. Or, consider the sales organization with a clever program for getting referrals from prospects that decide not to buy from them. Another example is the sales rep who prepares and sends helpful report cards to his customers that remind them when they need maintenance or upgrades, shows them how to save money on supplies, and advises them when equipment should be replaced.

Summary and Conclusions

In the new competitive landscape, the winners will be those companies better able to nurture the entrepreneurial spirit in every facet of their operations. Nowhere is this more critical than the sales function. Sales is arguably the single greatest source of ongoing interaction between a firm and its external environment. As such, it is in a unique position to recognize and exploit new opportunities and to help the firm adapt to emerging customer and competitive circumstances.

Entrepreneurship in sales is not about chaos or out-of-control innovation. It involves positive collisions between disciplined management and innovative concepts that fit the strategic direction of the firm. It involves a logical process that can be applied to the job of the sales manager and the sales rep. This process is opportunity driven and requires certain skills and abilities, including the ability to think and act as a guerilla.

Sales managers should be held accountable for creating work environments that encourage innovativeness, calculated risk-taking, and proactiveness. This challenge can be met by developing goal structures, territory designs, evaluation mechanisms, and administrative procedures as well as methods of resource allocation that allow for a level of autonomy, encourage experimentation, and reinforce healthy discontent.

Success requires that the sales manager develop a personal approach to the identification and pursuit of entrepreneurial opportunity. The approach should reflect skills in obtaining sponsors, building a flexible team structure, insulating projects, building project momentum, obtaining resources that have not been formally assigned to a project, developing internal support networks, and managing expectations. In effect, the manager is challenged to redefine the rules of the competitive game in terms of how sales resources are acquired and used.

A beginning point concerns the design of the sales job itself. A sales position must be fundamentally defined as an entrepreneurial pursuit. Entrepreneurial behavior is more likely where jobs are designed more broadly, with the salesperson responsible for creating total value solutions for customers by addressing a range of marketing tasks. The employee is given significant discretion in how the job is accomplished, with strong pressure for results. The job is less structured and less constrained by rigid organizational policies. Employees are also highly involved in designing their jobs. Turning to recruitment and selection processes, the entrepreneurial organization looks for employees who have demonstrated traits and characteristics associated with entrepreneurship, such as strong achievement motivation, comfort with ambiguity, an internal locus of control, calculated risk-taking, and a results orientation. As a case in point, some companies (e.g., Nordstrom) hire salespeople based on their ability to run a business within a business. In addition, significant effort is devoted to employee orientation and socialization, where the entrepreneurial values and behaviors are reinforced. Training and development programs in entrepreneurial firms, in addition to technical training (e.g., selling skills, product knowledge, an understanding of customers and markets), stress skills and methods related to opportunity identification, creativity, risk management, and innovation. Emphasis is also placed on political skills and techniques for gaining managerial support for new ideas and approaches.

The sales manager communicates performance expectations and reinforces desired employee behaviors through the performance appraisal and reward systems. Motivation to act in an entrepreneurial fashion requires that management make clear the types of behaviors expected, evaluate effort allocated to the behavior, assess results of the effort, and reward and reinforce the effort. Accordingly, appraisals of the sales force must go beyond standard performance measures such as exceeding quotas, generating new accounts, and building satisfactory relationships. Specific evaluative criteria must also assess the salesperson's innovative, risk-taking, and proactive behaviors in creating value for customers. In terms of rewards, the classic question in designing compensation programs for salespeople concerns the relative emphasis on incentive pay versus a fixed salary. Entrepreneurial behavior tends to be more associated with incentive compensation, and companies get quite creative in the ways in which they design the awards and rewards that support innovations by salespeople. They create point systems, bonus pools, stock options, on-the-spot cash awards, frequent innovator clubs, and other novel programs. Entrepreneurial companies have cultures of celebration, where they regularly create opportunities to recognize employee innovativeness, and they award everything from plaques and pins to a desired parking spot, gift certificates, innovator jackets, vacation trips, and large-screen televisions. Some go so far as to create scholarships in a salesperson's name in their hometowns or to donate funds to the salesperson's favorite charity.

In the final analysis, salespeople must see themselves as entrepreneurs, and their territories as entrepreneurial ventures. Training programs, resource pools, compensation systems, and symbolic recognition all represent vehicles for redefining the sales job and for honoring attempts at innovation. Complacency, not failure, should be penalized. Tolerance for bending the rules and skepticism toward established rules of thumb should guide the manager's behavior. The goal should be to get all the members of the sales force thinking about innovation on a daily basis so that business as usual is subject to experimentation.

Key Terms

- collaboration
- empowered sales force
- entrepreneurial selling
- leveraging resources in the selling environment
- strategic sales management

Questions

1. Given the dramatic changes affecting the modern sales force, why do you think some people argue that the sales force is becoming obsolete? Alternatively, why might it be argued that the sales force is more important than ever?
2. How can a sales force be "entrepreneurial"? What exactly does this mean? How do the elements of creativity, innovation, empowerment, technological competence, collaboration, and strategic thinking interact with one another to produce an entrepreneurial sales force?
3. Can you provide some examples of entrepreneurial things that salespeople might do as they attempt to meet a company's sales goals?
4. How is a sales territory similar to an entrepreneurial venture? If a salesperson views his or her territory as an entrepreneurial venture, how might this change the way in which he or she approaches the management of the territory?
5. Can salespeople be too entrepreneurial? Is it possible to be too innovative or proactive? What are some of the considerations that might determine how entrepreneurial a sales force needs to be?

Resources and References

1. For an expanded treatment of the material in this chapter, see Harris, A., Ingram, T., Jones, E., LaForge, R., Leigh, T., & Morris, M. (2005). *Strategic sales leadership: Breakthrough thinking for radical results.* Cincinnati, OH: Texere/Thomson.
2. Jones, E., Roberts, J. A., & Chonko, L. B. (2000). Motivating sales entrepreneurs to change: A conceptual framework of factors leading to successful change management initiatives in sales organizations. *Journal of Marketing Theory and Practice* 8(2): 37–49.
3. Morris, M. H., Kuratko, D., & Covin J. (2008). *Corporate entrepreneurship and innovation.* Mason, OH: Thomson Publishers.
4. Marchetti, M. (2000). Number 1 sales force: Cisco Systems. *Sales and Marketing Management* 152(7): 60–61.
5. Strout, E. (2003). Blue skies ahead. *Sales and Marketing Management* 155(3): 24–30.
6. Henderson, J., & Crawford, G. (2002). Ten ways to wire sales training. *T + D* 56(4): 48–57.
7. Kelly, P. (1998, July). Fast track. *Inc.,* pp. 33–36.

CHAPTER 14

MARKETING STRATEGY IN THE DIGITAL AGE
THE INTERNET CHANGES EVERYTHING

INTRODUCTION—TRADITIONAL STRATEGY AND KILLER APPLICATIONS

A leading influence on strategic thinking throughout the 1980s and 1990s was Michael Porter, a Harvard Business School strategy professor. Practitioners, academics, and consultants alike have used his well-known "five forces" model to evaluate industry attractiveness as strategic positioning. Porter's model[1] is very orderly and structured—and very applicable in the 1980s, which was a far less fragmented era than what the late 1990s, and especially the new millennium, have proven to be. It neatly explains why some industries are more attractive than others in a way that at least gave managers confidence in their judgment, even if it didn't make them feel better about being in a dead-loss market. Similarly, the forces were all about business and management issues: customers and suppliers, barriers to entry and substitute products, and of course, good old firm-to-firm competition itself. Small wonder then that practitioners, consultants, and academics loved the approach—it gave reasonable predictability in a reasonably predictable world.

The traditional view of strategy in organizations has been that it is possible to understand fully the environment in which the organization functions, and therefore to plan for the firm's future accordingly. This view might be acceptable when the environment changes slowly and the future is reasonably predictable. It might even be gratifying when trends are linear. However, in recent years, some observers have noted that the environment is changing so swiftly that it is not possible to strategically plan for the future (see, e.g., Downes and Mui[2]). As we saw in Chapter 1, current trends are usually paradoxical and contradictory rather than linear. The new environments that emerge, especially as the result of phenomenal changes in technology, have profound effects on society—and not just on the firms that operate within it.

If we were to study the occurrence of inventions in history, one phenomenon is particularly prominent—the rate at which technological change occurs over time. During the Middle Ages, for example, significant innovations appeared at a very slow rate—sometimes as infrequently as 200 or 300 years apart. During the time of the Renaissance, new technologies begin to emerge slightly more rapidly—for example, the invention of movable type by Gutenberg. In the era of the Industrial Revolution, inventions begin to surface far more frequently, now at the rate of one every 5 or 10 years. Entering the 21st century, we begin to see major innovations break the surface every year. The kinds of innovations that we are talking about are not simple improvements—rather, we are referring to what have become known as "killer applications."

A killer application or "killer app"[3] is not merely an innovation that improves the way something is done. It is not even something that merely changes a market or an industry; indeed, a killer application is one that changes the way society itself works and functions. The automobile was a killer app because it didn't just simply replace horse-drawn carriages or alter the way people traveled, it transformed the way we live, shop, work, and spend our leisure time. It also changed the appearance of the physical environment in most countries. In the past 10 or 15 years, we have seen killer applications arise at the rate of more than one a year, and this frequency is increasing in an exponential fashion at the moment due to "spreading" technologies such as the Internet. Thus, a strategy that attempts to plan 5 years ahead is befuddled by the fact that society and the way the world works may indeed change at the rate of one or two killer applications a year. The more traditional strategic planning models, such as those of Michael Porter, are less effective at dealing with the kind of strategic planning problems killer applications and rapid technological changes cause.

THE FIVE NEW FORCES

We need to develop a perspective on the new forces that affect strategy and the way organizations deal with the future. One possibility is that, in the spirit of Porter's five forces, we consider five new forces that will affect the way the business and management environment works. We also illustrate these forces and their effects using two cases: the music industry worldwide and the online betting exchange, **Betfair.com**. (These two industries are briefly described in the vignettes illustrated in Exhibits 14-1 and 14-2, discussed later). The effect of these forces on individuals and organizations is illustrated and summarized in Figure 14-1. Let's examine these forces in more detail.

FIGURE 14-1   The New Five Forces

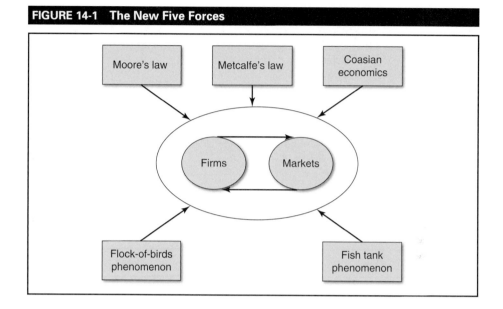

MOORE'S LAW

In 1965, an engineer at Fairchild Semiconductor named Gordon Moore noted that the number of transistors on a computer chip doubled roughly every 18 to 24 months. A corollary to Moore's law, as that observation came to be known, is that the speed of microprocessors, at a constant cost, also doubles every 18 to 24 months. Moore's law has held up for more than 40 years. It worked in 1969 when Moore's startup, Intel Corporation, put its first processor chip (the 4-bit, 104-kHz 4004) into a Japanese calculator. It worked at the turn of the century for Intel's 32-bit, 450-MHz Pentium II processor, which had 7.5 million transistors and was 233,000 times faster than the 2,300-transistor 4004. And it works today, when Intel's Rio Rancho factory is expected to begin producing 45-nanometer chips (meaning they will have features as tiny as 45-billionths of a meter) in the second half of 2008. The transistors on such chips are so small that more than 30 million can fit onto the head of a pin. Intel says it will have a 1-billion-transistor powerhouse performing at 100,000 MIPS in 2011.

For users ranging from vast organizations to children playing computer games, it's been a fast, fun, and mostly free ride. But can it last? Although observers have been saying for decades that exponential gains in chip performance would slow in a few years, experts today generally agree that Moore's law will continue to govern the industry for another 10 years, at least. Moore's law is illustrated graphically in Figure 14-2, which shows the increases in computing power over time.

The implications of Moore's law are that computing power becomes ever faster, ever cheaper. This means not only that just about everyone can therefore

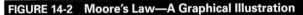

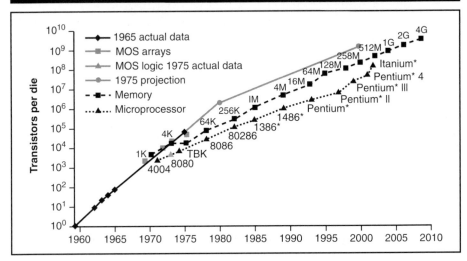

FIGURE 14-2 Moore's Law—A Graphical Illustration

Source: Intel Corporation.

have affordable access to powerful computing, but also that the power of computers can be built into devices other than computers themselves. Moore's law also drives convergence by placing computer chips into objects that previously had nothing to do with them: today there is more processing power in the average cellular telephone or digital television set than the National Aeronautics and Space Administration (NASA) had access to when Neil Armstrong landed on the moon in 1969. Already, computers are used in products as diverse as vehicles, surgical equipment, and elevators, enabling these machines to operate more efficiently, predictably, and safely. We are beginning to see computer chips in disposable products such as packaging, as the costs continue to decline. Hitachi, Ltd., a Japanese electronics maker, recently showed off radio frequency identification (RFID) chips that are just 0.05 millimeter by 0.05 millimeter and look like bits of powder. They're thin enough to be embedded in a piece of paper, yet they are able to store considerable amounts of information, which can then be read and processed. Computers have become ubiquitous—they are everywhere, but we don't consciously think of them or notice them.

The primary question that Moore's law should prompt in strategic planners is this: What will our industry or market be like when computers or chips are literally everywhere—in every product we make or part of every service we deliver? Some managers may think this is silly, simply because it is difficult for them to imagine a computer or chip in their product or service. Yet there are countless products or services being delivered today that have computers as an integral part and that the same reasoning would have applied to just 20 years ago: hotel doors with chips installed that facilitate card access and record entry and exit; microwave ovens; digital television. In the recent past, we have witnessed the demise of the videocassette recorder (VCR), as home owners turn to hard drives to record many hours of television entertainment. An 80-gigabyte hard-drive recorder costs less than $300. In the lifetime of most readers of this book, there was a time when the combined computer storage of most countries didn't reach 80 gigabytes.

METCALFE'S LAW

How useful is a piece of technology? The answer depends entirely on how many other users of the technology there are and on how easily they can be interconnected. For example, the first organization with a facsimile machine had no one to fax *to* and no one to receive faxes *from!* One telephone is useless; a few telephones have limited value. Many millions of telephones create a vast network. These effects are known as Metcalfe's law. Robert Metcalfe, founder 3Com Corporation and the designer of the robust Ethernet protocol for computer networks, observed that new technologies are valuable only if many people use them. Roughly, the usefulness (or utility) of the network equals the square of the number of users, the function known as Metcalfe's law. This is illustrated in the simple line graph in Figure 14-3.

The more people who use software, a network, a particular standard, a game, or a book, or indeed a language such as English, the more valuable it becomes and the more new users it will attract. This in turn increases both its utility and the speed of its adoption by still more users. The Internet is perhaps the best illustration of Metcalfe's law. While it began in the 1960s, it is only in the past dozen years that it has gained momentum—as more users joined the medium, it became more useful to even more users, thus accelerating its growth. Now its potential to

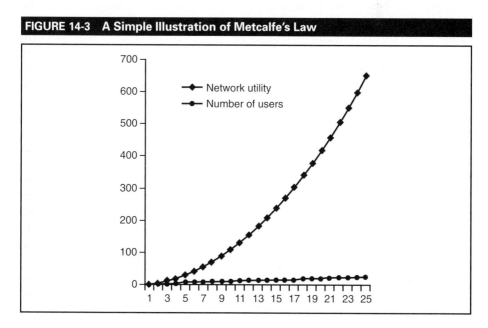

FIGURE 14-3   A Simple Illustration of Metcalfe's Law

spread new ideas, products, and services is awesome. Other good examples of Metcalfe's law in recent years have been cellular telephones and the ubiquitous handheld personal digital assistant (PDA). In the case of the latter, for example, most adopters of the earliest Palm device recommended the product to friends and colleagues, and the Palm succeeded not because of a large advertising budget but because of word of mouth. The early adopters insisted that others buy the product not just because it was good, but because it increased the size of their network, which made their own Palms more useful. One of the key factors in this success was the Palm's ability to "beam" to other Palms via a built-in infrared device. Palm users were proud not to carry paper business cards and preferred to beam their details to others.

Networks are important because they create shortcuts. Anyone who is part of the network can contact anyone else who is part of it and bypass more traditional channels and structures. This is important for planners, who should consider what the effects of technology will be that enables their customers to talk to each other, suppliers to talk to each other, and customers to talk directly with suppliers, wherever in the world they may be. As networks grow, their utility increases, so Metcalfe's law tells us; this is true for those who are part of the network and for those who then choose to join it.

COASIAN ECONOMICS

Ronald Coase, a Nobel Prize winner in economics, made a discovery about market behavior that he published in a 1937 article entitled "The Nature of the Firm."[4] Coase introduced the notion of "transaction costs"—a set of inefficiencies in the market that add or should be added to the price of a good or service to measure the performance of the market relative to the nonmarket behavior in firms. They include the costs of searching, contracting, and enforcing. Transaction cost economics gives us a way of explaining which activities a firm will choose to perform within its own hierarchy and which it will rely on the market to perform for it. One important application of transaction cost economics has been as a useful way to explain the outsourcing decisions that many firms face (e.g., whether the firm should do its own cleaning, catering, or security or pay someone else to do this).

The effect of communication technology on the size of firms in the past has been to make them larger. Communication technologies permit transaction costs to be lowered to the extent that firms are capable of subsuming many activities within themselves; thus, they are able to operate as larger entities even across continents. This has permitted multinational corporations such as General Motors, Sony, and Unilever to operate as global enterprises, essentially managed from a head office in Detroit, Tokyo, London—or anywhere. Communication technology (such as telephones, fax machines, and telex machines) enabled these operators to communicate as easily between Detroit and Sydney as between Detroit and Chicago. Smaller firms found this more difficult and more expensive. Thus, large firms brought more activities within the firm (or the "hierarchy" in transaction cost terms) because it was cheaper to do this than to rely on the market.

What strategic planners overlook at their peril in the age of the Internet is that these same communication capabilities are now in the hands of individuals, who can pass messages round the world at as low a cost as the biggest players — essentially, for free. Free voice over Internet protocol (VOIP) services such as Skype allow individuals to talk for free, regardless of location or distance. They can also hold multi-user conferences, including live video, for free and can simultaneously transmit documents and images. The effect of the new communication technologies, accelerated by Moore's law and Metcalfe's law, will be to reduce the costs of the hierarchy. But more especially, they will reduce the costs of the market itself. As the market becomes more efficient, the size of firms might be considerably reduced. More pertinently, as the costs of communication in the market approach zero, so does the size of a firm, which can now rely on the market for most of the activities and functions that need to be performed. A very thorny strategic issue indeed!

A simple illustration of the effects of transaction cost reductions in an industry is shown in Figure 14-4. When banking is done across the counter with a teller, the average cost per transaction exceeds a dollar; when the same transaction is conducted online, the costs reduce to nominal cents. Yet most banks charge their customers *more* for online banking! How long will banks continue to do this, and how long will customers tolerate it? Already, alternative services are beginning to emerge that may prove more appealing to many customers.

There are many strategic questions that Coasian economics prompts in the age of the Internet. However, what should undoubtedly top the agendas of many strategic planners in this regard is the issue of what functions the Internet will permit them to outsource. Allied to this is the matter of responding to competitors who do not carry the burden of infrastructure normally borne by traditional firms, having relied on technology to effectively outsource a variety of business activities and functions to the market.

FIGURE 14-4   Costs of Bank Service Delivery by Mechanism

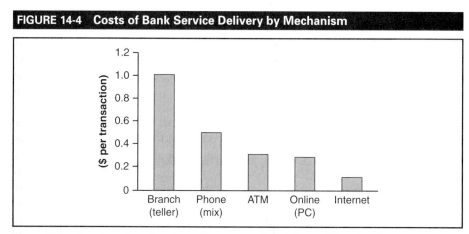

Source: Taken from http://search.techrepublic.com.com/search/Booz+Allen+Hamilton+Inc..html. Accessed September 5, 2006.

THE FLOCK-OF-BIRDS PHENOMENON

A feature of many new communication technologies has been the fact that in most cases they do not "belong" to any one institution, nor does any particular authority control them. The Internet is a case in point. Some have referred to this as the "flock-of-birds phenomenon."[5] When we observe a flock of birds flying in formation, or fish schooling in a distinct pattern, we are tempted to speculate whether there is or could be a "bird in charge" or an "alpha fish." Naturalists will explain that flocking is a natural phenomenon and that there are indeed no "head" fishes or birds in charge. The network becomes the processor.

Humans have been conditioned to seek a controlling body or authority for nearly all of the phenomena that we experience in life—because that is indeed how most modern societies have been organized. The response to questions such as "Who's in charge?", "Who controls this?", or "Who owns it?" is generally, "Some large firm," or "The government," (i.e., a government department or ruling institution). In the case of many of the phenomena observed on the Internet, there is indeed no one in charge. They are like giant flocks of birds or schools of fish. The response to questions such as "Who owns them?" or "Who's in charge?" is either "We all do," or "No one does." These are great mechanisms for democracy, but their effects can also be anarchic, and society may have to develop new ways to deal with these liberating effects.

The effect of the flock-of-birds phenomenon is that access is equalized, unlike what occurs in traditional media. In a very real sense, no one has a "better right of access," and no one, not even the largest corporation, can shout louder. The smallest player, the individual, has a right and opportunity to be seen and heard. Furthermore, many laws designed to regulate a physical world don't work as effectively when no one owns or controls the medium.

THE FISH TANK PHENOMENON

Moore's law and Metcalfe's law combine to give individuals inexpensive and easy access to new media such as the Internet. This means that anyone can set up a website and, theoretically at least, be seen by the world. As a result many have noticed the so-called fish tank phenomenon,[6] named after the fact that in the early days of websites, people used to put a video camera on top of their tropical fish tank (or coffee percolator, for that matter), so that when you logged on to their site, that is what you saw. This added to the clutter and junk on display— today there are hundreds of thousand of silly, futile, "junk" sites that only do something silly—let the viewer build a cow, tickle Elvis Presley's tummy, cure their addiction to lip balm, or whatever. The question that this prompts is this: Would it be better if, rather than relying on individuals for their input on the net, we depended instead on the considerable resources of large institutions and corporations?

The answer to this question really lies in another: What is more profound? And the answer to this second question is that, actually, it is the creative inputs of millions of individuals, all over the world, who now have the ability to show us what they can do. In other words, the creative outputs of millions of individuals will beat the doings of large institutions in a great majority of cases. So, while we may see lots of junk, such as fish tanks, coffee percolators, and devices to tickle a long-dead rock artist, every now and then some individual (probably a 17-year-old in his or her bedroom) is going to produce something so revolutionary that it will change our world. For strategists, this means that many firms may find themselves threatened by small startups that were previously unable to get access to the market. No longer will it be good enough to merely observe our close and known competitors; in the future, these competitors could be anyone and anywhere. They may be difficult to see before it is too late—they usually fly under the radar.

HOW THE NEW FIVE FORCES WORK IN INDUSTRIES AND MARKETS

The music industry[7] (see Exhibit 14-1) and Betfair[8] (see Exhibit 14-2) represent classic cases of the five technology-related forces that, when working in concert, cause radical change in industries and markets. Observers of industries as diverse

---

EXHIBIT 14-1   The Global Recorded Music Industry

For many years—indeed since Edison's invention of the phonograph in 1877—the music recoding industry didn't change much. While technological changes did come to the market for recorded music over the years, in the form of improved recording techniques, hi-fidelity stereo, and the advent of the compact disk (CD), essentially the industry remained stable, with its structure largely unaffected by technological developments. Recording companies found and recorded talent and marketed it, and the products of the industry—essentially disks and cassette tapes—were distributed through record stores. Artists were remunerated in the form of royalties and retailers in the form of margins, and the record companies kept the rest.

The fundamental distribution issue of assortment was (and in many ways still is) perhaps the most significant dilemma in the market for recorded music. The structure of the industry and the way the product was produced held an inherent problem for both the retailer and the consumer. The retailer's predicament is that of inventory—the need to hold very large stocks of records to provide a varied selection to customers, and to be able to make available to the customer the one that they will choose when they want it. This means that a lot of capital is tied up in stock, much of which moves slowly and often needs to be discounted to meet working capital requirements. The consumer is also in a quandary: Will the particular retailer stock the one album that they are looking for? And, will they be able to find it among the thousands of other items? Even once found, the consumer's problems aren't over—there may be 12 songs on the album, and they may really want only 3 or 4. But they are forced to purchase the entire album, with all 12 songs.

Source: Pitt, L. F. (2001). Total e-clipse: Five new forces for strategy in the digital age. *Journal of General Management* 26(4): 1–15.

EXHIBIT 14-2   The Market for Sports Betting

Players wishing to place a wager on a football game or a flutter on a horse race or to back up their opinions on a political election or the outcome of the Oscars have, until recently, had few alternatives. In a majority of European countries, Canada, and most states in the United States, their only option would have been to place a bet on a parimutuel or totalisator system, while in countries such as the United Kingdom and Australia, and in U.S. states such as Nevada, they would also have had access to licensed bookmakers. Both of these systems place the player at a significant disadvantage, not least of which is the fact that the "rake-off" or house percentage is considerable. This means that winners get paid well below the "true" odds against their choice. Furthermore, neither of the two systems allows a player to pick a "loser"—the player can stake on only a winning outcome. In simple terms, a player can't back a team to lose—they can only back the other team to win or play to a draw. A specific disadvantage of parimutuel systems is that the subsequent weight of money for a player's choice will reduce the payoff so that there is no opportunity to exercise any skill in the timing of a bet. Both systems profit not from the losers (as most inexpert gamblers believe) but from winners, by paying them out at less than true odds. In the case of parimutuels, the house percentage is around 20%, and even the most generous bookmakers make books that have an edge of around 14% in their favor.

Betfair (**www.betfair.com**), which commenced trading in 2002, is the world's largest betting exchange. As a business, Betfair has no interest in the outcome of any event it makes available to gamblers. It simply provides a market for opinions and trades to take place. It requires players to make and/or take fixed odds, and all income is derived from a small percentage commission (ranging between 2% and 5%, depending on a player's turnover) on a player's net winnings on an event. In general terms, the greater an event's turnover, the more revenue and profit Betfair generates, although Betfair's income is strictly a function of the total net winnings on an event, not turnover.

Source: Davies, M., Pitt, L. F., Shapiro, D., & Watson, R. T. (2005). Betfair.com: Five technology forces revolutionize worldwide wagering. *European Management Journal* 23(5): 533–541.

as music (e.g., the iPod), online betting (e.g., Betfair), and telecommunications (e.g., Skype) can immediately recognize the generalizable parallels between these innovations and the applicability of the five forces. An examination and comparison of the music industry and Betfair enable an intriguing examination and extension of these forces.

How Moore's Law Affects Music and Gambling

In the music industry, many consumers can now afford a relatively powerful computer and can use it as a device for recording and playing sound. The cost of storage media has declined exponentially—multi-gigabyte hard drives that would have exceeded the storage capacity of entire countries just a few years ago are now so inexpensive that individuals can use them not just to store complete music collections, but to carry around in their pockets. The success of Apple's iPod is testimony to this. The hugely popular devices—some as large as 60 gigabytes in capacity—have become fashion icons. No one thinks of them as computers with hard drives.

Similarly, it would be fair to say that without the effects of Moore's law, Betfair would not exist. On the one hand, just 10 years ago, the computing power required to process, manage, and store the millions of rapid betting transactions Betfair handles each day (Betfair processes more transactions each day than Visa) was simply unavailable. On the other, Betfair relies on the fact that its customers also have access to considerable computing power, in the form of affordable and easy-to-use laptop and desktop computers, and that these have access to the Internet. A generation ago, only parimutuels and the very largest bookmaking firms had access to computers, and the ordinary player had none.

METCALFE'S LAW—NETWORKS IN MUSIC AND WAGERING

Music consumers find that purchasing or obtaining music online suits them far better than acquiring hard-copy music products through traditional retail outlets. Napster, the first major advance in music downloads, provided a free music-sharing service that enabled consumers to choose and download only those songs they wanted. Its main problem was that it relied on one central exchange to facilitate the exchange of music; at its peak, its network consisted of more than 20 million users. The fact that it had a centralized server (or in network terms, one main hub) meant that it made an easy target for the organized music industry in its legal battle to close Napster down. Apple's iTunes service sells music (legally) under a similar system and charges around $1 per song, grossing more than $1million daily.

However, users no longer need to rely on centralized distribution or even central servers for their music. The Internet is a huge network of distributed power, which connects anyone to anyone else in a very short time. Services such as Morpheus permit users to share millions of files (including movies and pictures as well as music) daily (although the legality of these exchanges is questionable). The first of these distributed network systems was Kazaa, the brainchild of Niklas Zennström and Janus Friis. After numerous legal battles with the recording industry, these entrepreneurs used their peer-to-peer technology to create Skype, the Internet telephony network. Skype currently exceeds an average of 9 million daily users worldwide. The network effects are immense—users encourage friends and family to download Skype so that they can all engage in free communication. Skype was acquired by eBay in 2006 in a multi-billion-dollar deal.

Metcalfe's law is a very real factor explaining Betfair's success. The fact that more than 50,000 players use the site to place and lay bets each day means that the likelihood of any individual player finding a match for what he or she wants (assuming that what he or she is asking for is reasonable) is very high. This, of course, results in highly efficient and very liquid markets, which are to the advantage of all players.

Networks are important because they create shortcuts. Anyone who is part of the network is, by definition, in contact with anyone else who is part of it and can therefore bypass more traditional channels and structures (such as conventional bookmakers and totalisators in this case). As networks grow, their utility increases, so Metcalfe's law tells us—this is true for those who are part of the network and for those who then choose to join it. Neither traditional bookmakers nor totalisators enjoy the same network advantages as Betfair—bookmakers have contact only with players in their geographic vicinity or those with telephone access. Totalisators are on tracks only in some countries, where they will be affected by liquidity problems on quiet days, and even when they are not, they are restricted by local geography. Betfair faces none of these restrictions and can enable the world to wager.*

COASIAN ECONOMICS: TRANSACTION COSTS IN ONLINE MUSIC AND WAGERING

Hierarchies such as large music companies and their distribution networks are no longer able to achieve the lowest transaction costs in the recording industry. The low costs of communication and distribution have made the market more efficient, and millions of individuals benefit as a result. After the invention of the tape recorder, copying music became technically feasible, but of course the network effects were very limited: the song had to be played while it was being copied, and distribution was limited to a few local friends who had tape players. Computers and the Internet mean that a song can be copied very quickly and distributed, theoretically (if not always legally) at least, to a multitude of other users in a few seconds.

When contrasted with traditional bookmaking firms, Betfair is a fine example of the potential of low-cost, networked computing to make markets more efficient by lowering transaction costs. Traditional bookmakers need to be well informed (studying horseracing and sporting events carefully) to make odds and need to monitor market changes constantly to avoid being taken advantage of, or being overexposed. Betfair simply provides the platform for many individuals (theoretically, "firms of one") to do this for themselves. These individuals do not have to rent space or equipment, advertise, or employ staff. With a click of a mouse they can essentially either do what leading betting and gaming companies such as Ladbrokes or William Hill do—or, if the fancy takes them, play their fancies.

THE FLOCK-OF-BIRDS PHENOMENON: LAWLESSNESS IN MUSIC AND GAMBLING

The exchange and distribution of recorded music has become very difficult to legislate and control. While it eventually became possible for the Recording Industry Association of America (RIAA), after extensive legal and political efforts, to take action against and eventually close Napster, it is unlikely that it can have the same results against millions of individuals all over the world. When it has attempted

*While this is true in principle, in reality there are some exceptions. For example, wagering online with sites outside of its jurisdiction has been outlawed by the U.S. government. While many other countries decry this as just another example of American government bullying and blatantly disregarding all of the initiatives on free global trade, the U.S. government has been ruthless in pursuing this policy. It has arrested executives of foreign online wagering operations on entry into the United States; these include Canadians and U.K. citizens.

to pursue these, it has come out looking simply like a blundering bully. Also, just because it may succeed in one country (e.g., the United States) does not mean it will succeed in another with a different legal system. Technologies like Gnutella, Kazaa, and Morpheus have made this even more unlikely and complex. Commenting on the RIAA's attempts to block Napster, Charles Nesson (cited in Pitt[9]), professor at the Berkman Center for Internet and Society at Harvard Law School, had this to say of Gnutella: "There is a generation of young people out there who have already learned that music is something you get on the net, rather than buy. The only way for the music industry to stop Gnutella is to turn off the Internet." He added, "And, as no one owns it or controls it, that is impossible."

The case of Betfair has seen some interesting reactions from incumbents and also governments at various levels. Traditional competitors have attempted to cry "No fair" as they struggle to contend with a player whose methods they don't fully understand. Sports bodies are anxious to understand the possible impact of a firm such as Betfair on the potential for financial abuses in their domains. Governments, while supposedly welcoming competition as a force in consumer interest, will immediately seek new ways to tax new entrants such as Betfair, because it seems like, yet is not like, traditional firms such as bookmakers and totalisators.

In the United Kingdom, Betfair has been the focus of lawsuits by the major British bookmaking firms such as Coral, William Hill, and Ladbrokes. They have charged that by allowing individuals to lay bets (rather than merely take them), they are acting as bookmakers, and Betfair is not licensed to do so. Graham Sharpe, spokesman for William Hill, argues, "If you have a bet on an exchange, you don't know who it's with; if [the person] is offering extravagant odds, you don't know why."[10]

The British courts have thrown out all the cases and rejected the bookmakers' arguments, and Betfair has been allowed to proceed with its business. While bookmakers might not like the idea of the site, it is evident that many of them are using it, either to buy back bets at advantageous prices or to lay bets for which they might otherwise not have been able to find takers. The substantiation for this is the significant amounts of money that are available to be traded on many events.

In Australia, not only have bookmakers objected to the site and attempted to close it down through legal action, it has also been the focus of an aggressive advertising campaign by Tabcorp (essentially a consortium of totalisator operators), a listed company that is the world's fourth largest gambling and entertainment business. Its advertising has attempted to cast Betfair in a negative light by claiming that betting on exchanges encourages dishonesty in sporting events and racing, a similar argument used in the United Kingdom by bookmakers. Betfair has disabled certain features on its Australian site to comply with Australian gambling legislation (e.g., Australian players are not able to bet "in the running"—that is, after an event has started or a race is running). Gambling is more a matter of state than federal legislation in Australia. While the legislation is not quite clear regarding whether it is legal or not for Australians to bet on betting exchanges or online casinos outside of Australia, there is no legislation prohibiting players in one state betting on operations in another.

The real effect of the flock-of-birds phenomenon is that access is equalized by mechanisms such as Betfair when they operate online, unlike what occurs in traditional operations such as bookmakers and totalisators. In a very real sense, no one has a better right of access, and no one, not even the largest corporation, can shout louder. The smallest player, the individual, has a right and opportunity to be seen and heard. Furthermore, many laws designed to regulate a physical world don't work as effectively when no one owns or controls the medium. This has been apparent in the lack of success in the traditional incumbents' attempts to fight Betfair in courts of law. It has also been demonstrated by Betfair being a better, not less effective, mechanism for the detection of dishonest dealings in sport. If a particular player has inside information on an event, there is nothing stopping him or her from exploiting this advantage by placing large cash bets either with bookmakers or totalisators and anonymously reaping the benefits of this insider trading. Betfair is arguably in a better position to deal with this type of problem. For example, in July 2004, Betfair was dragged into the spotlight when it reported suspicious betting patterns on its exchange to the Jockey Club in the United Kingdom just before the Lingfield race in which leading jockey Kieren Fallon, riding favorite Ballinger Ridge, lost to Rye after seemingly easing down before the finishing line. *News of the World* alleged Fallon had told an undercover journalist that Rye would win. No proof was found that the race was fixed, but a Betfair spokesperson was quoted as saying: "We are putting a searchlight on the sport and helping it clean up its act. There is a clear paper trail on our site that doesn't exist in high-street [betting] shops. We are entirely transparent. We have no vested interest in the outcome of a horse race."[11]

As observed, there is also the issue of how governments will attempt to tax firms such as Betfair. Ideally, from the firm's point of view, tax would best be levied on net profits (which, in simple terms, would amount to net commissions on winnings less other direct costs). However, governments might not see it in that way and might attempt to tax market makers such as this based on other measures, such as sales revenue. Such a measure could be very detrimental to the firm and its thousands of players because revenue is not an accurate measure of financial performance.

THE FISH TANK PHENOMENON: THE POWER OF CREATIVE INDIVIDUALS IN MUSIC AND WAGERING

While there is a great deal of junk as well as stupid schemes placed on the Internet, there are also an incredible number of good ideas developed by everyday people that can now finally see the light of day through this medium. In the latter half of 1998, the ground shifted in the music business when MP3 arrived on the web. MP3 (or more correctly, MPEG3, short for Moving Picture Experts Group Audio Layer III) is the acronym for a type of data storage that allows recorded sound files to be compressed in a way that makes them quite small without sacrificing much sound quality. While there is an inverse ration of sound quality to degree of compression, the typical MP3 file is compressed at a 10:1 ratio, which means that the average

3 minute song takes up about 4MB of storage space. MP3 was invented in the mid-1980s as a dual project between Professor Dieter Seitzer of the University of Erlangen, and the Fraunhofer Institut in the same German city. The Fraunhofer Institut was granted the MP3 patent in Germany in 1989, and this was submitted to the International Organization for Standardization a few years later.

A software mechanism for playing back MP3 recordings, called the AMP MP3 Playback Engine, was developed by a programmer at Advanced Multimedia Products in 1997, and it became the first serious MP3 player. A few months later, university students Justin Frankel and Dmitry Boldyev augmented the AMP software with a Windows interface, and called it "Winamp". The real MP3 craze began in 1998 when Winamp was offered as a free download. Music enthusiasts around the world began to offer downloadable music (much of it copyrighted) for free. Other programmers joined the fray, and provided a plethora of MP3 tools, including search engines that made it easy to find music. Portable MP3 players (the forerunners to today's Apple iPod) appeared on retail shelves, which allowed enthusiasts to carry their newly downloaded music around with them.

Napster made its debut in 1999, and this allowed anyone with an Internet connection to find, download, and share music with others all over the world in a matter of minutes. Napster created a virtual global community of music enthusiasts by connecting users to other users' hard drives through a central server. The server was developed by Shawn Fanning, a 20-year old university student who simply wanted to make it easier for his friends to share their music. By the end of 2000, Napster had more than 20 million users around the world.[12]

The common thread through all of this online music history is the absence of any major, for-profit recording company in any of the technological developments. Indeed, the only role played by any of the incumbents was that of stifling, or attempting to stifle, progress. The major innovations came from academic institutions, students, and penniless enthusiasts, whose only real resources were talent, persistence, creativity . . . and an Internet connection. Sean Fanning was a young, not very wealthy student—not the research department of a major recording company. A firm's next serious competitor might not be a multinational conglomerate, but an individual operating from home. This individual now has a unique mechanism for bringing good ideas to market.

Similarly, Andrew Black invented Betfair and changed sport wagering forever. He never worked for a government totalisator or parimutuel agency, nor was he availed of the significant resources of one of the major traditional bookmaking firms. He was simply a very talented, frustrated individual, who decided that trying to pick a winner was difficult enough without having the odds truly stacked against the player. There had to be a better way—and that way was through the Internet. Neither Sean Fanning nor Andrew Black had previous experience of the industries that they changed forever, and neither had ever worked for any of the established incumbents. The incumbents' only action was to try to smother the innovations that they saw as threats, rather than opportunities at best, or at worst, the writing on the wall. Recent evidence is that their attempts at suppression have failed miserably.

Summary and Conclusions

In the future, firms may still need to consider five forces—but they will be a very different set of forces than those originally offered by Michael Porter. There will be the technological effects of Moore's and Metcalfe's laws, hyper-accelerating change and spreading it like a deadly virus. There will be the contradictory effects of transaction cost economics, not only making firms smaller but virtual as well. There will be the societal effects of the flock-of-birds phenomenon bringing undreamed of democracy along with the threat of anarchy. And the fish tank phenomenon brings access to all.

Michael Porter argues that his five forces determine the attractiveness of an industry, which in turn strongly influences the profitability of firms within that industry. The five new forces of the information age are more ethereal and affect firms and industries in ways that are far less predictable or structured. To use the new five forces astutely, the decision maker must depend on them not so much as guidelines and prescriptions, but as prods from behind to keep challenging oneself, one's firm, and one's market.

The technological forces of Moore's and Metcalfe's laws accelerate change not only within a firm, but also within industries and markets, and this acceleration tends to be exponential. The decision maker must consider what will happen when computer chips are not just in computers but also in every device and product, and what will happen when these computers, like all computers, in their turn become part of an exponentially growing network.

Transaction cost economics, and technology's effects on the efficiency of firms and markets, means that the manager must constantly reflect on what will happen to the shape and size of the firm. The decision maker must continually evaluate what activities the technology will allow to be performed in the market and what functions may indeed be brought back within the firm itself. In channels of distribution, managers will have to observe the constant tussle between disintermediation and reintermediation. In the case of the former, many traditional intermediaries will disappear from channels as their roles are either usurped by technologies or performed more efficiently by other channel members. Already the Internet is having a profound effect on institutions such as travel agenies and financial brokerages, and the long-term impact of online music on conventional record stores is obviously of great concern to those institutions. In example after example of reintermediation, we are seeing new intermediaries enter channels using technology to improve the channel's efficiency while taking a share of the margins available in the channel for themselves. Online consolidators such as Priceline.com in the travel industry and Autobytel.com for new and used cars are prime examples of this.

The social forces of the flock-of-birds and the fish tank phenomena will require managers to work in a new environment—one where control and governance are not as structured and clear as they have been throughout most of our lives. Managing in a world where significant issues are not really within the control of a government or a government department, or under the remit of a large organization, will be a new and often scary experience for most executives. Not knowing where competition may come from (because it may not be up-front and visible) will also require a constant revisiting of strategy. When competition comes head on, or at least from the side or from behind, it can be seen and dealt with, even if slowly. When competition has the potential to come from a computer in the bedroom of a 17-year-old in another country, life becomes less predictable.

Many managers may take cold comfort from an identification of the five new forces and what they will do to the business environment. They are not neat and structured, like Porter's five forces, nor do they seem to suggest much in terms of strategic direction, as do popular analysis tools such as the Boston Consulting Group grid. Much of the recent writing on strategy emphasizes the effects of these forces, however, and suggests that conventional approaches to strategy will at least be insufficient, if not ineffective, for coping with corporate survival. A number of these authors (see, e.g., Downe & Mui,[13] Kelly,[14] Shapiro & Varian,[15] and Schwartz[16]) offer perspectives that are worth considering. While, as would be expected, there is no absolute concurrence on their advice for strategy in the future, these authors do tend to agree on certain fundamentals.

In closing, it is worth summarizing some of these basics:

1. Change is too rapid for anyone anywhere to feel comfortable—success has an anesthetizing effect that becomes its own enemy.
2. It may be a good idea to continually seek ways of destroying your own firm's value chain and putting yourself out of business—if you don't, someone else will.
3. Resources are increasingly less about tangible assets and more about knowledge and the ability to constantly innovate.
4. Firms should constantly find and exploit ways to give the customer as much of an opportunity to do as much of the work as possible. Technology offers great opportunities in this regard. Strangely (and as we pointed out in Chapter 1), customers don't want more service, they want less. They want control, and the power to solve their own problems, and victory will go to those players who find ways for them to do this well.[17]
5. Strategy is no longer long term, as the half-life of ideas diminishes. The 5-year plan or the long-term strategy is no longer viable, and the value of the annual strategic planning session is to be questioned. Strategy becomes incremental, rather than planned. It is revisited and revised not annually or even bi-annually, but monthly, probably weekly, and possibly daily. It's not that strategy should be thrown out with the bath water. Rather, perhaps, managers should consider that the strategy needed for the 21st century might indeed be a new baby, born of five new forces in an age of convergence.

Key Terms

- Internet
- new five forces
- Moore's law
- Metcalfe's law
- Coasian economics
- flock-of-birds phenomenon
- fish tank phenomenon

Questions

1. Explain in your own words what is meant by a "killer app," and find some examples not discussed in the text.
2. Identify five more examples of the effects of Moore's law in products or services not already discussed in the text.
3. What is mean by "transaction costs"? Explain these by using practical examples from an existing organization.
4. It has been said by many observers that Google is the most important new firm for the new millennium. Is Google an example of the new five forces at work? Explain how the forces apply to Google.
5. Do a "new five forces" analysis for the organization you work in or for one that you are very familiar with. List ways in which the forces apply to this organization and how they represent either opportunities or threats.

Resources and References

1. Porter, M. E. (1998). *Competitive advantage: Creating and sustaining superior performance.* New York: Free Press; Porter, M. E. (1980). *Competitive strategy: Techniques for analyzing industries and competitors.* New York: Free Press.
2. Downes, L., & Mui, C. (1998). *Unleashing the killer app.* Boston: Harvard Business School Press.
3. Ibid.
4. Coase, R. H. (1937). The nature of the firm. *Economica* 4: 386–405.
5. "The accidental superhighway." (1995, July 1). *The Economist,* special supplement.
6. Ibid.
7. For a full description see Pitt, L. F. (2001). Total e-clipse: Five new forces for strategy in the digital age. *Journal of General Management* 26(4): 1–15.
8. For a full description see Davies, M., Pitt, L. F., Shapiro, D., & Watson, R. T. (2005). Betfair.com: Five technology forces revolutionize worldwide wagering. *European Management Journal* 23(5): 533–541.
9. Pitt.
10. Downes & Mui.
11. Davies et al.; Betfair.com.
12. Jones, C. (2000, July 27). MP3 overview. Webmonkey. Accessed November 13, 2007, http://www.webmonkey.com/00/31/index3a.html?tw=multimedia.
13. Downes & Mui.
14. Kelly, K. (1998). *New rules for the new economy: 10 radical strategies for a connected world.* London: Fourth Estate.
15. Shapiro, C., & Varian, H. R. (1998). *Information rules: A strategic guide to the network economy.* Boston: Harvard Business School Press.
16. Schwartz, E. (L. Marino, ed.) (1999). *Digital Darwinism : Seven breakthrough business strategies for surviving in the cutthroat web economy.* New York: Broadway Books.
17. Berthon, P. R., Pitt, L. F., Katsikeas, C., & Berthon, J.-P. (1999). Virtual services go international: International services in the marketspace. *Journal of International Marketing* 7(3): 84–105.

CHAPTER

CUSTOMER CAPITAL
WHEN THE RELATIONSHIP
COMES FIRST

BEYOND MAKING A SALE

Marketing is ultimately about transactions—with making exchanges happen between buyers and sellers. However, today's companies find that they often must go beyond the simple transaction to the building of a relationship. At the same time, the idea of having a relationship with a customer is not well understood in many companies. Is it really possible to have relationships in the marketplace in the same way we have a relationship with a spouse or best friend? Even more elusive for many firms is a clear understanding of how relationships can be creatively managed.

Marketers are beginning to recognize that cooperative relationships between buyer and seller have a greater long-term payoff than do approaches that are one-way, competitive, or even adversarial. Long-term relationships are vital in many product and service areas, especially where products or services are fairly customized, market growth is slower, or the number of users is comparatively small. Further, technology makes it possible for all firms to get closer to customers. As a result, the trend toward closer relationships will only continue to grow in the years to come.

As we have suggested throughout this book, marketing is a field in transition. The changes are dramatic and ongoing, and this is likely to be a fairly permanent state of affairs. Only a few years ago, the core problem in many organizations was to move from thinking of marketing as selling to approaching marketing as a set of value-creating activities that are captured in the marketing mix. Today, the problem is much more complicated. Organizations must make fundamental decisions regarding how to approach different market segments and individual customers. Simply making a sale or achieving a transaction is not enough. In this chapter, we explore the changes that are occurring in how buyers and sellers interact with one another over time.

MAKING SENSE OF THE WAYS FIRMS INTERACT WITH CUSTOMERS

Companies can have great products, attractive prices, and superb employees, but they have nothing without a customer. No company can survive without making sales to customers, and this is the fundamental task assigned to the marketing function. Yet, the objective must be to achieve profitable transactions over time, and this can mean making a sale to a given customer at a given point in time, or it can mean much more. For instance, it may mean building a long-term relationship with a given account, such that the customer places all of its orders with the same seller for the next 10 years. Alternatively, it may mean making occasional sales to a wide number of different customers. The reality is that a range of possibilities exist in terms of how the marketer approaches the marketplace.

Figure 15-1 summarizes five different approaches marketers rely on when dealing with customers. It is an evolutionary perspective, in that it captures the pattern in which marketing practice has tended to develop over time. However, as we shall see, companies can operate at a number of points along this continuum at the same time, depending on the market, segment, and particular customer in question.

The historical focus in marketing has been the transaction. In essence, a transactional focus stresses doing what is necessary to make individual sales happen. This approach is somewhat analogous to someone attempting to catch fish. The person relies on experience, skill, the selection of an appropriate lure, and the right type of bait to catch as many fish as possible. Transactional marketing can vary in terms of how proactive and aggressive versus reactive and passive the

---

FIGURE 15-1 How Marketers Approach the Customer

Making a Transaction Happen

⇓

Encouraging Repeat Transactions

⇓

Achieving Loyalty

⇓

Investing in Relationships

⇓

Forming Strategic Partnerships

company and its representatives are. However, it typically relies on a stimulus-response type of approach, and a shorter term time horizon, much like that of our fisherman as he or she tries to stimulate the fish to respond to the lure and bait. Further, this approach entails a one-way flow of activities from the marketer to the prospective customer, as pictured here:

Stimulus	$\Rightarrow$	**Object**	$\Rightarrow$	**Response**
The marketer		The customer		Buying behavior
(4 P's: marketing tools)				

A step beyond the simple transaction is the repeat transaction. Here, the marketer is attempting to reinforce the buyer so that he or she repurchases from the same seller whenever he or she has a need. The more they can make this a routine, automatic, or conditioned response on the part of the buyer, the better. Marketers look for ways to "lock customers in" or to create disincentives for them to consider alternative sources of supply. An airline's frequent flyer program is an example of a program aimed at encouraging repeat transactions by travelers. So, too, is a cumulative volume discount program, where price per unit drops based on how much the customer purchases over time.

Loyalty is more than repeat-buying behavior. There is an attitudinal as well as a behavioral component to loyalty. This means that the buyer tends to repurchase from the same seller, not because he or she is locked in or believes he or she has no real option, but based on a strong personal preference. The buyer is, in effect, biased toward a particular seller and will make a special effort to buy most or all of their requirements from that vendor on an ongoing basis. Although the customer will listen to presentations from other suppliers, the situation is usually one where the out-supplier has to offer a product or service of superior value or significantly lower cost to regain a place in the buyer's purchasing habits. Because of its importance, we will elaborate on the complexities involved in creating and managing customer loyalty in the next section of this chapter.

The most prevalent trend today is toward "relationship marketing." As we shall see, relationship marketing is not well understood by many managers, and companies are engaging in a wide array of practices under the generic banner of relationship marketing. At the root of a relationship approach is the abandonment of the unidirectional, stimulus-response approach described earlier. The buyer is not viewed in isolation as an object responding to a set of stimuli controlled by the marketer. Rather, a "dyadic" or two-way perspective is adopted. In a sense, the fish and the person doing the fishing interact with one another.

A dyad is a fundamental unit consisting of two members or, in this case, of a buyer and a seller. Each party affects and is affected by the other, and a complete appreciation for what is taking place requires that both be considered simultaneously. Both parties to any transaction are seeking certain attributes. The seller is trying to satisfy specific objectives through the buyer, while the buyer is doing the same with regard to the seller. Both have expectations, and the exchange between the two involves products, money, knowledge, information, and social interaction

TABLE 15-1 A Two-Way Street: What Sellers and Buyers Want	
Traits of a Good Buyer	*Traits of a Seller*
Does not act aloof toward seller or seller's products	Offers thorough presentation and good follow-through
Does not try to get a lower price to use as leverage with a competitor	Has a good working knowledge of his or her product or service line
Has a clear understanding of his or her needs and requirements	Is willing to go to bat for the buyer with higher-ups in the selling firm
Allows adequate time for sales presentation	Shows knowledge of the market and willingness to keep the buyer informed
Makes reasonable demands given the type of purchase situation	Has a good working knowledge of the buyer's needs and requirements
Maintains good credit standing and pays bills or invoices promptly	Uses imagination in applying his or her products or services to the buyer's needs
Will work cooperatively with the seller when there is a problem or error	Does not try to oversell or get the customer to buy beyond what he or she needs
Behaves in an ethical manner	Prepares for sales calls or interactions
Provides accurate projection of future needs or requirements	Behaves in an ethical manner, including meeting commitments and delivering what was promised

(see Table 15-1). Each dyadic relationship is likely to have its own distinct nature. Further, dyadic relationships tend to evolve and become more personal over time. That is, they move beyond formal discussions of task-related product and seller performance variables to informal social interaction and personal friendships. In the process, long-term buyer–seller arrangements are established, with both parties investing in the ongoing development of a mutually beneficial relationship.

In some instances, companies go beyond relationships and form strategic partnerships. A partnership involves the buyer and seller working together on some major initiative. This occurs more typically in business-to-business markets than in consumer markets. For instance, a buying firm and a selling firm might jointly create a new product or collaborate on the development of a new technology. Together they might enter and develop a new market that neither has been in before. The creation of a new just-in-time inventory program or an electronic data interchange network among all of the locations of the buyer and the seller would also be examples of partnerships. Shared risks and resources are defining characteristics of partnerships.

BUILDING A FOUNDATION: CUSTOMER LOYALTY

Because buying decisions are normally negotiated compromises, once a seller is selected by the buyer, there is a tendency for the customer to buy from that seller again. To the extent that the customer has viable alternatives but continues to rely on the same source, positive attitudes are reinforced and loyalty begins to

FIGURE 15-2   Different Types of Loyalties of a Customer Purchasing a PDA

Loyalty to a Technology
(e.g., the Windows platform)

⇓

Loyalty to a Product Class
(e.g., pocket PCs)

⇓

Loyalty to a Manufacturer's Product or Brand
(e.g., Palm versus BlackBerry)

⇓

Loyalty to a Retailer or Seller
(e.g., RadioShack)

⇓

Loyalty to a Person
(e.g., Bob Johnson, salesperson)

emerge. Loyalty can prove to save time and effort for the buyer, while also reducing risk. As noted earlier, loyalty implies an attitudinal predisposition or personal preference to favor a particular supplier. The customer will make a special effort to buy from the seller. Also, where they exist, loyalties are often divided. That is, loyalty does not necessarily mean that customers buy all of their requirements from one seller, or buy from that vendor every time they are in the market.

In trying to understand loyalty, it is imperative for marketers to determine "loyalty to what." Buyer loyalty or commitment can be to a brand, a store, a manufacturer, a product category, a technology, or a person. Figure 15-2 illustrates possible buyer loyalties when purchasing a PDA, or personal digital assistant. This is a rapidly changing industry with a range of technological solutions. The typical PDA device can include some of the functionality of a computer, a cell phone, a music player, and a camera. The different brands provide an array of features and accessories. Naturally, different customers seek certain features over others. Therefore, a customer has many options. He or she could remain loyal to the old technology, be an advocate for the new, or be indifferent. The customer could also be loyal to a particular product category, such as a cell phone that has some of the features of a PDA. Alternatively, the customer could be a strong proponent of a particular brand of PDA, such as BlackBerry. Or, the loyalty may be to a retailer, such as Best Buy or RadioShack, perhaps because of the company's reputation or service policies. Another possibility is that loyalty is not to the product or vendor, but instead to a salesperson, such as Mr. Johnson. If Johnson went to work for another company, the customer might then switch to the products of the new company.

In the coming years, marketers are likely to witness changes in the amount of, and reasons for, loyalty. Strategies should be developed that explicitly attempt to manage loyalties. When loyalty exists, the marketer must be wary of becoming complacent, taking customers for granted, or abusing his or her company's position. Even a marketer who conscientiously manages customer relationships can lose part or all of an account if the wrong variables are emphasized when dealing with the customer. And when the marketer is an out-supplier trying to break into a loyal relationship, the challenge is even greater, as he or she is trying to change customer behavior. In such situations, the real problem becomes the attitudinal component of loyalty. Marketers must focus on the underlying reasons that actually drive the buyer's favorable attitudes toward his or her current seller. And these reasons are often subtle and complex. Simply providing the buyer with reasons not to be loyal to their current supplier, or offering a price discount, will seldom be a successful strategy.

FROM LOYALTY TO RELATIONSHIPS

Over the past decade, a large number of companies have adopted new approaches to the way they interact with customers. While they take various forms, we will refer to these novel approaches to customers as "relationship marketing," or RM. We can define RM as the establishment of strong, lasting ties with individual customers for the purpose of mutual benefit and ongoing value creation.

Relationships represent both a way of thinking and acting. They depend on a high level of personal interaction, trust, and the need to meet *mutual* expectations. They can require a level of product and service customization and an adaptation of the selling firm's operations or logistical arrangements to reflect unique customer requirements. A company that adopts the RM approach might argue, "Our competitors sell boxes; we create mutually beneficial customer solutions." It is a mindset that prizes innovative ways to discover new sources of value hand-in-hand with customers, not just for customers. The customer is integrated into the business. This is different than aggressive selling and more than increasing the firm's attention to customer service.

Companies that have adopted and practice relationship marketing select clients that can be satisfied over time at a profit. Through consistent, positive actions, the seller and customer learn to trust one another. Each party believes the other will not take advantage of them and each attempts to transform all encounters into win-win situations. Dependency (and hence vulnerability) of both parties on one another increases. Information is freely exchanged between the buyer and seller, and collaborative efforts are made to solve problems before they occur, whenever possible. As captured in Table 15-2, there is a clear recognition that both parties to a transaction are playing roles; both are making certain assumptions about the other; and each has goals, expectations, resources, and constraints. By building on this mutual awareness and respect, each party benefits.

In relationship marketing, the seller's goal is to delight the customer on an ongoing basis. While many companies appreciate the concept of having relationships, fewer have formal, effective programs for doing so. To gain a better insight

TABLE 15-2 Seeing Both Sides of the Buyer–Seller Dyad		
Marketer	$\longleftrightarrow$	*Customer*
Goals		Goals
Expectations		Expectations
Experiences		Experiences
Resources		Resources
Products/services		Needs and requirements
Prices		Willingness and ability to buy
Marketing programs		Perceived alternatives
Expertise		Expertise
People		People
Other partners		Other users or decision participants
Operating constraints		Usage constraints

about this concept, assume that two competitors, Sky Airlines and Northeast Airlines, each have a problem with an instrument on one of their aircraft. The supplier of instruments to Sky Airlines follows a nonrelationship approach. Accordingly, they might handle the problem in this way. First, Sky Airlines would have to call the main number of the supplier and request assistance through customer service. Most likely, if Sky was not aware if the part was under warranty, the customer service representative would instruct Sky to return the part (at Sky's expense) for rework or replacement. A new instrument would be sent out by overnight shipping, probably also at Sky's expense. Once the instrument was repaired, it would be shipped back to Sky with a repair bill and possibly no explanation for the failure or for why it was being returned.

Contrast this experience with what happened to Northeast Airlines when its instrument failed. Northeast sent a message electronically to its supplier explaining which instrument had broken. The manufacturer immediately shipped, at its own expense, a replacement part. When the part arrived the next morning, a supplier maintenance specialist was waiting to assist in the replacement of the instrument. The defective instrument was collected by the specialist and shipped to the factory, where it was analyzed to determine the cause of failure. Once accomplished, the supplier electronically communicated the cause of the failure and the design changes taken to ensure this defect did not happen in the future. Finally, Northeast's maintenance supervisor received a phone call from her supplier counterpart apologizing for the incident and thanking her for using the supplier's components. Given these two scenarios, which supplier would you prefer to continue to do business with—the one who sold you a part or the one who provided a solution to your problem?

To accomplish RM, all employees within a marketer's firm must understand the concept of the relationship and what it means. In different ways, some more direct and others fairly indirect, every employee in the selling firm contributes to the relationship.

MYTHS AND REALITIES OF RELATIONSHIP MARKETING

Has there really been a paradigm shift in terms of how marketers approach their customers? The trend is certainly away from adversarial buyer–seller transactions and toward collaboration. But are marketers really adopting one-to-one marketing programs, where the marketing mix is tailored to the individual customer? Are marketers really doing anything new?

The answer appears to be a qualified "yes." In practice, the way many firms implement a relationship approach contrasts significantly with the RM concept as we have presented it. Marketers hesitate to make the necessary level of commitment to relationship development. They find that customers seem willing to make even less of a commitment to forming a close relationship. The reality is that many firms are currently approaching relationships more tactically than strategically. Shortsightedness can lead companies to misinterpret RM in the following ways:

- *Trying to lock the customer in:* The mistaken motivation of many marketers in forming relationships is less one of mutual investment and benefit over time and more one of securing as much of the customer's business for as long as possible. The outcome of successful RM is that customers will want to purchase from a seller that is interested in their well-being because of the benefits each party receives from the relationship. Rather than locking the customer in, each party enters a mutually beneficial, or win-win, relationship.

- *Failing to formalize:* Firms approach relationships too informally, creating little in the way of structure, formal goal setting, or mechanisms for measuring the quality or effectiveness of relationships. Likewise, it is important that two parties involved in a relationship share information and have some mutual goals. Relationships require systems, structures, guidelines, and assessments—together with a willingness by both parties involved to nurture the relationship.

- *Making only nonfinancial investments:* Marketers are more likely to invest time and effort into customer communications and less apt to incur costs in customizing what they sell to address unique needs of particular customers. They are hesitant to change equipment, operating processes, personnel, hours of operation, or technologies to reflect the customer's requirements. For RM to work, firms must pay more than lip service to relationships.

- *Avoiding dependency:* Relationships are a source of competitive advantage today, but so is flexibility. Some companies appear to want closer linkages with customers while keeping their options open. They also do not let the customer "too far" into their own operations. Relationship marketing implies that sellers and buyers work in concert to be successful. Mistrust and apprehension about sharing information or becoming too dependent are certain to preclude establishing a true and lasting relationship.

- *Pursuing unilateral efforts:* The evidence indicates that selling organizations are doing more to initiate and sustain relationships, including more investment and adaptation, than are customers. Relationship marketing is a two-way street. The buyer wants to deal with a great seller, and the seller wants to deal with a great customer. Thus, customers must also invest time and effort (and more of their purchases). Customers must be willing to share information about themselves, and to anticipate their needs. If customers do not want to enter into a close relationship with a seller, and contribute to the relationship, then it will not happen. Sellers must carefully determine who could benefit from a closer relationship. They also must realize this relationship will occur only over a period of time, after both parties come to believe they can depend on one another, and that a closer relationship will result in increased benefits for all.

- *Avoiding difficult choices:* Marketers fail to appreciate that investing more in certain customers means investing less in obtaining and serving other customers—they attempt to be all things to all people. However, if a company follows a true relationship marketing path, it chooses its clients carefully, knowing that not all customers or opportunities can or should be pursued.

- *Believing one size fits all:* Firms do not define different types of relationships for different categories of customers. Rather, they seem to have a general notion of a relationship, which applies to those key accounts with whom they have been dealing for some time. Hence, many firms have determined that their A accounts will receive different levels of service (and perhaps prices) than other customers. Instead, marketers must organize their accounts by A, B, C, or D, or Key, Promising, Small, and Other categories. Each category warrants a different type of relationship, and some may not involve a relationship at all. The levels of investment and customization will be unique to each of these categories.

In reality, then, companies "talk the talk" about relationships but don't "walk the walk." There is a need to approach RM more systematically, to be willing to make mutual investments and to design operating policies, systems, and organizational structure around relationship requirements. There is also a need to expect more from customers. Many firms are only beginning to truly think in relationship terms, and they are learning how to manage relationships through a process of trial and error.

RELATIONSHIPS LEAD TO CHANGES IN GOALS: THE LIFETIME VALUE CONCEPT

As companies move from transactional marketing to relationships and partnerships, a change also occurs in the objectives the marketer seeks to accomplish in the marketplace. Marketers strive to accomplish a wide array of objectives, ranging from the profit contribution from a given market segment to numbers of new

FIGURE 15-3 Changes in the Way Marketers Assess Performance

Sales Revenue
(close the deal)

⇓

Market Share
(own the market)

⇓

Operating Profit
(generate acceptable profit contributions from
investments in products, segments, channels)

⇓

Customer Equity
(capture a desired proportion of the customer's lifetime value)

accounts to awareness levels achieved among key target audiences. However, it is worth examining the overarching concern of those in marketing, or the performance variables for which they are held most accountable. Again there has been an evolution, as shown in Figure 15-3.

Consistent with the transactional focus, and the fact that sales are the lifeblood of any company, the traditional concern of marketers has been to generate sales or "close the deal." A sales orientation tends to be somewhat shortsighted, as the company becomes more preoccupied with the tactics necessary to make a transaction happen than with considering the total value proposition as it relates to the customer over time. Performance in this situation is simply measured by the number of closed sales and the total revenue generated by those sales.

Subsequently, driven by competitor pressures, as well as the desire to achieve production economies through volume, the concern of many marketers moves to achieving a certain share of the total market. Maintaining and increasing market share leads to a greater emphasis on customer retention, which means repeat business and customer loyalty. This orientation is driven by the belief that market share is correlated with profitability. However, many examples exist where the most profitable company in an industry was not the market share leader. In some instances, the cost of additional market share exceeds the benefit. Further, markets today are continually redefining themselves, and the firm finds that competition is coming from very nontraditional sources, making market share a less meaningful performance indicator.

As companies become more strategic in their marketing operations, they tend to move beyond sales and market share to an emphasis on profitability. Thus, marketers begin to focus on the margins achieved on a given sale, and on generating profitable sales over time. Efforts and resources are allocated based on which products, market segments, territories, and distribution channels generate the greatest profit or rate of return. Similarly, bonuses and commissions are tied to multiple measures of profit performance.

In many markets, companies find that the large proportion of their actual profits (as opposed to sales) come from a relatively smaller proportion of customers. This reality tends to reinforce the importance of relationship building. It also leads firms to examine the profitability of individual accounts. Customer profitability is an important issue, but it is not sufficiently comprehensive. The profitability of a given customer can vary, depending on what she or he buys, at what prices, in what quantities, at what times, and with what sort of customer support and servicing requirements. Profitability can also be enhanced where the marketer gets intimately involved with the customer, such that she or he is continually identifying new needs and opportunities for value creation.

Recognition of these ways to improve the profitability of a given account has led some companies to prioritize a concept called "customer equity" and the related notion of "customer lifetime value" (CLV). Simply put, *customer lifetime value* refers to the total amount a customer will spend on a given product category over a strategically meaningful time period (e.g., the next 10 years). *Customer equity* refers to the proportion of the customer's total expenditures or lifetime value that the marketer seeks to capture. By placing a value on customer equity, the marketer knows what the customer is "worth" and, correspondingly, how much the firm can invest in marketing efforts directed toward the customer. The marketer also starts to modify the product/service mix to better reflect the customer's evolving requirements over time.

The calculation of CLV is not as difficult as it may sound. Table 15-3 provides an illustration of a simple table that any marketer could use. Here, we have assumed a life of 10 years, meaning it is realistic to expect the customer could spend at least 10 years interacting with our firm if the relationship is properly managed. Further, it is assumed that we will acquire 1,000 customers in the first year of the calculation and that we will lose 9% of them in each ensuing year. Further, the typical customer is generating $150 in sales each year. Given the time value of money, a 20% discount rate has been applied to the future sales from the customer. A great source for further insights on the CLV concept can be found at **www.customerequity.com**.

An important implication of this discussion is that the ability to engage in successful relationship marketing requires that firms change the types of objectives they are setting. Developing meaningful relationships with customers is unlikely if the firm is preoccupied with sales and market share. Alternatively, relationships are facilitated when the measure of marketing performance is long-term customer value and the percent of customer equity the company seeks.

TYPES AND DEGREES OF RELATIONSHIPS

We believe the goal of the marketer is not to establish relationships with every customer. Many companies discover that they are investing considerable financial and nonfinancial resources trying to form relationships with unwilling and/or

TABLE 15-3 Sample Table for Use in Calculating a Customer's Lifetime Value

Revenue	Year 1	Year 2	Year 3	Year 4	Year 5	Year 6	Year 7	Year 8	Year 9	Year 10
Customers	1000	910	828	754	686	624	568	517	470	428
Retention rate	91.00%	91.00%	91.00%	91.00%	91.00%	91.00%	91.00%	91.00%	91.00%	91.00%
Ave ann sales	$150.00	$150.00	$150.00	$150.00	$150.00	$150.00	$150.00	$150.00	$150.00	$150.00
Total revenue	$150,000.00	$136,500.00	$124,215.00	$113,035.65	$102,862.44	$93,604.82	$85,180.39	$77,514.15	$70,537.88	$64,189.47
Costs										
Cost%	50.00%	50.00%	50.00%	50.00%	50.00%	50.00%	50.00%	50.00%	50.00%	50.00%
Total costs	$75,000.00	$68,250.00	$62,107.50	$56,517.83	$51,431.22	$46,802.41	$42,590.19	$38,757.08	$35,268.94	$32,094.74
Profits										
Gross profit	$75,000.00	$68,250.00	$62,107.50	$56,517.83	$51,431.22	$46,802.41	$42,590.19	$38,757.08	$35,268.94	$32,094.74
Discount rate	1.00	1.20	1.44	1.73	2.07	2.49	2.99	3.58	4.30	5.16
NPV profit	$75,000.00	$56,875.00	$43,130.21	$32,707.07	$24,802.86	$18,808.84	$14,263.37	$10,816.39	$8,202.43	$6,220.17
Cum NPV profit	$75,000.00	$131,875.00	$175,005.21	$207,712.28	$232,515.15	$251,323.99	$265,587.36	$276,403.75	$284,606.17	$290,826.35
CLTV	**$75.00**	**$131.88**	**$175.01**	**$207.71**	**$232.52**	**$251.32**	**$265.59**	**$276.40**	**$284.61**	**$290.83**

Notes: 1. Assume a firm acquires 1000 new customers in Year 1
2. Average annual sales per customer is $150
3. Costs = 50% of sales
4. Assume a 20% discount rate
5. The result is the CLTV of one of the customers acquired in year 1
6. Numbers of Customers have been rounded to the nearest whole number

inappropriate customers. What becomes important is the need to recognize that not all customers are necessarily treated in the same way. Some accounts warrant significant investment and customization of marketing efforts, while others warrant less investment. Another way of thinking about it is that there are degrees of relationships, where some are very deep and intimate and others are more shallow and short term.

Before attempting to establish a long-term relationship, there is a need for the marketer to examine such variables as the nature of the customer requirements, the ease of doing business with the customer, the likelihood that doing business with this particular customer will attract other customers, and the extent to which the customer has alternative choices to which he or she could easily switch. Ultimately, the focus should be on estimating customer lifetime value. Then, all of the customers in the firm's client base need to be put into categories or groups. After a thorough analysis, firms can classify their customers as single or occasional transactions, repeat or multiple transactions, loyal accounts, or relationships.

1. *Single or occasional transactions:* The customer does business rarely or infrequently with the seller, usually because he or she has an immediate need, is seeking the lowest price and/or fastest delivery, or because the seller is the most convenient to purchase from. There is no loyalty in this form of relationship. The marketer makes no unique investment in the customer.

2. *Repeat or multiple transactions:* Customers purchase on a repeat basis but will purchase from another supplier when conditions warrant doing so. There is little loyalty, with the buyer using the seller principally because of price or convenience. The marketer may develop incentives for repeat buyers, and these are offered to all buyers.

3. *Loyal accounts:* Customer has a strong preference for, and is loyal to, the supplier. In all but the most unusual circumstances, the customer will not purchase from a competitor. The marketer will frequently develop a loyalty program for these types of customers. Loyal customers receive more sales and service attention, and the company will make an effort to respond to special requests from the account.

4. *Relationships:* Customer and supplier share information and seek to make each interaction a win-win encounter. Each party believes it is in his or her best interest to cooperate with the other. There is a high level of loyalty exhibited by both parties. The marketer tailors the marketing mix to the account and looks for unique ways to create value for the customer. A formal program is put in place for working with the customer, often involving close interaction between the seller and buyer.

A firm may find itself simultaneously pursuing adversarial, competitive, cooperative, and partnering/networking approaches, depending on the category into which a customer falls. And yet, this strategic maze of transactions/relationships is easier said than done. It is apparent that firms need better guidance regarding how to distinguish among customers in their client base in terms of levels of investments, customization, and intimacy.

UNDERLYING CHARACTERISTICS OF RELATIONSHIPS

Relationships can be better understood by considering some of their underlying characteristics (see Table 15-4). Any relationship involves trust, commitment, information exchange, mutual goals, interdependency, player traits, roles, norms, adaptation, and value creation. Chief among these is trust, which refers to seller or buyer confidence in an exchange partner's reliability and integrity. Given the realities of competitive markets (e.g., buyer beware), and the diverse experiences of sellers and buyers, there is a natural tendency for both parties to limit the amount of trust they place in one another. Trust must be earned, which takes time, and it can easily be undermined.

Trust leads to commitment and a greater willingness to share key information with the other party. In a sense, information is the lubricant that makes the relationship work smoothly. Selling organizations are hesitant to share information regarding their needs, capabilities, limitations, future plans, and costs, just as buyers will hold back information regarding their ability to pay, knowledge of competitors, current and future needs, and personal demographics. With greater information exchange comes the ability to better understand both the goals and needs of the other party and to move toward a situation where mutual goals are shared.

Interdependency can explain many of the dynamics within a relationship. It is concerned with how much the seller and buyer need one another. Both parties

---

TABLE 15-4 13 Questions for Marketers to Consider about a Relationship

1. How dependent are we on this customer?
2. How dependent are they on us?
3. What are the sources of our respective dependencies?
4. What are the implications of these dependencies for the way in which we interact with the customer?
5. Where are potential sources of conflict between the seller and buyer?
6. What are the buyer's unique needs? What are the seller's unique capabilities?
7. Who actually makes the buying decision? Is the buyer different from the decider or user?
8. What are the demographic and personality characteristics of the players, both on the selling and buying side of the relationship?
9. Do the seller and buyer have similar experience levels, values, and backgrounds? In what areas are they similar or dissimilar, and how might this relationship affect their interactions?
10. Are there certain rules of the game or unwritten norms that determine acceptable and unacceptable tactics on the part of the seller and buyer?
11. What are our expectations of the role played by the customer in their dealings with us?
12. What are the buyer's expectations of our personnel in terms of both their actions and authority?
13. Are there differences between our perceptions and their perceptions of roles and norms?

need each other to some degree, meaning they are dependent on one another. The question becomes "Who needs who the most?" What is the degree to which either party meets the requirements of the other that are not immediately available from alternative sources? If there are few competitors and the item being purchased is a key necessity to the buyer, he or she will be more dependent; when demand is down and the economy is in recession, the seller may be more dependent. Examining the relative dependencies can suggest insights into the behaviors and relative flexibility of each party. Relationships imply that neither party takes unfair advantage of her or his relative position.

An especially interesting characteristic of any relationship concerns the traits of the parties involved. Sample traits might include age, gender, educational background, charisma, expertise, personality, and communication style, among others. If we think about the buyer and the representatives of the selling organization, both sides have traits that affect how they interact with the other. Some companies attempt to hire salespeople or store personnel with characteristics that are similar to those of customers. They assume customers are more likely to do business with people like themselves. Others might work on the theory that opposites attract, and so they hire individuals with distinctive traits that make them more interesting to buyers.

In any relationship, both parties play certain roles. Buyers act in particular ways so they will not be taken advantage of and to obtain desired outcomes from sellers. Sellers do the same. Both parties have certain expectations regarding how the other plays his or her role. Certain norms and rules of the game can emerge. Hence, it may be inappropriate for the buyer to use a promised price from some competitor to try and get an unreasonably low price from the seller. Alternatively, for the seller, norms may emerge where it is understood that she or he will not try to sell the customer something she or he does not require. In a sense, unofficial rules exist that are understood by each party. Frustrations and anxieties are less likely to exist when sellers and buyers agree on these rules.

As these various characteristics of a given relationship become more apparent over time, the seller and buyer are better able to adapt to one another. This kind of adaptation on both sides makes it possible for the seller to recognize new ways to create value for the customer. Value creation is the heart and soul of any relationship. But the amount of value created depends on the active participation of the buyer in the value-creation process. There is an important dynamic here, in that strong relationships make it possible for more value to be created for a customer than would otherwise be the case.

CREATING A RELATIONSHIP MANAGEMENT PROGRAM

The larger question faced by many firms is "How is a relationship marketing program implemented?" There is no one right way, and it should always be kept in mind that each relationship is unique and will require the marketer to modify his or her approach. At the same time, it is helpful to have a general framework for managing relationships. Here is an eight-step framework that can be easily adapted to different types of customer situations:

Step 1:   Establish criteria for selecting relationship customers

Step 2:   Define the purpose of the relationship

Step 3:   Set the boundaries

Step 4:   Establish expectations

Step 5:   Formulate performance goals

Step 6:   Establish communication channels

Step 7:   Create value

Step 8:   Measure performance

In applying this framework, consider the case of a small local bank. The bank has decided to establish a relationship management program with some of its customers. The bank's customer base is first classified into three categories, with the most attractive of these targeted for relationships. The relationship group is defined using the following criteria:

- The risk of losing the account is moderate to high.
- The customer is among the top 30% of accounts in terms of the balances kept.
- The customer is receptive to relationship formation.
- Opportunities exist for improvement in relationships with the account.
- A match exists between the values of the seller and buyer.
- Potential exists for mutual benefit to the two parties.
- There is scope for adding service benefits.

The next step is to establish the purpose of the relationship. Let's assume, from the bank's perspective, its purpose is twofold: to retain the account and discourage the customer from lowering his or her bank balances and to find ways to increase the bank services used by the customer. From the customer's vantage point, the purpose of approaching the bank as a relationship partner might be to ensure a consistently high level of personal service, to eliminate nuisance fees, and to get proactive advice regarding how best to manage his or her money. In defining the purpose of the relationship, both parties are identifying expected benefits.

The two parties also establish boundaries for the relationship. This involves determining the issues that are and are not on the table for discussion. Examples of issues on the table might include interest rates on particular types of loans, fees charged for particular services such as traveler's checks or international transfers of funds, information requested of the customer by the bank, the availability of the bank manager for consultations, and the ability to conduct business outside of normal banking hours. Issues that are not on the table could include flexibility in terms of late loan payments, availability of certain types of loans, and the time involved in clearing a check deposited into the customer's account.

The buyer and seller must also appreciate the expectations each has of the other. For instance, the customer makes it clear that he or she does not want to find other customers are getting better deals from the bank than he or she is, that he or she would receive adequate warning of fee increases, that his or her bank account information would be treated confidentiality, and that the bank would not provide its customer list to other firms. The seller makes clear its expectations in the areas of bank account balances maintained, how the customer voices complaints, on-time loan payments, and advance warning regarding large withdrawals.

Performance goals are then set for both parties. For the bank, standards are agreed to with regard to customer service levels, promptness in handling customer inquiries, the total fees charged to the customer over a year, and an overall customer satisfaction rating. For the customer, standards are established in terms of the balances kept in the bank, the number of accounts that he or she has, timely supply of information requested by the bank, timely payment of loans, and ease of doing business.

Attention is also devoted to ongoing communications between the parties. A distinction is drawn by the bank between standard marketing communications and technical communications regarding aspects of the bank's services or the customer's accounts and needs. There is an understanding regarding who the customer is able to communicate with in the bank for various purposes. Similarly, it is understood that the bank will communicate personally with the customer when certain types of issues or problems come up, rather than sending communications in the mail. This process is facilitated by mapping all the points of contact that tend to occur between the bank and the customer over a given year. Attention is also devoted to dispute resolution and how disagreements will be handled.

The buyer and seller also examine areas where each of them would need to make investments in the relationship. The bank proactively identifies new areas where it might be able to create value for the customer over the next year. The customer agrees to work with the bank on these opportunities. Finally, each party commits to evaluating the other by completing a report card every 6 months. It is agreed that the results will be compiled by the bank, and the data tracked over time. Further, an annual meeting is scheduled between the bank manager and the customer to review the relationship.

There is no one right way to establish a relationship program. Marketers will find that buyers vary widely in terms of how much time and effort they are willing or able to dedicate to interactions with a given seller. Further, the relationship can be expected to evolve, such that the buyer is not initially willing to do much about the issues of greatest concern to the marketer but that with time they will become more sensitive to those issues. At the same time, it is vital that the spirit of a relationship be established up-front, such that what evolves is not a one-way street in terms of how much the marketer gives up without any reciprocation from the customer.

THE NEED FOR IMAGINATION
IN MANAGING RELATIONSHIPS

There is no formula for how to manage a relationship. Although the process just described suggests key steps for marketers to follow, the best relationships are managed creatively. Imagination is used in finding ways to get close to customers but also in getting customers closer to the firm.

Consider an example involving the owner (Mr. Watters) of a gasoline station in a mid-sized town located in a remote part of Texas, just off a major highway. While the business seems relatively simple, in fact the owner recognizes that he has different types of customers whom he needs to approach differently. Consistent with our earlier discussion, Mr. Watters organizes the customer base into three basic categories: random drop-ins, repeat patrons, and high-value loyalists. With the random drop-ins (40% of the customer base), many of whom are travelers pulling off the highway for a fill-up, the owner makes relatively little effort or investment, other than having clear signage on the highway and friendly service. The repeat patrons are customers who purchase gas at any number of stations in town, often depending on which is cheaper or more convenient at a moment in time (25% of the customer base). Here, the station owner has an incentive program that gives customers a free gallon of gas for every 10 gallons that they buy.

The third group, labeled high-value loyalists by the proprietor, accounts for 35% of the total customer base. It is with these customers that Mr. Watters attempts to develop a relationship. Consider a typical customer in this group. Alice Moran is an accountant in the local town, where she has been practicing for the past 12 years. She does the accounting for the local school district and has a client base that includes a number of the professionals (doctors, lawyers, architects) in town. She has been frequenting Mr. Watters's gasoline station for 3 years, initially because it was on her way to work. She also began having her oil changed at the gas station a year ago. Ms. Moran more recently moved to a new house a little further from the station, but she continues to buy much of her gasoline requirements (now about 60% of her needs over a year) from Mr. Watters.

How does the owner create a relationship strategy for customers such as Ms. Moran? This is where creativity comes into the picture, as the owner must build the relationship around the needs and characteristics of the customer. A beginning point is to build a knowledge base about Ms. Moran in terms of the type of car she drives, when she tends to purchase gas, how often she buys, the type of fuel she buys, and what else she purchases when she stops in, as well as personal information such as her use of the car for work purposes, long-distance automobile trips she tends to go on, and even her birthday. Mr. Watters also takes time to estimate Ms. Moran's lifetime value—that is, what she is likely to spend on automobile maintenance and fuel over the next 10 years. He would like to capture at least 70% of that lifetime value. Clearly, Mr. Watters will make a point to offer Ms. Moran friendly service. But relationship marketing goes much further.

What if Mr. Watters makes a value proposition to Ms. Moran, based on his understanding of her needs? They agree that he will come to her office on the first Tuesday every third month and pick up her car. He will take it to his station, change the oil, check all other lubricants and water levels, check the air pressure and rotate her tires, wash and wax the car, and get it back before the end of the work day, all for a very attractive price. Further, he will provide Ms. Moran with a report card on her car every 6 months. His goal is to know her car and her associated needs better than she does. In addition, he will send a regular newsletter to clients such as Ms. Moran, advising them about things like battery maintenance, when to use which types of fuels, updates on new developments with hybrid cars, and the use of bio-fuels. It would not be unusual for him to tell Ms. Moran that she is buying a higher grade of gasoline than she really needs, in effect saving her money and costing him money (but only in the short term). He ultimately becomes an advisor and problem solver to Ms. Moran, rather than a seller of gasoline. For her part, Ms. Moran not only gives Mr. Watters more of her business, she shares more information with him and adapts her behavior over time to facilitate the relationship.

This example makes clear that relationships can apply in any kind of business and do not require huge expenditures. The keys to relationship success are a willingness to invest in customers, to think about them strategically, to know them well, and to apply creativity and imagination to the creation of value and the building of long-term connections.

Summary and Conclusions

Nowhere are the dramatic changes in contemporary marketing practice more evident than in the ways firms approach customers. An environment where change is fast, competitive pressures are intense, and much more choice exists means that companies must rethink the role of the customer. A focus on managing various types of relationships must replace the old emphasis on transactions. As we move toward a relationship mindset, marketing efforts become more intense and more one-to-one, with greater customization of the marketing mix and higher investment levels in individual customers.

The extent to which managers understand relationships remains in the formative stages. While embracing the concept, relationship marketing has a variety of different practical meanings and applications. Too many marketers are pursuing a conservative approach, and this caution may reflect their understanding of marketplace realities. But it also means missed opportunities.

Firms wishing to pursue the RM approach should recognize that it involves a fundamental change both in how managers and employees think and in the everyday operations of a company. It is critical to manage relationships strategically, not just tactically. This first means determining the firm's competitive advantage(s) and the type(s) of customers that would benefit from long-term relationships. It requires that marketers diligently work to gain trust while demonstrating how the customer will benefit from a closer relationship with the firm. The marketer must acquire intimate knowledge of customer goals, needs, concerns, and characteristics. Further, it may be appropriate to share information with customers about the firm's capabilities, operations, goals, priorities, and limitations. There is an understanding that relationships have ups and downs, but there is always an attempt to turn customer experiences into win-win situations. Relationship marketers also compute the overall worth of the customer and base their actions on the lifetime value of the relationship.

RM is not a "one size fits all" strategy. Relationships should not be formed with every customer. Not all relationships are profitable, and firms cannot usually afford to make unique investments with their entire customer base. In a given period, it is likely that customers will range from transactional to relationship oriented. The bottom line is to behave toward customers in such a way that maximizes the mutual benefit for both parties over time.

Finally, relationship management requires imagination. In a sense, a relationship is a special context that allows the marketer to explore new ways for continually discovering sources of value. The company and customer are both adapting toward one another. The RM approach recognizes that value creation is not fixed or limited—it is a dynamic process that unfolds as creativity is applied to a growing knowledge base regarding customers.

Key Terms

- buyer–seller relationship
- customer equity
- loyalty
- mutual relationships
- relationship marketing
- relationship types

Questions

1. Why do you think the marketer's approach to the customer is evolving from a transactional perspective to relationships and partnerships?
2. What are some of the challenges you think might be involved in measuring customer lifetime value and customer equity? Why is it critical to measure these things?
3. How is loyalty different from repeat buying behavior?
4. Why is it true that the marketer might not want to have a relationship with every customer?
5. Assume you were a company like Google. Identify three different types or categories of relationships you might have with different customer segments.

CHAPTER

THE ACID TEST

INTRODUCTION: DILEMMAS FACING THE CORPORATION

Every chapter in this book offers a set of questions at the end of the chapter to stimulate additional thinking about a particular topic—except this one. This chapter *starts* with a set of questions, and every section is infused with questions. Because the questions deal with the "grey areas" of the marketer's world, there are no definitive answers. Rather, each question raises even more questions. Moreover, if you have read some or most of the previous chapters and heeded the lessons offered, doing things differently than before has become second nature by the time you've reached this point. The logic behind this approach will reveal itself in due course—start with the end in mind. To gain maximum benefit, please take a moment to reflect on each question and write down your thoughts before proceeding to the next section. Knowing where you stand on a certain issues before you continue will enhance your understanding of dilemmas discussed in this chapter.

Despite unprecedented global prosperity, the gap between the haves and the have-nots is widening, with more than 2.8 billion people living on less than $2 per day, 1.2 billion people not having access to running water, and 2.9 billion people without adequate sanitation. Some people believe multinational corporations should use their economic resources to tackle global social problems such as poverty, hunger, and injustice, while others argue this is the domain and responsibility of governments. What is your opinion? Ideally you should answer the following three questions before proceeding:

1. Does the modern corporation have a role in pursuing such goals as ending world hunger, seeking social justice, and cleaning up the environment?

2. Good intentions aside, do corporations have the capacity to have an impact?

3. How should this capacity be exercised?

Your answers will depend on your views regarding the responsibility of corporate citizens and the role of the marketer.

Shortly after 9/11, a group of 20 thought leaders were asked to address the same three questions you were asked to consider. Their respective viewpoints were published in an article entitled "Below the Bottom Line,"[1] which is available at: **http://www.conference-board.org/articles/atb_article.cfm?id=58**. You might recognize some of the names in this group of 20 individuals, for instance, Richard Mahoney, Henry Mintzberg, C. K. Prahalad, Jeremy Rifkin, Chris Trimble, Charles Handy, and Art Kleiner. It is recommended that you read this article to get a clearer sense of both your own perspective and the conflicting forces affecting the dashboard for marketing performance. Record your observations regarding the implications for marketers before continuing.

How did your suggestions for the three questions about a better future for all compare with those of the 20 thought leaders in "Below the Bottom Line"? Did you suggest corporations should help eradicate poverty and hunger through their philanthropic efforts as good corporate citizens, or did you instead propose that a solution must come from the governments who are faced with these problems? Perhaps you suggested this is something development agencies or nongovernmental organizations (NGOs) should be doing? Or perhaps you approached the problem from a different perspective? In the following quotation, from one of David Suzuki's inspirational works, he calls attention to the challenge facing everyone today: "to look at the world from a different perspective" because "the way we see the world shapes the way we treat it."

"The way we see the world shapes the way we treat it.
If a mountain is a deity, not a pile of ore;
if a river is one of the veins of the land, not potential irrigation water;
if a forest is a sacred grove, not timber;
if other species are our biological kin, not resources;
or if the planet is our mother, not an opportunity;
then we will treat each one with greater respect.
That is the challenge, to look at the world from a different perspective."

—DAVID SUZUKI

Enter the marketer. What should marketers do given the contemporary environment described in the article entitled "Below the Bottom Line"? Let's consider three key activities that directly relate to the topics in this chapter: marketers are responsible for customer communications (in Chapter 8), brand management (in Chapter 9), and customer relationship management (in Chapter 14), among other important things. Which of the following options reflect your personal opinion regarding the marketer's job? The marketer should:

1. Use the marketing toolkit to sell more of the company's products and services.

2. Produce profits for the shareholders in legally sanctioned ways.

3. Make the world a better place by improving the quality of life for all human beings.

4. Make a fair profit by providing beneficial products to the marketplace.

5. Search for new markets in which to sell the company's offerings.

6. Optimize financial performance of the company.

7. Something else not mentioned here.

Jot down your answer, especially if it is something that is not listed as an alternative in the options provided here.

A TRANSFORMATION: FROM EFFICIENCY AND EFFECTIVENESS TO SUSTAINABILITY

The story continues with excerpts from the 2006 report, "The Next 4 Billion," by the World Resources Institute International Finance Corporation[2]:

> The 4 billion people at the base of the economic pyramid (BOP)—all those with incomes below $3,000 in local purchasing power—live in relative poverty. Their incomes in current U.S. dollars are less than $3.35 a day in Brazil, $2.11 in China, $1.89 in Ghana, and $1.56 in India. Yet together they have substantial purchasing power: the BOP constitutes a $5 trillion global consumer market.
>
> The wealthier mid-market population segment, the 1.4 billion people with per capita incomes between $3,000 and $20,000, represents a $12.5 trillion market globally. This market is largely urban, already relatively well served, and extremely competitive.
>
> In contrast, BOP markets are often rural—especially in rapidly growing Asia—very poorly served, dominated by the informal economy, and, as a result, relatively inefficient and uncompetitive. Yet these markets represent a substantial share of the world's population. Data from national household surveys in 110 countries show that the BOP makes up 72% of the 5,575 million people recorded by the surveys and an overwhelming majority of the population in Africa, Asia, Eastern Europe, and Latin America and the Caribbean—home to nearly all the BOP. . . .
>
> That these substantial markets remain underserved is to the detriment of BOP households. . . .
>
> The development community has tended to focus on meeting the needs of the poorest of the poor—the 1 billion people with incomes below $1 a day in local purchasing power. But a much larger segment of the low income population—the 4 billion people of the BOP, all with incomes well below any Western poverty line—both deserves attention and is the appropriate focus of a market-oriented approach. . . .
>
> There are distinct differences between a market-based approach to poverty reduction and more traditional approaches. Traditional

approaches often focus on the very poor, proceeding from the assumption that they are unable to help themselves and thus need charity or public assistance. A market-based approach starts from the recognition that being poor does not eliminate commerce and market processes: virtually all poor households trade cash or labor to meet much of their basic needs. A market-based approach thus focuses on people as consumers and producers and on solutions that can make markets more efficient, competitive, and inclusive—so that the BOP can benefit from them.

Traditional approaches tend to address unmet needs for health care, clean water, or other basic necessities by setting targets for meeting those needs through direct public investments, subsidies, or other handouts. The goals may be worthy, but the results have not been strikingly successful. A market-based approach recognizes that it is not just the very poor who have unmet needs—and asks about willingness to pay across market segments. It looks for solutions in the form of new products and new business models that can provide goods and services at affordable prices.

Up to this point in the chapter, there are at least six different approaches for tackling societal problems such as poverty: governments, corporate engagement, development agencies, NGOs, market-based options, and of course your own innovative solutions. "The Next 4 Billion" report proposes that the answer to poverty may lie in providing products to jumpstart local economies—some 4 billion potential consumers are viewed as the next market to exploit. Was this the solution you had proposed when you answered the first three questions at the beginning of this chapter? Cigarette companies realized a long time ago that the developing world was their next target market when they were forced to put warnings on their packets in the developed world. It just took most other companies a while longer to catch on to the fact that the aggregate purchasing power of consumers, not their individual means, constitutes a significant opportunity.

Every company aims to maximize profit. Some would even argue that maximizing shareholder profits is the *only* goal of a company. However, history has shown that an exclusive focus on financial results (and especially shorter-term financial results) can have disastrous effects on management's ability to plan for the future and might even encourage fraudulent behavior, as was seen in the criminal actions of executives at Enron and WorldCom. Others take a broader and longer term view that includes the interests of numerous stakeholders (not just the shareholders), where profit is a means to an end, with customer value and corporate social responsibility in the foreground. And so, firms may try to position themselves somewhere along a continuum between two poles: a focus on shareholder value, profit maximization, multiple stakeholders (e.g., customers, employees, community, environment, society at large) on one end and corporate social responsibility on the other end. This positioning, in turn, affects the way value is defined and created. As discussed in earlier chapters, value creation is intricately connected to opportunities pursued (see Chapter 5), innovation (see Chapter 6), and strategic options (see Chapter 10), all of which are central to long-term company survival. However, taking a longer term view might not necessarily

FIGURE 16-1   Stages in the Evolution of Corporate Social Responsibility

Environmental management plan	Customer orientation	Supply chain management
Environmental benchmark	Investment in people	Corporate governance
Sustainability	Transparent organization	CSR
Social ecological and economic targets	CSR	Stakeholder dialog

be aligned with short-term financial performance objectives, and the types of objectives emphasized in short- versus long-term approaches might lead managers to interpret ethics in very different ways.

The growing convergence between corporate reputation and social responsibility is worth noting. Initially corporate social responsibility (CSR) was at the margins of management's thinking—viewed as an additional cost of doing business. Driven by criticism from human rights and environmental activists, together with heightened visibility from the mainstream media, the questionable activities of multinationals (e.g., Nike's sweatshop factories and Shell's Brent Spar oil spill disaster in the North Sea) have become difficult to hide—and impossible to ignore. With this kind of detailed scrutiny, companies started making environmental and socially responsible investments, moving CSR center stage as shown in Figure 16-1.

The emergence of CSR as a central strategic concern has important implications for marketers. On the one hand, the core values of the company are articulated by the brand—it projects who the company is and what the company stands for. On the other hand, brands are becoming indistinguishable from the value chain, placing corporate reputation at risk at numerous points anywhere along the line. From suppliers at one end of the value chain to distributors, consumers, and the public at the other end, company reputation is increasingly affected by the actions of others with whom the firm interacts. More critically, companies that strive to be socially responsible are finding that the ability to have any impact requires collaboration and integration among all stakeholders—to solve real problems, answer real needs, and in doing do, make real profits for and with other people.

THE NEW CALCULUS: PEOPLE, PLANET, AND PROFITS

How does the marketer reconcile the conflicting demands of shareholder value, profit maximization, corporate social responsibility, and customer engagement? In the search for some answers to this fundamental question, the remainder of

FIGURE 16-2 Integration of Company and Stakeholder Requirements

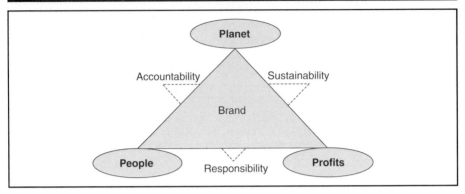

this chapter is organized around the 3 P's: people, planet, and profits. In the triple bottom line (3BL) as shown in Figure 16-2, people and their well-being come first. Here, the spotlight falls on corporate social responsibility, managerial ethics, and brand values. The second focal point is the ecological quality of our planet and environmentally responsible practices that minimize the company's carbon footprint. Profits and economic responsibility are the third and last element in the triad. The triple bottom line calls for responsibility, accountability, and sustainability.

Companies are only starting to realize the importance of integrating responsibility, accountability, and sustainability into a comprehensive approach that has substance, as opposed to just being part of the firm's annual report or enlightened self-interest in public relations campaigns. This creates a challenge for marketers who make substantial investments in creating goodwill through brand communications and customer affinity programs, particularly because marketing budgets allocated to social causes are dwarfed by other sponsorship activities. In 2005, sponsorship spending in North America was around $12.1 billion, of which 69% was allocated to sports; 10% to entertainment, tours, and attractions; 5% to the arts; 4% to festivals, fairs, and annual events; 3% to associations and membership organizations; and only 9% (about $1.15 billion) to social causes.[3] According to numbers reported in a study conducted in 2001, about $9 billion was spent by corporations on all types of social initiatives, which include strategic philanthropy.[4] It isn't clear which of these sponsorship activities ultimately achieve the intended objectives,[5] such as improving overall corporate reputation, brand differentiation, increasing awareness and interest of targeted consumers, stimulating brand preference and loyalty, and increasing profits and stock prices. However, it does appear that marketing programs built around social causes might be of secondary importance compared with a broader interest in sports and entertainment.

With the new calculus of people, planet, and profits, both the priorities of marketers and their mindsets must change. The ability of marketers to think differently is the key to sustainability—and specifically, the sustainability of companies, markets, relationships, resources, and ultimately, the larger environment in which we live, work, and play. To appreciate this new way of thinking, let's explore each of these three critical elements.

PEOPLE: MIRROR, MIRROR, ON THE WALL, WHO IS THE GREATEST SPIN-MASTER OF ALL?

Our attention now shifts to a different story, one that places the marketer directly in the spotlight. "All marketers are liars." In his book with this title, Seth Godin[6] distinguishes between the stories marketers tell that are fibs (perfume and cosmetics) and those that are frauds (Nestlé's baby formula debacle). Do you agree that "all marketers are liars"? It is well known that marketers (advertisements in particular) are viewed by the public as not being especially honest or ethical. In the marketing business, the focus is on promises such as eternal youth, irresistible attraction, and other impossibilities relating to money, fame, or power—the consumer is promised the proverbial pot of gold at the end of the rainbow. Does this mean a marketer's world, by definition, involves shades of grey, rather than black and white?

> *There are now two types of corporation: those with a marketing DEPARTMENT and those with a marketing SOUL. . . . The latter are the top performing companies, while the former, steeped in the business traditions of the past, are fast disappearing.*
> —ANTONY BROWN (IBM, 1995)

Ethics is defined as "the set of rules, principles, and beliefs about right and wrong, good and bad, justice and injustice, duty and obligation which govern people's behavior, or which they believe ought to govern their behavior."[7] Who makes this set of rules—corporate policies, religious institutions, the government? Given that laws and rules differ by country, and that government regulations and society's moral code often fail to provide the necessary guidance, is it up to individual marketers to make the distinction between right and wrong?

These are not hypothetical questions. Just ask the executives at Adelphia Communications, Arthur Andersen, Conseco, Credit Suisse, Enron, Global Crossing, HealthSouth, ImClone Systems, Livedoor (Japan), Martha Stewart Living Omnimedia, Parmalat (Italian food producer), Royal Ahold NV (Netherlands), Skandia (Sweden), Tyco, and WorldCom—firms that have failed to distinguish what is proper from what is improper. The impact of a wrong decision does not have to reach the magnitude of these ethical scandals to ruin people's lives.

Some general guidelines exist to help marketers make good choices. Unfortunately, close scrutiny of the American Marketing Association (AMA) code of ethics seems to suggest there might be degrees of honesty:

> *Don't knowingly do harm.*
> *Adhere to all applicable laws and regulations.*
> *Accurately represent education, training, and experience.*
> *Be truthful in your advertising or promotional claims.*

TABLE 16-1 The Six Pillars of Marketing's Code of Ethics

1. Honesty
2. Responsibility
3. Caring
4. Respect
5. Fairness
6. Citizenship

Source: Josephson, M. (n.d.). The six pillars of character. Making ethical decisions. http://www.charactercounts.org/defsix.htm.

Is the prevalence of unethical marketing practices to be blamed on the marketing profession's unclear line in the sand? Just where do *you* draw the line? The challenges are illustrated by considering the six pillars of the marketing code of ethics shown in Table 16-1. It's not hard to see how easily the marketer can cross the line, and, knowingly or unknowingly, do significant harm.

PILLAR #1: HONESTY

Be trustworthy—the bedrock of the model. Do not deceive, cheat, or steal. Be reliable—do what you say you will do. Have the courage to do the right thing.

"Of course I won't use lying and cheating as a marketing tactic," you think to yourself. But what about stealth marketing or subversive marketing mentioned in Chapter 8? "Stealth marketing attempts to catch people at their most vulnerable by identifying the weak spot in their defensive shields. . . . [Stealth marketing] is considered to be a viable alternative to conventional advertising because it is perceived as softer and more personal than traditional advertising."[8] The example given in Chapter 8 was that of Sony Ericsson, which used models in a street campaign for their new T68i camera phone without disclosing that they had been enlisted to promote it to passers-by. What do you think? Chances are that if you ask 10 people this question, you will get some answers you didn't expect.

The problem that arises here is that many people fail to distinguish what is ethical when it comes to the innovative, unconventional, guerrilla marketing practices outlined in Chapter 8. While the majority of marketing campaigns that incorporate a word of mouth element (which can be either buzz or viral marketing) do so in an ethical manner, the introduction of stealth marketing tactics frequently crosses the line. Consider two examples that clarify the differences between stealth and buzz marketing.[9] In the first example, the "Raging Cow" campaign by Dr. Pepper (http://www.slate.com/id/2081419/), teenage bloggers were paid to post comments (pretending to be the cow mascot) without disclosing this fact. By contrast people using Hotmail (**http://hackvan.com/pub/stig/etext/viral-marketing.html**) passed the message on voluntarily, without any incentives. The second example is the make-believe movie *campaigns* of Mercedes-Benz and BMW, that use stealth marketing and buzz marketing tactics, respectively. While Mercedes-Benz (**http://film.guardian.co.uk/features/featurepages/0,4120,752100,00.html**)

dressed up an advertisement to look like a preview for an upcoming film and the ad was screened with other trailers in the movie theater, it actually was not "coming soon" to any theater near you. By contrast, BMW (**http://www.bmwusa. com/uniquelybmw/bmw_art/films**) really created eight short films.

These stealth marketing practices have angered marketers and the public alike, enough to warrant an investigation by the Federal Trade Commission and resulting in a negative perception of buzz marketing as a promotional tool. The Word of Mouth Marketing Association (WOMMA) has stepped in, condemning and opposing stealth tactics. In an effort to delineate more clearly between buzz/viral marketing (people passing messages on without compensation) and stealth tactics, WOMMA published a Code of Ethics, which they refer to as the "Honesty ROI":

> The essence of the WOMMA Code comes down to the Honesty ROI:
>
> — Honesty of Relationship: You say who you're speaking for.
> — Honesty of Opinion: You say what you believe.
> — Honesty of Identity: You never obscure your identity.

PILLAR #2: RESPONSIBILITY

Do what you are supposed to do. Always do your best. Think before you act—consider the consequences. Be accountable for your choices. Sell products and services that are beneficial. Provide living wages. Curb child labor. Eliminate sweatshop labor practices. Consider the environment. Limit carbon emissions. Uphold stringent guidelines on product safety.

As discussed at the beginning of this chapter, companies' foray into developing countries are not motivated by altruistic intentions to address the gap between rich and poor. Instead they see the bottom of the pyramid (BOP) as the next attractive market opportunity, which could potentially contribute to an overall improvement in the lives of the disenfranchised. Companies have realized that good deeds are actually good business, shifting attention to company initiatives such as *cause-related marketing* (in which every unit of a brand sold triggers a donation to a cause), *green marketing* (where the environmental friendliness of a company or brand is stressed as a differentiating attribute), *cause sponsorship* (in which a brand is clearly identified as a cause supporter), and *social advertising* (where a cause is promoted in a brand's advertisements.)[10] Cause-related marketing is defined as "the process of formulating and implementing marketing activities that are characterized by an offer from the firm to contribute a specified amount to a designated cause when customers engage in revenue-providing exchanges that satisfy organizational and individual objectives."[11]

Examples of socially beneficial causes include Target's "Take Charge of Education" program, which has donated more than $200 million to different schools since 1997; Yoplait's campaign for breast cancer awareness, which has raised over $18 million by paying 10 cents per yoghurt container lid sent back to the company after purchase; and the Lance Armstrong Foundation's yellow LIVE-STRONG bands. Societal marketing initiatives at companies such as Timberland,

Ben & Jerry's, Avon, and Stonyfield Farm have received countless mentions in the press and are well-known case studies in business schools.[12]

More and more, companies are merging social and financial imperatives by creating an association in the minds of consumers between a cause and the company's brand. This can result in considerable consumer mindshare and, in turn, it can lead to greater efficiency for other marketing activities, increased market share (enabling the firm to charge premium prices), enhanced brand loyalty, and more favorable opinions by investors. But many are questioning whether achievement of superior performance is a valid reason for acting in a socially responsible manner. As companies continue to find new ways to tug at customers' heartstrings and bank goodwill with employees and shareholders, critics argue that cause-related marketing is very self-serving. Others say it is better than doing nothing. Opinions on this question cover a wide spectrum—from seeing it as enlightened self-interest, to viewing companies as naïve do-gooders trying to be something they are not, to mere corporate grandstanding, and everything in between. As a marketer, where do you stand on this issue?

PILLAR #3: CARING

Do not take advantage of others. Do not charge exorbitant prices—strive for a fair profit. Share. Be open minded. Listen to others. Do no harm.

Is the marketer simply giving the customer what he wants or in fact taking advantage of those who are vulnerable? Again, the line in the sand is not clear. Consider one side of the story: taking advantage of a moment of weakness—candy at the checkout for a mother with young kids who is tired after a long day; taking advantage of the innocent—promoting "the forbidden," which has irresistible allure to teens (cigarettes and alcohol); taking advantage of those who are uninformed—promoting cigarette smoking as a weight-loss option in Third World countries; taking advantage of those who are less fortunate—state lotteries.

Here is a different side of the story: Is customer choice always right? What if the customer wants something that isn't good for her or him, such as products that harm health, safety, and well-being (e.g., tobacco or hard drugs) or products that harm when taken in excess (e.g., alcohol, sweets, high-calorie foods, fast food)? What if the product/service is good for the customer but not for society or other groups (e.g., rap music, gun ownership)? What if customer communication is offensive or intrusive (e.g., new media, infomercials, text messages on cell phones, online advertisements)? What if the product harms the environment (e.g., Hummer)? Is there a difference between "questionable" products and "harmful" products? What should the marketer do in the case of questionable products?

PILLAR #4: RESPECT

Treat others with respect. Follow the Golden Rule—unselfishly treating others in the manner you would like to be treated. Respect human rights. Heed labor relations. Be tolerant of differences.

Of course society cannot condone Nike's behavior when the company expected Indonesian children to work in unhealthy environments. Of course Shell's alleged complicity in human rights abuses in Nigeria should be condemned. These examples are clearly not acceptable. And yet, there are numerous examples of companies that do what is clearly morally reprehensible. But things get a lot more complicated when it comes to treating others with respect, because there is a wide range of possible interpretations of what is acceptable. For instance, some people admire Donald Trump's hardnosed demeanor, while others find the same style somewhere in the range between offensive and rude. There is also the question of putting the customer first—doing what is best for the customer regardless of what is in the best interest of the company. Would you walk away from a big potential sale because you know there is a better solution for the customer, perhaps available only from your competitor? Companies such as Integrity Systems have been recognized for doing exactly this—even though the customer was keen on going through with a deal.[13] This company's choice relates to the notion of "decent" marketing.

Decent (adj.): 1. Respectable, worthy; 2. Kind.

Pillar #5: Fairness

Be open. Share the hard facts—the good, the bad, and the ugly. Do not sugarcoat reality. Just talk. And listen. Strive for a fair profit.

When Gap and Nike came under fire, they demonstrated forthrightness and transparency by disclosing violations at supplier factories. Shell had to learn the lesson the hard way that communicating during times of trouble is a dialog. So did Coca-Cola when it tried to deny any wrongdoing after people in Belgium experienced symptoms of poisoning. People are showing zero tolerance with any attempts to disguise the truth—companies must be transparent when communicating with the public or customers.

The need for openness is at all levels of communication. A case in point is so-called branded entertainment (see advertisement in Chapter 8), which has recently come under fire. The Screen Actors Guild and the Writers Guild of America filed formal complaints with the Federal Communications Commission (FCC) because actors are, in effect, forced to implicitly endorse a product by association. They argue that the endorsement is effectively written into a script over which the actor has no say and for which the actor does not receive compensation. Moreover, companies are concealing their identities through product placement in film and television programs in ways they could not get away with in advertising. The FCC continues to investigate ways in which clearer guidelines can be set for full disclosure in all media, including branded entertainment.

Pillar #6: Citizenship

Cooperate. Show you care. Stay informed. Help others in need. Build a good reputation.

EXHIBIT 16-1   The Body Shop's Annual Values Report

We aim to achieve commercial success by meeting our customers' needs through the provision of high-quality, good-value products with exceptional service and relevant information, which enables customers to make informed and responsible choices.

Our trading relationships of every kind—with customers, franchisees, and suppliers—will be commercially viable, mutually beneficial, and based on trust and respect.

Our trading principles reflect our core values.

We aim to ensure that human and civil rights, as set out in the *Universal Declaration of Human Rights,* are respected throughout our business activities. We will establish a framework based on this declaration to include criteria for workers' rights embracing a safe, healthy working environment, fair wages, no discrimination on the basis of race, creed, gender, or sexual orientation, or physical coercion of any kind.

We will support long-term, sustainable relationships with communities in need. We will pay special attention to those minority groups, women, and disadvantaged peoples who are socially and economically marginalized.

We will use environmentally sustainable resources wherever technically and economically viable. Our purchasing will be based on a system of screening and investigation of the ecological credentials of our finished products, ingredients, packaging, and suppliers.

We will promote animal protection throughout our business activities. We are against animal testing in the cosmetics and toiletries industry. We will not test ingredients or products on animals, nor will we commission others to do so on our behalf. We will use our purchasing power to stop suppliers animal testing.

We will institute appropriate monitoring, auditing, and disclosure mechanisms to ensure our accountability and demonstrate our compliance with these principles.

Source: http://www.thebodyshop.ca/body.asp?Lang=EN&CName=ProfitsMain. Reproduced with the kind permission of The Body Shop International plc.

Microsoft often receives bad press for its proprietary systems, and DeBeers is no one's best friend—even though a diamond is forever. Brands that consistently deliver on a brand promise built around core values, such as The Body Shop, are rewarded for good corporate citizenship with loyal, returning customers, motivated employees, and satisfied investors. Exhibit 16-1 is a statement from The Body Shop's annual "Values Report." The Body Shop is one of only a handful of companies that produce such a report in addition to the traditional annual report and demonstrate this kind of accountability.

PLANET: IT MIGHT BE A BLUE OCEAN, BUT THE FUTURE IS G-R-E-E-N

The story of our planet: blue skies and blue oceans with birds in the sky and fish in the ocean; shiny crystals and energy-rich liquid deep in its belly. Bountiful. Graceful. And also under threat.

The great thing about creating a sustainable future is that it is an inspiring ideal: something that, like the elephant, is bigger than ourselves—a little frightening, somehow magical, an exciting challenge at the very least. And in today's barren desert of materialism and secularism, people are crying out for something inspirational, even sacred, to quench their thirst for meaning. Sustainability is that oasis shimmering on the horizon. It is what we call the "wow calling," the hunger for something to believe in, the eternal yearning to make a positive difference.[14]

Although people are concerned about the environment, they are not willing to pay more for green products, which they believe are often inferior and therefore overpriced. Moreover, with the general distrust of advertising, consumers have been skeptical of products that are presented as beneficial or less harmful to the environment, viewing these claims as yet another marketing ploy. This inconvenient attitude is referred to as the *boiling frog syndrome*[15]—"if you throw a frog into a pot of boiling water, he'll jump out. But if you place a frog into a pot of lukewarm water and slowly turn up the heat, it will boil to death." The moral of this story is that people, companies, and the governments have been denying the reality that consumerism is killing the planet, because it is politically and economically more expedient to ignore the signs of adverse changes that would require them to change their habits.

> *Every second, five people are born and two people die, for a net gain of three people each second. That means that 12 people were added to the world's population in the time it took you to read the previous sentence. The world is adding about 78 million more people every year: the population of France, Greece and Sweden combined, or a city the size of San Francisco every three days.*
> —SIMON ROSS AND JOSEPH KERSKI (IN "THE ESSENTIALS OF THE ENVIRONMENT")

Like ostriches in the sand, people prefer to believe they are not to blame or that the problem is too big to be solved by them, or anyone else for that matter.

Green minded activists failed to move the broader public not because they were wrong about the problems but because the solutions they offered were unappealing to most people. They called for tightening belts and curbing appetites, turning down the thermostat and living lower on the food chain. They rejected technology, business, and prosperity in favor of returning to a simpler way of life. No wonder the movement got so little traction. Asking people in the world's wealthiest, most advanced societies to turn their backs on the very forces that drove such abundance is naïve at best.

With climate change hard upon us, a new green movement is taking shape, one that embraces environmentalism's concerns but rejects its worn-out solutions. Technology can be a font of endlessly creative solutions. Business can be a vehicle for change. Prosperity can help us build the world we want. Scientific exploration, innovative design, and cultural evolution are the most powerful tools we want. Entrepreneurial zeal and market forces, guided by sustainable policies, can propel the world into a bright green future.[16]

It has been impossible for the mainstream to accept personal responsibility for the earth until environmental problems became a part of everyday social life. The documentary narrated by Al Gore, *An Inconvenient Truth,*[17] combined with extensive media attention, has helped to get the message through that consumer attitudes and behavior will have to change, while at the same time reaffirming the important role technology can play in changing current predictions.

> Sir Nicholas Stern, the lead economist for the British government, recently published the most comprehensive report to-date on the consequences of global warming. The report concluded, that left unchecked, global warming will reduce the global economy by 20%. Conversely, however, it will only cost 1% to prevent it. This report has confirmed what is now a fact of mainstream thought; the global economy, our health, and natural environment depend on rapidly implementing innovative ways of living that are "lighter" on the planet. In addition to climate change, businesses are also grappling with the social consequences of global capitalism, such as growing inequality, poverty, and marginalisation that threaten the very foundation of the economic system.[18]

Old-style thinking has created the problem. People need to change their perspectives if they want to find a solution. Ethical consumerism and commerce require a different paradigm—a shift in the concept of value, where personal commitments that involve costs in the short term are reinterpreted by considering enormous long-term benefits for future generations and the planet. As a first step, the concept of *sustainable development* is being replaced by the concept of *development for sustainability;* that is, sustainability is the outcome of responsible company practices and governance.[19] An excellent example of development for sustainability can be found with the renowned Spier wine estate (**www.spier. co.za**) in the Stellenbosch Winelands of South Africa (see Exhibit 16-2).

In line with this shift in perspective, many companies have accepted their responsibility for product life-cycle assessment and ecoefficiency (see Figure 16-3), in which the watchwords are *reclaim, reuse,* and *recycle.* Companies are accountable for the products they bring to life—from "cradle to grave" and beyond, and this accountability sometimes comes at the expense of short-term profits.

Further, ecologically and socially conscious businesses in the blue oceans[20] of untapped market potential are becoming part of a positively green future. Companies are creating new business models and new market spaces that reverse or minimize further damage to the environment. Already quite sizable, the Lifestyles of Health and Sustainability (LOHAS) market keeps growing, with a number of niche segments such as renewable energy, resource-efficient products, alternative transportation, environmental management services, and green building or industrial goods within the sustainable economy sector. Beyond various environmentally friendly products, other prominent niches include ecotourism and environmental technologies.

The basic premise here is that if companies demonstrate they care for the environment, they get noticed by consumers who care. Further, marketers need

EXHIBIT 16-2 Spier—In Search of a Sustainable Future with a Triple Bottom Line Focus

In South Africa, the Spier company is another example of visionary elephant leadership. Set in the idyllic landscape of Stellenbosch in the Cape, Spier had operated as a wine farm for three centuries before the (then) 90 hectare estate was bought by businessman, Dick Enthoven. Having led an extremely successful career in South Africa's mainstream business sector, Enthoven wanted to leave a legacy, to give something back. Transforming Spier became the centre-point of his vision quest. "In 150 years from now," says Enthoven, "I want people to look back and say that they did a good job".

The way this vision has unfolded in practice is a colourful story full of inspiration. It started with Enthoven embracing the cultural heritage of the area. Spier set about restoring the old Cape-Dutch historical buildings on the estate that date back to 1680, and turning these into conference and restaurant facilities. Next, a hotel complex named The Village was constructed, drawing on the Cape's Malay influences for its architectural style and on ecological principles for its design. An open-air amphitheatre was also built and an Arts Trust started to develop and showcase local talent. The last initiative led to the recent performance of Carmen in the West End of London by a South African cast of newcomers, which drew rave reviews from music critics of leading English newspapers.

One of Enthoven's key concerns in the Spier project was "the restoration of equity in a society that has been distorted by social engineering." For this reason, former farm labourers have been given an ownership and management stake in the vineyards and vegetable farming enterprises. In addition, Spier has embarked on establishing an off-site eco-village, which will eventually incorporate schools, offices, craft workshops, an arts venue, a community centre and homes for almost 150 local families.

There have been various ecological reforms at Spier as well. With 140 hectares of land set aside for organic farming, it is now one of the largest commercial organic farms in South Africa, cultivating both vegetables and vines. Spier has also formed a subsidiary called Green Technologies which acquired the South African licence for an environmentally-friendly waste treatment system called the Biolytix Filter. The installation of this Biolytic Filtration system at The Village at Spier is the first of its kind on this scale in the world.

The vision around which Enthoven has been building Spier's renaissance is now classic triple bottom line thinking, underpinned by a set of inspiring values. The latter include the following: custodians of culture; financial viability and economic sustainability; unexpected pleasures; places of the soul; sustainable resource use; community building; and learning for development. As 'airy fairy' as these values may sound, Eve Annecke, who is the Spier executive responsible for implementing them in all operations, can certainly not be accused of living with her head in the clouds. "We are not on some sort of moral trip here," she says. "We're dealing with practical technologies and looking for better ways of doing things. We learn as we go and we face contradictions all the time: what good is organic farming when women are subject to regular abuse at home, or when babies are born with foetal alcohol syndrome? We live in a violent society. We are not pretending to solve all the problems but we are acknowledging that the problems exist and we work at resolving them where we can.

Adrian Enthoven, chairman of Spier Holdings and a director of Biolytix, sums up their philosophy as follows: "Our view is not purely altruistic. The whole world is moving in this direction – towards ecological sustainability. Economic imperatives are driving it, and economics relies on social sustainability. These three issues are inextricably linked and this is why, at Spier, we call for accountability in terms of the triple bottom line: financial viability, social equity and ecological sustainability."

Source: Visser, W., & Sunter, C. (2002). *Beyond reasonable greed: Why sustainable business is a much better idea!* Cape Town: Human & Rousseau.

FIGURE 16-3 Life-Cycle Thinking

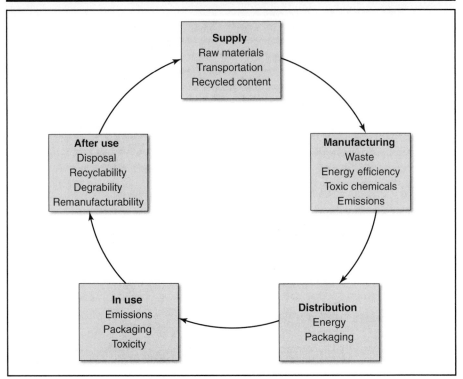

to think and act entrepreneurially to create sustainable enterprises in a connected world. This represents a fundamental change in the way the corporate world does business. It's an even more profound change than the quality movement in 1980s. Then it was about efficiency and effectiveness; now it is about sustainability—more importantly, it's about doing what's right in the first place. Singular pursuit of profits with no responsibility for the negative externalities created in the process of making those profits is counterproductive. By respecting the planet, firms can enhance rather than destroy the context in which they operate. Ultimately, it is about interconnectivity—among the planet, people, principles, and profits.

PROFIT: RETOOLING THE MARKETING DASHBOARD

Profit is the third element in the triple bottom line. To ensure the story has a happy ending, marketing typically adheres to a recipe for success similar to the following:

Take six ounces of mass media advertising, two cups of relationship marketing, one pound of online marketing, three tablespoons of brand management mixed with a dash of intuition, and add a pinch of strategy. Add as many dollars as the budget allows. Mix and stir for 90 minutes during a marketing planning session. Wait until the mixture separates into market share and then freeze the profits.

The myth: the more you spend on marketing, the higher the profits.

Within an organization, the marketing department is often known for its ability to "pour money down the big black hole"—it is the first budget other departments would cut if it were up to them. Why? They believe marketing practitioners are not held accountable for their contribution to the company's performance.[21] Although there are several plausible reasons the impact of a marketing campaign might lag short-term sales revenues, the results from marketing spending are often disappointing.[22] The fact of the matter is that marketers have found it easy to hide behind arguments that creating brand awareness, building relationships, and other activities do not translate into a direct net increase in sales at the end of the fiscal year.[23] Another argument used in defense of increased spending despite disappointing results is that media proliferation, intensified competition, and multiple distribution channels make it more difficult to reach potential customers effectively and efficiently.

Yet, the historical absence of sufficient accountability has swung the pendulum the other way. This swing has been aided by the growing recognition of the high impact (at low cost) of novel guerrilla, buzz, and viral marketing efforts. As a result, instead of viewing marketing as just another expenditure required to run the business, chief executive officers (CEOs) have started to view it as an investment. As with any investment, this means managing risk-return trade-offs. It finds the company imposing extensive metrics for assessing the returns from marketing activities. To do more with less, marketers are using various analytical tools that might help them get the most from every marketing dollar. Some companies use a "magic number" (e.g., a 4:1 ratio where every $1 invested in marketing should yield $4 in sales revenue) or some other rule of thumb for various marketing activities. Others have developed quantitative tools such as marketing mix models to determine the return on investment (ROI) of marketing spending.

Within marketing, adopting this sort of performance orientation is complicated by the relatively long list of activities that must be monitored. There is a need to assess performance or returns in such areas as marketing planning, branding, advertising campaigns, direct-mail or permission marketing initiatives, telemarketing and contact management, online marketing, websites, tradeshows and events, sales promotions, the sales force, public relations and internal communications, stakeholder relationships, channel performance, channel marketing efforts, customer relationship management systems, market research efforts, budgeting, and so forth. Many of these activities require objective as well as subjective measures for adequate monitoring. For the sake of simplicity, the various areas of measurement are organized into four categories as shown in Figure 16-4:

1. Key marketing performance metrics (factors that affect above-the-line revenue).[24]

2. Brand management metrics (to maximize long-term value of the brand because there is a causal link between brand equity and stock return).[25]

3. Customer management metrics.

4. Online marketing metrics.[26]

FIGURE 16-4   The Dashboard—Key Performance Indicators of What Happens and Why

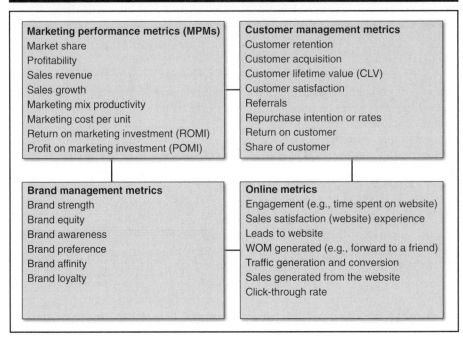

While the overall objective is fairly simple (i.e., generate loyal and committed customers at an acceptable cost), measurement is not as straightforward. The various tools available to the marketer include marketing science models, portfolio analysis, demand analysis, marketing mix measurement, shareholder value, brand valuation tools, and so forth. Two things can go wrong in marketing efforts: the wrong people are marketed to or the right people get marketed to in the wrong way. All marketing metric programs should aim to assess both effectiveness and efficiency. Effectiveness is increased when customers give the company "share of wallet." Efficiency relates to a cost-benefit analysis—marketers aim to maximize the input-output ratio of the marketing function for individual customers. Making marketing more effective and efficient means the company can sell more products (higher effectiveness) while incurring less marketing costs (higher efficiency).

Marketers also consider customers as investments.[27] After all, a customer is the basic building block of cash coming into the company. Thus, the customer base is probably the single best measure of the company's true value, similar to that of a "going concern" value. According to this view, customer capital is the value the company creates from its customer activities, which is tied to customer lifetime value, or CLV (i.e., the present value of all current and future profits generated from the entire duration of the company's relationship with a particular customer; see Chapter 15 for more details on calculating CLV). This implies a customer value portfolio (i.e., the value of a customer to the firm based on a future stream of profits through purchases, not the value the firm offers the customer through its products and services). It also explains the importance of the term "return on customer" as one of the performance metrics under customer management in Figure 16-4. One example of a company that has a clear focus on their customer value portfolio is BMW. Some insights regarding the metrics used for one of BMW's marketing campaigns are provided in Exhibit 16-3.

EXHIBIT 16-3   Marketing Metrics for BMW's "The Hire" campaign

BMW owns "performance" as a differentiating factor associated with the premium image of its cars. The company wanted its agency, Fallon, to reach its target market of men, between the ages of 25 and 35 years, cost effectively and in an innovative and unique manner. Having made a product placement decision with James Bond driving the Z3 sports car in *GoldenEye*, BMW had established a relationship with MGM, and thus Fallon decided to create short films instead of traditional 30-second TV advertisements, because that was where the majority of luxury car shoppers were searching for information related to intended purchases.

The marketing campaign, The Hire, consisted of a series of short films (about 7 to 8 minutes long) to promote various BMW models. Produced by a group of A-list movie directors, each film followed a mysterious character for hire. "The driver" played by Clive Owen, represented the ultimate personification of BMW's message of superior performance. He would get anyone (or anything) from point A to point B through each of the plot dramas in his various BMW automobiles, using few words and effortless movements. The resulting series of high-caliber, action-packed, and compelling films was an exquisite showcase for BMW's line-up.

The short films were positioned as entertainment, not a marketing campaign. Each film was promoted as if it were a big budget Hollywood production that was only screened at bmwfilms.com. To create awareness for The Hire, opinion leaders were seeded to build buzz. This was followed up by screening film-style trailers, "leaking" news to popular Internet movie sites, targeted insertions in magazines for the movie-reporting industry (*Hollywood Reporter* and *Variety*), and TV teasers on selected cable networks (e.g., A&E and The Independent Film Channel). Huge movie posters were displayed in hip, urban areas, and postcards were distributed in trendy clubs. The films were listed alongside theatrical releases in regular movie listings in various media. Additionally, radio DJs on 59 stations in 20 key metropolitan markets were recruited to talk about the films in their shows. VIP recipients of advance copies of *Vanity Fair* also received copies of the films on DVD prior to the official release, accompanied by an endorsement from the editor-in-chief (Graydon Carter). In a final daring move, the films were entered in the Cannes Film Festival, causing controversy and immediate interest among the world's top film critics.

About 75% of the budget was allocated to production and only 25% to efforts that would drive traffic to the BMW website—another unconventional move. Given the innovative nature of the marketing initiative, measurement tools were built into campaign plans so that impact could be assessed in real time and to determine the relative efficiency of the short-film approach compared with the reach and frequency of traditional TV campaigns. Facilitated by technology readily available for its website (i.e., data on server logs), the following information was gathered and evaluated on an ongoing basis: film views, time spent on the site, and discrete users. Additionally, an online study of film viewers was conducted to profile the audience and to ensure the right target group was reached.

A comprehensive pre- and post-study was designed to drill deeper into the effects of the overall campaign. In the first phase, 1,200 BMW owners and luxury car purchase intenders were interviewed to gather information about BMW and its competitors. In the second phase, 400 of these respondents were re-interviewed, and they were asked the same set of questions as before. This established proven awareness of advertising/films for BMW and of competitors, which made it possible to isolate the individuals who were exposed to the short films. Based on information from this group, it was possible to determine the impact of The Hire on brand perceptions, purchase intentions, and plans to visit a dealer. The final metric used was actual sales units.

Within the first 9 months after the first film premiered on bmwfilms.com, 10 million film views by 2.13 million people were registered, more than half of which were from the intended target group. By the end of the campaign, more than 93 million film views were recorded. Results indicated the short films engaged people in unexpected and entertaining ways, which led to improvements in brand image, performance, value for money, and safety. All objectives for The Hire campaign were met and exceeded, with substantial improvements in both sales growth rate (12%) and marketing efficiency. The cost of a "brand minute" for the BMW films campaign proved to be 44% lower. Moreover, BMW received $26 million in free media coverage. As an additional bonus, demand for access to the short films continued after the campaign ended, which maintained positive word of mouth. Overall, BMW was credited with "first-mover" advantage as a halo for its cars.

Source: Fallon, P., & Senn, F. (2006). *Juicing the orange.* Boston: Harvard Business School Press.

It is not possible to cover all the metrics in a single chapter, and it certainly is not the intent in this chapter given the numerous books available on this topic.[28] However, the argument here is that it is time to rethink metrics in this new era of marketing. It is necessary for the organization to justify its existence not only in the marketplace but also in the larger society within which it operates. While it is reasonable to argue that this is the responsibility of the CEO, senior executives, or the board of directors, change starts with each employee. Any individual can take the lead and become an idea champion. Moreover, the public is becoming increasingly willing to vote for or against companies with the choices they make in spending their hard-earned money. No longer confined to a limited number of activist groups on the fringes of society who stage loud protests but achieve relatively little, the power of individual consumers who rise up against perceived injustices is increasingly becoming a major force to be reckoned with. Thus, the reality is that if the marketer doesn't choose to include the planet and people into its equations, people who do care have enough power to force a company to care, or face the consequences.

Admittedly, the relationship between profits and balance (people, planet, and profit) is not a straightforward one. If done in the right way, balance could have a multiplicative effect instead of being a cost or merely an additive outcome. It is difficult to argue for an inclusive and balanced approach as long as companies are making large profits while disregarding the other two factors (people and planet). For example, in mid-year reports for 2007, one oil company announced profits of $9 billion during a year of severe oil shortages around the world that resulted in record-high gasoline prices at the pump. Additionally, during this same year of extraordinary profit, oil companies were lamenting their increased costs at the refinery, presumably to further justify their record-high prices to the consumer. Yet, this oil company is also directly responsible for significant environmental pollution, as well as exploitation of human and other resources. It is but one example out of many where an imbalance in the people, planet, and profit equation tends to swing the argument toward profits, and away from people and the planet. A myopic view in the short term is favored above the inconvenient need attitude of caring for the planet and its people.

Organizations and marketers need to stop assuming that profit and "doing good" involve a zero-sum game, where one side can gain only if the other is sacrificed. However, this requires a shift in mindset—a rethinking of priorities in view of the company's primary role as a "citizen of the world." On the one hand, profit can be defined in terms of financial outcomes—income, earnings, revenue, return, yield, and so forth—all of which imply "taking" and *making money on*. One the other hand, profit might be defined as advantage—gain, benefit, reward, aid, serve, and so forth—*be of advantage to*. Instead of thinking about these two perspectives as "either-or" options or two opposite points on a continuum of profit, Figure 16-5 illustrates how viewing profit in terms of *advantage* includes (not excludes!) positive financial outcomes as well as advantageous ecological outcomes. In the center of the diagram, examples of possible value-added opportunities are shown. *Value* means that the benefits exceed the costs; it has tangible and intangible components, and it doesn't mean the company throws good money down the black hole. Taking care of people means they are better able to care for the environment, and profit (advantage) follows. It is time to put the old profit dinosaur in the museum. Place people before short-term profits.

A rethinking of marketing metrics is predicated on a five-pronged approach:

1. Anticipating the future, rather than just measuring the past.
2. Using multidimensional success criteria, many of which are nonfinancial.
3. Combining value-based issues at various levels of impact—from the individual level to company, community, society, global, and, finally, planet levels.
4. Complementing a measurement approach that is actionable in real time with insightful analysis in an iterative process to make sure future marketing initiatives achieve better performance.
5. Identifying marketing management decisions and their consequences to manage marketing as the driver of business strategy and growth (value management).

FIGURE 16-5 Value Creation Integrated with Triple Bottom Line Objectives

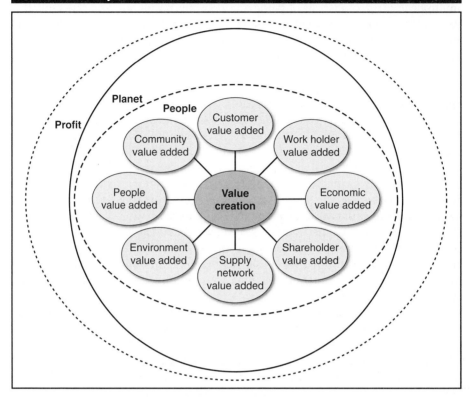

The ultimate marketer's dashboard combines all the data sources available from as many measurement tools as are relevant and ties the effectiveness of campaigns that are in progress directly into the sales performance data in the company's customer relationship management (CRM) system. As seen in the introduction to this chapter, being "of benefit" is a choice the company makes. The firm can choose to turn a financial profit in a narrow-minded view, or it can choose to extend the profit horizon of the company that will benefit its shareholders, the planet, and its people.

RETHINKING THE PROFIT MAXIM: THE ENTREPRENEURIAL IMPERATIVE

But what if the truth is elsewhere? What if it isn't merely a marketing or PR problem, but a substantive problem (as identified in the introduction to this chapter) that cannot be "fixed" with a corporate social responsibility campaign? CSR initiatives aim to protect companies' most valuable asset: the brand and its reputation. But can CSR move beyond concerns about corporate reputation to address two sets of intertwined challenges:[29] contributing to a better world and improving business success? What if the problem requires strategic redirection rather than tactical solutions? Have we even asked the right questions? This brings to the foreground the question of how a company can be "for benefit" instead of "for profit." Is this necessarily a trade-off or can a company be "for benefit" as well as "for profit"?

Entrepreneurs are breaking the old rules and discarding long-held assumptions that you cannot do charitable deeds and make a profit.[30] In the words of Steve Case (founder of AOL):[31] "I'm aiming for a more flexible tool box, not just looking at things through the prism of philanthropy or the prism of business but a fresh creative approach that uses the best of both." Examples of hybrid philanthropy to tackle major global issues like poverty and climate change abound. For instance eBay's founder, Pierre Omidyar, uses investment capital and donations to expand the micro-credit industry. In 2007, Muhammed Yunus (founder of Grameen Bank) won the Nobel Peace Prize for his innovative banking practices that make micro-loans available to those who would never qualify for financial assistance from traditional banks. Ted Turner (founder of CNN) also melds business and philanthropy, as does Sir Richard Branson, who invested $3 billion in a venture capital fund to develop greener fuels instead of making a donation toward alternative energy resources.

This is the entrepreneurial imperative: thinking and doing things differently. The traditional model of philanthropy by foundations that use fortunes of entrepreneurs such as Andrew Carnegie, John D. Rockefeller, and, more recently, Bill Gates and Warren Buffett have proven to be ineffective in providing long-term solutions for the problems of the underdeveloped world. According to Bill Drayton (founder of Ashoka),[32] "Our job is not to give people fish, it's not to teach them how to fish, it's to build new and better fishing industries." This new and better fishing industry is what philanthropreneurs are doing. As seen in Chapter 5, entrepreneurs create new products/services, new markets, and new customer value. They create change and respond to change. Entrepreneurs create new worlds—they make the world a better place and improve the quality of life for all. This is where "the rubber hits the road," and the example in Exhibit 16-4 illustrates how one entrepreneur has broadened the profit horizon in a way that transcends traditional boundaries between financial, social, and environmental objectives.

This is the twist in the tale—finding real solutions for real problems, not temporary Band-Aids for social problems to make the company look good to its shareholders and consumers. Organizations do not solve problems, people do. It is not the big government agencies nor the large corporations, but the entrepreneurs among us who conceive the appropriate solutions—not in the traditional way, but by rethinking old models. Let's return to where we started in this chapter. Did you see the entrepreneurial imperative prior to it being presented to you? Increased interest in BOP markets have led to innovative solutions from entrepreneurs who address BOP consumer needs in housing, agriculture,

EXHIBIT 16-4 All in a Day's Work: How Playing Can Be Profitable

In rural villages across South Africa, some 5 million people don't have access to clean drinking water. To get a sense of the severity of the water scarcity there, you have to go back to the early 1800s when Europeans and others started colonizing the country.

When these settlers arrived, they brought with them nonnative seeds and plants with the idea that they would be able to re-create the thick forests and vegetation of their homeland.

Two hundred years on, the pines and eucalyptus trees, along with 161 other invasive plants introduced to the country, are soaking up billions of gallons of water that used to flow into mountain streams and support wetlands and other precious arteries in this largely arid country. Add to that the needs of South Africa's growing population and you have a situation in which the competition for water has become fierce. . . .

Trevor Field, a retired advertising executive, had done well in life and wanted to give back to his community. He noticed that in many rural villages around the eastern Cape, the burden of collecting water fell mainly to the women and girls of the household. Each morning, he'd see them set off to the nearest borehole to collect water. They used leaky and often contaminated hand-pumps to collect the water, then they carried it back through the bush in buckets weighing 40 pounds. It was exhausting and time-consuming work. . . . He knew there had to be a better solution.

Field then teamed up with an inventor and came up with the "play pump"—a children's merry-go-round that pumps clean, safe drinking water from a deep borehole every time the children start to spin. Soup to nuts, the whole operation takes a few hours to install and costs around $7,000. Field's idea proved so inventive, so cost-efficient and so much fun for the kids that World Bank recognized it as one of the best new grassroots ideas. In true ad-man style, Field's next idea was to use the play pump's water towers as makeshift billboards, selling ad space to help pay for the upkeep. . . .

The indefatigable entrepreneur wants to build thousands of these pumps to help water-stressed communities across South Africa, then expand to other African countries. He says, "It would make a major difference to the children, and that's where our passion lies."

Source: http://www.pbs.org/frontlineworld/rough/2005/10/south_africa_th.html.

consumer goods, and financial services through new startups and social entrepreneurship initiatives, rather than relying on NGOs and multinational corporations. There is general agreement that a bottom-up market approach is essential in developing countries, and this has resulted in increasing support (financial, institutional, and governmental) for small and medium-sized enterprises. One noteworthy example of a BOP success story is that of Celtel, in the area of mobile telephony. By crafting a strong value proposition for low-income consumers in some of the poorest and least stable countries in Africa, Celtel grew from startup to a telecom giant.[33] It now has operations in 15 African countries in only 7 years, after being acquired for $3.4 billion (in U.S. dollars) in 2005.

Summary and Conclusions

At a time when boundaries between marketers' fabricated needs and reality are increasingly blurred, marketers and society coexist in a complex, symbiotic relationship. This creates a dilemma because marketers are both the provider of solutions and the cause of problems. On the one hand, marketers must find entrepreneurial solutions to the world's needs through the products and services they provide. On the other hand, marketers are faced with the problem of fabricated needs and exerting influences that shape popular culture through mass media. The outcome is an economy based on greed and the consumer treadmill, in which more is just never enough. Forever prone to the boiling frog syndrome, some consumers behave as if problems do not exist. On the other extreme are consumers who are lashing out in revolt against marketing and its hold on shaping society's views of the world and how to live in it.

A nascent yet budding domain, anti-consumption has gained prominence with the rise in social networking that has contributed to the socialization of marketing resistance. People's dissatisfaction with consumerism can take the form of avoidance, grudge-holding, active retaliation, or civil disobedience; in one form or another they challenge the ideology of consumerism that manifests itself in unnecessary consumption with bouts of retail therapy and expressions of personal identity. Anti-consumption tactics range from activist movements to anti-brand discourses, from ignoring commercial radio and television to hiding behind technologies (e.g., TiVo) that facilitate avoidance of advertising messages, from anti-globalization demonstrations to utopian communities who vow to buy nothing new for a year (e.g., Compact[34]), from culture jamming[35] and alternative Podcasting to voluntary simplicity,[36] and from brand avoidance to careful carbon-counting "green" consumption. The realization that psychological desires and possible ways to satisfy "hyper-wants" are infinite, but that environmental and human resources are limited, has led to the rising popularity of frugality and downshifting. Much of this resistance is related to the globalization of culture (also referred to as Americanization of the world) and companies' focus on the value in exchange (profit) rather than the value in use (based on need) that has been fueling materialism and addictive consumption.

What should a marketer do in view of this see-saw? There are no universal truths to guide actions in the marketplace because the notion of what is right or wrong differs among people, organizations, and cultures. This brings us to the "acid test" for marketers—it consists of three intertwined challenges as depicted in Figure 16-2, each of which relates to people, planet, and profit, respectively:

1. The first challenge is *accountability* (passing the "butterfly test" in decisions that affect all stakeholders, not only shareholders).
2. The second challenge is *sustainability* (ensuring solutions pass the "green test").
3. The third challenge is *responsibility* (avoiding the "red face test" when facing stockholders with disappointing financial results).

While it is possible to achieve financial success by meeting the demands of any one of the three challenges, prosperity requires that the company meet each of the three challenges in the ultimate acid test for every aspect of the company's operations—from cradle to grave and beyond for all its products, including behaviors of far-flung suppliers and others in the value chain, potential activities of end users, and the impact of its marketing practices. This requires an attitude of ongoing healthy self-criticism, rather than finding loopholes in the system or hiding behind minimum laws or regulations. It goes beyond social responsibility and cause marketing. This means going beyond the company's self-interests and success to create a better world for all people.

A concern for the well-being of people and the planet, in addition to the company's success, requires a different kind of bottom line. A marketer must have the moral courage to do what is right and the courage not to do what is wrong. Character is shaped not by what happens to us, but rather by how we respond to what happens to us. This is the lesson of the movie *Groundhog Day*. Bill Murray (in the role of weatherman Phil Connors) finds himself trapped in a constantly repeating day as he gradually changes from a selfish, egotistical, and manipulative individual into a person who acts with integrity, humility, and a sharing mentality. He learns to care for the well-being of others regardless of whether or not they meet his expectations or act the way he would have in a specific situation.

This chapter poses numerous questions to encourage you to explore the issues and develop novel solutions to complex problems. Are you thinking differently yet? Consider this: when thinking about ethical issues, asking "How can good be produced?" instead of "How can harm be avoided?" changes the focus of the issue. When thinking about what really matters about the effectiveness of activities, a question such as "Are we competing successfully?" is quite different when it is stated as "Are we pursuing the highest human potential?" When considering social responsibility, a different emphasis results when asking "How can we benefit from our efforts (e.g., do well) while doing good?" instead of asking "How can we help others to flourish?" The simple act of asking the questions differently reframes the issues and probes the underlying premises of marketing. It calls attention to a change in perspectives—rethinking the role of marketing; this is a theme that permeates every aspect of marketing (and this book). It is up to you. The time is now.

Key Terms

- profit maximization
- triple bottom line
- ethics
- social responsibility
- environmental responsibility
- economic responsibility
- sustainability
- carbon footprint

Resources and References

1. Bartlett, C. A., & others. (2002, January/February). Below the bottom line. *Across the Board:* 20–32. Accessed November 14, 2007, http://www.conference-board.org/articles/atb_article.cfm?id=58.
2. Hammond, A. L., Kramer, W. J., Katz, R. S., Tran, J. T., & Walker, C. (2007). *The next 4 billion: Market size and business strategy at the base of the pyramid.* World Resources Report. Accessed April 6, 2007, http://archive.wri.org/publication_detail.cfm?pubid=4142#1.
3. "Sponsorship spending to see biggest rise in five years." (2004, December 27). IEG Sponsorship Report, p. 1.
4. Cone, C. L., Feldman, M. A., & DaSilva, A. T. (2003), Causes and effects. *Harvard Business Review* 81(7): 95–101.
5. Cornwell, T. B., Pruitt, S. W., & Clark, J. M. (2005). The relationship between major-league sports' official sponsorship announcements and the stock prices of sponsoring firms. *Journal of the Academy of Marketing Science* 33(4): 401–412; Speed, R., & Thompson, P. (2000). Determinants of sports sponsorship response. *Journal of the Academy of Marketing Science* 28(2): 226–238; Cornwell, T. B., & Maignan, I. (1998, Spring). An international review of sponsorship research. *Journal of Advertising* 27(1): 1–21.
6. Godin, S. (2006). *All marketers are liars: The power of telling authentic stories in a low-trust world.* New York Portfolio.
7. Wallace, G., & Walker, A. D. M. (1970). *The definition of morality.* London: Methuen.
8. Kaikati, A. M., & Kaikati, J. G. (2004). Stealth marketing: How to reach consumers surreptitiously. *California Management Review* 46(4): 6–22.
9. "Counterpoint on stealth marketing." (2006, July 18). Accessed November 14, 2007, http://viralone.wordpress.com/2006/07/18/counterpoint-on-stealth-marketing/.
10. Bloom, P. N., Hoeffler, S., Keller, K. L., & Meza, C. E. B. (2006). How social-cause marketing affects consumer perceptions. *MIT Sloan Management Review* 47(2): 49–55.
11. Varadarajan, P. R., & Menon, A. (1988). Cause-related marketing: A co-alignment of marketing strategy and corporate philanthropy. *Journal of Marketing* 52(3): 58–74.
12. Drumwright, M., & Murphy, P. E. (2000). Corporate societal marketing. In P. N. Bloom & G. T. Gundlach (eds.), *Handbook of marketing and society* (pp. 162–171). Thousand Oaks, CA: Sage Publications.
13. Stout, E. (2002). Selling on a prayer. *Sales and Marketing Management* 154: 38–42, 44–45.
14. Visser, W., & Sunter, C. (2002). *Beyond reasonable greed: Why sustainable business is a much better idea!* Cape Town: Human & Rousseau.
15. Boiling frog syndrome. Accessed January 15, 2007, http://en.wikipedia.org/wiki/Boiling_frog.
16. Steffen, A. N. (2006, May). The next green revolution. *Wired.* Accessed January 15, 2007, http://www.wired.com/wired/archive/14.05/green.html.
17. *An Inconvenient Truth.* Directed by Davis Guggenheim. (2006). Hollywood, CA: Paramount Studios.
18. Kotler, P., & Lee, N. (2004). Best of breed. *Stanford Social Innovation Review* 1(4): 14–23.

19. Visser & Sunter.
20. Kim, W. C., & Mauborgne, R. (2004). *Blue ocean strategy.* Cambridge, MA: Harvard Business School Press.
21. Webster, F., Malter, A., & Ganesan, S. (2005). The decline and dispersion of marketing competence. *Sloan Management Review* 46(4): 35–43.
22. Morgan, N. A., Clark, B. H., & Gooner, R. A. (2002). Marketing productivity, marketing audits, and systems for marketing performance assessment: Integrating multiple perspectives. *Journal of Business Research* 55(5): 363–375.
23. Adler, L. (1967). Systems approach to marketing. *Harvard Business Review* 45(3): 105–118.
24. O'Sullivan, D., & Abela, A. V. (2007, April). Marketing performance measurement ability and firm performance. *Journal of Marketing* 71: 79–93.
25. Aaker, D. A., & Joachimsthaler, E. (2000). *Brand leadership: The next level of the brand revolution.* Washington, D.C.: Free Press.
26. Rosenfeld, L., & Morville, P. (1998). *Information architecture for the World Wide Web: Designing large-scale web site.* Sebastopol, CA: O'Reilly Media.
27. Gupta, S., & Lehmann, D. (2005). *Managing customers as investments.* Philadelphia, PA: Wharton School Publishing.
28. Lilien, G. L. L., & Rangaswamy, A. (2003). *Marketing engineering: Computer-assisted marketing analysis and planning.* New York: Pearson Education.
29. Freeman, B. (2006, Winter). Substance sells: Accountability and sustainability. *Market Leader* 35. Accessed November 14, 2007, www.warc.com.
30. Strom, S. (2006, November 13). What's wrong with profit? *New York Times.*
31. Strom.
32. "Bill Drayton: Entrepreneur for society." Accessed March 20, 2007, http://www.ashoka.org/node/4211.
33. Hammond, A. L., Kramer, W. J., Katz, R. S., Tran, J. T., & Walker, C. (2007), The next 4 billion: Market size and business strategy at the base of the pyramid. World Resources Report. Accessed November 14, 2007, http://www.wri.org/.
34. "Group sold on buying nothing new for a year." (2007, January 16). *St Petersburg Times,* http://www.sptimes.com/2007/01/16/Business/Group_sold_on_buying_.shtml.
35. Lasn, K. (1999). *Culture jamming: The uncooling of America.* New York: William Morrow.
36. Maniates, M. (2002). In search of consumptive resistance: The voluntary simplicity movement. In T. Princen, M. Maniates, & K. Conca, (eds.), *Confronting consumption* (pp. 199–235). Cambridge, MA: MIT Press.

NAME INDEX

A

Aaker, D., 184, 195
Aaker, D. A., 325, 335
Abela, A. V., 325, 335
Achrol, R. S., 23, 41
Adler, L., 325, 335
Ahonen, T., 159, 167
Alderson, W., 238, 239, 250
Aldrich, H., 114, 127
Allen, J., 134, 144
Allen, K., 90, 107
Allen, T. J., 110, 126
Alvarez, S. A., 99, 107
Amabile, T. M., 87, 106
Anderson, E., 238, 250
Anderson, J., 160, 167
Andreasen, A., 64, 69, 83
Andreasen, A. R., 69
Atkin, D., 189, 195

B

Band, J., 110, 126
Bandura, A., 242, 250
Barber, B., 8, 19
Barnett, W., 198, 213, 215, 217
Barney, J., 200, 215
Barney, J. B., 99, 107
Baron, R. A., 98, 107
Bartlett, C. A., 124, 128, 310, 334
Bedbury, S., 193, 195
Beeby, W., 123, 128
Bennet, P. D., 22, 41
Berry, J., 158, 166
Berthon, J. P., 7, 18, 122,
    240, 250
Berthon, J. -P., 287, 288
Berthon, P., 169, 194
Berthon, P. R., 7, 11, 18, 19, 44, 45,
    50, 54, 61, 110, 115, 127, 240,
    250, 287, 288
Bhave, M. P., 99, 107
Bickhoff, N., 102, 108
Bieger, T., 102, 108
Biever, C., 58, 61
Blackshaw, P., 157, 166
Blainey, G., 240, 250
Blattberg, R. C., 23, 41, 247, 250
Bloom, P. N., 317, 318, 335, 336
Bourdieu, P., 53, 61
Bourgeois, L. J. III, 213, 217

Bower, J., 110, 112, 126
Brown, M., 118, 128
Brown, S., 101, 108, 193, 195
Brown, S. L., 205, 216
Bruner, J., 186, 195
Bruno, A. V., 35, 42
Bulgin, R., 113, 127
Burns, T., 114, 127
Butler, J., 208, 216

C

Cairncross, F., 240, 250
Campbell, D. T., 197, 215
Carpenter, G. S., 114, 127
Carroll, L., 197, 203, 215, 216
Chonko, L. B., 255, 270
Christensen, C., 53, 61, 110, 112,
    118, 126, 128
Clark, B. H., 325, 335
Clark, J. M., 314, 335
Clark, K. B., 110, 126
Clewett, R. M., 238, 250
Coase, R. H., 276, 288
Collis, D. J., 200, 215
Conca, K., 333, 336
Cone, C. L., 314, 334
Corballis, M., 103, 108
Cornwell, T. B., 314, 335
Coughlan, A., 238, 250
Courtney, H., 205, 216
Covin, J., 266, 270
Cowen, T., 8, 19
Crawford, G., 267, 270
Cummings, L. L., 124, 128

D

DaSilva, A. T., 314, 334
Davidow, E., 225, 233
Davies, M., 279, 280, 284, 288
Dawkins, R., 187, 195
Day, G. S., 23, 41, 110, 126
Deighton, J., 247, 250
Deming, W. E., 114, 127
Derrida, J., 176, 195
Deschamps, J. -P., 118, 128
Deshpande, R., 22, 31, 41
Desiraju, R., 225, 233
Dew, N., 90, 96, 107
Dickinger, A., 160, 167
Dickson, P., 35, 42

Dickson, P. R., 113, 127
Dodgson, C. L., 197, 215
Dollinger, M. J., 89, 107
Downes, L., 114, 127, 272, 283,
    287, 288
Draper, T., 148, 166
Drayton, B., 331, 336
Dru, J. M., 148, 166
Drucker, P., 91, 107
Drucker, P. F., 110, 111, 126
Drumwright, M., 318, 335
Duhigg, C., 209, 217
Duncan, R., 114, 127
Duncan, R. B., 112, 124,
    126, 128

E

Eckhardt, J. A., 90, 107
Eisenhardt, K. M., 139, 144, 205,
    213, 216, 217
El-Ansary, A., 238, 239,
    242, 250
Eldredge, N., 17, 19
Ettlinger, N., 184, 195
Euster, C. C., 230, 233

F

Fahey, L., 22, 41
Fallon, P., 328
Farley, J. U., 31, 41
Feldman, M. A., 314, 334
Fielding, M., 78, 83
Fjellman, S. M., 112, 126
Freeman, B., 331, 336
Freeman, J., 114, 121, 127, 128
Frelinghuysen, J., 147, 165
Frery, F., 199, 215
Friedman, T. L., 205, 216
Friesen, P. H., 28, 41
Fujimoto, T., 110, 126

G

Gallaugher, J. M., 247, 250
Ganesan, S., 325, 335
Gatti, J., 247, 250
Getz, G., 23, 41
Ghiselin, M. T., 16, 19
Ghoshal, S., 124, 128
Giglierano, J. J., 35, 42

Gilfillan, D. P., 208, 216
Gilmore, J., 192, 195
Gilmore, J. H., 12, 19
Girotto, J., 139, 144
Glazer, R., 114, 127
Godin, S., 11, 19, 147, 148, 152, 165, 166, 177, 195, 315, 335
Gooner, R. A., 325, 335
Gouillart, E., 115, 127
Gould, S. J., 17, 19
Green, P. E., 117, 127
Grönroos, C., 23, 41, 148, 165
Grousbeck, H. I., 27, 32, 41, 42
Gundlach, G. T., 318, 336
Gunther, R. E., 149, 166
Gupta, A. K., 110, 126
Gupta, S., 326, 336

H

Haghirian, P., 160, 167
Haire, T., 71, 83
Hamel, G., 21, 32, 40, 42, 101, 108, 114, 127, 148, 165
Hammond, A. L., 311, 332, 334, 336
Hannan, M. T., 114, 121, 127, 128
Harris, A., 251, 270
Hauser, J. R., 81, 83
Heath, C., 190, 195
Heath, D., 190, 195
Hedberg, B., 124, 128
Henderson, J., 267, 270
Hertz, N., 9, 19
Heylighen, F., 197, 215
Hill, S., 35, 36, 42, 148, 166, 190, 195, 202, 203, 216
Hills, G. E., 94, 107
Hitt, M. A., 202, 216, 225, 233
Hoeffler, S., 317, 335
Holbek, J., 114, 127
Holloman, J. H., 110, 126
Holt, D. B., 187, 195
Howe, J., 25, 41
Hudson, E. E., 47, 61
Hufbauer, G., 4
Hughes, M., 151, 153, 166
Hulbert, J. M., 44, 45, 110, 115, 127

I

Ingram, T., 251, 270
Intel Corporation, 274
Interbrand, 14
Ireland, R. D., 202, 216, 225, 233
Ito, M., 160, 167

J

Jacobson, R., 184, 195
Jantsch, J., 149, 166
Jaworski, B., 37, 42
Jaworski, B. J., 111, 126
Joachimsthaler, E., 325, 335

Johansson, J., 115, 127
Jones, C., 285, 288
Jones, E., 251, 255, 270
Jones Soda Company, 27
Josephson, M., 316
Joslyn, C., 197, 215
Jurvetson, S., 148, 166

K

Kaden, B., 184, 195
Kahwajy, J. L., 213, 217
Kaikati, A. M., 316, 335
Kaikati, J. G., 316, 335
Kakkar, J. N., 230, 233
Kallianpur, A., 31, 41
Kanter, R. M., 208, 216
Kates, S. M., 50
Katsikeas, C., 287, 288
Katz, R. S., 311, 332, 334, 336
Keith, R. J., 113, 127
Keith, T., 208, 216
Keller, E., 158, 166
Keller, K. L., 317, 335
Kelly, K., 287, 288
Kelly, M., 149, 166
Kelly, P., 268, 270
Kerski, J., 322, 335
Kilman, R. H., 112, 126
Kim, W. C., 99, 100, 107, 108, 211, 217, 322, 335
Klein, N., 15, 19, 187, 195
Kocak, M., 37, 42
Kodama, F., 110, 126
Kohli, A. K., 37, 42, 111, 126
Kotha, S., 142, 144
Kotler, P., 23, 37, 41, 42, 322, 335
Kramer, W. J., 311, 332, 334, 336
Kumar, N., 37, 42
Kuratko, D., 266, 270
Kwak, M., 205, 216

L

Lachenauer, R., 204, 216
LaForge, R., 251, 270
LaForge, R. W., 28, 41
Laidler-Kylander, N., 15, 19
Lasn, K., 333, 336
Lee, N., 322, 335
Lefebvre, H., 185, 195
Lehmann, D., 326, 336
Leigh, T., 251, 270
Levine, R., 24, 41, 145, 165
Levinson, C., 148, 166
Levitt, T., 12, 19, 130, 144
Lilien, G. L. L., 328, 336
Locke, C., 24, 41, 145, 165
Lodish, L., 31, 41

M

Macdonald, S., 112, 126
Macrae, C., 169, 194
Madden, T. J., 174, 194

Mahajan, V., 149, 166
Maignan, I., 314, 335
Malter, A., 325, 335
Mander, J., 116, 127
Maniates, M., 333, 336
March, J., 99, 107
March, J. G., 206, 216
Marchetti, M., 267, 270
Mauborgne, C., 99, 100, 107, 108
Mauborgne, R., 211, 217, 322, 335
McCarthy, I., 50
McGee, L. W., 111, 126
McIntyre, S., 35, 42
McKelvey, B., 114, 127
McKenna, R., 39, 42, 148, 166, 213, 217, 241, 250
McKitterick, J. A. B., 112, 126
McLuhan, M., 248, 250
McVey, P., 237, 250
Menon, A., 317, 335
Meza, C. E. B., 317, 335
Miller, D., 28, 41
Mintzberg, H., 206, 209, 216
Mollick, E., 52, 61
Molloy, T., 51, 61
Montgomery, C. A., 200, 215
Montgomery, D. B., 23, 41
Moore, A., 159, 167
Moorman, C., 23, 41
Morgan, H. L., 31, 41
Morgan, N. A., 325, 335
Morris, M., 134, 144, 251, 270
Morris, M. H., 28, 37, 41, 42, 266, 270
Morrissey, B., 51, 61
Morville, P., 326, 335
Mui, C., 114, 127, 272, 283, 287, 288
Muniz, A. M. Jr., 53, 61
Murphy, J. S., 160, 167
Murphy, P. E., 318, 335

N

Naisbitt, J., 1, 18
Nakamoto, K., 114, 127
Narver, J. C., 23, 41, 110, 111, 126
Naumann, E., 110, 126
Neisser, D., 162, 167
Nel, D., 122
Nicholls, A., 103
Nonaka, I., 114, 115, 127, 213, 217
Nystrom, P. C., 124, 128

O

Ohmae, K., 199, 215
O'Reilly, C., 112, 126
O'Sullivan, D., 325, 335
Otlacan, O., 77

P

Parsons, A., 148, 166
Pelofsky, M., 235, 250
Peppers, D., 148, 166
Peteraf, M. A., 201, 216
Peters, T. J., 12, 19
Pilzer, P. Z., 114, 127
Pine, B. J., 12, 19
Pine, J., 192, 195
Pitt, L. F., 7, 11, 18, 19, 44, 45, 50, 54, 61, 110, 115, 122, 127, 169, 180, 183, 194, 195, 240, 250, 279, 280, 283, 284, 287, 288
Pondy, L. R., 112, 126
Poole, M. S., 31, 41
Popcorn, F., 1, 18
Porter, M. E., 271, 288
Powell, W. W., 124, 128
Prahalad, C. K., 21, 32, 40, 42, 101, 108, 114, 127, 148, 165
Prandelli, E., 98, 107
Princen, T., 333, 336
Pruitt, S. W., 314, 335

Q

Quelch, J. A., 15, 19
Quinn, J. B., 113, 118, 127, 128

R

Raj, S. P., 110, 126
Rajeski, D. W., 198, 215
Rangaswamy, A., 328, 336
Rayport, J. F., 241, 250
Rifkin, G., 35, 36, 42, 148, 166, 190, 195, 202, 203, 216
Rindova, V. P., 142, 144
Rivkin, J., 139, 144
Roberts, J. A., 255, 270
Roberts, K., 171, 176, 178, 191, 194, 195
Roberts, M. J., 27, 32, 41, 42
Roegner, E. V., 230, 233
Rogers, M., 148, 166
Ronstadt, R., 94, 107
Rosen, E., 149, 166
Rosenfeld, L., 326, 335
Ross, S., 322, 335
Rothenberg, R., 147, 165
Rushkoff, D., 148, 158, 166
Rust, R. T., 23, 41
Ryans, J. K. Jr., 110, 126

S

Sahay, A., 37, 42
Salehi-Sangari, E., 122
Sarasvathy, S., 90, 96, 97, 107, 208, 216
Sarasvathy, S. D., 31, 41, 90, 107
Sawhney, M., 98, 107

Sawyer, C. A., 58, 61
Scarborough, M., 117, 127
Schau, H. J., 53, 61
Scheer, L., 37, 42
Schindehutte, M., 28, 37, 41, 42, 134, 144
Schlesinger, L. A., 235, 250
Schmitt, B. H., 148, 166, 175, 194
Schotter, A., 124, 128
Schumpeter, J., 28, 41, 88, 106, 114, 127
Schumpeter, J. A., 88, 107
Schwartz, E., 245, 250, 287, 288
Searls, D., 24, 41, 145, 165
Senn, F., 328
Shane, S., 88, 107
Shane, S. A., 90, 107
Shanklin, W. L., 110, 126
Shapiro, C., 287, 288
Shapiro, D., 279, 280, 284, 288
Sharma, A., 149, 166
Shervani, T. A., 22, 41
Sheth, J. N., 149, 166
Shifflet, D., 117, 127
Shimp, T. A., 174, 194
Shrader, R. C., 94, 107
Shugan, S., 225, 233
Siklos, R., 154, 166
Simon, H., 10, 19
Sirbu, M. A. Jr., 110, 126
Sirmon, D., 225, 233
Sirmon, D. G., 202, 216
Sisodia, R. S., 149, 166
Slater, S. F., 23, 41, 110, 111, 126
Slevin, D. P., 112, 126
Smilor, R. W., 28, 41
Smith, L., 110, 126
Sonnack, M., 54, 61
Souder, W. E., 110, 126
Speed, R., 314, 335
Spiro, R. L., 111, 126
Springwise, 25, 41
Srivastava, R. K., 22, 41
Stalk, G. Jr., 204, 216
Stalker, G. M., 114, 127
Starbuck, W., 209, 216
Starbuck, W. H., 124, 128
Staw, B. M., 124, 128
Steffen, A. N., 321, 335
Stern, L., 239, 242, 250
Stern, L. W., 238, 250
Stevenson, H. H., 27, 32, 41, 42
Steyaert, C., 90, 107
Stout, E., 318, 335
Strauss, K., 103, 108
Strom, S., 331, 336
Strout, E., 267, 270
Sturdivant, E., 115, 127
Sull, D., 139, 144
Sunter, C., 321, 322, 335
Sun-Tzu, 204, 216

Sviokla, J. J., 241, 250
Swartz, B., 169, 194

T

Takeuchi, H., 213, 217
Tapscott, D., 27, 41
Thomas, J. S., 23, 41
Thomke, S., 54, 61, 207, 216
Thompson, P., 314, 335
Timmons, J., 95, 107
Top Mobile Applications, 161, 167
Tran, J. T., 311, 332, 334, 336
Tuan, Y. F., 185, 195
Turchin, V., 197, 215
Tushman, M., 112, 126
Tyebjee, T. T., 35, 42

U

UN Population Division, 5
Uncles, M. D., 169, 194
UNCTAD, 9
Urban, G. L., 81, 83
Utterback, J., 110, 126

V

Van de Ven, A. H., 31, 41
Van Valen, L., 197, 215
Varadarajan, P. R., 317, 335
Varian, H. R., 287, 288
Velamuri, R., 90, 96, 107
Venkataraman, S., 31, 41, 88, 90, 96, 107
Verona, G., 98, 107
Visser, W., 321, 322, 335
Vollmer, C., 147, 165
von Hippel, E., 53, 54, 61, 79, 83, 98, 107, 114, 127

W

Waitman, R., 148, 166
Walker, A. D. M., 315, 335
Walker, C., 311, 332, 334, 336
Wallace, G., 315, 335
WARC Report, 149, 166
Warner, F., 177, 195
Waterman, R. H. Jr., 12, 19
Watson, R. T., 11, 19, 54, 61, 169, 194, 279, 280, 284, 288
Webber, A. M., 211, 217
Webster, F., 325, 335
Webster, F. E. Jr., 31, 41, 110, 112, 126
Weick, K. E., 208, 209, 216
Weigand, R. E., 231, 233
Weimann, G., 193, 195
Weinberger, D., 24, 41, 145, 165
Westley, F., 206, 216
Wiener, N., 116, 127

Wilemon, D., 110, 126
Williams, B., 160, 167
Wind, J., 117, 127
Wind, Y. J., 149, 166
Winston, R., 50, 61
Woodruff, R. B., 101
World Advertising Research
    Center, 148, 165

Wynn, D., 169, 194
Wynne, D., 54, 61

Y

Yamanouchi, T., 114, 127
Yarger, R. H., 199, 215
Yoffie, D. B., 205, 216

Z

Zaltman, G., 73, 83, 114, 127
Zedong, M., 204, 216
Zeisser, M., 148, 166
Zineldin, M., 210, 217
Zinkhan, G., 54, 61,
    169, 194
Zinkhan, G. M., 11, 19

SUBJECT INDEX

A

abrasion, highlighting natural differences, 257
access web, 161
accountability
  challenge of, 333
  triple bottom line (3BL) calling for, 314
accumulation, 239
acid test, for marketers, 333
act marketing, 175
actionable research findings, 68–69
AdSense platform, 163
advantage, internal source of, 136
advergaming, 155
advertainment, 154–155
advertising, 146
affective domain, of reciprocal space, 188–189
Age of the Brand, 14
aggregators, 160
AiboPet, hacking of, 57
allocation, 239
AMA (American Marketing Association)
  brand definition, 169
  code of ethics, 315
  definition of marketing, 22
  redefining marketing, 23–24
Amazon.com, 202
  compared to a conventional bookstore, 241
  creative use of databases, 75–76
  introducing a rival online DVD rental service, 226
ambitions, of the entrepreneur, 137
ambush marketing. See subversive marketing
America Online. See AOL
American Express Travelers Cheques, 95
American Marketing Association. See AMA
AMP MP3 Playback Engine, 285
analysis, of creative consumers, 59
anti-brand, era of, 15–16
anti-branding movement, 15
anti-consumption tactics, 333
anti-globalization protesters, 8
AOL (America Online)
  acquired Third Screen Media, 162
  changes of mode, 123
Apple
  as always market-driving, 40

entry into the music industry, 198
espoused attitude to podcasting, 56
influencing effects of, 118
"Think Different" attitude, 191
The Apprentice, as an infomercial, 155
archives, sifting, 80
The Art of War, 204
aspersion, 47, 49–50
Association of Southeast Asian Nations (ASEAN), 7
assorting, 239
AT&T, sales force performance, 267
attention economy
  shift to an attraction economy, 178–179
  shift to the attraction economy, 171
attitude, to consumer innovation, 56
attraction economy, 171, 178
audiences, media fragmentation of, 11
augmented product, 131, 132
authentic stories, 177
auto theme park, 236
Autobyte1, 249
automation, of transactions, 239
Avila, Jose, 51
awareness, of creative consumers, 59

B

baby boomers, 101
backstage website, 51
backward marketing research, 68–70
balance
  in judo strategy, 206
  relationship with profits, 329
bank service delivery, cost by mechanism, 277
Bare Escentuals QVC television, 71
base of economic pyramid. See BOP
BBC
  giving access to its content, 51
  making content freely available, 58
  news program based on user-generated content, 158
BeingGirl interactive site, 179
Ben & Jerry's flavor world, 169
Betfair, 272, 280
  attempting to tax, 284

as the focus of lawsuits, 283
invention of, 285
processing millions of rapid betting transactions each day, 281
Biolytix Filter, 323
Black, Andrew, 285
black holes, 104
Blackspot Unswooshers, 16
Blockbuster, competing service to Netflix, 226
Blodgett, Leslie, 71
blogs, monitoring, 80–81
blue ocean strategists, 211
Bluetooth, 49
BMC, 100
BMW
  clear focus on customer value portfolio, 327–328
  feature in *James Bond* films, 155
  gathering customer ideas, 53
  movie campaign, 316–317
The Body Shop
  annual Values Report, 320
  as a market driver, 37
Boeing
  moving from shaper to interact mode, 123
  settling into a follow mode, 123
Boeing 777
  designed in interact mode, 119
  in interact mode, 123
Boldyev, Dmitry, 285
bookmakers, 282
bootstrap grassroots methods, 150–151
BOP (base of economic pyramid), 311, 332
boss model, death of, 262
boundaries, meaningless of traditional geographic, 6
boundary rules, 139
brand(s)
  age of, 14–15
  being hijacked by consumers, 192
  brief history of, 170
  changing role of, 169–171
  defining, 169
  embracing ambiguity, 192–193
  future for, 192–193
  global, 6
  indistinguishable from the value chain, 313
  least loved, 183

brand(s) (*Continued*)
  making a statement, 186–187
  most loved, 183
  people's interest in, 184
  people's perceptions of, 184
  value of, 14–15
  virtues of, 172
brand archetype, 193
brand companies, MNCs
    vulnerable to, 10
brand democratization, 162
brand equity, 14
brand loyalty, 184
brand management, at Proctor &
    Gamble, 177–178
brand management metrics, 325, 326
brand message, repeating, 172
brand narratives, 186
brand protection, as paramount, 59
brand-as-experience-provider, 175
brand-centric managers, 192
brand-consumer relationship, 173
branded entertainment, 155
branding challenge, 190
brand-in-the-hand marketing, 160
Branson, Sir Richard
  influenced by Freddie Laker, 118
  melding business and
    philanthropy, 331
  radical results for Virgin, 153
breaking bulk, 239
bundling, as a pricey
    approach, 228
business concepts, 133
  characteristics of, 94
  compared to opportunities, 93–94
business model, 129–130,
    133–134
  core components of, 135
  elements defining, 134–137
  emergence of, 142–143
  as a platform for innovation, 130
  purpose of, 134
business model framework
  applying in mainstream industry,
    139–141
  considering decision variables at
    different levels, 137–138
business operations, key pricing
    questions, 231
business purpose, creating a
    customer, 111
businesses or organizations
    (B2B), 136
business-to-business
    marketers, 79
butterfly test, passing, 333
buyers
  tapping into the unconscious
    mind of, 71
  traits of good, 292
buyer-seller dyad, 295
buyer-utility map, 100
buzz
  creating, 151
  generated by Snapple, 187
buzz marketing, 149

C

Café TuTu Tango, 181
calculated risk-taking, 28, 33–34
capacity to innovate, 114
capital-intensive purchasing
    situations, 119
car cup holder, 45
carbon footprint, minimizing, 314
Case, Stephen M., 331, 332
Case Foundation, 332
catalyst, role of, 103, 104
Caterpillar, online purchasing by,
    246–247
causal ambiguity, 201
cause sponsorship, 317
cause-related marketing, 317
causes, examples of socially
    beneficial, 317
Celtel, 332
CGM. *See* consumer-generated
    media
champion, role of, 103, 104
change
  accelerated rate of, 16
  capitalizing on, 96–98
  as constant, 85
  dominant forces of affecting the
    sales force, 252–255
  opportunities arising as a result
    of, 87
channel inertia, 237
channels, of distribution, 237–238
character in a story, brand
    as, 176–177
character with personality, brand
    as, 172
chat rooms, 156
chemicals, entrepreneurial pricing
    in, 224
chief experience officer
    (CXO), 192
China, 2
choice and convenience, 25
choices, avoiding difficult, 297
Chrysler, defining the minivan
    market, 118
Cirque du Soleil, 214
Cisco Systems, empowered sales
    force, 267
cities, most populated, 5
citizenship, as a pillar of ethics,
    319–320
clever consumers, 52
Cluetrain Manifesto, 24
CLV (customer lifetime value),
    254, 299, 326–327
  calculation of, 299, 300
CNN
  broadcasting to the world, 11
  core value proposition, 133
Coase, Ronald, 276
Coasian economics, 276–277
Coca-Cola
  26 kinds of, 169
  global scope of, 8
co-created solutions/experiences, 25

coffeehouse community, 189
cognitive domain, of ideological
    space, 186–187
collaboration, within the modern
    sales organization, 262
collaborative sales force, 262–263
commoditization, rise in, 248
communicated product, 131, 132
communication
  costs of approaching zero, 277
  entrepreneurial pricing in, 224
  ongoing between parties in a
    relationship, 305
  openness at all levels of, 319
communication technology, effect
    on the size of firms, 276
communication within
    communities, 25
communications mix,
    optimizing, 146
communities, communication
    within, 25
community-supported information
    services, 156
company, as co-creator of value,
    180–181
competition
  changing the economics of
    selling, 254
  making irrelevant, 212
competitive advantage
  defined, 199–200
  sources of, 114–115
competitive factors, in mode
    selection, 120
competitive landscape, forces
    characterizing, 21
competitors
  as anyone, 279
  capitalizing on opportunities, 55
  cooperation between, 209
computer hardware and software,
    intense competition in, 120
computing power, as ever faster,
    ever cheaper, 273–274
conscious process, 54
consistency, describing in terms of
    fit, 141–142
constituencies within the firm, 120
construction, entrepreneurial
    pricing in, 224
consumer(s), 25
  finding connections with, 179
  innovative products and services
    initially rejected by, 100
  participating, 174
  reinventing marketing
    communications, 147
consumer behavior, study of, 43
consumer creativity, compared to
    creative consumers, 55
consumer engagement, 179
consumer innovation
  action on, 56
  attitude toward versus action
    on, 56
consumer panels, forming, 78

consumer-generated media (CGM), 156–159
consumers (B2C), selling to, 136
consumption, in the world's richest countries, 8
container shipping, 6–7
content
downloading of, 11
generation of, 25
context, continually changing, 22
conventional marketing, contrasted with entrepreneurial, 29, 30
conventions, questioning certain, 187
convergence marketing, 149
conversation, 119
conversation-starter methods, 151–152
Converse Gallery, 158
cool places, 97, 104
cooperative relationships, between buyer and seller, 289
co-opetition, 210
core competency, 136, 139
core principles, governing the sales function, 252
core product, 130, 131, 132
core value proposition, 133
corporate reputation, convergence with social responsibility, 313
corporate social responsibility (CSR), 313
corporations. See firms
cost based pricing, versus market based, 223
cost leadership, 200
cost per thousand impressions (CPM) rates, 149
Counter-Strike, creation of, 58
countries, most populated, 4–5
Country Business Patterns, 80
Counts Media, 161
creation of value, 90
creative abrasion, 257
creative consumers
capturing and creating value from, 59–60
compared to consumer creativity, 55
compared to lead users, 53–54
defined, 52
dilemmas caused by, 51
firms' stances toward, 56–59
ignoring or mismanaging, 55
as an intriguing paradox for business, 52
lack of control over, 54
not benefitting directly from innovations, 53
overlap with lead users, 54
rarely asking permission to experiment, 54
reasons for treating them strategically, 54–55
utilizing as a form of outsourcing, 55
working on personal interests, 53

working with all types of offerings, 53
creative destruction, 88–90
concept of, 28
Silicon Valley's economy relying on, 124
creative individuals, in music and gambling, 284–285
creative problem solving, fostering, 257
creative sales force, 256–257
creativity
as a basic survival tool, 87
role in entrepreneurship, 88
as the soul of the sales organization, 256
crowd-sourcing, 25, 27
cult, characteristics of, 189
cult brand, 189
cultural icons, 187
cup holder, 45
Current TV, view-generated content, 181
curveball, of a blue ocean strategy, 212
customer(s)
as active participants, 180
classifying, 301
as co-creator of value, 181
co-developers of products, 181
driving innovation in follow mode, 116
economic power of existing, 120
effects of products on, 44–50
flow from to innovative technology, 115
giving opportunity to do work, 287
interacting with firms, 290–292
as investments, 326
leading, 258
marketers approaches to, 290–292
observing in action, 76, 77
redefining marketer's role, 24
trying to lock in, 296
types of loyalties, 293
customer behavior, unconventional look at, 44
customer community, as co-creator of value, 181–183
customer creation, 113
customer creativity
firms' stances toward, 56–59
researched at a conceptual level, 55
customer equity, 299
customer evangelists, 182
customer experiences, 175
customer interactions, 174–175
customer intimacy, 32–33, 36
customer lifetime value. See CLV
customer loyalty, building, 292–294
customer management metrics, 326
customer orientation, 110
entrepreneurial orientation key to achieving, 266
reexamination of, 110–112

customer purchasing behavior, 43
customer relationship management (CRM), 174
customer value, 100
customer wants, 114
customer-brand relationships, 174
customer-centric marketing, 149
customer-made, 25
customer-made products, at Jones Soda, 26
customer-product debate, 110
customizable personal value, 25

D

Dada.net, Google partnership with, 163
daily operations, building research into, 74
Dans le Noir restaurant, 181, 182
databases, creating and mining, 75–76
Dealmaker online planning and knowledge management tool, 267
death of distance
reassortment/sorting and, 243
routinization and, 243
searching and, 243–244
decent marketing, 319
decision-making models, comparison of, 207
defining strategy, 117–118
Dell
business concept, 134
business model of, 133–134
electronic commerce success story, 246
products, 134
questioning industry orthodoxy, 202
Dell Direct Method, 138
Dell Hell, from the *Buzz Machine,* 157–158
demographics, market change due to, 91
dependency, avoiding, 296
development for sustainability, 322
dialogue, between customer and technology in interact mode, 118–119
differentiating identifier, brand as, 171–172
differentiation, 200
bases of, 136
lasting point of, 200
sources of, 136
digital marketing, 148
digital technology, displacing traditional film, 86
diminished service, 12–13
directly lived space, 185
discount structure, 230
discourage stance, good reasons to follow, 58

discouraging, creative consumers, 56, 57
disintermediation, 248–249
Disney
    barring Jim Hill, 51
    creating a fantasy world, 181
DisneyFord, 236
disparities, effects of economic, 3
disposable camera technique, 81
disruptive marketing, 148
distance, death of, 240
distinct identity, of a brand, 172
distribution, effects of technology
    on, 240–241
distribution channels, 237–238
    defined, 238
    effects of technological changes
        on, 242–247
    essential purposes of, 239
    inertia built up by, 237
    long-term effects of the impact
        of technology on, 247–249
    purpose of, 238
distribution media, versus
        distribution
        channels, 247–248
distribution strategy
    purpose of, 238–240
    redefining, 235–249
diversion, 47, 48
doing first approach, to decision
    making, 207
Dominatrix Barbie, 59
Don't Play Hardball-Throw a
    Curveball approach, 210–212
drafting, 209
Drucker, Peter, 110–112
duct tape marketing, 149
dyad, 291
dyadic relationship, 291–292

E

Eastern Roll, in high jumping, 212
eBay, Skype acquired by, 281
ecological sustainability, moving
    toward, 323
e-commerce, changing pricing, 227
economic man, model of, 43
economic model, of a firm, 137
economies
    nation states compared to
        corporations, 9
    providing products to jumpstart
        local, 312
economies of scope, intermediaries
    supporting, 239
education
    as a growth sector, 3
    online, 244
effectiveness, 326
    of a sales force, 260
effectual action, 208
    entailing curiosity-driven
        ideas, 97
efficiency, 326
    not implying effectiveness, 260

EM. *See* entrepreneurial marketing
e-mail, as an example of
    emersion, 49
e-mail marketing, 11
emergence, offerings as, 48, 49–50
emerging trends, confluence of, 154
emersion
    unintentional, 49–50
    of unintentional processes, 47
emotion
    language of, 190
    providing motivational
        energy, 176
emotional arousal, critical for
    sustained interest, 73
emotional aspect of successful
    market actions, 33
emotional responses, 71
empowered sales force, 258–259
enable position, 58
enable stance, 59
enablers, 160
enabling, creative
    consumers, 57, 58–59
enactment, 207, 208
encourage position, 57
encourage stance, 59
encouraging, creative consumers,
    57–58
enhanced service, 12
enlightened experimentation, 207
Enthoven, Dick, 323
entrepreneurial action
    outcome of, 89
    results of, 88, 89
entrepreneurial actor, roles played
    by, 103, 104
entrepreneurial enactment, 208
entrepreneurial imperative, 331
entrepreneurial intensity, 265–266
entrepreneurial marketers
    doing different things, 138
    personally identifying with
        products, 132
entrepreneurial marketing
    as central concept, 31
    versus conventional marketing,
        29, 30
    defined, 29
    interactions among components,
        34–36
    need for, 29
    underlying dimensions of, 31–34
entrepreneurial marketing
        construct, 28–31
entrepreneurial opportunities
    compared to others, 90
    views of, 96
entrepreneurial pricing, 223–224
    coming of age, 225–228
    integrative framework for, 229
    manifestations of, 224
    reflected in value-based
        strategies, 228
entrepreneurial research, 64, 71
    principles guiding, 72–76
entrepreneurial researcher, 70–71

entrepreneurial sales force, 263
entrepreneurial sales organization,
    elements of, 256–263
entrepreneurial strategy, 204
entrepreneurship
    calculated risk-taking and, 33
    crafting strategy in, 198–202
    defined, 27, 88
    as everyday activity, 88–89
    examples of, 267–268
    as imperative, 86
    need for, 27–28
    sales in, 263–265
    versus selling, 263
    time and money constraints, 64
    underlying dimensions, 28, 265
environment, concerns about, 321
environmental factors, in mode
    selection, 120
environmental influences, effect on
    pricing trends, 227
environmental turbulence,
        managerial implications
        of, 225
Estrada, Joseph, 45
ethics, defined, 315
ethnography, 81
European Union (EU), 7
    agricultural tariffs, 3
    population, 5–6
Every Battle Is Won Before It Is
        Ever Fought approach,
        203–205
evolutionary change, versus
        revolutionary change, 16,
        17–18
evolutionary economic problem,
        requiring social institution, 124
exclusivity agreements,
        Pepsi, 200
expectations, forming of, 117
Expedia, 244
expeditionary marketing, 148
expeditionary sales force, 257–258
experience economy, advent of, 171
experience provider, brand as, 172
experience-based marketing, 192
experiential domain, of
        transformational space, 188
experiential marketing, 148
experiment(s), simple,
        conducting, 81
experimenting organizations, 124
exploitation
    of opportunities at Harley-
        Davidson, 36
    in value-creation process, 99
exploration, in value-creation
        process, 99
extension, of intentional processes,
        46
external environment, 225
external fit, 142
extreme sporting events, Jones logo
        promoted at, 27
eye-tracking methodologies, in
        marketing research, 75

F

Facebook, 86, 87
fairness, as pillar of ethics, 318
Fallon, Kieren, 284
Fanning, Shawn, 285
Fantasy football, 181–182
FantasyFootball.com, 183
Federal Express (FedEx),
   12, 136
   as market driver, 37
   reaction to Jose Avila, 51, 57,
      58–59
Federal Express boxes, furniture
   from, 51
feel marketing, 175
Femcare division (P&G), 179
Fidelity Investments, 153
financial performance
   entrepreneurial intensity and,
      266
   exclusive focus on, 312
financial services, entrepreneurial
   pricing in, 224
Financial Times, 11
firms
   customer interactions
      with, 290–292
   dilemmas facing, 309–311
fish tank phenomenon, 278–279,
   284–285
five forces model, 271
five new forces, affecting marketing
   strategy, 272–279
flexibility, pricing, 223
flock-of-birds phenomenon, 278
   equalized access and, 284
   lawlessness in music and
      gambling, 282–284
Fluevog fanatics, 27
focus (cost/differentiation), 200
focus groups, 78
follow mode, 116–117, 123
follow strategy
   among suppliers, 120
   in evolving environment, 120
Foose, Chip, 58
Foose Design, 58
for benefit, versus for profit, 331
Ford Motor Company
   alternative business models
      explored by, 236
   "Project Olympus", 235
   working with individuals, 58
Ford of Europe, Mk4 Escort poor
   reception, 113
foreheADs campaigns, 156
foresight, 201
Formula 1 motor racing, 48
Fosbury, Dick, 212
Fosbury Flop, 212
foundation level, 137
   Southwest model, 139, 140
Four Seasons Hotels, 12
4 C's, shifting to, 25
4 P's (product, price, place, and
   promotion), 17, 24

fragility, multinational
   corporations, 10
fragmentation, media and
   audience, 11
framework, for business model
   design, 134–137
franchises, predictable future
   for, 98
Frankel, Justin, 285
free markets, versus protectionism,
   3–4
friend$, 163
Friss, Janus, 159, 281
functional magnetic resonance
   imaging (fMRI), 152–153
functional silos, firms organized
   as, 17
future
   creating, 211
   for marketers and brands,
      192–193
   mental time travel into, 103

G

gap between rich and
   poor, 2–3, 309
garbage, checking, 79–80
garbology, 79
Generation C, 25
global bliss, 6–8
global brands, 6
   top five, 183
global enterprises, 276
global gloom, 6–8
global recorded music industry, 279
global trends, diverging, 16
global warming, consequences
   of, 322
globalization, 8, 85, 86
GM cars, 169
Gnutella, 283
good deeds, as good
   business, 317
good opportunity, identifying, 95
Google
   innovations by, 210–211
   rule breaking by, 202
Gore, Al, 322
grassroots methods, 150–151
green marketing, 317
green products, pricing of, 321
Green Technologies, 323
green test, passing, 333
Gremban, Ron, 51
Groundhog Day, 334
growth and prosperity, versus
   poverty and despair, 2–3
growth model, of entrepreneurship,
   137
guerrilla marketing, 72,
   148, 150
   disadvantages of, 204
   in pricing arena, 230
   principles of, 204
guiding principles, at rules level,
   138–139

H

Habitat for Humanity, 15
Half-Life game, 58
Harley Ownership Group (HOG),
   36
Harley-Davidson, 35–36
Harley-Davidson ownership
   groups, 182
Hawkins, Gary, 75
healthy dissatisfaction, sense of, 258
Hertz, Noreena, 9
Hewlett-Packard, 98
hidden champions, MNCs
   susceptible to, 10
high net worth individuals
   (HNWIs), 2
high-consumer-involvement
   media, 156
Hill, Jim, 51
The Hire campaign, 327–328
HOGs, 182
homogenization of time,
   7, 240–241
   reassortment/sorting and, 244
   routinization and, 244–245
   searching and, 245–246
honesty, as pillar of ethics, 316–317
hostile environment,
   characterization of, 225
Hot Spots, 97, 104
how question of strategy, 199
hub-and-spokes model, 212
Human Genome Project, 27
hypercompetitive markets, 254
hypothesis formulation, research
   guided by, 66–67

I

IBM, 38, 267
ICON grid (innovation or
   customer orientation), 115
ICON Scale, amended, 121–122
iconic brand, 187
idea(s)
   brand as conveyor of, 187
   versus opportunities, 91–92
   as unattractive opportunities, 92
ideal self, relating individual to, 175
identifier, brand as, 172
ideological space (cognitive
   domain), 185, 186–187
IKEA
   crowd-sourcing by, 27
   flat-pack furniture concept, 94
   as market driver, 37
   market ownership, 39
   rule breaking by, 202
iMac, 191
imagination, in relationship
   management, 306–307
imitation, protection against, 201
imperfect information, living
   with, 206
improvisation, effective, 208
In Search of Excellence, 12

income model, of
    entrepreneurship, 137
An Inconvenient Truth, 322
India, 2
individual sales territories, versus
    entrepreneurial ventures,
    263–264
"The Industrialization of Service",
    12
industry market structures, changes
    in, 91
influencing mode, 118
inkjet technology, Hewlett-
    Packard, 98
innovation, 28, 33, 265
    as business function, 111
    by consumers, 54, 114
    defined by Drucker, 111
    flowing to customers, 115–116
    marketing and, 113–114
    as prerequisite for creating
        customers, 112
    return to, 112–113
    in sales, 257
    shaping the market, 117
    sources of, 114
    without value, 99
innovation orientation, 110
    components of, 114
    rationale for, 114
    traditional marketing and, 114
insights, in ordinary things, 72–73
Integrity Systems, 319
intellectual property protection, 10
intentional processes, of offering
    evolution, 46–47
interact mode, 118–119
interacting firm, most radical
    organizational form, 124
interactive voice response
    (IVR), 159
interactivity, notion of, 248
Interbrand, 14
interdependency, relationship
    dynamics and, 302–303
intermediaries
    between buyer and seller, 237
    elimination of, 134
    entering channels to facilitate
        search, 249
    providing economies of
        distribution, 239
internal collaboration, 262
internal fit, 141–142
Internet
    changing distribution, 238
    as distributed power
        network, 281
    evolution of, 153–162
    as illustration of Metcalfe's
        law, 275
    people-power through, 158
    as three-dimensional experience,
        154
Internet distribution matrix,
    240, 242
Internet pure-plays, 241

Internet technologies, effects on
    distribution, 240
Internet-based industries, 120
intrapreneurial marketing, 29
inventory, excess, disposing of, 249
iPod, 56, 191, 280–281
irrelevance of location, 241
    reassortment/sorting and, 246
    routinization and, 246–247
    searching and, 247
Islamic divorce, sent by SMS, 45
isolation mode, 116
    of AOL, 123
    benefits of, 121
    in stable environment, 120
Issigonis, Alec, 100
It Takes Two To Pass One
    approach, 209–210
iTunes, 56, 191, 243, 281

J

Janus, 1–2, 16–18
jazz, 208
Jeep, 117
Jet2 website, 244
JetBlue, 99
John Fluevog Shoes, 27
Jones Independent Music
    website, 26
Jones International University, 244
Jones Soda Co., 25, 26–27
Jones Team Riders, 27
Joost (a.k.a., the Venice Project),
    159
judo strategy, 205–206

K

Kazaa, 281, 283
Keith, Robert J., 112–113
killer applications, 272
Klein, Naomi, 15
Knight, Cindy, 51
knowledge, changes in, 91
Kodak, 85, 86

L

labor unions, 120
Laker, Freddie, 118
Lance Armstrong Foundation, 152,
    317
Land of Possibilities, 96
land of promise, 104
Land Rover, 117
Landreth running shoe, 48
Lastminute.com, 249
lawlessness, in music and gambling,
    282–284
lead user
    concept of, 53
    versus creative consumer, 53–54
    finding, screening, and
        selecting, 54
    identifying, 53
    managerial attention to, 54

overlap with creative consumers,
    54
    talking to, 78–79
lead user research, 78
learning, three-step approach to,
    207, 208
legal and ethical environment,
    defining acceptable sales
    behavior, 255
leverage, in judo strategy, 206
leveragers, salespeople as, 254
Levi Strauss, 8
Levitt, Ted, 12
life, individual's, spaces in, 185
lifestyle ventures, 137
Lifestyles of Health and
    Sustainability (LOHAS)
    market, 322
lifetime value concept, 297–299
linear, supply-based view of
    marketing, 24
linguistic analysis of blog
    discussions, 80
The Little Red Book, 204
lived space, people's, being part of,
    190
LiveStrong bracelet, 152
location. *See* irrelevance of location
logical process, approaching
    research as a, 64–68
London Times, Higher Education
    Supplement, 245
long-term relationships, vital, 289
lovemark
    brand as, 172, 176
    defined, 176
loyal accounts, 301
loyalties
    managing, 293–294
    as more than repeat-buying
        behavior, 291
    types of, 293
Lundgren, Gillis, 94

M

Macintosh, 118
magazines, global publishing of,
    10–11
management, existing mode of, 120
management decision, market
    research and, 64–66, 68
managerial reports, in database
    management, 76
Mao Tse-Tung, 204
margins, on products and services,
    137
market
    constantly leading, 40
    geographic scope of, 136
    owning, 213
market discontinuities, identifying,
    87
market fragmentation, price
    differentiation resulting from,
    226
market leadership, 38–39

market opportunities, expiration date of, 205
market orientation, 31, 110
market ownership, 38–39
market research, in follow mode, 116
market shapers, pricing secrets of, 219–232
market share, maintaining and increasing, 298
market spaces, new, creating, 101, 129
market-based approach, to poverty, 311
market-based pricing, 223
market-driver approach, 37, 38, 213
market-driving firms, 37, 39
marketers, 146
    approaches to customers, 290–292
    as customer agent, 153
    future for, 192–193
    honesty or ethics of, 315–320
    as servers of customers, 25
marketing
    according to Drucker, 111
    aligning more closely with science and engineering, 124
    alternative approaches, 23
    approaches, spectrum of, 29
    communication in post-World War II era, 146
    as context dependent, 22
    contrasting conventional and entrepreneurial, 29, 30
    defined, 22
    department, 113
    efforts, characteristics of successful, 147
    under an evolutionary scenario, 17
    innovation and, 113–114
    interactions and evolution of within a firm, 35
    juju, 189–192
    logic, 24–25
    metric programs, 326
    metrics, rethinking, 329
    mix, 17, 24, 25
    network, 180
    perspectives on emerging nature of, 148–149
    redefined, 23–24
    under revolutionary change, 17–18
    sole purpose, 25
    technology and, 50
    traditional activities, 22
    velocity, 25
    viewing as an investment, 325
marketing code of ethics, six pillars of, 316
marketing performance, forces affecting the dashboard for, 310
marketing performance metrics (MPMs), 325, 326

marketing practice, new developments in, 147–153
marketing research
    as a logical process, 64–68
    uncertain conditions defining the role of, 63–64
marketing strategy, in the digital age, 271–287
marketing theory, trying to keep pace, 23–24
marketing thought and practice, developments in, 22–24
marketplace
    conversations and social value of, 145
    lessons from, 145–147
market-research input, Ford avoiding, 113
markets
    creating entirely new around discontinuities, 101
    freeing up of, 3
    misleading, 113
marketspace, 146
    move to, 241
market-technology relationship, as dialogue, 119
Marriott Hotels, Courtyard concept by, 117
Mary Kay, relying on social networks, 163
mass customization, 179
mass market, as dead, 252
Mattel Inc. versus Susanne Pitt, 59
Mazda, development of the M5 (Miata), 117
MBA programs, entirely virtual, 244
McDonald's
    global scope of, 8
    label action in British High Court, 15
McElroy, Neil, 178
McFord business model, 236
McWorld, spread of, 8
meaning
    making out of something, 190
    transforming to the symbolic, 193
means extension, offerings as, 47
measurement
    as the end result of research, 66
    of market research, 67–68
measurement approaches, 76–81
media, worldwide reach versus fragmentation, 10–11
media options, proliferation of, 146
medium, defining, 247–248
memes, ideational, 187
mental models, rejection and replacement of previous, 102
Mercedes-Benz, 316–317
mergers and acquisitions (M&As), cross-border, 9
metaphors, endowing brands with connotations, 176
Metcalfe, Robert, 275
Metcalfe's law, 275–276
    explaining Betfair's success, 281

metrics, rethinking, 328
MG brand subculture, 186
MGM, BMW relationship with, 327
micro-credit industry, expanding, 331
microprocessors, speed of, 273
Microsoft, 123–124
Mini (car), 100
minivan market, defined by Chrysler, 118
missing-the-boat risk, 35
missionaries, for brands, 182
mixed reality entertainment experience, 161
M(or mobile)-media, personalized messages posted to, 11
MNCs (multinational corporations), 9–10
mobile advertising campaigns, responses to, 161
mobile ASPs, 160
mobile content as premiums to drive sales, 161
mobile marketing
    advent of the era of, 160
    categories of, 161
    defined, 160
    vertical segments, 160–161
Mobile Marketing Association (MMA), 161
mobile marketing ecosystem, 159–162
mobile phone
    becoming a platform complementing traditional media, 159
    distinct role in consumers' lives, 160
    essential features, 160
    as an example of emersion, 49
    uses of, 160
mobile subscribers, 159
mobile video, 159–160
mobile-phone-based panels, 78
mode, implications of changes of, 123–124
mode of focus, diagnosing a firm's, 121
Model T Ford, adapted by farmers as power source, 52
modern age, linear trends of, 1
modification, 89
mom and pop ventures, 137
monolinear information, shift to polyrhythmic interactions, 21–22
Monster, 245
Moore, Gordon, 273
Moore's law, 273–275, 280–281
Morpheus, 281, 283
morphing power, of offerings, 45
Morris, David, 15
MP3
    arrival of, 284–285
    changing the music industry, 198
MPEG3. See MP3
MPMs (marketing performance metrics), 325, 326

MRI (magnetic resonance), 149
MTV, broadcasting to the world, 11
Muji, crowd-sourcing by, 27
multinational corporations
  (MNCs), 9–10
multi-user conferences for free, 277
music
  networks in, 281–282
  production and consumption
    of, 50
music industry, worldwide, 272
music service, from a soda
  company, 26
mutual expectations, meeting, 294
myjones.com business operation,
  patent for, 26
MySpace, advertising revenues, 157
mystery shoppers, 81

N

Naisbitt, John, 1
Napoleon, 206
Napster
  debut in 1999, 285
  forced to suspend services, 48
  free music-sharing service, 281
NASCAR axiom, 209
negatives, turning into positives, 36
negotiated prices, at Priceline.com,
  219
negotiation, 119
negotiation interact mode, 119
Netflix
  price setting by, 226
  use of databases, 76
networks
  becoming the processors, 278
  creating shortcuts, 276, 281–282
neuro-marketing, 149, 152–153
neuroscience tools, in marketing
  research, 75
new marketing logic, fundamental
  rethinking required, 24–25
new media
  emergence of, 156
  non-Internet, 156
new technologies
  changing markets, 116
  failure rates in developing, 118
News Group Newspapers, 161–162
news reporting, changes in, 10
newspapers
  facing a calamity, 162
  global publishing of, 10–11
Newton PDA
  active community
    surrounding, 53
  market research effort on, 118
niche, finding and owning, 214
nichemanship, 225
Nike
  e-mail exchanges "Sweat-shop"
    slogan, 15
  emotional connection with
    consumers, 176
  shoes as fashion accessories, 48

No Logo, 15
nonfinancial investments, making
  only, 296
Nordstrom, 12
North American Free Trade
  Agreement (NAFTA), 7
nostalgia, creating value around,
  100–101

O

obesity, epidemic linked to fast
  foods, 49–50
objectives
  of the entrepreneur, 137
  as SMART, 199
observational methodologies, in
  marketing research, 75
oceans, sorts of, 211
offerings
  defined, 44
  as means extension, 47
  paths taken by, 46–47
  role of, 45
  unintended consequences of, 49
offline WOM conversations, 158
Olympics, high jump event, 211
Omidyar, Pierre, 331
O'naturals restaurants, 177
one size fits all, believing, 297
one-to-one marketing, 148
online betting exchange
  (Betfair.com), 272
online marketing metrics, 326
online stores, 156
online surveys, tools for creating, 77
online video games, advertising and
  product placement in, 155
online WOM, 158
Open Source Footwear, 27
open systems, 25
openness, as a pillar of ethics, 319
openness to innovation, 114
open-source software
  community, 54
operating leverage, of a firm, 137
opportunities
  availability of, 32
  change as the genesis of, 85–88
  compared to ideas, 91–92
  defined, 90
  finding, 93
  frequently asked questions
    about, 90–95
  identifying for new ventures,
    94–95
  methods for evaluating, 95
  obsession with, 32
  recognizing, discovering, and
    creating, 96–98
  rules of thumb for attractive, 95
  source of, 91
opportunity creation, 96, 97
opportunity discovery, 96, 97–98
opportunity identification, 94
opportunity recognition, 96, 98
organizational ambidexterity, 112

organizational structures, best
  suited to innovation, 124
orientation modes, strategic, 116
origination, 89
outsourcing decisions,
  explaining, 276

P

Palm PDA, 276
panel methodology, 78
paradox of choice, 169
paradoxical trends, 1
parimutuel systems, 280
path dependency, 201
patterns, identifying trends, 73
pay-to-say marketing, 149, 152
peer-to-peer file sharing, 198
peer-to-peer forums, 188
peer-to-peer technology, 281
people, putting before short-term
  profits, 329
people-powered marketing, 162
Pepsi, exclusivity agreements, 200
perceptions, of brands, 184
Peretti, Jonah, 15
performance goals, 305
performance standards, setting
  high, 259
permission marketing, 11, 148, 152
permission marketing
  campaigns, 149
personal identifier, brand as, 186
personal selling, 146
  technology impacting, 261–262
personalized TV channel, 159
pessimism. *See* global gloom
petrol heads, 52
Peugeot, crowd-sourcing by, 27
phenomena, emersion (or
  revealing) of, 49
photographic film market, maturity
  of, 86
Pillsbury, progression of, 113
pixel-selling, on the Internet, 156
playfulness, as vital, 213
PlayPumps International, 332
podcasting, 11
point system, for software
  pricing, 224
point-of-sale system
  data produced by, 75
  as a living laboratory, 81
political factors, in mode
  selection, 120
polyrhythmic interactions, shift to,
  21–22
Popcorn, Faith, 1
population
  growth versus shortages, 4–6
  shortages, 5–6
  world's, 4
portable MP3 players, 285
Porter, Michael, five forces
  model, 271
Porter's generic strategies, 200

post-modern 21st century, trends of, 1
poverty and despair, 2–3
power
  of multinational corporations, 9
  shifting from marketer toward the market, 22
Prada, embracing ambiguity, 192–193
pre-call preparation, 252–253
price
  as both noun and verb, 221
  key characteristics of, 221
price avoidance, 220
price differentials, charging, 229
price innovator, Netflix as, 226
price levels, 222, 230
price management, 220
price objectives, 222
price promotions, 222
price strategy, 222
price structure, 222, 228
price variables, 228
Pricesearch service, 219
pricesetters, customers as, 181
pricing
  conventional turned on its head, 219
  creative potential of, 220–221
  examples of emerging practices, 224–225
  magic of, 219–220
  strategic perspective on, 221–222
pricing orientation, 222–224
pricing program, 228–230
pricing secrets, of market shapers, 219–232
primary research, pursuing, 67
priority rules, 139
proactive legal steps, against innovating consumers, 57
proactive orientation, at Harley-Davidson, 36
proactive pricing, 223
proactiveness, 28, 31–32, 265
  in instituting price moves, 231
process innovation, 265
process needs, changes in, 91
processes, interrelationships of, 50
Proctor & Gamble, evolution of brands and branding, 177–179
product(s)
  defined, 110
  defining from a marketing standpoint, 130
  effects on customers, 44–50
  essential in shaping the market, 117
  existing on four levels, 130–132
  framework for viewing, 130–132
  influencing market expectations and trends, 118
  starting with new, 130–132
product innovation, creating customers, 112
product support, 132
product-centric managers, 192

product/company identity, brand as, 172–173
production processes, globally integrated, 6
production/operating system, at Southwest, 139
profit(s)
  coming from a relatively smaller proportion of customers, 299
  relationship with balance, 329
  retooling the marketing dashboard, 324–330
PROFIT acronym, 200, 201
profitability
  challenge of, 333
  emphasis on, 298
  proprietary level, 137–138
  exploring, 138
  at Southwest Airlines, 140
  Southwest model at, 139
  as strategy specific, 138
protectionism, growing, 3–4
prototypical preferences, forming of, 117
PSS/World Medical, sales force in reserve program, 267–268
public relations, 146
public spaces, colonization of, 187
public utilities, entrepreneurial pricing in, 224
pull model, shift to, 153
punctuated equilibrium, 17
punitive action, against consumer innovation, 57
purposeful enactment, proactive behavior as, 31
push model, shift from, 153

Q

qualitative techniques, of low-cost but effective research, 77
quantitative techniques, of low-cost but effective research, 77
QVC, customers providing immediate feedback, 71

R

radical innovations, producing a lock-out, 39
radical marketing, 148
radio frequency identification (RFID) chips, from Hitachi, 274
Raging Cow campaign, by Dr. Pepper, 316
rapid movement, in judo strategy, 205–206
rate of response, speeding up, 205
rational choice theory, 43
reactive pricing, 223
Ready! Fire! Aim! approach, 206–209
real time, 241
real-time marketing, 148

real-time pricing, achieving, 221
reassortment/sorting
  death of distance and, 243
  homogenization of time and, 244
  irrelevance of location and, 246
reassortment/sorting activities, 239
reciprocal space, 185, 188–189
recorded music, exchange and distribution of, 282
Recording Industry Association of America (RIAA), 282–283
recruitment market, 245
Red Bull, embracing ambiguity, 192
red face test, avoiding, 333
red oceans, of bloody competition, 211
Red Queen effect, lessons in escaping, 202–212
Red Queen's race, 197–198
Reflect.com, 179
regulatory boundaries, fall of, 7
Reimann, Joerg, 53
reintermediation, 248
  opportunities for, 249
relate marketing, 175
relationship builder, brand as, 172, 174
relationship management program, 303–305
relationship marketing, 148, 152, 291
  approaching more systematically, 297
  compared to EM, 32
  described, 294–295
  misinterpreting, 296–297
  myths and realities of, 296–297
relationships, 294
  classifying customers by, 301
  establishing boundaries for, 304–305
  establishing the purpose of, 304
  failing to formalize, 296
  framework for managing, 304
  keys to success, 307
  leading to changes in goals, 297–299
  need for imagination in managing, 306–307
  types and degrees of, 299, 301
  underlying characteristics of, 302–303
relevance, increasing for brands, 173–174
repeat or multiple transactions, 301
repeat transactions, encouraging, 291
representational space, 185, 186
research design, 67, 70–71
research methods
  building into daily operations, 74
  as eclectic, 71
  traditional, 71
research objectives, establishing, 66
research project, basic logic of any, 64–68

research questions, speaking to the unconscious brain, 73
resist stance, 57
resisting, creative consumers, 57
resource leveraging, 34
  emphasized in emergent practices, 147
  at Harley-Davidson, 36
resource-based view (RBV), 200
resources
  as increasingly less tangible, 287
  leveraging, 34
  utilization of existing, 32
respect, as a pillar of ethics, 318–319
response, to creative consumers, 59
responsibility
  as a pillar of ethics, 317–318
  triple bottom line (3BL) calling for, 314
retail store discount card, data produced by, 75
retention, 207, 208
rethinking, of old rules, 25
retro autos, 100
retro celebrities, 101
retro commercials, 101
retro communities, 101
retro house-furnishings, 101
retro movies, 101
retro radios, 100
retro rock music, 101
retro sneakers, 100
retro television, 101
retro video games, 101
return on customer, 327
revenue drivers, for a firm, 137
revolutionary change, versus evolutionary, 16, 17–18
revolutionary thinking, 201
RIAA (Recording Industry Association of America), 282–283
Rider' Edge programs, 36
risk management, at Harley-Davidson, 36
risk manager, marketer as, 33–34
risk profile, characterizing company operations, 33
risk-assumptive pricing, 223
risk-aversive pricing, 223
risk-taking, 265
RM. *See* relationship marketing
roach-bait marketing. *See* subversive marketing
Roddick, Anita, 37
role overload (burnout), salespeople experiencing, 253
roles, played by the brand, 171–177
Rolls Royce, 119
Roundabout Outdoors, 332
routinization
  death of distance and, 243
  facilitating exchange, 239
  homogenization of time and, 244–245
  irrelevance of location and, 246–247

rule of thumb, for various marketing activities, 325
rules, breaking, 102–104
rules level, 138
  at Southwest Airlines, 140
  understanding, 138–139

S

sale force automation (SFA) systems, 255
sales culture, changes in, 255
sales force
  external changes affecting, 252–255
  linking to the overall strategies of the firm, 260
  new concept of, 255–263
sales force in reserve program, at PSS/World Medical, 267–268
sales function
  aligning with other areas of the firm, 260
  role of, 251–252
sales management
  as entrepreneurial, 263
  information technologies impacting, 261
sales organizations
  placing limitations on claims, 255
  rating on entrepreneurial intensity, 265–266
sales orientation, tending to be short-sighted, 298
sales professional, leading customers, 258
sales promotion, 146
salespeople, treated as replaceable objects, 251
Savvy.com, 159
SBC, race with Verizon, 202
SCA (sustainable competitive advantage)
  obtaining, 200–201
  sources and criteria for obtaining, 201
  strategies for creating, 202
Schengen zone, in Europe, 6
Scissors technique, for high jumpers, 211
Sculley, John, 87
search marketing, 149, 152
searching
  death of distance and, 243–244
  homogenization of time and, 245–246
  irrelevance of location and, 247
searching process, intermediaries facilitating, 239
Second Life, 154, 155
secondary data, 67
seeing first approach, to decision making, 207
Seitzer, Dieter, 285
selection, 207, 208
self-redesign, constant state of, 124
sellers, traits of good, 292

sense marketing, 175
serendipitous process, 54
serendipity, in market opportunities, 97
service
  enhanced versus diminished, 12–13
  versus problem solution, 13
  push for diminished, 12
service deliverers, 12
services
  entrepreneurial pricing in, 224
  starting with new, 130–132
set up, of market research, 64–67
shape mode, 117–118, 124
shaping strategies
  failure of, 118
  on rapidly evolving technology, 120
share of mind (SOM), of brands, 163
share of voice (SOV), consumers' increasing, 163
short message system (SMS), 45
short-term tactics, in pricing, 230
Siemens, global scope of, 8
Singapore Airlines, 12
single or occasional transactions, 301
sinking-the-boat risk, 35
SKUs (or stock-keeping units), in a typical supermarket, 169
Skype, 58, 202, 277, 281
SMS service, 47
snack packs, ads on, 156
Snapple, critique of the establishment, 187
snowball sampling, 79
social advertising, 317
social change, entrepreneurial activity producing, 90
social complexity, 201
social consequences, focusing on, 88
social entrepreneurship, 103
social initiatives, corporate spending on, 314
social interaction, soda as a platform for, 26
social media, 163
social network
  analysis, 80
  brand becoming part of a, 188
social networking
  creative energy of, 157
  new and evolving trend of, 86
  rethinking, 159
  sites, 156
social text, brand as, 186
societal problems, approaches, 312
soda, all natural, 26
software, entrepreneurial pricing in, 224
Sony
  reaction to AiboPet hacking, 57
  reaction to hacking of the PSP game player, 56
sorting, 239
sorting out, 239

sources, of high-value ideas for new ventures, 94
South Africa, theft of copper wire and optical cable, 47
Southern African Development and Economic Community (SADEC), 7
Southwest Airlines
applying the business mode framework to, 139
creating a blue ocean, 212
as a market driver, 37
owning a market, 39
perception of new value, 99
spirituality concept, 33
superiority exploiting its model, 139
SparkleBodySpray.com, 179
special events, creating an emotional connection, 180
speculative model, for an entrepreneur, 137
speed, as a strategy, 205
Spier wine estate, as an example of development for sustainability, 322
sports betting, market for, 280
Stain Detective, 178
standardization, in pricing, 223
Staples, website as a catalog, 243
Star Wars videos, allowed by Lucasfilm, 183
Starbucks
financing *Akeelah and the Bee,* 155
owning a market, 39
recreating the Italian espresso-bar experience, 214
as a target of anti-globalization activities, 15
Starbucks brand
community formed around, 188–189
experience of, 189
state-of-the-art technologies, developing in freestanding technical units, 113
stealth marketing. *See also* subversive marketing
ethics of, 316
Steel, Helen, 15
Stellenbosch Winelands, 323
step backward to go forward approach, 205–206
stocks, aggregating from different suppliers, 239
Stonyfield Farm
lovemark created by, 176
unique kind of culture for consumers, 177
storage media, 280
store greeters, at Wal-Mart, 95
strategic balance, achieving, 16
strategic decisions, modes of, 206
strategic dynamics, 121–122
strategic entrepreneurship, 201–202
strategic evolution, by creeps, 16

strategic experiential marketing (SEM) framework, 175
strategic landscape, changes in, 200
strategic orientation in selling, 260
strategic partnerships, 292
strategic pricing
key to, 222
by Southwest, 212
strategic sales force, 260–261
strategy
advice for the future, 287
defined, 198–199
derivation of the word, 204
entrepreneurial world, 201
escaping the Red Queen effect, 203
as improvisation, 208
as no longer long term, 287
objectives of, 199
street marketing, 150
subsistence model, for an entrepreneur, 137
subversion, 48
intentional, 48
of intentional processes, 46–47
subversive activity, entrepreneurship as, 28
subversive marketing, 148, 150
Sun-Tzu, 204
superior market position, 200
suppliers, winning back power from the channel, 247
support services, augmenting products, 132
surgical strikes, 204
surroundings, making use of, 72
Survey Monkey, 74, 77
surveys, heavy reliance on, 71
survival, contest for, 197
sustainability, 321, 324
challenge of, 333
key to, 314
triple bottom line (3BL) calling for, 314
sustainable advantage, sources of, 39
sustainable competitive advantage. *See* SCA
sustainable development, replacing, 322
sustained innovation, at Harley-Davidson, 36
SUVs, 117
sweeps via SMS, 161
symbolic capitol, 53
symbolic domain, of representational space, 186
synthesis, 89

T

Tabcorp, 283
tangible product, 131, 132
Target, Take Charge of Education program, 317
Tate Britain, 180
tattoo brand, 35
team goals, putting ahead of self-interests, 262

technological change, rate over time, 272
technological innovation orientation, 110
technological sales force, 261–262
technology
enabling salespeople, 255
as a key driver of change, 85
marketing and, 50
transforming the capabilities of a company sales force, 261
using creatively for market research, 74–75
technology-facilitated methods, 152–153
teenage girls, online P&G communications, 179
television channels, proliferation of, 146
text messaging, 45
textbook marketing, 17
text-messaging users, 159
theme parks, branded experience through, 181
"Think Different" slogan, 191–192
think first approach, 206–207
think marketing, 175
thinking, discarding previous ways of, 102
third place, 188–189
Third Voice, 48
third-generation technology (3G), 160
third-screen marketing, 162
3 P's: people > planet > profits, 313–315
3M
bringing lead users into the process, 79
process to develop a new disposable surgical draping product, 54
Tide, role in family harmony, 178
tight community, characteristics of, 189
time, homogenization of. *See* homogenization of time
time-period pricing, 229
TiVo, customer acting as collaborator, 181
tokenism, 259
toothing, 49
Top App Award, 161
top-down organizations, 258–259
topsight, 201
totalisators, 282
Toyota
development of the Lexus, 117
reaction to Ron Gremban, 51
trademarks, 172
trade-offs, marketing research and, 64
transaction cost reductions, 277
transaction costs, 276, 282
transactions
as the historical focus in marketing, 290–291
intermediaries routinizing, 239

transactions (*Continued*)
  repeat or multiple, 301
  single or occasional, 301
transformational space, 185, 188
Travelocity, 244
trends
  Janus-like, 2
  linear, 1
  paradoxical, 1
tribal-like communities, 189
triple bottom line (3BL),
  313–314
trust
  brand as a symbol of, 173
  as fragile thing, 173
  in relationships, 302
trustmark
  brand as, 172, 173
  operating at a brand level, 176
Tupperware, relying on social
  networks, 163
turbulent environment, 225
Turner, Ted, 331
TV channel, personalized, 159
TV/video, 161

U

U-commerce, 11
unbundling, as a pricey
  approach, 228
unconscious, exploring, 73–74
undercover marketing. *See*
  subversive marketing
underground innovators, creative
  consumers as, 52
unidirectional, stimulus-response
  approach, abandonment
  of, 291
unilateral efforts, pursuing, 297
unintentional processes, of offering
  evolution, 46, 47
unique combinations, creating at
  the proprietary level, 138
unique models, cool businesses
  built on, 129–130
unique selling/value proposition
  (USP), 173
unit cost, determination of
  average, 220
unsustainable consumption,
  promoted by globalization, 8
Urban Juice and Soda Company
  Ltd. *See* Jones Soda Co.
Uruguay Round on Textiles and
  Clothing, 4
U.S. government, safeguarding
  quotas, 4
user-centric web, 211
user-generated content sites, 156
users, innovative ideas from, 114

V

value
  conceptualization of, 100, 101
  creating and capturing, 52

meaning of, 329
price as, 221
without innovation, 99
value chain
  destroying your own, 287
  modularization of activities, 10
value co-creation, forms of,
  180–181
value creation
  at the core of why question of
    strategy, 199
  for the customer, 25
  as the focal point of EM, 34
  foundation of all entrepreneurial
    opportunity, 98–101
  at Harley-Davidson, 36
  integrated with 3BL
    objectives, 330
  new ideas leading to, 90
value innovation, 99, 211
value proposition, 100
  defining for a firm, 136
value-creation process, dual nature
  of, 99
value-exchange model, 180
Valve Software, 58
van Stolk, Peter, 26
variability, of price, 221
variety, of pricing, 221
venture capitalist, sales manager
  compared to, 264–265
venture creation, 133
venture ideas. *See* business
  concepts
verbal terrorists, 157
Verizon, race with SBC, 202
vicarious learning, 242
video blogging, 158
video games, 156
  advertisements in, 11
video projection billboards, 156
video streaming services, 11
viral marketing, 148, 151
virtual communities, 248
virtual markets, 248
virtual reality presentation
  techniques, 75
virtual realms, conquering, 154
virtual worlds, 248
visibility, of price, 221
visionary methods, 153
visual stimuli, response to, 73
vlogging. *See* video blogging
voice over Internet protocol
  (VOIP) services, 277
VOIP (voice over Internet
  protocol) services, 277
von Hippel, Eric, 79
Vonage, 158, 202
VRIO acronym, 201
vulnerabilities, understanding your
  competitor's, 206

W

wagering, networks in, 281–282
Wal-Mart

achieving low prices based on
  superior supply chain
  management, 136
store greeters, 95
undercutting Netflix on
  price, 226
warranty, invalidation of, 57
wealthy nations, lip-service to trade
  liberalization, 4
web advertising, 163
Web-based surveys, 77
weblogs, monitoring, 80–81
website supplier bidding
  system, 247
Western Roll, introduced to high
  jumping, 212
what question of strategy, 200
white space, exploring, 101
white spaces, 104
Whole Foods brand, 188
why question, of strategy, 199
why question of strategy, 199
Winamp, 285
Windex, in *My Big Fat Greek
  Wedding*, 155
window of opportunity, 92–93
win-win encounter, making each
  interaction a, 301
win-win situations, transforming
  encounters into, 294
WOM (word of mouth)
  resulting from CGM, 158
  revival of, 151
WOM catalyst, marketer as,
  162–163
Woot, 249
Word of Mouth Marketing
  Association (WOMMA), 317
World Resources Institute
  International Finance
  Corporation, 311–312
World Trade Organization
  (WTO), 3
worldwide media reach, 10–11

Y

Yahoo!
  business model evolution, 142
  partnership with MobiTV, 162
  set of guiding rules, 139
Yellow Arrow campaign, 161
yield management systems, 224
Yoplait, campaign for breast cancer
  awareness, 317
Your News, 159
YouTube, 158
Yunus, Mohammed, 331

Z

Zaltman, Gerald, 73
Zazzle, crowd-sourcing by, 27
Zennström, Niklas, 159, 281
Zuckerberg, Mark, 87